TRICK OR TREASON

TRICK OR TREASON

The October Surprise Mystery

ROBERT PARRY

Sheridan Square Press
NEW YORK

Library of Congress Cataloging-in-Publication Data

Parry, Robert, 1949–
Trick or treason : the October surprise mystery / Robert Parry.
p.   cm.
Includes bibliographical references and index.
ISBN 1-879823-08-X : $24.95
1. Iran Hostage Crisis, 1979–1981.   2. Presidents—United States—
Election—1980.   I. Title.
E183.8.I55P37   1993
973.927—dc20   93-8831
                                  CIP

Published in the United States by
Sheridan Square Press, Inc.
145 West 4th Street
New York, NY 10012

Distributed to the trade by
National Book Network
4720A Boston Way
Lanham, MD 20706

10 9 8 7 6 5 4 3 2 1

To those I have met who care more about truth than their reputations. With special thanks to my wife Diane, and four children: Samuel, Nathaniel, Elizabeth, and Jeffrey. In memory of my mother and father.

CONTENTS

INTRODUCTION

David Henderson, a disgruntled State Department official, paced the narrow confines of his modest basement apartment. It was a cloudy fall day in Washington—October 18, 1980—and Henderson was awaiting the arrival of a journalist. Worried about deepening career trouble, Henderson was ready to take a gamble.

As the presidential campaign neared its close, Henderson had decided to throw in his lot with Republican challenger Ronald Reagan. Round-faced and quick-tempered, Henderson hoped that a Reagan victory might save his shaky future with the State Department. He didn't seem to have much to lose.

Henderson's relations with one of President Carter's ambassadors had frayed so badly that the tightly wound Henderson nearly snapped, almost coming to blows with his boss. Henderson was feuding with other superiors, too, and knew his days in the Foreign Service were numbered, unless there were changes at the top. A Republican president, he thought, might dismiss Carter's men before they got around to dismissing him.

So to help Reagan and hurt Jimmy Carter, Henderson had begun leaking information to the news media. Carter's presidency was already wounded, damaged by the near-year-long standoff with Iran over its seizure of 52 American hostages. Henderson, a Latin American affairs specialist, also saw Carter as vulnerable over his handling of Fidel Castro's communist government in Cuba. Castro's Mariel boat lift had disgorged thousands of

ix

Cuban dissidents and malcontents into south Florida. Henderson felt that Carter had been outsmarted.

Henderson believed his complaints might help secure Florida's electoral votes for the Republicans—and gain him some political favors from the Reagan administration. To leak the story, Henderson had opened channels to conservatives in Congress and in the press. Those contacts had led him to the interview he was about to have with John Maclean, a foreign affairs correspondent for the *Chicago Tribune* and son of the respected author, Norman Maclean.

The hum of the nearby Interstate could be heard as Maclean, a tall and dapper journalist, arrived on foot at Henderson's apartment. Henderson lived in a townhouse complex in southwest Washington, not far from the U.S. Capitol. The rows of two-story brick townhouses were set off from the street and formed a square around a simple concrete courtyard. Henderson shared one of the townhouses with another government official. Henderson had a bedroom-study on the basement floor.

Entering the townhouse, Maclean noticed a bike leaning against one wall and the under-decorated look of a graduate student's apartment. Henderson thought Maclean seemed excited, apparently by a hot piece of news that he had just heard. As the interview started, Maclean shared that information with Henderson. The reporter had gotten a tip about a secret diplomatic initiative that was supposedly in the offing or maybe already under way. According to one of Maclean's well-placed Republican sources, vice presidential GOP nominee George Bush was going to Paris for a clandestine meeting with the Iranians over the fate of the 52 American hostages then held in Tehran.

Maclean mentioned the tip to Henderson, possibly looking for confirmation or perhaps simply sharing an interesting rumor that was making the rounds of Washington. Henderson was perplexed by Maclean's account. It sounded odd: the Republican vice presidential nominee flying to Paris to meet with Iranians? But the junior Foreign Service officer remembered that Bush had been CIA director in the past. Maybe the Paris trip had the Carter administration's blessings? Henderson wondered out loud if the Bush mission might be part of a bipartisan initiative for freeing the hostages, whose fate had become a national obsession. But clearly, Henderson did not know anything independently.

Finding Henderson uninformed, Maclean changed the topic, back to the diplomat's complaints about President Carter's policy toward Cuba. Henderson then launched into a rambling tale about Carter administration incompetence. Though Maclean took notes and followed the account patiently, Henderson's complaints did not strike the reporter as very interesting. But Maclean thought Henderson's beef might have the makings of a front-page feature story if focused on the disillusionment of a young Foreign Service officer. Maclean recognized in Henderson the self-destructive tendencies common to government whistle-blowers.

After finishing the Henderson interview, Maclean thanked Henderson, left the townhouse, and went off to pursue the other, more intriguing story. He contacted the Reagan-Bush campaign and sought confirmation about the rumored Bush mission. The campaign's response was a firm and categorical denial. There was no secret Bush diplomacy on the hostage crisis, campaign spokesmen insisted. There was no Bush trip to Paris. Faced with a strong knockdown and with no other leads, Maclean set the tip aside as one of the many unfounded rumors that circulate in the overheated atmosphere of a presidential campaign.

Henderson's ploy to earn Reagan's gratitude by undercutting Carter in Florida also failed. Delayed by more pressing news, Maclean wrote the story about Henderson's complaints after the election was over, when the victorious Ronald Reagan needed no more help. Indeed, the *Chicago Tribune*'s airing of Henderson's personal gripes only stirred up more trouble for the embattled bureaucrat, who had leaked internal State Department documents to further his complaints. Henderson had lost his gamble for currying favor with the Republicans.

Early in 1981, Henderson was dismissed from the Foreign Service and moved West. In California, he taught at a small community college for a time and ran through a string of low-paying jobs. For years, he nursed his personal bitterness toward the government. But the meeting with Maclean never completely left Henderson's mind.

* * *

In 1991, a decade after Henderson left the Foreign Service, a public controversy arose over allegations that the Reagan-Bush campaign had interfered
with President Carter's negotiations to free 52 American hostages in Iran.
By the early 1990s, about a dozen international arms dealers, secretive
intelligence operatives, and expatriate Iranian officials had come forward
with accounts of the supposed meetings. Their stories varied, but some of
these "witnesses" cited the weekend of October 18–19, 1980, as the date
for secret negotiations in Paris between Reagan campaign representatives
and Iranians. A couple even claimed that they had seen George Bush.

The story reminded Henderson of his strange chat with a reporter in
October 1980. But Henderson could no longer remember the journalist's
name. Still, the ex-diplomat wrote to Senator Alan Cranston. Henderson
told Cranston about the peculiar meeting that had taken place two and a
half weeks before the 1980 election and the discussion of a rumored Bush
trip to Paris. He also reprised his long-held grievances with the State
Department.

A copy of Henderson's letter was sent to me because I had been the
reporter for a television documentary in spring 1991 that had examined
allegations of Republican interference on the hostage crisis. My immediate reaction to the account of the Bush-to-Paris conversation was that
Henderson must be some sort of crank. The letter's diatribe against his
former employers read like a case study of clinical paranoia.

But that letter eventually led me to Maclean by way of the front-page
feature story he had written about Henderson's complaints in November
1980. The reporter, still with the *Tribune* but back in Chicago, initially had
no recollection of the decade-old Bush-to-Paris tip that hadn't checked
out. But when reminded of the conversation, it came back to Maclean's
memory. He recalled that he had indeed told Henderson about the rumor of
Bush jetting to Paris. Maclean confirmed that he had been given that story
by what he regarded as a reliable source in Republican political circles.

Yet by the early 1990s, the Bush-Paris allegation was one of the most
repudiated claims about possible Republican interference in the 1980
hostage crisis. Those vague accusations of GOP shenanigans, known
collectively as the October Surprise conspiracy, were regarded by most of
official Washington with open disdain. The strongest contempt was reserved for the Bush story.

President Bush personally had denounced the accusation of a secret trip to Paris as "that ugly little word-of-mouth rumor." And with Bush residing in the White House, Republican and even Democratic congressmen rushed to endorse the president's emphatic denial. There was no truth, they agreed, to the charge that the president had joined in an act of international treachery.

Still, the coincidence of the Maclean-Henderson conversation and the later allegations of Bush's trip to Paris was puzzling. Did the Bush trip rumor, picked up by Maclean in October 1980, give rise to the later allegations? Had others heard the same rumor and begun claiming first-hand knowledge of the event? Or was the Maclean-Henderson discussion evidence that Bush indeed may have gone on a secret mission to Paris? At a minimum, the discovery of the decade-old story established that the October Surprise conspiracy had not been concocted years later, as some suspected. The rumors, it seemed, existed at the exact time of the alleged events.

But the strange tale of the reporter and the diplomat was only symptomatic of the larger mystery of the October Surprise. And some other allegations about Republican hostage-tampering were even tougher to disprove. Most focused on the whereabouts of Reagan campaign chairman William J. Casey during several time periods in the summer and fall of 1980 when he, too, supposedly met with Iranians. Despite careful investigations into Casey's 1980 schedule, the question "where was Bill?" seemed to defy a categorical answer.

Though hard evidence also was lacking to support the October Surprise charges, the doubts persisted: Was the October Surprise story a case of something close to politically motivated treason? Or was it a trick played by some disreputable characters who had stitched together scraps of coincidental information into a false accusation? Was the October Surprise conspiracy part of a long genealogy of Republican chicanery? Or was it a bogus scandal that derived its slim credibility from the Republican family reputation for electoral manipulation and intelligence abuses that both preceded and followed the 1980 election?

That history of GOP campaign dirty tricks did stretch back at least two decades—to the 1968 presidential race when Republican campaign activists intervened with South Vietnam's President Nguyen Van Thieu to discourage his participation in peace talks that President Lyndon Johnson had proposed. Thieu's cooperation with the Republican maneuver denied Democratic nominee Hubert Humphrey a last-minute boost in the polls and may have saved the close election for Richard Nixon.[1]

Then there were the two major Republican scandals of the modern era: the Watergate break-in and cover-up in 1972 and the complex Iran-contra arms-for-hostage affair which unraveled in 1986. Was the October Surprise conspiracy in 1980 a "missing link" between Watergate and Iran-contra? Did the anything-goes mentality demonstrated by those two scandals lead the Republicans to even worse abuses during the Carter-Reagan showdown of 1980? Or was the October Surprise just a conspiracy theory that had run wild, driven by low-life liars who hoped to profit from their charges or exact revenge for some personal wrong they had suffered?

A conclusive answer would not be easy. To solve the October Surprise mystery required reconstructing decade-old evidence—an extraordinarily difficult task given faded memories, lost documents, cold leads, and dead witnesses. But time was not the only problem. These were actions that, if real, would have been carried out by professional intelligence agents skilled in the art of deception and the fabrication of cover stories. The events would have played out over several continents and over a number of months. Plus, the available witnesses—arms dealers, intelligence agents, and Iranian officials—were far from trustworthy. Similarly, their allegations were often too vague to check against the verifiable record.

As hard as a serious investigation might be under those circumstances, it would be made immeasurably more difficult by Republican determination in the early 1990s to shut down any thorough inquiry. Angered by the insinuation of treacherous behavior and fearful that the allegations would destroy the legitimacy of 12 years of Reagan-Bush rule, GOP activists and their press allies made even consideration of the October Surprise a powerful taboo. Anyone in the press or Congress who challenged that taboo paid a very high price in terms of personal credibility and professional standing.

---

[1] Seymour M. Hersh, *The Price of Power* (New York: Summit Books, 1983), pp. 21–22.

Eventually, the October Surprise inquiry would turn into a nasty battle at the highest levels of Washington power politics. It was a battle that pitted George Bush's White House and its vast resources against a handful of scholars, journalists, and congressional staffers. But in a larger sense, it was a battle over what the American people would get to see, hear, and believe. It was a struggle over how far investigators could penetrate into an intelligence netherworld of intrigue and illusion, influence and money, espionage and betrayal. This book is an account of that investigation and that conflict. For me, the story started inauspiciously.

TRICK OR TREASON

1

THE TRANSLATOR-SPY

The shuttle flight from Washington banked eastward, skirting Manhattan island and turning toward the bright morning sun. It was February 27, 1990. New York City's familiar landmarks—the Empire State Building, the Twin Towers, the Chrysler Building—reflected the sunlight off their windows. The East River sparkled, too. But the winter-barren trees and the skyscrapers' long shadows made the city look bleak and cold.

The crowded jet coasted into its final approach to LaGuardia Airport. The plane was loaded with businessmen and lawyers commuting between the nation's two great power cities. As the flight attendants made a final pass down the aisle to collect coffee cups, the passengers hurried to put away work papers and fold up their laptop computers. But I wasn't paying much attention to the scenery below or to the people with me on the flight. My mind was on the unease in the pit of my stomach that always accompanied my pursuit of a news lead that my editors didn't want.

As a correspondent for *Newsweek* magazine, I was going to New York to talk to a federal prisoner who might hold answers to one of the deepest mysteries of all: the origins of the Iran-contra scandal. Or I might be wasting my time. The prisoner was Ari Ben-Menashe, an Israeli who had been linked to the clandestine supply lines that fed the Iranian war machine in the 1980s. Ben-Menashe had been arrested three months earlier on charges of plotting to sell three C-130 cargo planes to Iran.

After landing at LaGuardia, I took a taxi west toward Manhattan.

Through heavy morning traffic, the cab pushed its way around the repairs and the tie-ups, past decaying buildings and cemeteries packed with gravestones. The cab finally crossed the Brooklyn Bridge and took an immediate exit into a dreary urban stretch dominated by off-ramps, low-rise stores and the federal courthouse. Next to the courthouse was MCC-New York, the federal prison.

I paid the fare, climbed out of the cab, pulled my winter coat up around my neck, and approached the entrance marked by a Bureau of Prisons decal. New York's Metropolitan Correctional Center was a modern building that covered a full city block. Its light brown striated concrete exterior rose a dozen stories. MCC's windows were narrow, but except for that, a casual passerby might guess it was not a prison at all, but just another high-security New York apartment complex.

Since the interview had been pre-arranged, the guard at the front desk had a note anticipating my arrival. After checking my ID, he buzzed open the door to the visitors' holding area. I stuffed my overcoat and cloth L.L. Bean briefcase into a locker. I filled out a visitor's form, emptied my pockets, and walked through a metal detector. Then I was politely asked to step aside so I could be frisked with a metal-detecting wand. Having passed those tests, I had my hand stamped with fluorescent ink. Carrying only my notebook, pen, and locker key, I was instructed to sit down in the glass-enclosed holding room to wait for a prison official to escort me through the next series of locked doors.

Two years earlier, I had first run across the name Ari Ben-Menashe. He had been described by international arms dealers as an Israeli intelligence operative and a figure in the Iran-contra arms-for-hostage scandal that had tarnished the last two years of Ronald Reagan's presidency. But Ben-Menashe was a man of some mystery. I had heard he traveled often to South America. But I could never get a good line on his whereabouts.

Then, in early 1990, another journalist who knew of my interest in Ben-Menashe called me and asked if I was still looking for the shadowy Israeli. "Why not?" I thought. I had spent countless hours running down other Iran-contra leads. What was one more?

"Try MCC New York," the reporter told me. Ben-Menashe, it seemed, had run afoul of a U.S. Customs sting. He was in detention pending trial.

The prosecutors had blocked his release on bail because they feared that, as a foreign national, he would flee.

While working for the Associated Press in 1985, I began investigating the secret White House intelligence operations that would later take the title Iran-contra. One of my stories in June 1985 was the first news article to mention the workings of an obscure Marine officer named Oliver North. Over the next 18 months, I wrote a score of stories about the secret operations in Central America, before the scandal finally exploded into a major controversy that threatened the political survival of President Reagan and his top men at the end of 1986. So I had a longstanding interest in discovering individuals who could supply new clues to the mystery. To me, the Iran-contra story was like a maze, with no discernible beginning or end, no definitive conclusions, just innumerable paths to follow. Yet each path revealed more and more about the clandestine world that had enveloped U.S. foreign policy in the 1980s.

But in 1990, I could not help thinking that I was damaging my career by continuing to search for the Iran-contra secrets. My press colleagues in Washington had long ago lost interest in the scandal. My superiors at *Newsweek* had made clear, repeatedly, that they saw no story in the unanswered questions. Indeed, my persistence in investigating the scandal's hidden corners had poisoned my relations with senior *Newsweek* editors. They had considered the congressional hearings in 1987 the story's finale. To the editors, Iran-contra had dragged on too long. It was too complicated and too boring.

Still, I thought there was something wrong about the official story that blamed the mess largely on a few overzealous underlings. The American public deserved a straighter answer to questions about the White House decision to set up what amounted to an extra-constitutional intelligence network.

Where did the idea start? Who was behind it? Were there other secret operations mounted illegally by the White House and the CIA? Had foreign governments, such as Saudi Arabia, become a private piggy bank for an international apparatus for unsupervised intelligence activities? Had the nation's democratic process been systematically overridden by an

Executive Branch that had arrogated to itself the unrestrained power to wage covert wars? Had the Reagan-Bush administrations willfully covered up illegality? Were the highest officials in the land lying?

So here I was on a chilly morning in late February 1990 in a prison waiting room, following another lead to a story that no one wanted. My prison escort arrived and guided me through the locked doors, past one-way windows, up an elevator, and into an unadorned area for lawyers to talk with their clients. This glassed-in section had two soda machines and a table for a guard to sign visitors in and out. Off the soda-machine waiting area were small private rooms with hard plastic chairs and tables. The concrete-block walls echoed back every word.

Ben-Menashe was brought down another set of elevators from the cell block. A solidly built man of average height, he wore a tan prison jumpsuit open at the neck to reveal a hairy chest. He looked to be in his mid-to-late 30s, with Middle Eastern features, quick eyes, a swarthy complexion, and an expressive face. The dark wavy hair on his head was thinning. As he shook my hand, he was sizing me up. His quizzical expression suggested complex calculations already clicking away in his head. How much could he trust me? How should he play me?

We were given a tiny room with a fluorescent light overhead and diffused sunlight through a narrow window. We sat at a hardtopped table like those found in public schools. Either the table legs or the floor must have been uneven, because the table rocked whenever Ben-Menashe or I leaned on it. A heating vent behind me rumbled on and off every few minutes, making the acoustics even worse.

After we exchanged pleasantries, I explained my interest in the Iran-contra scandal and what he might know. But Ben-Menashe had something else he wanted to get off his chest: the injustice and humiliation of his arrest for the alleged C-130 plane deal. He had been apprehended on November 3, 1989, at a friend's house in Los Angeles.

"I was taking a shower when the police arrived," Ben-Menashe fumed, as he relived the indignity in his mind. "They ordered me out of the shower and took me into custody." He was allowed to dress and then was hustled, handcuffed, into a police car.

"I couldn't believe what was happening," he said, waving his arms and rattling the table with a slap of his hand. "The charges were insane. They said they were going to bring me back to New York, but not directly. I hop-scotched from one prison to the next. Each time, there was a body search."

He wanted *Newsweek* to write about his mistreatment, but his proposal sounded more like a demand than a request. Presumptuous, I thought. Clearly, Ben-Menashe was no run-of-the-mill criminal. He was brash and arrogant. He seemed a stereotype of an Israeli intelligence officer, a breed of operative known for swagger, toughness, and smarts. But who exactly was he? Was he an intelligence man as I had been told, or was he a freelancer who only claimed Israeli government sanction? Israeli authorities had already informed the federal prosecutor that Ben-Menashe's claim of a past association with Israeli military intelligence was bogus.

While I tried to show some sympathy for his plight, I also explained to Ben-Menashe that *Newsweek* would not be running anything about his case, at least not until I knew who he was. I suspected he might be just another private arms dealer, promoting himself with false assertions of official backing. Some arms dealers who claimed to know Ben-Menashe had said he worked for the Mossad, Israel's feared foreign intelligence service. But there was no solid evidence of that. At my request, *Newsweek*'s Jerusalem office had checked with the Mossad. Mossad officials denied that anyone named Ari Ben-Menashe had worked there.

"Some people think you work for the Mossad," I told him. "Is that true?"

Ben-Menashe looked annoyed. "I never said I worked for the Mossad," he responded, his voice rising again. "I held a very sensitive position in the External Relations Department of the Israel Defense Forces. I worked there from 1977 to 1987, for ten years."

The External Relations Department was a branch of Israeli military intelligence, he said. Though I had covered intelligence issues for a decade, I had never heard of such a department. From its name, it sounded more like a press office than a secret agency. But Ben-Menashe claimed otherwise. He said the External Relations Department—or ERD—was a prestigious arm of Israeli military intelligence, managing delicate relations with the armies of other countries and running sensitive intelligence missions, including transfer of weapons. Ben-Menashe said the ERD had even eclipsed the Mossad in standing inside Israeli intelligence.

"At first, I oversaw a small unit responsible for translations," Ben-

Menashe said. "But I soon advanced." He claimed that by 1979–80, he was assigned to handle arms transfers and risky contacts in Iran. He had been born in Iran and grew up in Tehran's tight-knit Jewish community. "My specific assignment was with the Special Aid Branch of the Intelligence Exchange Branch," he said. "Even the name of the unit is classified."

Ben-Menashe had a flair for the dramatic and for highlighting his personal role in history. He even boasted of having a hand in exposing the Iran-contra scandal. "In mid-1986, I was instructed to leak the story of secret White House arms sales to Iran," he told me.

Conservatives in Israel's intelligence services put out the arms-for-hostage story as retaliation for a U.S. Customs sting called the "merchants of death" case, Ben-Menashe claimed. In April 1986, Customs had rounded up 17 international arms dealers who were charged with conspiracy to supply billions of dollars worth of weapons to the Iranian war machine. One of the indicted "merchants of death" was a former Israeli brigadier general, Avraham Bar-Am, who had close ties to Israel's conservative Likud bloc.

The arms-smuggling charges angered Likud leaders, Ben-Menashe said, especially since the White House itself had been secretly trading arms for hostages with Iran for months. "But in the White House operation," Ben-Menashe continued, "the Reagan administration was working with Labor," then Israel's governing political party and Likud's chief rival.

Reacting tit-for-tat, Ben-Menashe said, his Likud superiors inside the intelligence community instructed him to slip the story of the White House arms shipments to American reporters. Ben-Menashe said he offered the story to journalists at *Time* magazine and *Newsday*, a Long Island-based daily, but the publications could not get adequate confirmation. So the story stayed hidden until the fall.

"Then we told our Iranian friends to leak it," Ben-Menashe claimed. He maintained that the story's eventual appearance in a Beirut weekly, *Al-Shiraa*, on November 3, 1986, resulted from that Israeli intervention. My brow furrowed over his unlikely reinterpretation of the series of events that had unlocked the secrets of the Iran-contra scandal. How could the Israelis have planted the *Al-Shiraa* story in Lebanon, I wondered. How could even the talented Israeli intelligence services finagle that?

Yet, I thought, why was Ben-Menashe giving me a revisionist account of the Iran-contra history? Normally when people lie, they embroider on a fabric of information that their listener already accepts as true. If Ben-Menashe wanted *Newsweek*'s help in bringing attention to his plight, why wasn't he giving me a version of events that I would be inclined to believe? The arrogant Ben-Menashe was not a witness who pandered to a listener's preconceptions. Rather, he seemed to delight in doing the opposite.

Whether the result of Israeli machinations or not, the case against the "merchants of death" did collapse after the *Al-Shiraa* disclosure. And the Reagan administration sank into the worst national security scandal of the decade. A year later, the bitterness and recriminations from the Iran-contra affair also ended Ben-Menashe's ten-year career with the IDF's External Relations Department, he said.

"I left ERD in 1987," Ben-Menashe said, conceding that he had burned too many bridges. "For a little while, I was unemployed." But his personal fortunes continued to turn. "Soon I was approached by someone who worked for the prime minister's office. I went to work personally for Prime Minister [Yitzhak] Shamir. I was handling special assignments for the prime minister when I was arrested."

As Ben-Menashe continued with his stories of internal intrigue in Israel's intelligence services, I grudgingly found myself interested in his tales. His version of events was provocative. His analysis of the political tensions inside Israel—between Labor and Likud—seemed insightful. But still the first step for Ben-Menashe was to supply documents that would establish who he was and what he had done officially for Israel. Without that corroboration, there was little reason to devote any more time to him or his stories.

I had grown tired of talking to arms dealers who insisted their work was cleared by the CIA, Mossad, or some other intelligence agency. Too often, their claims of official sanction evaporated under close inspection. "You have to give us something so we can verify who you are," I told him as politely as I could. "If we get that, then maybe I can do a piece. But first we need to know more about you. You know, your government is denying it's even heard of you."

Ben-Menashe responded with a short laugh. "I know that the government is denying me," he said. "But I made a decision when I realized that no one was coming to my defense to get me out of prison. I decided that my only chance was to talk about what I did for Israel and to tell the truth about everything. Telling the truth is my only hope." After pausing a moment, Ben-Menashe continued, "My mother is still living in Israel. I'll have her send you some of my papers and a plaque I got when I left ERD."

After about 90 minutes, the interview was over. A prison guard arrived and announced that my time was up. Over the course of the interview, Ben-Menashe's abrasiveness had softened. He seemed almost saddened to be losing his audience of one. I shook his hand, thanked him for his time, and watched as he was led back to the elevator heading to the cell block.

I followed my prison escort as we reversed our path out of the building, through the layers of locked doors, past the one-way mirror, back to the reception area. I put my hand under an ultraviolet light to show the stamp that I had gotten when entering, then I reclaimed my coat and briefcase from the locker. As I stepped out into the bracing February air, the ache in my stomach was still there.

Ben-Menashe had supplied a new batch of pieces to the Iran-contra puzzle. But it was as if he had scattered them on the floor and, at first glance, neither the colors nor the shapes matched the other pieces I had. I thought maybe my *Newsweek* editors were right. Trying to piece together the complete Iran-contra puzzle might be a hopeless task.

The first of Ben-Menashe's promised proof arrived at *Newsweek*'s Washington office several weeks later. Sent by his mother, the package contained a wooden plaque shaped like a fleur-de-lis and inscribed in Hebrew. The plaque appeared to be a going-away gift to Ben-Menashe from his friends at the External Relations Department of the Israel Defense Forces.

A *Newsweek* librarian who spoke Hebrew contacted the company that made the plaque in Tel Aviv. The proprietor said he made many plaques for the Israel Defense Forces but had no specific memory of that one. Of course, the problem with this "proof" was that anyone could have a wooden plaque made up for himself. So I put it aside on the countertop which passed for a desk in my *Newsweek* cubicle.

Delivered a week later, the second package from Ben-Menashe's mother was more helpful. It contained dozens of documents relating to Ben-

Menashe's business activities from the mid-to-late 1980s. Most of the papers seemed to relate to commercial deals and arms sales. Ben-Menashe's stationery carried a company name of the ORA Group. The documents showed that his travels took him to remote corners of the world, from Sri Lanka to Peru.

But to me the most riveting papers were three letters of reference from officials at the IDF's External Relations Department. The letters were dated September 1987 and were typed on Israel Defense Forces stationery.

One letter, signed by a Colonel Pesah Melowany, praised Ben-Menashe's work in "key positions" within the department. "As such, Mr. Ben-Menashe was responsible for a variety of complex and sensitive assignments which demanded exceptional analytical and executive capabilities. . . . He fulfills his assignments in a very efficient and reliable manner. I can vouch that Mr. Ben-Menashe combines a very astute mind and fine intelligence with exceptional understanding."

A second letter, signed by Colonel Arieh Shur, who was identified as chief of the IDF's External Relations Department, said Ben-Menashe had been "in charge of a task which demanded considerable analytical and executive skills. Mr. Ben-Menashe carried out his task with understanding, skill and determination, managing to adapt himself to changing situations."

A third, over the signature of a Dr. A. Granot, also of the External Relations Department, noted Ben-Menashe's work at the office for the last ten years and commended him for fulfilling "his duties in the department with great responsibility, expertise and dedication, down to the finest detail."

Even excusing the normal puffiness of letters of reference, the recommendations were important. If real, they would establish that Ben-Menashe had been working for the Israeli government during at least some of the days in the mid-1980s when he was also working as an arms dealer and when he claimed to be leaking the secrets of the Iran-contra scandal.

I summarized the letters in a cable to *Newsweek*'s Jerusalem office. I asked the office to seek verification of the documentation. Were the letters genuine or were they forgeries?

The response came back a few days later. IDF spokesman Moshe Fogel insisted that Ben-Menashe's actions trying to sell C-130s to Iran had not been sanctioned by the Israeli government. But Fogel confirmed that Ben-

Menashe had worked for the IDF's External Relations Department. The letters were real. And in calls to other Israelis who worked on intelligence matters, I discovered that the External Relations Department was, as Ben-Menashe had said, part of the Israeli government's intelligence community. The office handled contacts with foreign militaries and fit under the bureaucratic umbrella of Aman, Israel's military intelligence agency. So at least part of Ben-Menashe's story was true.

I called Baruch Weiss, the federal prosecutor in Ben-Menashe's case, to get his assessment of the new information. I had talked with Weiss earlier about Ben-Menashe and gathered that the prosecutor regarded the strange Israeli as little more than a fraud. When Weiss had inquired about Ben-Menashe's claim of official sanction, the Israeli government had told Weiss that Ben-Menashe was an impostor who had never worked for Israeli military intelligence.

Weiss still sounded doubtful even when I passed on our confirmation of Ben-Menashe's past government employment. But the prosecutor insisted that secrecy guidelines barred him from commenting on the case. After my call, Weiss wrote to Israel, double-checking on the letters that I had received at *Newsweek*. He asked the Israeli government if the letters might yet be forgeries.

To *Newsweek*, Israeli authorities were now acknowledging Ben-Menashe's employment, but they still were attacking his credibility. The government's new story was that Ben-Menashe served only as an office-bound translator who worked all day in a tiny cubicle and never traveled on official business. Ben-Menashe had no responsibilities for shipping weapons or engaging in intelligence activities, the Israeli government insisted.

But the solid confirmation that Ben-Menashe had worked for an Israeli intelligence unit was a breakthrough of sorts. Whatever Ben-Menashe's other demerits, he now had a documented relationship with a key government in the Iran arms sales. For me, the discovery also meant another trip to MCC-New York.

At this second prison interview, in spring 1990, Ben-Menashe was much more relaxed. He expressed a self-contented I-told-you-so smugness when

I informed him that his letters had checked out. He acted like a teacher pleased that one of his plodding students had performed surprisingly well on a test.

Ben-Menashe also informed me that while I was checking him out, he had been checking me out. He knew about my work as one of the original reporters unearthing the Iran-contra scandal. But he said I only knew a small part of the story.

"You think you know what happened," the Israeli said with a sly smile. "But you don't understand what really happened."

The story dated back not to 1984–1985, as most Iran-contra historians believed, but to 1980, Ben-Menashe claimed. Even as 52 American hostages were held by Iranian radicals in Tehran, Israel had started shipping military equipment to Iran. First went tires for F-4 fighters, then, in September 1980, some artillery pieces.

"The shipments were not authorized by President Carter and the Democrats," Ben-Menashe said. "They were authorized by the incoming administration." Behind the transactions, he insisted, were secret contacts between Israel's conservative Likud leaders, who ran the government in 1980, and Americans from the Reagan-Bush campaign and from the CIA.

I felt the visceral urge to stop Ben-Menashe right there. He was slipping into a discussion of what was known derisively around Washington as the October Surprise conspiracy. As dangerous to a reporter's career as the Iran-contra scandal had become by 1990, the October Surprise story was suicide.

The allegation that the Reagan campaign had interfered with President Carter's negotiations to free the hostages had circulated for years. But the story was deemed incredible by most mainstream journalists. It was the stuff of conspiracy fantasists. Its chief promoters were regarded as flakes and fabricators. Yet I swallowed hard and listened. At least this strange Israeli had the benefit of an official pedigree. He had indeed worked for Israeli intelligence in 1980. But Ben-Menashe would not make the story easy to take.

Ben-Menashe leaned forward and fixed my gaze. "The key American official in these early contacts with Iran," the Israeli said, "was Robert Gates of CIA."

"Robert Gates?" I choked in disbelief.

"Yes, Robert Gates," insisted Ben-Menashe.

I shook my head at the unlikely prospect that Robert Gates might somehow have been party to election shenanigans in 1980. Though a well-known hardliner on the Soviet Union, Gates was considered a career intelligence analyst and bureaucrat, not a covert operative or some master of the CIA's clandestine arts.

I had interviewed Gates several times in the late 1980s. Bright, clean-cut, self-assured, Gates had a youthful face and a Midwest twang more fitting a Boy Scout leader than a spy. He impressed me as an ambitious bureaucrat with a keen eye for pleasing his superiors, but not someone open to audacious risks.

In 1980, Gates was one of the CIA's rising stars. Still in his 30s, he was finishing a stint on President Carter's National Security Council staff. During the year, he returned to the spy agency as executive assistant to Carter's CIA director Stansfield Turner. The idea that Gates was secretly working with the Republicans seemed implausible, to put it mildly.

Under Ronald Reagan's CIA director, William J. Casey, Gates did rise rapidly. He was put in charge of the CIA's analytical division in 1982. In 1986, Casey jumped Gates over more senior CIA officials to be deputy director. Then, when the Iran-contra scandal broke in November 1986 and Casey collapsed with a cancerous brain tumor, Gates found himself acting CIA director. But his less-than-candid answers to the Senate's Iran-contra questions cost Gates the appointment as CIA director in 1987. When President Bush took office in 1989, Gates transferred back to the NSC staff as deputy to NSC adviser Brent Scowcroft.

In 1990, as I spoke with Ben-Menashe in prison, Gates was far from a well-known name. The reference was puzzling. Gates seemed an unlikely candidate for Ben-Menashe to pluck out of thin air as a behind-the-scenes intelligence operative for the October Surprise.[1] Again, I was baffled why Ben-Menashe was offering me a story that I would be inclined to disbelieve. My face contorted into its most annoyed and skeptical frown. But Ben-Menashe continued as if he didn't notice.

---

[1] In 1991, President Bush nominated Robert Gates, again, to be CIA director. After acrimonious hearings that included allegations that Gates had slanted intelligence estimates, Gates won Senate confirmation. In Senate testimony, Gates denied Ben-Menashe's allegations putting him in the middle of October Surprise intrigue.

Sitting in the cramped prison conference room, Ben-Menashe rambled on, outlining the historical background of his October Surprise story. His assessment of Middle East tensions made more sense. Israel had little sympathy for the new radical Islamic government in Tehran, Ben-Menashe said. But the conservative Likud government of Prime Minister Menachem Begin shared a *Realpolitik* interest in containing the ambitions of Iraq's Saddam Hussein. Saddam, who had vowed unrelenting Arab hostility toward Israel, coveted Iran's oil-rich Khuzistan province. The Iraqi dictator wanted to expand his oil riches to finance both economic and military development. So when Iraqi forces invaded Khuzistan on September 22, 1980, the Israelis felt an urgency to open up the Israeli-Iranian arms pipeline to help Iran avert defeat. Preventing military victory for Iraq's Saddam Hussein—a vital priority for Israel— hung in the balance.

But an obstacle to Israel's desire to save Iran was the lingering hostage crisis between the United States and Iran's Islamic fundamentalist leaders. For nearly a year, youthful Iranian radicals had held 52 American hostages in Tehran. Until Iran freed those hostages, President Jimmy Carter was demanding that U.S. allies keep a trade stranglehold on Iran, particularly over the shipment of military hardware.

So here was Israel's dilemma, Ben-Menashe said, his eyes narrowing. "Prime Minister Begin was desperate to assist Iran versus Iraq. But his advisers were very, very nervous about challenging the White House over Iran and the hostages. The Israelis wanted approval all the way from the top in Washington. But that approval was possible only from the Reagan-Bush campaign, not from President Carter. Besides, by September 1980, polls showed Ronald Reagan comfortably ahead. The Israelis were sure the Republicans were going to win.

"In September 1980, I received orders from my special assignment superiors in the Israeli government to go to Vienna for meetings with Khosro Fakhrieh, the secretary of Iran's Supreme Defense Council," Ben-Menashe continued as I took notes on his story. "Those meetings led to a general agreement on how relations between the two countries should go forward." The currency for the new secret relationship between Jerusalem and Tehran would be Israeli military supplies purchased with Iranian oil and money, Ben-Menashe said.

After Ronald Reagan took office, Israeli Defense Minister Ariel Sharon and U.S. Secretary of State Alexander M. Haig held secret talks in summer 1981 to permit American arms to flow to Iran, Ben-Menashe added. "Before that, there was approval, but it was not official. After that, I was all over Paris, Vienna, London, meeting with Iranian officials. NATO stuff was being sold with State Department okay beginning in 1981. The weapons were continuous, except for four months in late 1982 because of a fallout with Khomeini over Sharon's admission."

At that time, Sharon, the combative Israeli defense minister, embarrassed Iran's fundamentalist leader Ayatollah Ruhollah Khomeini by announcing in public that Israel was supplying the Iranian war machine. But tempers soon cooled, and weapons were flowing through the arms pipeline again. After all, both sides had powerful motives for their covert relationship.

The Israeli brokering of Iranian arms sales, through private and government channels, generated vast profits. Ben-Menashe estimated total Israeli sales for the eight-year war at $82 billion. Those arms deals created a slush fund that he claimed was spread through two dozen bank accounts and stood at about $800 million. He said much of that largesse filled Likud political coffers and paid for new Jewish housing on the occupied West Bank. That housing, in turn, cemented the settlers' political loyalty to the Likud and—in the view of Likud leaders—laid a strong foundation for continued Israeli control over the disputed lands.

As on my first visit, a prison guard arrived, saying my time was up. He cut off Ben-Menashe's discourse on the secret political history behind the Israeli-Iranian arms transactions. Except for Ben-Menashe's vague October Surprise claims and the staggering sums of Israeli weapons deals, I thought his story contained some elements that clearly were true and others that were at least plausible. The Haig-Sharon relationship indeed had been close, and Israel certainly had been rushing supplies to the embattled Iranians.

But at *Newsweek* there was little I could do with Ben-Menashe's information. My relations with the magazine's senior editors had gone from bad to worse. In June 1990, I left *Newsweek* and began work on a book about the phenomenon of Washington's "conventional wisdom"—the pedestrian thinking that had come to dominate the political-journalistic culture of the nation's capital. The book also was a way to recount what I had learned by following the Iran-contra scandal, from its hazy origins to its murky conclusions. Though I was sure there was much more to the story, the conventional wisdom on the Iran-contra scandal was that nobody cared anymore.

By summer 1990, I, too, had come to accept the accuracy of that conventional wisdom. The origin of the Iran-contra scandal, I felt, was on nobody's journalistic agenda. But I was wrong. There were still some news executives who believed, as I did, that the Washington press corps had missed the real story, that there were subterranean levels still to be explored. There were even a few editors who suspected that Ben-Menashe might be right on at least one point—that the genesis of the scandal traced back to 1980.

2

A PHONE CALL

I answered the phone in the kitchen of my home in Arlington, Virginia. On the line was the clear, reedy voice of Martin Smith, a senior producer at the Public Broadcasting System's news and documentary program *Frontline*. Smith reminded me that we had talked once some years before, in the mid-1980s, when I was investigating the activities of Marine Lt. Col. Oliver North. At the time, Smith was working on a documentary on the private funding for the Nicaraguan contra rebels. I had been digging into the same story for the Associated Press. "You probably don't remember," he said modestly.

I presumed the call related to an interview I had given a few weeks earlier to a producer for a Bill Moyers documentary on the Iran-contra scandal, "High Crimes and Misdemeanors," which was to air on *Frontline*. I had been interviewed as the reporter who, in 1985, disclosed North's secret White House role supporting the Nicaraguan contra rebels. The Moyers interviewer had been interested in how the White House had discouraged pursuit of the contra supply story. I thought Smith might be about to pose an Iran-contra question. He had something else in mind.

"We're thinking about taking a look at the October Surprise," Smith said, sounding hesitant when he got to the words, "October Surprise."

Smith asked me if I could come to *Frontline*'s offices in Boston to discuss what I knew about the long-whispered allegations that the Reagan campaign had contacted Iran before the 1980 election. The Reagan campaign and its director, William Casey, were said to have been so worried that Jimmy Carter would spring the 52 American hostages right before the election—the so-called October Surprise—that Casey secretly arranged to delay the release.

But I winced at the mere mention of the words, "October Surprise." It was a story that almost no one in Washington took seriously. On one side were prominent government officials and Republican businessmen denying that anything happened. On the other side, arms dealers, intelligence operatives, and Iranians were the source of vague rumors that Casey had engineered a hostage delay.

But anything approaching solid proof or a reliable witness was lacking. The story was filled with characters like Ben-Menashe, whose honesty was suspect and whose allegations were almost beyond belief. Though President Reagan's men had been tarnished by the lies of the Iran-contra mess, they still got the benefit of the doubt.

So when Martin Smith suggested an October Surprise investigation, I knew as instinctively as a deer sensing hunting season that it would only be trouble. Already, my career had been damaged by insisting that the Washington press corps had too readily accepted the Iran-contra cover story blaming the scandal on North and some of his expendable colleagues. Examining an even riskier set of allegations would alienate my mainstream press colleagues even more. But another part of me was drawn to the challenge. This would be an opportunity to track, for once, the origins of the Iran-contra arms deals.

Besides, I had grown annoyed by the unwitting news blackouts about such taboo subjects that had been informally decreed by Washington's "conventional wisdom" crowd. The herd mentality and professional timidity of the Washington press corps were, after all, at the center of the book I was writing. I could not very well succumb so easily to the same tendencies that I planned to criticize. Plus, I was going to Massachusetts soon anyway to visit my father, who lived about 20 miles west of Boston. So I agreed to a sidetrip to meet the *Frontline* producers and discuss what I knew about the October Surprise controversy.

* * *

Smith's call made me think back about the conspiracy story that had grown in fits and starts over the past decade. The October Surprise allegations had surfaced periodically as a theory to explain a string of anomalous events from the early 1980s: the remarkable timing of the hostages' release as President Reagan was giving his inaugural address, the mysterious flow of U.S. weapons to Iran through Israel in 1981, and the later arms-for-hostage swapping during the Iran-contra affair. But when the 52 U.S. hostages were freed on January 20, 1981, I recalled not having the slightest inkling that the fortuitous timing—Ronald Reagan's inauguration and the hostage release—might have been pre-arranged.

That inauguration day, I was working as a reporter at the Associated Press, the nation's largest wire service. It had been a hectic day at the AP, as it had been for news organizations throughout Washington. It had marked the start of a new era and the end to an old crisis. The country saw Ronald Wilson Reagan move into the White House and 52 American hostages leave Tehran.

Most Americans were simply relieved that the crisis was over. But there was talk that the arrival of a "cowboy" president might have spurred the Iranians to action. That day, a reporter friend had told me the nuke-'em-back-to-the-Stone-Age joke then circulating in Republican circles: "What's three feet deep and glows in the dark? Tehran ten minutes after Ronald Reagan becomes president." The neatly timed hostage release only minutes after Reagan was sworn in immediately enhanced the new president's reputation as a tough guy who won respect even from enemies.

Though I doubted that Reagan's macho image had scared the Iranians, I assumed that the Inauguration had become something of a deadline for both sides to work out the final details of the complex negotiations. It also seemed plausible to me that the Iranian radicals had held back the hostages in one final gesture of disdain for Jimmy Carter.

After finishing up work that evening, I headed home. I emerged from the subway stop at the Pentagon, where I would catch a bus to my home in Arlington. The night was dark and cold. Across the Potomac River fireworks were exploding, celebrating the arrival of the new president. The celebration could have been for the hostages' freedom, too. Inauguration Day had been a time of revival, catharsis, and hope.

When the hostages did return, they were greeted with an outpouring of national joy and, strangely, pride. Like millions of Americans, I felt a lump in my throat as the chaotic parade of buses carried the ex-hostages past huge crowds that had lined the roads near Highland Falls, New York, where the Americans had landed. As the nation cheered, the new president basked in the celebration. If there were any suspicions among disgruntled Democrats that a backdoor deal had been done, those questions remained dormant for years.

Then, in 1983, reporter Laurence Barrett's book about the 1980 campaign, *Gambling with History: Ronald Reagan in the White House*, highlighted a little-noticed admission from Reagan insiders. The Reagan-Bush campaign had obtained a copy of the briefing book that Jimmy Carter used to prepare for a pivotal presidential debate. In other words, Ronald Reagan's debate preparation advisers knew President Carter's arguments and answers before the debate started. They could prime candidate Reagan with just the right responses. Barrett's book touched off a political firestorm over a scandal quickly dubbed "Debategate."

A congressional investigation examined how the purloined briefing book found its way into the hands of Reagan's advisers. But the Debategate investigators also stumbled upon a larger intelligence operation. The congressional probe discovered that the Republican campaign's chairman, William Casey, had been receiving out-of-channel reports about some of the Carter administration's most tightly held secrets.

Casey, a World War II spymaster and a veteran of Richard Nixon's 1968 presidential campaign, was keeping a particularly close eye on Carter's progress in winning freedom for the American hostages. Apparently, Casey feared that a cynically timed hostage release in the weeks before the election might revive Carter's flagging re-election hopes. Casey assigned a special team of Republican staffers and volunteers to monitor hostage developments around the clock and around the world.

Though the Debategate investigation uncovered Casey's October Surprise concern, it failed to solve the mystery of the stolen briefing book. It remained unclear whether Casey, the campaign director, or James Baker III, the senior adviser in charge of debate preparation, had masterminded the debate book heist. The investigators also could not get to the bottom of the October Surprise intelligence network, but they thought they had touched a raw Republican nerve.

Press attention returned to Republican-Iranian contacts in early November 1986 when a Lebanese weekly newspaper disclosed that the Reagan administration was clandestinely shipping missiles to Iran. Three weeks later on November 25, 1986, the White House admitted that profits from the Iran arms sales had been diverted to support the Nicaraguan contra rebels. The Iran-contra scandal was born.

A shocked nation learned that President Reagan, the perceived no-nonsense tough guy, had privately approved the arms deals while publicly labeling Iran a charter member of an international "Murder, Inc." Reagan's understudy, George Bush, too, looked deceptive, having issued a report in February 1986 repudiating negotiations with terrorists. Again, Casey lurked in the background as the scandal's mysterious evil genius.

The Washington press corps, which had long pooh-poohed the outlandish tales of Oliver North's secret White House intelligence network, finally took stock of its own gullibility. Overnight, the flood of Iran-contra disclosures reshaped the landscape of Washington reality. What had seemed impossible before now looked plausible. What had been barely thinkable—like North's contra support operation—was now accepted fact. As reporters reassessed their sense of the real world, they began plumbing for the depths and origins of Reagan's arms trade with Tehran.

In late November 1986, I read with interest an article by the *Washington Post*'s Bob Woodward and Walter Pincus saying that the Reagan administration had approved arms sales to Iran, through Israel, as early as 1981, within a few months of taking office. But I still gave little thought to the prospect that those transactions might have predated Ronald Reagan's Inauguration.

The *Miami Herald*'s Alfonso Chardy found a new piece to the Reagan-Iran puzzle in April 1987. A hard-working reporter who had competed with me in investigating Oliver North's secret contra supply network, Chardy discovered that three Republican campaign activists had met a mysterious Iranian emissary in September or October 1980 at the L'Enfant Plaza Hotel in Washington. Supposedly, the Iranian emissary had proposed releasing the American hostages to the Reagan campaign. These Reagan advisers—Richard Allen, Laurence Silberman, and Robert McFarlane—insisted that they had spurned the offer, but they could not remember the emissary's name.

And then there was Flora Lewis, who wrote in the *New York Times* on August 3, 1987, that ex-Iranian president Abolhassan Bani-Sadr was alleging from exile in Paris that a Reagan representative had struck a hostage deal with Iranian hardliners in October 1980. Because of the deal, Bani-Sadr claimed, Iran's radical mullahs had blocked a hostage settlement with Carter. Still, few journalists in Washington took the word of the ousted Iranian president seriously.

But curiosity about the 1980 hostage question continued to bubble. In *Playboy*'s October 1988 issue, which was on the newsstands in late summer, ex-Yippie Abbie Hoffman and reporter Jonathan Silvers compiled a full-scale account of the October Surprise discoveries by the Debategate investigation five years earlier. But Hoffman and Silvers went further. They argued that Casey's intelligence operation that snared the debate briefing book had as its larger goal the countering of Jimmy Carter's frantic efforts to free the hostages before the 1980 election.

Besides constructing a circumstantial case that Reagan's hostage-release "miracle" had been pre-ordained, the Hoffman-Silvers story expanded on Bani-Sadr's account about the October 1980 meeting. Bani-Sadr told the writers that his source had claimed that George Bush was one of the American representatives sent to Paris to negotiate a hostage deal. Taking the allegation seriously, the writers asked the vice president's press office to reconstruct Bush's schedule for October 1980. The schedule left open a few weekend days, but showed no trip to Paris.

Also in summer 1988, a former Republican White House aide, Barbara Honegger, began hectoring national news organizations about their inaction on the October Surprise story. Honegger claimed to have heard an offhand remark inside the Reagan-Bush campaign headquarters in 1980 that the Reagan team had "cut a deal" on the hostages. But by 1988, Honegger had become obsessed with the October Surprise issue. Her style and manner had the intensity of a true believer, an approach that always alarms and annoys mainstream journalists.

When Honegger called me at *Newsweek* to complain that the magazine was ignoring the October Surprise mystery, I told her that *Newsweek* simply wasn't interested in pursuing the story. By then, my *Newsweek* superiors were bored with the Iran-contra affair and wanted nothing to do with some of the kooky side stories the scandal had spawned. But besides a general disinterest in the subject, Washington journalists reasonably felt that the 1980 allegations lacked specifics that allowed for a systematic follow-up. The October Surprise charges were hazy and poorly supported.

It was about this time—in late summer 1988 in the heat of the presidential election campaign—when an anonymous caller, using the pseudonym "Mr. Razine," and a shady arms dealer named Richard Brenneke began claiming detailed knowledge about the October Surprise story. Two years later, the unlikely results of their bizarre intervention were pulling me into a story that I had wanted no part of.

On August 7, 1990, a half dozen producers and reporters met with me at *Frontline*'s offices on the Boston side of the Charles River, opposite Harvard College. Like many other PBS series—*Nova, The American Experience, Mystery, This Old House—Frontline* was produced at WGBH, Boston's respected public broadcasting station. The national PBS shows were housed in a low-rise modern office building across Western Avenue from the television studios.

The offices for the national program were small and spartan, befitting PBS's reputation for frugality. Each show's area of rooms and cubicles was marked by a yellow diamond-shaped sign hanging from the ceiling. *Frontline*'s sign designated a corner of the second floor for the producers and office staff working on the independent-minded series.

As we discussed the October Surprise controversy, we were seated on couches and chairs in a lounge area where windows offered an unimpressive view of a back street and a parking lot. On one table was a bust of Robert F. Kennedy that had been awarded to *Frontline* for its coverage of the problems of the disadvantaged. It was one of the many journalism awards the PBS series had won during its eight years on the air. Though a prestigious award, the Kennedy bust seemed to have been placed casually on the table, like some household nicknack.

The *Frontline* producers were interested in examining the October Surprise issue because the federal government had lost a perjury case three months earlier against Richard Brenneke, the arms broker and money launderer who surfaced in the story during the 1988 election campaign. In federal court testimony in an unrelated case in Denver, Brenneke had claimed that William Casey, CIA officer Donald Gregg, and George Bush attended meetings in Paris in October 1980.

Convinced that Brenneke's testimony was false, a federal prosecutor obtained Brenneke's perjury indictment in 1989. But a federal jury, which heard the case in Portland, Oregon, had acquitted Brenneke on all counts in May 1990. Now, three months later, *Frontline* producers wanted to know whether the verdict might mean that there was some truth to the long-maligned October Surprise allegations after all.

Before Brenneke leveled his October Surprise allegations, I had interviewed him several times about his purported Iran-contra knowledge. He had claimed to know about guns-for-drugs deals in Central America and secret arms sales to Iran in the early 1980s. The weapons, he said, had passed through European middlemen with whom Brenneke had worked. From those interviews, I had come to think little of his credibility. But at times, he did have real nuggets of information.

As for his October Surprise claims, I doubted that he had any direct knowledge. Brenneke's claim to have seen Casey and Gregg sounded particularly ludicrous. I thought he might have heard rumors from friends in the arms-dealing community and inserted himself as a first-hand witness. Still, his perjury acquittal had surprised me. To other reporters, I had privately been predicting his conviction.

"I don't know how the government lost that case," I told the *Frontline* producers. "But I suppose if the government can't convict Richard Brenneke of lying about this, maybe there is something to it."

"Why was the case brought?" one *Frontline* producer wondered.

"I guess the prosecutor in Denver just was mad about Brenneke's testimony in the other case," I responded. "Maybe he thought that he might earn some brownie points in Washington." How wrong he had been. Instead, the prosecutor had brought unwanted press attention onto the ugly October Surprise allegations.

Frontline's interest in examining the October Surprise mystery came primarily from the senior producer who had called me. Martin Smith was a tall man, in his early 40s, who mixed an East Coast aristocratic look with a California casualness. Like me, Smith had lived through the deceptions of Iran-contra. In the mid-1980s, he had confronted editors' skepticism about the stories that Oliver North was running a secret intelligence network inside the White House.

Smith's sense of how far government malfeasance and deception might go had been stretched by the Iran-contra scandal, as had mine. A reporter's trust does not easily snap back to where it had been before. The other producers, while curious about the issue, responded cautiously to the feasibility of mounting an ambitious international investigation with no certainty that any story would result. *Frontline* would also be entering largely uncharted journalistic territory. Normally, TV documentaries follow a trail already marked out by the printed press. But in this case, the Washington press corps had shied away from the controversial October Surprise tale. There were few daring trailblazers whose work could be followed.

To ensure that the investigative work would not be wasted, *Frontline* could approach the story with a fall-back plan in mind, I suggested. If the October Surprise investigation went nowhere, perhaps *Frontline* could incorporate the reporting into a broader documentary about the changes in U.S.-Iranian relations or an examination of the mysterious U.S.-sanctioned arms deals in the early 1980s. Those shipments had never been fully explained nor even officially acknowledged. Smith agreed that the documentary should examine how those shipments occurred and who was responsible. He suggested that those secret arms sales might even help prove or disprove whether an October Surprise deal had happened. After about an hour, the discussion ended inconclusively.

Upon leaving *Frontline*, I drove up to southern Maine, where my wife and three of my four children had gone with my father in his new recreational vehicle. After a week's vacation, we returned to my father's home in Framingham, Massachusetts. There was a message for me from *Frontline*. The producers wanted to go ahead with the October Surprise project.

From its start, I suspected that the October Surprise investigation might be less a journey toward some heart of darkness than a voyage to the center of the modern world's complex duplicity. I doubted that we would ever find a definitive answer. But I thought we might recover pieces of a secret history from a remarkable era, glimpses of the behind-the-scenes reality that might otherwise be lost for good.

To join me on this historical search, *Frontline* recruited an independent producer, Robert Ross, who had formerly worked with ABC News on international investigative projects. Ross had shown up in Boston expecting to produce a documentary on real estate mogul Donald Trump. But a *Frontline* producer pulled him into an office, closed the door, and told him instead that *Frontline* was contemplating a program on the so-called October Surprise. "They almost whispered the words, 'October Surprise,' " Ross said.

Frontline's executives thought we might make a good team for investigating the mystery of the 1980 election. Ross knew his way around the Middle East and Europe—he spoke a variety of foreign languages—and I had written many of the major stories about the Iran-contra affair. While dubious about the assignment, Ross was an adventurous sort. He agreed to try.

Beyond the journalistic challenge, *Frontline*'s executive producer David Fanning saw the project as a chance to experiment with new, lightweight Sony Hi-8 video equipment in a complex investigation. Freed from cumbersome and costly TV lights, equipment, and crews, Ross and I would have the luxury of chatting with potential sources before coaxing them into on-camera interviews. The equipment was so simple that it could be set up in minutes.

The approach—what Ross called the "Hi-8 experience"—allowed for spontaneity and flexibility. We could jump from one city to another if an opportunity arose for an important interview. Ross and I would haul the camera and other gear with us to a home or office. Ross would run the camera himself. I would ask the questions. As Fanning would say, the Hi-8 camera had become "a video notebook."

The application of the new technology could make our investigation a kind of real-life "Where in the World is Carmen Sandiego?" game. Ross and I could hopscotch from city to city in the United States, Europe, and the Middle East in search of clues and informants.

On August 23, 1990, over lunch at a shabby Thai restaurant in lower Manhattan, Ross and I started mapping out our plans. I took an immediate liking to Ross, a low-key personality, polite and smart. He had dark hair and a medium build. Ross dressed presentably, but not expensively. He seemed comfortable in the artsy atmosphere of New York's Soho district, where he had his office. Ross also possessed a dry sense of humor, which would be vital for this assignment.

Though only in his mid-30s, Ross had accomplished more than many people do in a lifetime. After growing up in Hartford, Connecticut, he attended Harvard, graduating with honors. He then went to Paris, where he landed a job as a producer for Iranian television. He moved to Tehran in the go-go days before the Islamic revolution and lived there for two years. He taught filmmaking at an Iranian university and studied the Persian language.

But political tensions were mounting. While attending a lecture by a well-known dissident writer, Ross was caught up in the violence that was sweeping the nation. The SAVAK, the shah's secret police, attacked the crowd before the lecture started. In the melee, Ross was beaten with clubs and iron whips. The ulnar nerve in his right arm was severed. Soon after that, Ross left Iran. As the shah's forces disintegrated and Islamic extremists were seizing power, Ross made his way out of Iran through Pakistan.

After returning home, Ross joined the ABC News documentary unit. Then, shortly before that unit was phased out, Ross changed career course, opting for the world of international finance. He attended Wharton School of Business and took a job with Chase Manhattan Bank. But he was drawn back to filmmaking in 1989, opening his own independent video production company. He approached *Frontline* with a fistful of project ideas, including the one about Donald Trump.

Over the clatter of the noisy Thai restaurant, we talked about the October Surprise leads we had and the task ahead. I warned Ross that we'd be climbing onto a dangerous limb by taking on the 1980 election story. My press colleagues in Washington had long since closed off any respectful discussion of the issue. Like many other seemingly farfetched tales, it had been consigned to the loony bin of conspiracy theories. If we didn't go for an outright debunking of the allegations, we could expect to be derided as dupes or conspiracy nuts, real downers for a journalistic career.

So as we picked through the crispy spring rolls and fumbled with our chopsticks, we wondered how to approach the controversial project. There were a number of leads to follow. For one, we could re-contact Ari Ben-Menashe, the Israeli intelligence official who had annoyed me weeks earlier by asserting direct knowledge about the October Surprise mystery. I had found that claim implausible and tried to focus him on more verifiable tales about the early Israeli arms shipments to Iran in the 1980s. But this new *Frontline* assignment would require another talk with the arrogant Israeli to get down his detailed account about 1980.

Then, there was Brenneke, the defendant from the October Surprise perjury trial. Maybe, we thought, we could uncover some evidence missed by the Brenneke prosecutor. We might be able to prove that Brenneke's claims had been an elaborate trick played by arms dealers for revenge or money or God knows what other motive. If we could debunk the story quickly, Ross and I felt we could focus on the broader issue of the early U.S.-approved arms sales to Iran or work on a historic overview. Or maybe *Frontline* would have an entirely different idea.

Ross began taking notes. "We need Brenneke," he said. Since the trial in Portland, Oregon, had been in federal court, there had been no video-taped testimony. So we would need Brenneke and other key trial witnesses to repeat their stories again in interviews.

Also on the West Coast, we wanted to review the 1980 Reagan-Bush campaign records stored at the Hoover Institution on the campus of Stanford University in Palo Alto, California. We thought we might find travel or expense records for William Casey that would prove or disprove a possible trip to Europe. Former Attorney General Edwin Meese III had control over those papers. Ross scribbled down a note to submit an official request to Meese.

In California, too, was Houshang Lavi, an Iranian arms dealer who had brokered U.S. arms deals to Iran both before and after the Islamic revolution. Lavi claimed that he was the Iranian emissary who met with the three Republicans—Allen, McFarlane, and Silberman—at the curious L'Enfant Plaza get-together which had been discovered by Alfonso Chardy. The three Republicans acknowledged meeting with an Iranian emissary in 1980 about the hostages, but they denied that anything came of the conversation. They also insisted that they had forgotten the emissary's name, where he worked, and what he looked like.

I had interviewed Lavi once in 1989 about the early Iran-contra arms sales and his claims about 1980. He had not been a very good witness. He rambled and avoided the specifics that allow a story to be checked out. Still, it was worth another run at him. And we would need an on-camera interview anyway. But I no longer had a working phone number for Lavi. So a stop in Los Angeles might be needed to find him.

We had leads in Paris—names mentioned by Brenneke as well as hotel records to check and airport officials to question. We hoped we might find some evidence to establish what had or had not happened in mid-to-late October 1980. Ex-Iranian president Abolhassan Bani-Sadr lived outside Paris, in Versailles, and we would ask him to go on camera with his October Surprise story.

There were leads, too, in Great Britain. One potential witness was retired CIA officer Miles Copeland, who was living in the British country-side. Copeland, a legendary Middle East hand, had collaborated with other CIA veterans in early 1980 to draft their own plan for rescuing the American hostages in Iran. The volunteered scheme was rejected by the Carter administration in favor of the disastrous Desert One rescue mission that exploded in flames outside Tehran. But Copeland might know whether his spurned plan had kindled Republican thinking about a private strategy for resolving the hostage crisis.

There was also a chance that we could persuade Iranian arms dealer Jamshid Hashemi to agree to an interview. Jamshid Hashemi, living in London, was the older brother of the late financier Cyrus Hashemi, who had served the Carter administration as an intermediary on the hostage crisis. We had heard vague allegations that Cyrus Hashemi had betrayed the White House on the hostage negotiations and secretly had gone to work for William Casey.

Our *Frontline* superiors also wanted us to tie down a dangling loose end mentioned in the Hoffman-Silvers *Playboy* article: a claim by a senior Palestine Liberation Organization official that a Republican emissary had sought help in contacting radical Iranians in 1980. That, likely, would require a side trip to Tunisia, where the PLO had set up headquarters after its ouster from Lebanon in 1982.

In West Germany, we hoped to find two other witnesses: first, Sadeq Tabatabai, one of Ayatollah Ruhollah Khomeini's sons-in-law who had handled eleventh-hour negotiations with the Carter administration, and second, a mysterious figure who had intervened in the October Surprise story in September 1988 as an anonymous voice on the telephone.

The anonymous caller, who had contacted me and other Washington-based journalists during the 1988 presidential campaign, had used the pseudonym "Mr. Razine." He provided a detailed and what turned out to be a provably false account of the alleged Republican-Iranian meetings in Paris. It was also "Mr. Razine" who had first insisted to reporters that Richard Brenneke had joined the meetings. It had crossed my mind that "Mr. Razine" and Brenneke might somehow have been in cahoots. "Mr. Razine," I understood, now lived outside the city of Düsseldorf in West Germany.

3

A PERJURY TRIAL

In September 1990, Robert Ross and I—along with our compact video camera, tripod, and sound equipment—headed to the Pacific Northwest. Our investigation's first stop was Portland, Oregon. Ross wanted to get an interview on tape with the acquitted perjury defendant Richard Brenneke before the erstwhile arms dealer's heart gave out. Brenneke had been in and out of the hospital with severe heart trouble for months, even missing part of his own trial. We thought Brenneke might die before he could repeat his controversial story on camera.

From my earlier experience listening to Brenneke's tales about pre-Iran-contra arms trafficking, I had grown to dislike as well as distrust the man. Brenneke combined a remarkable number of character traits that struck me as irritating to the extreme. Simultaneously, he could be pompous and nerdy, self-righteous and deceptive. He would casually assert in-depth knowledge about important events and then phase out when pushed for details.

In his late 40s, Brenneke was a man of above average height, yet physically unimpressive. Before his heart problems, Brenneke had trained in martial arts and was described by friends who knew him then as a robust individual. But he no longer was. His sandy-colored hair was turning gray and thinning on top. He wore black wide wire-rim glasses and had a fondness for big cigars.

During the Iran-contra heyday, Brenneke had approached many reporters and investigators with his intriguing tales about secret deals and shipments of guns and drugs. A number of his prior claims of first-hand information had proved to be suspect, if not outright false. But some details did check out. He did have real connections to the arms-trading circles of Europe and the Middle East.

Though Brenneke was not indicted in the 1986 "merchants of death" case that rounded up 17 alleged weapons traders, federal prosecutors linked him to the Iranian arms pipeline. Government documents portrayed him as a friend of some of those defendants. Brenneke was an aspiring gunrunner angling for official permission to swap U.S. arms to Iran for an advanced Soviet T-80 tank that Iran had supposedly captured from Iraq.

But one internal government document, which I found in the confidential records of that case, established that Brenneke did possess genuine inside knowledge about secret White House activities. The handwritten Defense Intelligence Agency notation was dated January 3, 1986. It stated that one of Brenneke's attorneys had informed the Pentagon that Brenneke knew that Admiral John Poindexter was selling TOW anti-tank missiles to Iran. The DIA officer, Viekko E. Jappinen, wrote that Brenneke's lawyer, Richard Muller, had called to say that Brenneke had "learned that 'Admiral Poindexter had given permission to sell 10,000 missiles to Iran.' " Jappinen even added a footnote to clarify who Poindexter was: Ronald Reagan's newly appointed national security adviser.

Brenneke's knowledge was all the more remarkable because the DIA memo was dated three days *before* President Reagan secretly signed the first formal intelligence finding authorizing the TOW missile sales. In early January 1986, when Brenneke was talking to his lawyer about the sale of arms to Iran, that transaction was one of the darkest secrets in Washington. So my personal dislike for Brenneke was tempered by a recognition that somehow he did have access to some very sensitive information.

Brenneke met Ross and me at the door of his modest split-level home in a middle-class neighborhood of Lake Oswego, a Portland suburb. He looked older and weaker than when I had seen him last in 1988. He was wearing a black shirt opened at the collar to show a gold chain. Despite his declining health, he still smoked big cigars.

Brenneke introduced us to his wife, who sat on a living room couch and barely acknowledged our presence. Then he led us into the basement, where he suggested Ross set up for the interview in a wood-paneled den. The room smelled musty. A large tropical fish tank sat against one wall. Plaques and certificates commemorating martial arts accomplishments were displayed in several corners. Ross arranged the lamps to give off just enough light for the Hi-8 camera.

Though Brenneke had escaped a perjury conviction four months earlier, he was on the verge of losing his home as part of the personal bankruptcy that had swamped his life. Brenneke's lawyers had told us that despite his financial and medical problems, Brenneke rejected what they considered a generous plea bargain from the federal prosecutor—no fine or jail time in exchange for an admission that he had lied about a 1980 arms-for-hostage deal in Paris. Instead, Brenneke insisted on standing trial.

"I was offered a way out," Brenneke told us as the interview began. "I was offered a deal: just plead guilty and don't worry about it, you won't go to jail and you won't get fined. I was looking at a five-year jail term and a $10,000 fine. To a man who's just filed bankruptcy, $10,000 might as well be $1 million. And five years of my life, given my health, I didn't think I'd live five years in a prison." Brenneke spoke with a self-righteous passion, but strangely his voice stayed under tight control, softly modulated. It was as if the words and his voice were disconnected.

"But I turned down the deal," he continued in his monotone. "I elected to go to trial. I had to be found not guilty on all five charges by 12 people. In other words, the vote had to be 60-zero in my favor. And the vote was 60 to zero. There was never one guilty vote cast by any of those 12 jurors on any of those five counts."

In preparing for the Brenneke interview, Ross and I had read the trial transcript and examined the documentary evidence from the case. Though far from an ideal test of the October Surprise story, the Brenneke trial was the first time the allegations had been challenged in a government forum. The trial made for a fascinating story in its own right.

Brenneke's legal troubles began on September 23, 1988, in Denver, Colorado, at a sentencing hearing for his friend, Heinrich Rupp, a German pilot who had been convicted of bank fraud. In the closed hearing, Brenneke laid out a halting version of his October Surprise story. He told the judge that Rupp had been framed on the bank fraud charges to discredit him because he knew about Republican-Iranian meetings in Paris over the weekend of October 18–19, 1980. Brenneke personally claimed to have attended a meeting at Paris's Waldorf-Florida Hotel on or about October 20, 1980, along with Casey and CIA officer Donald Gregg, who in 1988 was national security adviser to Vice President George Bush. Brenneke told the judge that he had heard that Bush was in Paris, too. Brenneke said he and Rupp were there because of their long work as contract agents for the CIA—Brenneke moving money, Rupp as a pilot.

Brenneke's intervention had little effect on the judge who sentenced Rupp as though the strange interlude had never happened. But Brenneke incensed Rupp's prosecutor, Thomas O'Rourke, who decided to punish Brenneke for his grandstanding. In May 1989, O'Rourke took Brenneke's testimony to a grand jury. He returned with a five-count indictment accusing Brenneke of lying to a federal judge. Three counts dealt with the alleged presence of William Casey, Donald Gregg, and George Bush in Paris. The remaining two counts went after Brenneke's claim that he and Rupp had worked for the CIA.

Trial preparation took nearly a year. The FBI checked out the Secret Service report showing that Bush's protective detail had gone to the Chevy Chase Country Club in suburban Maryland on October 19, 1980. But the FBI could find no records of the visit nor anyone at the club who remembered seeing the vice presidential candidate that day. The government also appeared to have no conclusive documentary evidence on the whereabouts of Casey and Gregg.

The case went to trial in spring 1990 in Portland, Oregon, where it had been moved so Brenneke would be near his home and his heart specialists. The trial again pitted O'Rourke against Michael Scott, who had represented Rupp in the Denver bank fraud case. In that prior confrontation, the two lawyers had developed a genuine dislike for one another. O'Rourke— young, sharply dressed, good-looking—was known as a smart but hot-headed prosecutor. Scott—tall, balding, laid-back—was the brother of

Colorado's Democratic congresswoman Patricia Schroeder. But he didn't play the part of a high-powered attorney. In court, he sometimes had trouble phrasing questions to conform with courtroom style. Yet he was prepared to push to the limit in his defense of Brenneke.

The underlying issue in the trial was whom do you trust: the federal government or Richard Brenneke? Prosecutor O'Rourke thought the answer was obvious. Richard Brenneke was a low-life liar, and his October Surprise allegations were absurd. O'Rourke declared in his opening remarks that he would prove the falsity of Brenneke's claim that Casey, Gregg, and Bush traveled to Paris in October 1980 to negotiate with Iranians about the American hostages.

"What Mr. Brenneke said that day in Denver was not true," O'Rourke told the 12-member jury empaneled in the federal courthouse in Portland, Oregon. "What Mr. Brenneke said that day in Denver was a lie."

In his opening remarks, defense attorney Scott urged the jury to distrust the government denials. "I think what we're going to see in this case and what you will see and what will be very clear to you when the case is over is [that] the government, even in the presentation of this case, is going to still be hiding the ball," Scott said. "They're going to be hiding the ball from you."

O'Rourke started his case crisply. He called to the stand a CIA bureaucrat who testified that neither Rupp nor Brenneke had shown up in the spy agency's files as contractors. But the CIA officer did admit that in the 1960s, Rupp had received flight training from a CIA proprietary, Intermountain Aviation.

O'Rourke then summoned two Secret Service supervisors, William Hudson and Leonard B. Tanis. They were responsible for Bush's protection over the days of October 19th and 20th, 1980. Both denied that Bush left the country during that period. But under Scott's cross-examination, the pair acknowledged they would not have seen Bush for periods of time when he was at home. They also could not say precisely when their shifts started or ended.

Surprisingly, prosecutor O'Rourke failed to introduce any Secret Service records covering the days in question. Censored copies of those documents had been turned over to the defense and prosecution. But O'Rourke did not put the papers into evidence, nor did he ask the Secret

Service supervisors to refer to any notes to help them recall precisely what candidate Bush was doing on those days. Possibly O'Rourke feared that the heavily censored Secret Service records would raise suspicions among the jurors about why so many entries were hidden.[1]

The Secret Service men were followed by two secretaries who had worked for William Casey in 1980 at the Reagan-Bush campaign headquarters in Arlington, Virginia. When O'Rourke asked the secretaries, Barbara Hayward and Mary Costello, if Casey left the country during the last month of the campaign, they both answered no. But Scott elicited admissions from the women that they were not always with Casey, that he traveled from time to time, and that he did keep secrets from them. Again, O'Rourke failed to introduce any documents about Casey's travel or whereabouts into the court record.

The next witness was Donald Gregg, a CIA veteran who served as Bush's national security adviser during most of the Reagan administration and, in 1990, was U.S. ambassador to South Korea.[2] In October 1980, Gregg was detailed from the CIA to President Carter's National Security Council staff.

---

[1] After the trial, O'Rourke refused to answer any questions from us about his prosecutorial decisions.

[2] Gregg's career survived the Iran-contra scandal despite widespread allegations that he had helped construct Oliver North's secret contra supply network. Though Gregg's role was never proven, what was known certainly looked suspicious. To assist anti-communist forces in Central America, Gregg dispatched another former CIA man, Cuban exile Felix Rodriguez. His official job was to train Salvadoran helicopter units in counter-insurgency tactics. But Rodriguez later joined Oliver North's secret flyboy operation, dropping supplies to the Nicaraguan contra rebels after Congress barred continued U.S. military assistance in 1984. Throughout the Iran-contra scandal, Gregg would insist that he did not know that Rodriguez was moonlighting on contra resupply, even though the two men were in regular telephone contact. But Gregg's credibility suffered when a March 1986 memo surfaced about a planned meeting between Rodriguez and Bush to discuss "resupply of the contras." Gregg was at a loss to explain why this memo would have been written if his office had no idea that Rodriguez was participating in the resupply operation. Gregg first blamed a secretary for typing the incriminating phrase. But she recalled being told to include the line by one of her superiors. During Senate confirmation hearings in 1989, Gregg offered an even more imaginative explanation. He noted that Rodriguez had been assisting the Salvadoran military on airborne tactics. So, Gregg theorized, the secretary meant to type "resupply of the copters," not "resupply of the contras." It was one of those moments when Gregg seemed to overreach his personal talent for projecting honesty.

Gregg, a tall man with regular American good looks, resembled President Bush in many respects. In excellent physical condition, he looked younger than his age, then around 60. Competitive in his tennis playing, Gregg even marked down the scores of friendly games in his daily calendar. Still, Gregg had a compassionate personal style, like a man one could trust. He seemed the consummate CIA bureaucrat, mild-mannered, well-educated, a good listener, but driven by a personal ambition to win.[3]

Local TV news crews captured the image of Gregg arriving and departing the courthouse. The CIA veteran walked stiffly past knots of reporters and refused to comment on the trial. He seemed to enjoy the notoriety about as much as a dental appointment for root canal work.

At the trial, Gregg testified that on the weekend of October 18–19, 1980, he was nowhere near Paris. The CIA veteran said he had taken his wife and daughter to Bethany Beach, Delaware, where they stayed at a friend's summer home. The trio went swimming on one of the days, Gregg recalled.

"The water was still warm enough for that," Gregg testified. "We played some tennis, and we walked on the beach and read, took naps." He said he brought his wife and daughter back to Washington on Monday, October 20. He then returned to work at the National Security Council. He flatly denied traveling to Paris or meeting with Iranian representatives. But Gregg had no credit card slips, no restaurant receipts from the beach weekend, nor any clear-cut record of his presence at the NSC prior to mid-afternoon on Monday.

To buttress his testimony, Gregg did bring photographs of himself, his wife, and his daughter posing on the beach. But there were no recognizable landmarks nor any precise way to figure the date. Gregg was wearing swim trunks and the women were in light summer outfits. The pictures were shot on what appeared to be a partly sunny day, though in his testimony Gregg recalled the weekend to have been cloudy. Gregg did not remember if the

---

[3] When I first met Gregg in 1988, my strongest impression was that he must have made a wonderful CIA case officer. He had a knack for exhibiting empathy for another person's troubles and needs. When I spoke, he leaned toward me as though he wanted to catch every word. His face was lined with understanding and concern. I could almost imagine him persuading a foreign official to betray his country through a heartfelt appreciation of the gripes and grievances the targeted official might voice.

photos were taken on Saturday or Sunday, but he believed he went swimming in the early afternoon when the weather was warmest. Printing on the back of the photos showed they had been developed in "October 1980."

During cross-examination, Scott tried to dirty up the respectable image of Gregg. Scott reminded the jury that Gregg had spent thirty-one years working at the CIA, an agency known for deception and dirty tricks. Repeatedly, Scott pressed Gregg about the concept of "deniability," the necessity for CIA officers serving around the world to claim falsely that they worked for another U.S. government agency or a private business.

Gregg bristled at the suggestion of pervasive dishonesty at the CIA. "Intelligence work is based on relationships because the relationship has to stand up under tremendous pressure," Gregg told the jury. "And that's why I always felt that intelligence work was being in the people business because the people you were working with had to trust you and you had to trust them. And that's why the emphasis was so much more on truth than on deception."

But Scott wouldn't swallow Gregg's bromides about the integrity of the intelligence world. "When you were in Japan [on CIA assignment], did you go to work in an office that said 'Central Intelligence Agency' on it?"

"I didn't," Gregg answered.

"You might show up in an office that said 'U.S. Customs' or you might show up in an office that said 'State Department'?"

"That's correct. It was called cover."

"So that would allow you then to make the Japanese people or even the people you were working with in that State Department office, make them think that you were a regular employee of the State Department and not a person who was out gathering intelligence for the United States," Scott observed. "Isn't that correct?"

"More or less, yes," Gregg answered.

"So if the jury was walking down the street in Japan and they met you and said, 'I think I recognize you,' and you say, 'Yeah, I'm Don Gregg,' and they'd say, 'Oh, where do you work, Don?' you wouldn't say, 'I work for the Central Intelligence Agency,' would you?" asked Scott.

"That's correct," responded Gregg.

"So you would deceive them?" observed Scott.

"That's correct," acknowledged Gregg.

Given Gregg's battering over the CIA's practice and policy of deception, O'Rourke's failure to summon Gregg's wife or daughter as a corroborating witness would prove a critical error. To the jury, their failure to appear raised suspicions that the women could not or would not support Gregg's sworn testimony.

The swimsuit photos also boomeranged. The defense called to the stand Bob Lynott, a retired Portland television meteorologist known as "Mr. Weatherman" during his years on local Channel 6. The affable and aging Lynott testified that his review of weather reports from Bethany Beach for that October 1980 weekend revealed inclement weather that conflicted with the scenes in Gregg's photos.

"I am 100 percent certain they were not taken on the 18th [of October]," Lynott said. "I'm 90 percent certain that they were not taken on the 19th." Lynott described a cold front passing over Delaware in the early morning hours of Sunday, October 19, bringing moderate rain, cool temperatures, and a stiff northerly breeze onto the beach.

By late in the afternoon, there were some breaks in the clouds, creating the possibility that the sunlight on Bethany Beach could match the photos. But Lynott questioned whether the Greggs, smiling and comfortable in the photos, would have looked that way in the face of a chilly northerly breeze on October 19.

"So the temperature to the human being, lightly dressed or partly undressed as people with swim clothes are wearing, that's a little chilly," the aging weatherman said. "But these people [in the photos] don't seem to be chilly. They don't display any signs of shivering and I think I would."

On cross-examination, O'Rourke tried to recover the lost ground. He argued that the high temperatures for the weekend did reach the low 60s and, therefore, could fit with Gregg's account. "In fact, it was a little chilly, such that you would never go swimming on that day, isn't that correct?" the prosecutor asked. "But you're not trying to tell the jury, are you, that nobody could go swimming that day? Somebody who likes to swim, no matter what the weather, might take a dip in the ocean that day, assuming that it wasn't below zero, isn't that true?" Lynott agreed that a swim was possible.

As the trial neared its end, O'Rourke had one last chance to establish Brenneke's guilt—when the acknowledged money launderer and erstwhile arms dealer took the stand in his own defense. For his part, Brenneke tried to explain how an obscure businessman from Lake Oswego, Oregon, found himself in the middle of international intrigue. Brenneke first described his Jesuit educational background and his early work out of college, managing "offshore mutual funds" for Consolidated Business Management, a firm based in the Portland area.

Brenneke personally had set up two banking companies, one in Panama and another in Beirut, Lebanon. The defendant drew on an easel how money was shifted among the offshore mutual funds to Panama banks and Swiss accounts. By transferring the money through mutual funds, the company could shield the names of investors from government authorities. His lecture about the intricacies of money laundering impressed the jury.

Nervous but composed, Brenneke also recounted his controversial story about hostage talks in October 1980. "My purpose for being in Paris in October, approximately October 18th through the 20th, 21st, was to go to a meeting in which the release of the hostages was to be discussed," he testified. "My function was very simple. I was asked if I would handle the financial transaction, the money movement if necessary if this should come to pass. I agreed to do so. . . . In order to handle the financial transactions involved, I needed to know who was involved, what companies were involved, what the objective of the operation was, and where it started and where it ended."

Brenneke claimed the meeting was held at the Waldorf-Florida Hotel in the stylish Madeleine district in Paris. "The individuals I saw there included a man named Cyrus Hashemi, a man named Donald Gregg, Mr. William Casey, a number of Iranians, including a man named . . . Jalal al-Din Farsi, Bernard Veillot was there, John Delaroque by telephone from time to time was there. There were others who I didn't know and wasn't introduced to. My friend Robert Beneš, a colonel in the French intelligence service, was also there. Madame Robert, an intelligence officer for the French government, was also there."

On cross-examination, prosecutor O'Rourke seemed to have been in a perfect position to shred Brenneke's account with ridicule. Why was

William Casey, director of an American presidential campaign, present at a meeting with so many European and Iranian riffraff? Where exactly were these mysterious accounts that Brenneke was to control? How did he transfer the $40 million for the operation? Did he travel to the banks personally? If not, how were the wire transfers ordered? What were the details of Brenneke's travel to Paris? Did he have any stamps in his passport or travel records showing the trip? Was it on his personal calendar? Did he possess any records showing what he was doing during October 1980?

But O'Rourke failed to dissect Brenneke's curious tale. After asking Brenneke some questions about his background and getting him to repeat the 1988 testimony that he had given before the federal judge in Denver, O'Rourke rested. O'Rourke's summation to the jury focused on Brenneke as a man who lived in "a world on the fringes" and stressed the respectability of Donald Gregg and the government witnesses.

But the jury was unimpressed with O'Rourke's respectable witnesses. Gregg's long association with the CIA had severely damaged his credibility. O'Rourke apparently did not know how much.

"For myself, not knowing Gregg at all, I was truly excited when he first came in, thinking, 'Wow, we have someone very important here,' " jury foreman Mark Kristoff told me after the trial. "But the tie-in with the CIA—that he worked for them for many, many years—that all became a factor on exactly if we should totally believe when he said that he wasn't there. Listening to all the other evidence that we had, it came clear to us that there was a doubt. There was a doubt."

Other doubts were raised by Gregg's beach photos. "The evidence that was presented to us in actual concrete evidence was the snapshot photo of Donald Gregg on the beach," said Kristoff, an earnest young man. "The photograph itself on the back of it had the date October of 1980, but like all of us being just average people, we know that when you develop film, that's not when it was taken, that's when it was developed. And that left a wide open door for speculating when the photograph was actually taken."

The jury wasted little time in returning a verdict of not guilty. Brenneke was overcome with emotion. He called his wife over a cellular phone outside the courthouse. He choked back tears.

"We told the truth," Brenneke told reporters. "We told the truth all along and by God, it was believed." He vowed to recount his heroic tale in a book.

In our *Frontline* interview four months later, Brenneke reprised his now-familiar tale of flying to Paris in October 1980 on the instructions of a CIA man whom he knew only as "Bob Kerritt." He was equally vague on many of his other alleged intelligence contacts. He begged off our questions with claims that the individuals were still working under cover. As for personal records, he said he had none—no calendars, no credit card receipts, no flight records—covering the period that might help establish his whereabouts.

Brenneke's story went as follows: Once in Paris, he went to the Waldorf-Florida Hotel, where a large room on the top floor had been reserved for his use. He described a small elevator in the hotel lobby and the half-story staircase that leads up to the top floor of the intimate little hotel. Told to plan for a meeting the next morning, he arranged for extra chairs, coffee, and croissants to be brought to the room. First to arrive were two French arms dealers whom he had known—Robert Beneš and a woman identified as Madame Robert. They were followed by Gregg and Casey.

"I had never met Mr. Casey," Brenneke said. "The only knowledge I had of him was pictures in the newspapers and he was not bashful. It was 'Hi, I'm Bill Casey.'"

As Brenneke described the meeting, possibly two dozen people—Europeans, Iranians, and Israelis—entered that room at one time or another. The overriding topic was a future release of the American hostages in exchange for a supply of $40 million in light weapons.

"Isn't that a little surprising," I asked, "that you would have what sounds like a reception where something as sensitive as this is being discussed?"

"No," Brenneke answered, "because someone would come in the course of the conversation and the conversation at that point might not relate to the hostages at all. It might simply relate to the availability of tires for F-4s."

Brenneke claimed his job was to transfer money from various bank accounts, primarily from Mexico, to other banks in Europe. The approval for the money transfers, he said, came from Casey verbally.

"I don't recall what kind of reference name or code was used, but there was one," Brenneke said. "Generally, they ran more than one word—two or three words, separated generally by periods. You would spell the words out and appropriately separate them to the banker so that he would know who he was talking to."

He said he wrote down the account numbers and code words on his calendar or address book, while memorizing the banks and bank officers to be contacted.

"So have you gone back over your calendars for 1980 to see if you have such a thing?" I asked.

"I don't recall having any calendars," Brenneke answered. "I've looked for calendars for 1980 and I don't have anything, no."

"So you have no record of these arrangements and these transactions?"

"None that I can find. No. The last time I moved, which was maybe five years ago, I threw out most of this stuff."

Again and again, when pressed on specifics, Brenneke would claim a faulty memory or lost records. He would look away. Other times, as corroborating sources, he would mention the names of shadowy arms dealers or Iranians who were next to impossible to track down. Though the interview had covered about two hours, Brenneke had ducked and weaved on nearly every specific question we asked. He lit up a half-smoked cigar as Ross packed our video gear.

We left the split-level house in Lake Oswego. Brenneke walked us to our car and waved from the front lawn as we pulled away. "Now, you understand the Brenneke problem," I said to Ross. We wondered how to express our strong doubts about this oddball character. "Maybe we could use *Who Framed Roger Rabbit* animation techniques and paint Bart Simpson in as the questioner," I volunteered. "When Brenneke describes the Paris meeting, Bart could turn to the audience and say, 'cowabonga.' " We chuckled, shook our heads in dismay, and turned back onto the highway toward Portland.

*　*　*

Besides interviewing other participants in Brenneke's trial, Ross and I used our West Coast trip to locate the swank Santa Monica condominium of Iranian arms dealer Houshang Lavi, but he wasn't in at his ocean-view home. We left a message and snuck a look at his private phone number at the security guard's desk, so future contacts would be easier. We had even less luck reviewing Casey's campaign records. Edwin Meese would not give us permission to examine the 1980 campaign files at the Hoover Institution.

As we headed into the European leg of our investigation, we were still looking for the right route to follow in a search for some conclusive answers—and some reliable witnesses.

4

THE GAME PLAYER

After escaping the congested streets of London, Robert Ross and I drove west through the lush British countryside toward Oxford. About an hour later, still east of that famed university town, we turned off onto a winding country road. The road led to a little village called Aston Rowant, a community so small that it did not show on our map.

Through narrow streets, we passed well-kept English cottages, horse stables, and a stone church that dated back nearly 1,000 years to the Norman Conquest. Across the street from an English green was the red brick cottage of oldtime CIA officer Miles Copeland.

Ross and I had put Copeland near the top of our interview list as we started our trip to Europe in early fall 1990. We were searching for the right path to follow toward what had happened a decade earlier. We had other leads to pursue in Paris, Tunis, Brussels, Düsseldorf, and Jerusalem. But I thought Miles Copeland could help explain the hidden undercurrents that were pulling events in 1980 and might even know the genesis of the October Surprise mystery.

Copeland had close ties to the pro-Bush wing of the Republican party and to the potentates of the Arab world. I thought he might have started Jimmy Carter's adversaries thinking about alternative means for resolving the hostage crisis in early 1980. According to his autobiography, *The Game Player*, and some decade-old press reports, Copeland and his CIA chums had drafted their own hostage rescue plan in March

46

1980, a month before Carter's commando raid went up in flames at Desert One.

Ross and I were met at the door by Copeland's elderly British wife, Lorraine, who led us into the cluttered study where the CIA veteran worked at his word processor. Copeland, hobbled by arthritis, rose painfully to greet us. He was a big man with a deeply lined face and a shock of white hair. He still spoke with the Southern drawl of his youth and moved slowly with the aid of metal crutches that strapped to his forearms.

Copeland had settled in the English countryside after retiring from his two careers, one at the spy agency and the other as a Washington-based international consultant. A garrulous and immodest sort, Copeland called himself "the CIA's original political operative." He was known as a loose-lipped intelligence man who loved recounting his exploits as a behind-the-scenes adviser to Egypt's president Gamal Abdul Nasser and other Arab leaders. On the overnight flight to Europe, I had reread *The Game Player*. In it, Copeland recalled how he scouted out the weaknesses of Iran's nationalist government in 1953, prior to a CIA-sponsored coup that reinstalled the shah of Iran.

Wearing a beige-colored flannel shirt, Copeland shuffled into the cramped living room of the cottage and painfully lowered himself into a chair. Around him were pictures of his handsome children, a few of whom had made careers in the music business. One had been the drummer for the rock group, The Police; another was manager for the rock star, Sting. Although his body was crippled by arthritis, his mind was alert. He talked with openness and pleasure about politics and world events.

Like many of his CIA colleagues, Copeland was a strong supporter of George Bush, who had served one year as CIA director in 1976. That, plus Bush's schooling at Yale, a primary CIA recruiting ground, and membership in secret clubs like Skull and Bones, made the president a trusted figure to CIA veterans. I had been told that "Bush For President" signs had been plastered on walls all over the CIA in 1980. Copeland was so personally impressed with Bush's year as director that the CIA oldtimer founded an informal political support group called "Spooks for Bush." But as Ross began filming, Copeland offered a surprising analysis of Jimmy Carter, who was held in contempt by many CIA men.

"Let me say first that we liked President Carter," Copeland said, causing my eyebrows to rise. "He read, unlike President Reagan later, he read everything. He knew what he was about. He understood the situation throughout the Middle East, even these tenuous, difficult problems such as Arabs and Israel.

"But the way we saw Washington at that time [1980] was that the struggle was really not between the left and the right, the liberals and the conservatives, as between the Utopians and the realists, the pragmatists. Carter was a Utopian. He believed, honestly, that you must do the right thing and take your chance on the consequences. He told me that. He literally believed that." With those words, Copeland's voice registered a mixture of amazement and disgust, as if he were talking about a hound dog that wouldn't hunt. To Copeland and his CIA friends, Carter deserved respect for his first-rate intellect, but only contempt for his idealism.

The rift between the CIA and the president widened as the shah, ailing from cancer, lost American backing for a violent repression of the popular unrest in 1978–79. As the Pahlavi dynasty tottered, hundreds of thousands of Iranians took to the streets demanding the shah's ouster. This time, it was the shah's turn to seek shelter in exile. He fled Iran on January 16, 1979. Ayatollah Ruhollah Khomeini, who had been forced into exile by the shah in 1964, returned on February 1, 1979.

"Most of the things that were done [by the United States] about Iran had been on a basis of stark realism, with possibly the exception of letting the shah down," Copeland told me. "We believed on a basis of experience back in 1953 that the crowd could be turned as long as it didn't gather such tremendous momentum. Then there's no stopping it.

"In 1953, we had a crowd of about 20,000 yelling 'death to the shah, long live Mossadegh.'[1] And the ones that we used, who yelled 'death to Mossadegh, long live the shah,' were the same 20,000. All we had to do was to get at them, they were in a mob anyhow, and turn it around. I think we had about 80,000 at the end yelling, 'Long live the shah, death to Mossadegh.' But they [Khomeini's supporters in 1979] got up to a million. You don't turn a million people. You can't do it."

Copeland, however, thought early detection and fast action could have

---

[1] Mohammed Mossadegh, Iran's elected prime minister, was removed from office in the CIA-sponsored coup that reinstalled the shah in 1953.

saved the shah from the Islamic fundamentalists who seized power. "There are plenty of forces in the country we could have marshaled," he believed. "We could have sabotaged [the revolution]. I think in the long run we'd have had a hard time to do it because Islam is the march of the future. But, yes, we could have done something about it.

"But we had to do it early. We had to establish what the Quakers call 'the spirit of the meeting' in the country, where everybody was thinking just one way. The Iranians were really like sheep, as they are now. That's what Islam is all about. They go along with whatever the current momentum happens to be."

But, frozen by President Carter's idealism, the U.S. government missed the moment of opportunity, Copeland complained. Carter committed a cardinal sin as far as the aging spooks were concerned. He sacrificed a trusted ally on the altar of idealism. Carter criticized the shah's use of arrest, torture, and killings to stifle dissent.

"Carter really believed in all the principles that we talk about in the West," Copeland said, shaking his head from side to side in dismay and disbelief. "As smart as Carter is, he did believe in Mom, apple pie, and the corner drugstore. And those things that are good in America are good everywhere else."

Though Copeland was unusual in his bluntness, other veterans of the CIA and of the Nixon and Ford administrations agreed. Carter had dallied, and the delay destroyed the shah's hope for political survival.

But the trouble was not just Iran. The shah's fall capped a depressing decade for U.S. intelligence. Its secret wars in Indochina were lost; its "family jewel" secrets about assassination plots and domestic spying spilled out; its freewheeling ways were curtailed by intrusive oversight from Congress; and many covert operatives were dismissed unceremoniously by Jimmy Carter's CIA director, Stansfield Turner. Then, the shah of Iran, who owed his throne to CIA political action, fell to mobs of angry Iranians who made CIA interference in their domestic affairs a chief rallying cry.

"There were many of us—myself along with Henry Kissinger, David Rockefeller, Archie Roosevelt in the CIA at the time—we believed very strongly that we were showing a kind of weakness, which people in Iran and elsewhere in the world hold in great contempt," Copeland said. "The fact that we're being pushed around, and being afraid of the Ayatollah Khomeini, so we were going to let a friend down, which was horrifying to us. That's the sort of thing that was frightening to our friends in Saudi Arabia, in Egypt, and other places."

The shah's influential American friends prevailed upon Carter at least to let the exiled and ailing monarch enter the United States. "They got one concession after another," Copeland said. Carter agreed to a series of steps to ease the shah's isolation, including admission to the United States for treatment of terminal cancer. Carter felt that shunning a friend in need would not only send a dangerous message to American allies, but it would be wrong, morally. "Carter, I say, was not a stupid man," Copeland recalled, though adding that Carter had an even greater weakness: "He was a principled man."

The shah's welcome to New York for cancer treatment angered the radicals in Tehran who saw the United States again coddling the man they considered their tormentor. Angry students targeted the U.S. embassy for reprisal. Surging over the embassy walls on November 4, 1979, they captured the hapless American personnel inside and touched off the hostage crisis.

Copeland and his friends whose insistence on the shah's cancer treatment had contributed to the crisis now put their minds to work on how to undo the damage. "First of all," said Copeland, "there was very little sympathy for the hostages. We all have served abroad, served in embassies like that. We got additional pay for danger. I think, for Syria, I got fifty percent extra in salary. So it's a chance you take. When you join the army, you take a chance of getting in a war and getting shot. If you're in the diplomatic service, you take a chance on having some horror like this descend upon you.

"But on the other hand, we did think that there were things we could do to get them out, other than simply letting the Iranians, the students, and the Iranian administration know they were beating us. We advertised it. The fact that they were holding us by a certain part of our anatomy, which since I'm not President Johnson, I can't mention on PBS television. We let them know what an advantage they had. That we could have gotten them out is something that all of us old professionals of the covert action school, we said from the beginning. 'Why don't they let us do it?' "

According to his autobiography, Copeland got his first insight into the hostage crisis when he met his old friend, ex-CIA counter-intelligence chief James Angleton, for lunch. The famed spyhunter "brought to lunch a Mossad chap who confided that his service had identified at least half of the 'students,' even to the extent of having their home addresses in Tehran. . . . He gave me a rundown on what sort of kids they were. Most of them, he said, were just that: kids."[2]

Though Angleton and Copeland were friends, they represented two competing elements of the CIA. Angleton had fathered and fostered the close historic ties between the CIA and the Israeli intelligence service, Mossad. Copeland, one of the CIA's leading Arabists, had nurtured the spy agency's relationship with Arab leaders such as Nasser.

But the interests of the pro-Israel and the pro-Arab wings of the intelligence community suddenly converged on the question of Iran in 1980. The pro-Arab side feared the spread of radical Islamic fundamentalism as a destabilizing force in the oil-rich region; the pro-Israel faction saw the loss of a powerful ally in the disappearance of the shah. Both sides wanted to contain or reverse the revolution in Iran. But President Carter seemed immobilized by the hostage crisis.

Copeland formulated his hostage rescue plan, he claimed, at the request of a State Department official looking for alternatives to the hostage stalemate. At Copeland's Georgetown apartment the plan was hammered out on March 22, 1980, by CIA veterans: Steven Meade, the ex-chief of the CIA's Escape and Evasion Unit; Kermit Roosevelt, who had overseen the Mossadegh coup; and Archibald Roosevelt, who had a long and storied career as a CIA officer before taking a job as Middle East adviser to David Rockefeller and Chase Manhattan Bank.

"The details of the plan are now lost to history," Copeland told me. "But essentially, the idea was to have some Iranians dressed in Iranian military uniform and police uniform go to the embassy, address the students and say, 'Hey, you're doing a marvelous job here. But now we'll relieve you of it, because we understand that there's going to be a military force flown in from outside. And they're going to hit you, and we're going to scatter these [hostages] around town. Thanks very much.' "

---

[2] Miles Copeland, *The Game Player* (London: Aurum Press, 1989), p. 256.

Copeland's Iranians, posing as soldiers and police, would then move the hostages out of the embassy and drive toward the edge of town. There, the hostages would be loaded onto American helicopters and be flown out of the country.

"That essentially was the plan," Copeland said with a contented look on his large and craggy face. "I'm oversimplifying, but that would have worked."[3]

Copeland's plan made no dent at all in the Carter administration's rescue preparations, which relied heavily on U.S. military forces, with only modest help from Iranian assets in Tehran. Called Operation Eagle Claw, Carter's rescue mission ended in disaster as three helicopters suffered mechanical troubles en route to Tehran on April 24, 1980. At a rendezvous point called Desert One, the agonizing decision was reached to scrap the operation.

The worst, however, was still to come. As one of the helicopters maneuvered to leave the landing zone, it collided with a C-130 refueling plane, which exploded in flames. Eight American crewmen died. Later, their charred and twisted bodies were ghoulishly displayed by the Iranians to the world's press in another humiliation for the United States.

Copeland said the Desert One tragedy and the resulting dispersal of the hostages to locations scattered around Iran also killed any hopes for his scheme. But Copeland's plan may have had a second life, as its implicit criticism of Carter's strategy gave vent to the Republicans' contempt for the president.

"Well, officially the plan went only to people in the government and was top secret and all that, but as so often happens in government, one wants support, and when it was not being handled by the Carter administration as though it was top secret, it was handled as though it was nothing," Copeland said, with a flash of anger in his voice. "Yes, I sent copies to everybody who I thought would be a good ally. Here we'd made a proposal, endorsed by the CIA, that we thought would work, and it had been turned down by the Carter administration.

---

[3] Others, however, were a lot less sure. Carter's CIA director Stansfield Turner told Ross and me that the Copeland plan envisioned arming the rescue team with a knockout gas that the CIA never had.   ▽ suspiciously

"Now I'm not at liberty to say what reaction, if any, ex-President Nixon took, but he certainly had a copy of this. We sent one to Henry Kissinger, and I had, at the time, a secretary who had just worked for Henry Kissinger, and Peter Rodman, who was still working for him and was a close personal friend of mine, and so we had these informal relationships where the little closed circle of people who were a, looking forward to a Republican president within a short while, and b, who were absolutely trustworthy and who understood all these inner workings of the international game board."

One consummate international game player, Richard Nixon, still wondered if some independent action might not work where Jimmy Carter had failed. According to a 1989 article that we had found in the London *Sunday Telegraph*, Nixon consulted in late July 1980 with Alan Bristow, a helicopter specialist with close ties to the British Special Air Services, SAS, a clandestine military arm used for intelligence and paramilitary operations. *Sunday Telegraph* reporter Simon O'Dwyer-Russell had interviewed Bristow, who had described Nixon's detailed interest in the theoretical possibility of a second rescue mission, one which might be mounted privately.

When I called O'Dwyer-Russell, he elaborated on his story, saying that Bristow had described an angry Nixon pacing the floor and fuming about Carter's ineptness. But Bristow had clammed up after the *Sunday Telegraph* story. Though he came to the phone when I called, he refused to comment. But pointedly he did not deny O'Dwyer-Russell's account. Copeland told me that he had talked with Bristow about his contacts with Nixon and other prominent Republicans and that Bristow acknowledged the contacts described in the *Sunday Telegraph* article.

"But," Copeland added, "there was no discussion of a Kissinger or Nixon plan to rescue these people, because Nixon, like everybody else, knew that all we had to do was wait until the election came, and they were going to get them out. That was sort of an open secret among people in the intelligence community, that that would happen." Copeland then startled me by claiming that this sense was more than intuition.

"The intelligence community certainly had some understanding with somebody in Iran in authority, in a way that they would hardly confide in me," he added calmly. Copeland said his CIA friends were quietly informed by contacts in Iran that the mullahs would do nothing to help Carter or his re-election.

"At that time, we had word back, because you always have informal relations with the devil," the old CIA man said. "But we had word that, 'Don't worry. As long as Carter wouldn't get credit for getting these people out, as soon as Reagan came in, the Iranians would be happy enough to wash their hands of this and move into a new era of Iranian-American relations, whatever that turned out to be.' "

Though Copeland would not explain who handled these "informal relations with the devil," he insisted there was no formal deal with the Iranians, only another convergence of interests. Neither the Iranians nor the Republicans wanted Carter to gain political capital from a last-minute hostage release. There was also a mutuality of interest in freeing the hostages after Carter left office. The Iranians could punish Carter while currying favor with the new American administration. President Reagan would be seen as a tough new player on the international game board.

But how had this informal "understanding" come about? What did the Iranians expect to get by denying the hostages to Carter? Who had talked to whom? Who were the intermediaries? Copeland wouldn't say. He only assured me that there were people deep inside the intelligence community who understood what had to be done for the good of the United States. He called these professionals "the CIA within the CIA."

The interview came to a premature close when Copeland's wife, Lorraine, began yelling from another room that they were late for an appointment as house-sitters for a neighbor's home. The gruff CIA veteran put his wife off several times. Each call of "Miles!!" from Lorraine would draw an "Okay!" or "All right!" from Copeland. He would go back to talking for a few more minutes before the next interruption. Finally, the interview ended. The white-haired CIA veteran rose slowly from his chair and shuffled painfully toward the door with us.

Enlightening though he was about the political background of the events we were investigating, Copeland had steered clear of a full discussion about the October Surprise. He outlined the strategy that had prevailed in the Iranian test of wills against President Carter. But he volunteered no secrets about whether the CIA old boys' private maneuvering had interfered with Carter's negotiations to win the hostages' release.

Ross and I hoped we could interview Copeland again on a later visit to England. Perhaps he would tell us which representatives of the "CIA within the CIA" had passed on hostage messages to Iran in 1980. Why were his friends certain the hostages would be freed after Carter's defeat? What had Copeland meant by "informal relations with the devil?" But we never got that chance. Miles Copeland died in England on January 14, 1991. He was buried in the small graveyard next to Aston Rowant's Norman-era church.

5

LEADS AND LOSERS

We turned slowly into a dark, narrow street of a middle-income neighborhood in Paris. I peered out the window looking for the right number. Finally, I spotted it over the doorway of an old stone apartment building on the Rue Jean-Richepin. It was the address of Nicholas Ignatiew, a reserve officer in the French cavalry. Ignatiew was an acknowledged arms dealer and past associate of Richard Brenneke.

While Robert Ross parked the car in the crowded residential street, I rang the bell for Ignatiew's first-floor apartment. The entryway was dark, but I could see through the wrought-iron bars of the door. A short man, with close-cropped hair and a square face, hurried to answer the bell. The man's jacket and trousers didn't match. He was wearing white socks which stood out because his pants legs were too short. I thought for a moment that the man must be the concierge. But he greeted me in English. "Oh hello, hello," he said, ushering me inside. The man was Nicholas Ignatiew.

Ignatiew, who looked to be in his late 40s, led Ross and me into his apartment. The hallway was poorly lit. Dusty oil paintings of family ancestors hung from the walls. The apartment, with its high ceilings, must have been elegant once, but now looked worn and tattered. The red velvet wallpaper in the living room was dulled by age.

Ignatiew's bookshelves were filled with obscure volumes about European wars and the glory days of the royal armies. Above one desk was a photograph of Ignatiew as he was inducted into the Knights of Malta, a conservative Catholic lodge that was renowned for its militant anticommunism. Ignatiew claimed to have descended from a royal Russian family.

"Would you care for something to drink?" Ignatiew asked, pouring each of us a J&B whiskey. "I normally don't," I began to respond, but thought better of it. I accepted the glass, took a sip—I had hated whiskey since getting drunk on it once in my youth—and thanked him.

Though excessively polite, Ignatiew talked guardedly about his acquaintances in the arms business. He acknowledged knowing Richard Brenneke. He also knew the French man and woman—Robert Beneš and Madame Robert—whom Brenneke placed at the October Surprise meeting in Paris.

"I know them through the arms business," Ignatiew said. Through his own weapons dealing, Ignatiew had helped the French government free French hostages in Lebanon. His assistance was even admitted by the tight-lipped French secret services. Before calling Ignatiew, Ross and I had given his and several other names to a former French intelligence officer we knew. Only Ignatiew's name had come back circled as having legitimate connections to "le Service." Ignatiew's chief contact in the Middle East was Manzar al-Kassar, a notorious supplier of weapons to Arab terrorists.

Ignatiew was hesitant to appear on camera, but he did accept our dinner invitation. "I know a very good place," he said as he led us out of his apartment building. We walked several blocks to the Place Victor Hugo, a large traffic circle which featured a well-lit fountain in the center. Ignatiew picked out a restaurant with open-air tables. The restaurant's food was good quality, as was the red wine, which Ignatiew drank in some volume. We sat and talked for two hours. It was nearly midnight when we finished.

After dinner, we returned to his apartment. Ignatiew finally relented and agreed to an on-camera interview. Ross quickly pulled the equipment out of the car trunk and set up in Ignatiew's study. He sat Ignatiew down in front of his liquor case with bottles of whiskey visible behind the Frenchman's head.

Ignatiew started his account of what he knew about the October Surprise. The Frenchman said he had first heard the allegations in the fall of 1988, when Richard Brenneke visited Paris with Martin Kilian, Washington correspondent for the German newsmagazine *Der Spiegel*. Killian was checking out what Brenneke really knew of the Republican-Iranian hostage deal. Brenneke had arranged a dinner with two of his French associates, Robert Beneš and Madame Robert, and Ignatiew had joined them.

"At the meeting there was a discussion, but I should say a rather difficult discussion, because on one side you had people who tried to ask Robert Beneš and also Madame Robert about their attendance at 1980 meetings with Republicans and Iranians, which they denied, of course, and then there was me, who didn't know anything about that."

"Mr. Brenneke's claim," I interjected, "was that there was a meeting at the Waldorf-Florida, that he was in attendance, and that Robert Beneš and Madame Robert were there along with Mr. Casey, Mr. Gregg, and some others. Now, when he presented that to Robert Beneš and Madame Robert, how did they react?"

"They denied," said Ignatiew.

"After that meeting, you then checked on some of these October Surprise allegations with contacts you had in the French government?"

"Well, first I did not try to find out in a very precise way," Ignatiew responded about the possibility of Republican-Iranian contacts. "What was my interest was to know whether really it existed or not, because as I told you previously, until that day in 1988 I more or less never heard about that. Or, even if I heard, it was just heard, not more.

"And here, as I felt more or less involved at that moment, I wanted to know about what we're speaking. And after having spoken with a few friends of mine, I was convinced that some very important meetings really took place, let us say, between 19th and the 22nd of October 1980 in Paris, in Hotel Raphael first and, I think, then two meetings in the Florida.

Ignatiew said his "reliable" contacts in French intelligence circles differed on whether George Bush had joined the meetings. "I was told, but after that it was denied, that the former boss of the CIA was there," he said. "I should say, first, it seems logical, and second, I think it shows extraordinary patriotism because he was running for vice president, he was working to obtain the release—the immediate release—of the hostages."

"But doesn't it seem odd to you," I inquired, "that the actual release would have been several months later, on the day that President Reagan is inaugurated?"

"I very strongly believe," he responded, "that the Americans tried to obtain an immediate success. Well, they obtained a delayed success."

Ignatiew was less certain if Richard Brenneke had actually attended one of the Paris meetings.

"I have not the slightest proof that he really attended these meetings," the French arms dealer said. "Sometimes he claimed that he has. At other points, he seemed to deny it."

Ross and I had less luck getting videotaped interviews with Robert Beneš and Madame Robert. When we tracked down the two Brenneke associates, neither chose to be cooperative. But they did deny being present at the alleged Casey-Gregg meeting. They also denied having any hand in the arms business. Beneš called himself a simple mathematician, and Madame Robert was just a housewife, she said. But neither would state a denial on camera nor provide any other help in debunking Brenneke's claims. Madame Robert acknowledged having two fax machines running in her house, and Ignatiew had been clear on at least one point—that he knew Beneš and Madame Robert through the arms business.

Ross and I also checked with the Hotel Waldorf-Florida, where Brenneke claimed he had met William Casey and Donald Gregg. Brenneke had accurately described the hotel—its intimate lobby, its small elevator, and its top floor rooms. But all that meant was that he likely had stayed there. We could neither prove nor disprove that Brenneke was there in October 1980. Since then, the hotel had been sold, and the new owners could not locate the decade-old registration cards.

During our several days in Paris, Ross and I took a side trip to Versailles to interview Abolhassan Bani-Sadr, Iran's president in 1980. The exiled leader, best remembered for his thin mustache and finicky mannerisms, was living in a ramshackle country estate that fronted on the main road used by tourist buses heading to Louis XIV's palace.

Bani-Sadr repeated his claims to us of a Republican hostage deal with radical elements in Tehran. "If there had not been contacts with the Reagan-Bush group, the hostages would have been let go six months before the U.S. elections," Bani-Sadr told us.

As evidence of Paris meetings in October 1980, Bani-Sadr waved a letter from an associate who had supplied general information about the talks. The letter writer was still in Iran, Bani-Sadr said, so he could not give us a copy, nor would he let us examine it.

"It's a text which was sent a long time before the Irangate affair," said the ex-president in fluent French. "No one knew at the time what was going on between the White House and Tehran. It says, 'point number five,' the various points are numbered, 'the meeting was at the Hotel Raphael in Paris.' It didn't give the exact date, but it was just before the 23rd of October."

Even though he had been president, Bani-Sadr did not claim first-hand knowledge of these contacts. By fall 1980, he was in disfavor with the chief religious leaders and might not have known the mullahs' confidential activities. He had been an ineffectual president who eventually fled from Iran in disguise. But as the nation's president during the turbulent year 1980, Bani-Sadr could not be totally dismissed either. Still, the October Surprise leads were taking us farther afield with no clear answers. Our next stop was north Africa.

The Palestine Liberation Organization's office was located in a well-to-do residential neighborhood of Tunis. The only marking for the PLO safe-house was the police checkpoint outside the walled front entrance to the house. The guards were courteous and friendly, though they searched our gear carefully. We then walked through a small courtyard and up a flight of stairs to the sparsely furnished, airy rooms of the house. The young PLO functionaries who greeted us were hospitable, bringing tea and pastries. One wall of the living room was decorated with a poster of Sabra and Shatilla, the Palestinian refugee camps where Lebanese Christian militias under the protection of the Israeli army slaughtered hundreds of civilians in 1982.

After a brief wait, we were escorted in to talk with a PLO deputy spokesman, Marwan Kanafani. The silver-haired Kanafani looked more like a European jetsetter than a revolutionary. Dressed in chic clothes, his stylish glasses perched on his head, he worked the phones with the aplomb of a Washington public relations specialist. He nodded to us to sit down as he continued talking in Arabic to a caller. We wanted to know when our

requested interview with the PLO's senior spokesman, Bassam Abu
Sharif, would be granted. During a break between calls, Kanafani told us
that Bassam had been delayed. He would not return until the next night,
but he would see us. Until then, Kanafani suggested we visit the ruins of
Carthage, shop in the bazaar, and enjoy the other sights of Tunis.

Tunis, a tidy Arab city on the north coast of Africa, had become home to
the PLO after the organization's forced departure from Beirut in 1982 at
the point of Israeli guns. With its Mediterranean breezes and elegant
gardens, Tunis blends European flair with rich Arab traditions, a reflection
of the city's own conflicted history. On the outskirts of the city are the ruins
of Carthage, one of the great capitals of the ancient Mediterranean world
until it was sacked by Rome in 146 B.C. In the Seventh Century, Tunis fell
to the Arabs and became an important crossroads in the Muslim world.

In today's Tunis, the narrow tunnels of the city's bazaar seem to run on
endlessly, in classic Middle Eastern fashion. But the main boulevards are
wide and modern, like those in Paris and Rome. Unlike more conservative
Islamic countries, Tunisia permits its women to dress in Western-style
clothes rather than the traditional chador which covers a woman head
to toe.

Midway through a two-and-a-half-week trip to Europe and the Middle
East, Ross and I were thankful for the respite of Tunis, where we had
nothing to do besides sightsee and wait for Bassam. In other cities on our
itinerary, there were always other interviews that could be squeezed in.
The delay also gave us a chance to take stock of our investigation. While
wandering through Carthage and visiting the bazaar, Ross and I assessed
the shape of the October Surprise story as it had begun to emerge for us so
far. We had pinned down little evidence that an outright deal had been
struck. But there were indications that some secret contacts had occurred
between the Republicans and the Iranians in 1980.

There had been Miles Copeland's oblique acknowledgement that pro-
Reagan-Bush CIA officers had made their own contacts with the Iranian
"devil." The Iranians, Copeland said, had promised the hostages after
Carter's defeat. Frenchman Nicholas Ignatiew claimed that French intelligence officials told him that the Republicans had contacted Iranian
representatives in Paris. But those overtures, he said, had sought the
earliest possible freedom for the hostages, not a delay. On the other hand,

Iran's ex-president Abolhassan Bani-Sadr continued to insist that the Republican overtures had blocked an early release. His evidence, however, was shaky.

There also were some new sources who were alleging that a hostage deal did happen, though their credibility was dubious. Ex-Israeli intelligence official Ari Ben-Menashe had sketched out his October Surprise claims in prison. But I had yet to have Ben-Menashe spell out precisely what he claimed to know. Nor was I sure that what he might tell me could be trusted. He was, after all, in prison on federal arms smuggling charges. Plus, the Israeli government continued to picture him as a Walter Mitty character sitting in a tiny translator's office only imagining that he was circling the globe in pursuit of international intrigue and profit. Yet, if Ben-Menashe were telling the truth, the Israelis certainly wouldn't rush to confirm it. So, at this point, he could best be rated a question mark.

Ross and I also had hopes to get an insight into what the late Cyrus Hashemi might have done with the Republicans. While in London, we had extracted a promise for an interview from his brother, Iranian arms dealer Jamshid Hashemi. Cyrus had played a key middleman role for Jimmy Carter in 1980. Jamshid, we understood, was ready to discuss his brother's Republican contacts and Jamshid's own first-hand involvement in negotiations between Casey and the Iranians. That interview was scheduled for a stop in London on our return trip to the United States.

Then, of course, there was Bassam Abu Sharif. We had come to Tunis to follow up on his claim in the 1988 *Playboy* article that in 1980 a Reagan backer had sought the PLO's help as intermediaries to the Iranian militants.

Bassam told *Playboy* reporter Morgan Strong that "one of Reagan's closest friends and a major financial contributor to the campaign said he wanted the PLO to use its influence to delay the release of the American hostages from the embassy in Tehran until after the election."[1]

Bassam said he could prove his assertion and wanted to drop his "bombshell" if his allegation was denied. Since his charge of improper contacts between the Reagan campaign and Tehran had been denied, we

---

[1] Abbie Hoffman and Jonathan Silvers, "An Election Held Hostage," *Playboy*, October 1988.

felt it was worth giving him a chance to prove his case. We also had a hunch we might know who the Reagan friend had been. So we had brought along a photo of the Republican businessman to show Bassam and test his reactions.

By the time Bassam arrived, another day late, Ross and I were impatient for the interview. Called to the PLO offices after dark, we carried our camera gear out of the hotel, dumped the equipment into a cab, and gave the driver directions back to the quiet residential neighborhood with the police checkpoint. We went through the screening procedure again to gain entrance and then were escorted into Bassam's office.

The senior PLO spokesman was a cautious yet friendly man. His face was badly scarred and part of his right hand blown off by an Israeli letter bomb sent to him during the violent days of terrorism and counter-terrorism in 1972.[2] He wore sunglasses to cover his damaged eyes, but did not hesitate to extend his stunted hand in welcoming us. Gracing the office on a bookcase was a photograph of a smiling Yasser Arafat playing with two children.

"What I can recall is that in the beginning of the Iran crisis, the contacts between the Carter administration and the PLO were, in fact, the main channel of the Americans to the Iranians in order to solve the problem of the hostages, to release them," Bassam began. "And as long as that channel was kept as the main, sole channel, the PLO succeeded in releasing some of the hostages. President Arafat contacted the highest level in Iran. But the fact that the American administration started to contact other Iranians through other channels complicated the whole issue. We were always saying that too many cooks spoil the broth. That's why we gave up and decided to draw back."

But Bassam also claimed knowledge about overtures to the PLO from the Reagan campaign. "I can't go into details, but I can tell you that, yes, someone contacted us from the Reagan group. That was during the campaign. Carter and Reagan were competing for president. Someone from the Reagan election group contacted us on that issue, also, the issue of the hostages. The issue of the hostages at that time was very, very sensitive

---

[2] Dan Raviv and Yossi Melman, *Every Spy a Prince* (Boston: Houghton-Mifflin, 1990), p. 183.

and very delicate and it seems it was important for Reagan not to have any of the hostages released during the remaining days of President Carter. But PLO refused utterly to deal with such a proposal."

"Are you certain this person was with the campaign?" I asked.

"Yeah, I am sure, but I am not going to talk about it. I am not authorized to release names or to give names because we don't want to be involved in internal American intricate matters."

"How would someone know if someone is involved with a campaign?"

"We have our ways of knowing what people do," Bassam said with a laugh. "We have checked about him, the same way we have checked about you!"

"Where did you meet him?"

"I met him in Beirut," Bassam responded, but he refused to go further. "I'm not going to go into details of that, for one simple reason, I'm not authorized. I have checked with my president [Arafat] on the issue, and I didn't get the okay to talk about the details. I know the details would mean probably a big scandal to some people in the United States, but I'm not going to talk about it, because I'm not authorized."

I reminded him of his vow in the *Playboy* article that he could prove his claims if they were denied, as they had been. "Nevertheless," he responded, "I didn't get an authorization from my president to talk about that, but we have the proof. We have the proof of what I have told you."

I then handed Bassam a photograph of a Reagan campaign aide whom we suspected might have been the man who approached the PLO. It was a glossy, black-and-white head shot of a California businessman who was close to both Reagan and Edwin Meese III. Bassam smiled when he saw the picture. There seemed to be a glint of recognition. But his response was inscrutable. "Is this the only picture you have?" he asked me.

"That I have right here with me, yes," I responded.

The silence, as Bassam studied the photo, was broken by dogs barking outside. A breeze rustled through an open window.

"Is this the gentleman that you met with?" I finally asked.

"No comment, no comment," Bassam said. "I am not authorized. I'm a responsible person. I'm in an official position. I'm not authorized by my president to talk about it. We have the evidence as I told you."

I then mentioned the name of the man in the photograph and asked: "Is that a name that's familiar to you?"

"No comment. I'm not—please, don't, don't embarrass me by keep asking me. I'm not authorized. I might open this drawer and give you the evidence, if he [Arafat] gives me the green light. He did not. My president refuses to use such means because he respects himself and respects others. If the United States, the administration, wants to support the Palestinian cause, it should support it for principles, for basic rights of the Palestinian people—and not through blackmailing."

"Well, I think that blackmail is not what we're talking about here," I said, stunned. "This is a historical question at this point. It's ten years ago; much has happened since. It is important, I think you would agree, at some point to try clarify the history and what the record is."

"You know very well," Bassam proceeded hesitantly, "that some of the people who were working closely with President Reagan are still working closely with President Bush."

"Well, do you have any reason to think that President Bush was knowledgeable about all this?"

"We don't know," he responded. "And embarrassing the Reagan administration might mean embarrassing those who were involved at that time." He then grew more adamant. "I'm not, as I told you, I'm not ready to talk about that. Reagan tried to use that to block Carter's success. We have nothing to do with that. But we have rejected a request to block the release of hostages before the election. We turned that down."

Trying a different tack, I asked, "What would the PLO have gained, had it gone along? Was there some offer made by the Reagan emissary?"

"The offer was, 'if you block the release of hostages, then the White House would be open for the PLO.' In spite of that, we turned that down, because we are people of principles. We've helped release the hostages for humanitarian reasons; of course, for political reasons. But we cannot possibly play tricks of this sort. I think every one of you understand what that meant, what it meant to the PLO, to have a promise from a coming administration to deal with the PLO, but we have turned that offer down.

"I guess the same offer was given to others, and I believe that some accepted to do it and managed to block the release of hostages. You have to look for that. It was not PLO. PLO had turned down the offer, but probably others did not."

Having waited two days in Tunis, I was in no mood to accept idle speculation. "But you had very good contacts into the Iranian government, as you said, and you might know if not just hypothetically, but that in reality something happened."

"I'm sure someone in the Iranian government knows what I am talking about," Bassam said. "I am sure some of Reagan's people contacted or had contacts with some Iranian to block that."

"You say you're certain," I followed. "There's some evidence?"

"It's unfortunate that I'm not in a position to give information," he retreated. "What I'm giving you is in the context of analysis, general information. I'm sorry I cannot give you further information, which we probably possess. But I'm not authorized to do it."

I took one more run at prying loose some hard evidence, knowing that the word of a PLO official would count for little in the court of American public opinion.

"Have you asked Chairman Arafat recently about whether or not he might be willing to release the evidence?"

"President Arafat knows about that," Bassam said with growing annoyance in his voice. "He has the information. President Arafat, until now, doesn't want to release any of that information."

Frustrated, Ross and I wrapped up the interview, packed up the video equipment, and began to take our leave. Bassam looked nervously down at a briefcase in the corner of his office.

"Is that yours?" he asked with more than idle curiosity. For a man who has lost his fingers and part of his face to a letter bomb, such questions are not paranoia. The satchel did not belong to either Ross or me. But one of Bassam's aides stepped forward to claim it and relieve the worries of his skittish boss.

6

THE DISINFORMATIONIST

Oswald LeWinter, huffing and puffing, walked hurriedly into the Hilton Hotel in Düsseldorf, Germany. He spotted me sitting at a small table in the glittering lounge, situated off the main lobby. He apologized for being late. But I was surprised that he had shown up at all. He must have known the interview was not going to be pleasant.

In his 50s, LeWinter looked like an out-of-shape fireplug. His face was bloated, and his tired eyes were those of a man who had fallen woefully short of his potential in life. For the on-camera interview, LeWinter was wearing an inexpensive sports jacket and tie. He was freshly shaven and had neatly combed his thinning hair. When he crossed his legs, he showed off a pair of dark leather cowboy boots. While nervous, LeWinter seemed to have come to grips with telling at least part of his story on camera. He was prepared to explain why he had called journalists in Washington in 1988, identifying himself only with the pseudonym "Mr. Razine," and why he had outlined a provably false version of the October Surprise story.

I led him upstairs to a conference room where Robert Ross had set up the videocamera. LeWinter sat down, wriggled in the chair to get comfortable, and listened to my first question: Why had he deceived journalists during the middle of the 1988 presidential race? Why had he told a story of October Surprise meetings that, for one, placed Reagan's foreign policy adviser, Richard Allen, at a meeting in Paris when Allen was on a live TV talk show in the United States?

LeWinter looked glumly at me and the camera. He began in a soft, slow voice to tell an equally amazing tale. "I was asked by some people to mount a disinformation campaign," LeWinter said haltingly. "Barbara Honegger [the ex-Republican aide who was demanding a press inquiry into October Surprise] had started enough interest in the newspaper community and the media to throw a negative light on George Bush's candidacy, potentially a negative light. The people who asked me to intervene felt that the country could not stand another Watergate, another major political scandal and upheaval, and also worried that the Democratic party's candidate might have hurt the intelligence community, which was just in the process of recovering from the damage that had been done to it during the Carter administration."

But LeWinter would not identify his supposed employers, except to say they were associated with the U.S. intelligence community. "I'm not going to mention any names," he told me. "And I don't think the names are important. But these are people who are in their own estimation patriots and people who believe that a country like the United States, for its leadership role, needs a strong intelligence community. I met with four people, basically, and was given to understand that there were a number of others who were interested in seeing this succeed. In other words, making sure that the media lost interest, that the story was discredited."

"Were you paid for it?" I asked.

"Yeah, but that wasn't the reason I did it," LeWinter responded. He put his payment at $100,000.

"I contacted Barbara Honegger through another person," LeWinter continued in a slow monotone. "I managed to pass on some information to her which had factual elements in it, but also elements that with a little bit of digging could be discovered to be questionable. The story would lead some investigators to spend time and effort running into blind alleys, with the result that eventually the whole story would be discredited."

If fouling up the October Surprise investigation had indeed been LeWinter's goal, he, along with Richard Brenneke, had succeeded. Their intervention in September 1988 sent reporters off on wild goose chases and left journalists frustrated and furious. Many reporters, who wasted time checking out LeWinter's false leads, concluded that the entire story was a fraud, some elaborate and crazy conspiracy theory. That thought had crossed my mind, too.

I was one of those who had received evening phone calls from "Mr. Razine" starting in the late summer of 1988. I was a correspondent for *Newsweek* at the time, and Mr. Razine would play classical music in the background as he spun out his curious tales. But the anonymous voice did offer what had previously been lacking in the vague October Surprise allegations. He pinpointed times, places, and participants for the alleged Republican-Iranian meeting in Paris. These were details that could be checked against known facts and official records.

Over the phone, Mr. Razine told me that he was a retired CIA officer. He said he knew about the October Surprise meetings because he had read a French intelligence report inside CIA headquarters. He offered up the obscure names of alleged Iranian emissaries as well as four American principals: George Bush, William Casey, CIA officer Donald Gregg, and Richard Allen. Mr. Razine also alleged that there was one other American eyewitness: Richard Brenneke.

As reporters began methodically checking out Mr. Razine's claims, the disembodied voice upped the ante. On September 17, 1988, Mr. Razine repeated his story on a talk radio show broadcast by KFI in Los Angeles. He had been persuaded to make the call by Barbara Honegger, who saw the anonymous talker as an important new source in establishing the reality of the October Surprise conspiracy.

"The name I'm going to use this evening is Mr. Razine," the voice began, affecting a lousy Southern accent.

KFI Host Bill Moran got immediately to the point: "Mr. Razine, tell us about the George Bush connection to this alleged deal. Was he there?"

"Sure as God made little green apples," Mr. Razine responded, trying to sound folksy.

But in the weeks ahead, it quickly turned out that there were problems with Mr. Razine's story. For instance, he had accused Richard Allen of attending one of the meetings on Sunday, October 19, at 1:00 p.m. When reporters checked, they learned that Allen had appeared on a live Sunday morning network interview program that day. Given the seven-or-so-hour flight to France, he could not have been in Paris at 1:00 p.m., which was 7:00 a.m. in Washington. Other Razine references also turned sour. CIA officials denied the existence of a French intelligence report. The Secret Service denied that Bush had left the country at all in October 1980. Although Brenneke "confirmed" his role in one meeting under oath in a Denver courthouse, the story was getting more and more unbelievable.

Mr. Razine's voice had been like an audible Cheshire cat grin that had directed journalists down wrong paths into a wilderness no less fantastic than Alice's Wonderland. Almost as suddenly as it arrived, the voice faded from the scene. There were no more evening phone calls from Mr. Razine. But the voice had left behind one tell-tale clue, the call he had made to KFI.

While Mr. Razine's call-in may have made no more than a blip in the strange world of talk radio, it had an unintended consequence in the weeks after George Bush's election as president. Tapes of the performance circulated among reporters on the West Coast in fall 1988, and one columnist in San Francisco recognized the lightly disguised voice of Mr. Razine as the real voice of a New York literature professor named Oswald LeWinter.

Martin Kilian learned of the identification and went to work locating LeWinter. Kilian had been another recipient of Mr. Razine's anonymous phone calls in 1988. When Kilian started investigating Razine's allegations, he did so with the enthusiasm of a reporter grabbing onto his first potentially big story. Kilian even went with Richard Brenneke to Paris to interview the French arms dealers, Nicholas Ignatiew, Robert Beneš, and the mysterious Madame Robert.

While that and other leads led into dead ends, Kilian and his *Der Spiegel* colleagues did find several independent European sources—including a senior French intelligence officer and a Swiss-based arms dealer—who told them that October Surprise meetings between Republicans and Iranians indeed had happened. Those off-the-record confirmations were at least enough to keep Kilian on the trail.

Tall, dressed in a rumpled European Bohemian style, intellectual but earthy, Martin Kilian did not fit my middle-American idea of a German. He loved American jazz, blues, and progressive rock 'n' roll. He adored the rich diversity of American culture. A Ph.D. in American history, Kilian had done work on his doctorate at the University of Georgia, an experience that gave him a slightly idealized vision of the American South. He had even learned to root for the Georgia Bulldogs football team.

Kilian was a foreigner who could shame me with his depth of knowledge about my own country. The details he knew about the American colonial experience were only vague high-school lessons to me. He could expound in rich detail about the writings of the Founding Fathers and their theories of personal liberty. Those theories he had embraced as his core beliefs. A child of post-war Germany, Kilian grew out of a counterculture that had repudiated the traditional German values of odedience in favor of free-thinking and intellectual inquiry. He expressed unabashed affection for the United States for "liberating" his nation from Adolf Hitler and the Nazis.

Kilian was fond of telling how, after the war, U.S. GIs had helped his father, a German artillery officer, return home to his family. As the war ended, Kilian's father was captured by the Soviets and was interned in a POW camp in Poland. But he and a friend escaped. Hiding out during the day and stumbling along back roads at night, they started a furtive trek westward. For weeks, half-starved, the two men struggled on toward southern Germany where their families had lived. They were constantly fearful of Soviet recapture. It was not until they forded the river into the American sector of occupied Germany that the two Germans finally felt safe. They approached American GIs at a checkpoint. The Americans gave them food, a chance to rest, and directions for the final leg of their journey.

Kilian saw ferreting out the truth about the 1980 election as a kind of repayment for what American democracy had meant to him and his family. Kilian was personally offended that anyone might have tampered with the election of a president. But as a journalist and a historian, he wanted answers, one way or the other, to the dangling October Surprise questions. He repeatedly put his career at risk by pushing his editors back in Hamburg to authorize expenses for an investigation that had little interest to *Der Spiegel*'s German readers.

Joking once about his self-sacrifice in pursuit of this frustrating story, I asked Kilian what kind of statue the American people should erect for him if a hostage deal had been struck and the culprits were finally exposed.

Amused by the question, Kilian thought for a moment and answered that he would like to be shown with Thomas Paine's "Rights of Man" in one hand, the score for Duke Ellington's "New Orleans Suite" in the other—and a bottle of good red California wine at his feet.

In fall 1988, after learning the real identity of the mysterious Mr. Razine, Kilian tracked Oswald LeWinter to the War and Peace Foundation in New York, where he was assisting on a television project about the United Nations. The War and Peace Foundation, a reputable organization that promotes international understanding, was one place where reporters had been instructed to leave messages for Mr. Razine. Kilian then contacted LeWinter directly.

LeWinter/Razine went into a panic when he learned that he had been unmasked. He remonstrated himself for being so foolish as to have gone on the radio talk show in the first place. "He didn't like the idea that all of a sudden we knew who he was," Kilian recalled. "Then a couple of weeks later, he turned up in my office. He still told me that he was a veteran of the CIA, that he had worked for them for 20 years. So I thought this guy was rather strange, and also my fears increased that perhaps this Mr. LeWinter had worked in tandem with Mr. Brenneke.

"I started looking into who this man might be. We were told by German police that Mr. LeWinter had worked for the CIA and for 'another friendly service.' But it was made clear to our Stuttgart bureau that Mr. LeWinter had not worked for the CIA as an agent. As far as they knew, he apparently had done contract stuff for them and that was all they knew about him. So the mystery deepened."

LeWinter was yet another October Surprise paradox. He was no ordinary con man who survived on the sleazy edges of the intelligence world. He was smart and well-educated, though he had clearly turned onto the wrong track in life. In the early 1960s, he taught English at the college level. He won awards for his poetry and edited a book on Shakespeare's influence in Europe. He counted as friends some of the leading New York literati, including novelist Saul Bellow.

In the late 1960s, LeWinter got excited about politics in reaction against the antiwar demonstrations sweeping the nation's campuses.

LeWinter saw himself as a pro-Vietnam War Democrat and went to work for Hubert Humphrey's presidential campaign in 1968. His political dabbling continued into the next decade. In 1976, he volunteered his assistance as a negative campaign researcher to conservative Democrat Vance Hartke of Indiana. LeWinter had dug up dirt on Republican challenger Richard Lugar. But Hartke would not use the information and went down to defeat.

By the early 1980s, LeWinter had moved to West Germany and was working as a psychologist, with a clientele drawn from the ranks of American servicemen stationed at German bases. But in 1984, his life took an ugly turn. LeWinter was charged in New Jersey with conspiracy to smuggle designer drugs into the United States. His alias for that endeavor, the federal government alleged, was "Mr. Wamma." LeWinter pled guilty and served a two-year sentence. In 1988, after completing his jail term, LeWinter turned to some old friends in New York who helped him land a temporary job with the War and Peace Foundation. It was from those offices that he began his curious phone calls to reporters.

In early December 1988, LeWinter agreed to a face-to-face meeting with Kilian and me in Washington at the Melrose, a quiet restaurant on M Street, between the city's business district and Georgetown. That night, I had finished up a late story at *Newsweek* and arrived after dinner. Kilian and LeWinter had finished eating and were seated at the table. The elegant restaurant was dark and nearly empty. I accepted the pleasantries of an introduction to LeWinter curtly. LeWinter was smiling, but I didn't find what he had done very amusing.

"So why did you lie?" I asked, as an opening question.

"Well, I didn't exactly lie," LeWinter answered, moving uncomfortably in his seat. "I told some things that were true and some things that weren't."

From his gravelly voice, it was clear that he was the same man who had called me three months earlier. But LeWinter's new story was almost more bizarre. He now claimed that he had been recruited by several American intelligence figures to spread a version of the October Surprise allegations that was skewed enough from the truth to be debunked.

The idea of the disinformation campaign, he told Kilian and me, was to discourage reporters from continuing their pursuit of what happened in 1980. LeWinter claimed that he had been paid for his work, but he insisted that he had a higher motive. He believed that the October Surprise story deserved to be sidetracked to clear the route for George Bush's election.

The dinner ended unpleasantly. As we walked toward the door, LeWinter extended his hand. I ignored it. I found his new story as implausible as his original one. Who could know when a man like LeWinter had stopped lying? Maybe not even LeWinter. But two years later, as Ross and I examined the October Surprise mystery for *Frontline*, I thought that LeWinter's strange tale fit in the story somewhere. So, through Kilian, I had contacted LeWinter in his new home in Germany.

Only reluctantly had LeWinter accepted *Frontline*'s request for a videotaped interview. He seemed afraid that if he did not cooperate, Kilian might write a story about him in *Der Spiegel*. One such article in the large-circulation magazine could destroy LeWinter's reputation in Germany, where he lived quietly and edited a small Jewish publication. So he apparently judged that the interview with *Frontline* would be the lesser of two evils.

Though nervous in the interview, LeWinter showed no signs of remorse. When I asked how effective his deception campaign had been, he responded flippantly: "Well, you probably know better than I. The October Surprise story did not break before the election, and, to my knowledge, it hasn't broken yet. The promised critical mass never came to be."

While admitting that he had salted the story with false information, LeWinter insisted that some parts of his story were true. He even claimed some limited firsthand knowledge. He said that in mid-October 1980, he was in Paris working on the outskirts of hostage negotiations involving Americans, Europeans, and Iranians.

"I was working at the time within the American intelligence community, and this was in the form of an assignment. I was part of a team of people that was composed of people from various countries in Europe that were there for the purpose of cleaning up any evidence that these meetings had taken place. It was October, 18th, 19th. It was a weekend."

According to LeWinter's new version of events, he still insisted that Casey, Gregg, and Bush had been in Paris, but he admitted that he had lied about Richard Allen. LeWinter insisted, too, that Richard Brenneke was there.

"There's a problem in talking to you about this," I noted, grasping the obvious, "and the problem is that you presented the media with false information in 1988. Why should someone believe what you're saying now?"

"I'm not asking anyone to believe what I'm saying now," LeWinter answered slowly. "All I'm asking them is to ask themselves what purpose could I possibly have in speaking at this time to an American audience and admitting my complicity in a disinformation campaign aimed through the media at the American people? I'm not exculpating. I'm just simply saying that's how it was."

LeWinter's new twisted tale seemed no more credible than his old one. Now, he had been in Paris on the fringes of the October 1980 meetings. He was cleaning up incriminating records left behind by the participants. But all he could give us was his word, a highly questionable commodity.

LeWinter also had no proof that he had been hired for a disinformation campaign in 1988 by four intelligence operatives whose names he wouldn't divulge. His friends in New York did say LeWinter had shown up suddenly with large sums of cash in fall 1988. But there was no evidence linking that money to his phony phone-in performance as the fictitious Mr. Razine.

As Ross and I completed the interview, we were shaking our heads. Though LeWinter had influenced the direction of the October Surprise mystery at a key moment in 1988, it was unclear what we could do with his strange story. I wanted to have a segment in the documentary exposing this slippery character. But his continued insistence that some Paris meetings occurred complicated matters.

While I was willing to report that LeWinter had lied, I was uncomfortable mentioning that he was now insisting on a first-person role and was defending some of his earlier allegations. I doubted that we could overcome that dilemma; we might have to drop LeWinter altogether. Maybe LeWinter had figured that out, too. Maybe he was that sophisticated about manipulating the news media.

7

MAN WITH A MEDALLION

The lunchtime traffic clogged the crisscrossing streets near Victoria Station, one of London's busiest railway hubs. Robert Ross and I had returned to London as a final stop on our grueling two-and-a-half-week trip through Europe and North Africa. We had hauled our video gear through airports in London, Paris, Brussels, Düsseldorf, Tunis, and now back to London. We were exhausted and grouchy—and had one more interview to go.

During our previous stop in London, we had wrung an agreement from Iranian financier Jamshid Hashemi for an interview by enlisting the help of Gary Sick, a former National Security Council aide at the Carter White House. Sick was also investigating the possibility of Republican tampering with the hostage issue and had known Jamshid since 1980. At our request, Sick recommended that Jamshid talk with us, and Jamshid had agreed.

Jamshid Hashemi's brother, Cyrus, had been a key intermediary between Iran and the Carter administration on the hostages. In 1980, Cyrus, a balding, portly businessman, ran a small merchant bank, First Gulf Trust, with offices in London and New York. Cyrus was a man of many faces and many agendas. Some Carter aides who had dealt with Cyrus came to suspect that the clever financier had turned into a double agent, cooperating behind-the-scenes with the Republicans.

But some of the suspicions about Cyrus's double-dealing might have been hindsight. During the Iran-contra investigation, it was discovered that Cyrus brokered early contacts between the Reagan administration and the Iranians in 1984 and 1985. Cyrus offered his help in recruiting Iranians to negotiate freedom for American hostages, including CIA Beirut station chief William Buckley, who had been seized by pro-Iranian militants in Lebanon. Cyrus's assistance was proffered to CIA director William Casey, through Casey's close friends and Cyrus's business associates, John Shaheen and Roy Furmark.

The Lebanese-born Shaheen had known Casey since their World War II days together in the Office of Strategic Services, the CIA's forerunner. Furmark had worked for Shaheen's financial and energy companies before joining Saudi financier Adnan Khashoggi, who also played a key role in the Iran-contra affair. I had come across the names of both Hashemi brothers during my work on the Iran-contra affair, though I had never talked with either one.

In 1990, however, the question was: Did Cyrus's activities in 1985 have a historical precedent—in 1980?

In 1980, the Hashemis were known mostly as globe-trotting businessmen with diverse connections in the Persian Gulf and Republican business circles in New York. Though younger than Jamshid, Cyrus was the mover and shaker. He was well-tailored, well-schooled, and well-connected. Politically savvy, he could put together deals in a variety of profitable commodities, but most importantly, oil and weapons. When he crossed the Atlantic, as he did often, he flew the supersonic Concorde. When he visited the glamour cities of Europe, he stayed at the best hotels. While a big spender, he cultivated a conservative public image as a responsible businessman.

"When I first met Cyrus," former Attorney General Elliot Richardson told us, "he was elegantly turned out by a Bond Street tailor. He was very personable, unassuming, soft-spoken, intelligent, gracious in manner. He seemed in every way consistent with being a well-educated Iranian with an advanced degree from Oxford that he was said to have, a person who would have moved comfortably in international banking circles. Every-thing about him was perfectly consistent with that image. He lived on a very opulent scale, not ostentatiously so, more Oxfordian than blatantly *nouveau riche*."

Richardson had encountered Cyrus in 1979 when the Iranian business-man was offering to help broker an end to the embassy hostage crisis. Richardson put Cyrus in touch with officials in the Carter administration who were overseeing the hostage negotiations. The Cyrus Hashemi whom Richardson knew seemed like the "kind of moderate, responsible, interna-tionally oriented Iranian who would have been embarrassed by fundamen-talism and would have been embarrassed by the seizure of the hostages. He would have seen it in the long-term interest of his own country to re-establish relations with the United States."

But Cyrus had a darker side. His respectability cloaked a private life as a high-rolling gambler, a womanizer, and a man who misled his associates about his finances. Cyrus died owing London casinos three million pounds, or about $5 million at that time. His bank was a shell. He left his family destitute. "He was by no means the urbane, civilized, decent banker/economist that he seemed to be when I met him," Richardson told us. "Hashemi was a person capable of playing more than one role simul-taneously and seeming quite convincing to his audience whoever it was. So what I know now is not wholly inconsistent to his having been playing a double or a triple game."

Cyrus collapsed and died in London on July 21, 1986. An autopsy attributed the death to acute myeloblastic leukemia, a rare disease. But his older brother, Jamshid, became convinced that Cyrus had been murdered to silence him. In press interviews in 1987 during the Iran-contra scandal, Jamshid also began to intimate that there was another dimension to the story, one that dated back to 1980. But he would tell reporters nothing more.

During our stops elsewhere in Europe, I had called repeatedly to Jamshid's London office to remind him of his agreement to be interviewed. Nor-mally, I talked with a secretary, who promised to convey my message to him. Perhaps naively, I hoped that this persistence would protect us from getting stood up at the last minute.

Our other ploy was to show up at Jamshid Hashemi's office near Victoria Station with all our video gear: the camera, tripod, and bags of tapes and microphones. Jamshid had not explicitly agreed to an on-camera interview. I chose not to press the point on the telephone for fear he would cancel us out altogether. But I figured that if our camera gear was there, he might consent to a full-fledged interview.

But Jamshid was cleverer than we were. He had chosen not even to be present for our little performance. As we lugged our equipment through his office doorway, his secretary looked at us, smiled, and coolly suggested that we put our gear down. "Mr. Hashemi has already gone to lunch," she said. "But he's expecting you." She instructed us to wait downstairs for a driver to take us to Grosvenor House, an elegant hotel and restaurant across from Hyde Park. Jamshid Hashemi would be our host for a midday meal.

We deposited the camera and other equipment in a corner and took the elevator back down. The chances for an on-camera interview were fast approaching zero. But at least the weather was pleasant. It was a mild fall day in London, damp from a morning rain but now sunny. Soon a powder-blue Rolls Royce pulled into the driveway. A driver, who identified himself as Bill, invited us to climb in. The limousine had polished wood interior and white leather seats. The business of finance and weapons apparently had been good to Jamshid Hashemi.

As we climbed out of the Rolls at Grosvenor House, we were greeted in the open-armed Persian style by an overweight man with white thinning hair. He wore an expensive suit and turtleneck and carried a cellular phone. Around his neck was a gold medallion bearing the face of the prophet Mohammed. Jamshid Hashemi looked like a stereotypical rich Persian businessman.

Jamshid warmly shook our hands and invited us to follow him into the hotel's high-ceilinged dining room. The airy restaurant had the hushed tones of a classy eating establishment. The tables were far apart so conversations didn't carry. The most noticeable noises were the clicking of plates and an occasional polite laugh. Jamshid motioned for us to sit at a well-placed center table. The maitre d' smoothly eased our chairs out from the table. We sat down and exchanged pleasantries about our recent travels. We accepted Jamshid's advice to try the poached salmon and placed our orders with an attentive waiter.

As I started to phrase a question about the events of 1980, Jamshid apologized and said he needed to make a call on his cellular phone. When he finished, he started some more small talk about lunch. He acted like a man unsure exactly what he wanted to tell two reporters. Slowly, I eased him into the substance of the interview. But I was nervous that if we didn't bring Jamshid to the point soon, he might find enough excuses to stall so lunch would be over before the interview had begun. I continued to push him toward the reason for our meeting. He took a deep breath and began his tale. When Jamshid did talk, I scribbled notes furiously, suspecting that we might never get a second chance to interview him.

Jamshid's October Surprise story began New Year's Day 1980. A minor official in the Iranian government's Ministry of Information, Jamshid arrived in Washington carrying, he told us, a special State Department visa. His first important stop was CIA headquarters in Langley, Virginia, where the spy agency was considering what steps might be taken to moderate Tehran's radical Islamic policies. Jamshid said he had traveled to the United States to help arrange covert campaign financing for Admiral Ahmad Madani, an old friend in Iran who was running for president in the Islamic government's first national election.

With his weathered good looks and military bearing, Admiral Madani had cut an imposing figure in Iranian government circles for decades. He also was respected for his integrity as one of the few senior military officers who had dared to oppose the shah's rampant corruption. He had been forced out of the navy and spent the last several years of the shah's reign as a teacher, constantly harassed by SAVAK.

After the revolution, Madani was rewarded for his courage by gaining important posts in the post-revolutionary government. Madani was named the new government's first defense minister and then was appointed governor general of oil-rich and strategically vital Khuzistan province.

Madani's chief rival in the presidential election was Abolhassan Bani-Sadr, an academic who had stayed with Ayatollah Khomeini during his long exile in Paris. But the U.S. government, looking for any sign of rationality in Tehran, favored Madani. Responding to the pro-Madani appeals of the Hashemi brothers, the CIA agreed to funnel a modest sum of covert aid to the admiral's campaign. Madani had known the Hashemi brothers since childhood.

At lunch, Jamshid said his brother handled $500,000 in campaign money for Madani, but "very little, too late, reached Iran." At the polls, in the Islamic republic's first presidential election, on January 25, 1980, Madani garnered only 17 percent of the vote, losing handily to Bani-Sadr. The CIA demanded an accounting of the money and concluded that only about $100,000 had reached Iran. To blunt CIA anger, Cyrus returned $290,000.

Between bites of poached salmon at Grosvenor House, Jamshid claimed that Madani's defeat did not end his brother's wheeling and dealing with the U.S. government. Instead, Cyrus continued to trade on his contacts in Iran, offering to help the Carter administration settle the hostage crisis. To that end, and with the State Department's blessing, Cyrus ferried messages to and from Europe, typically jetting to the Continent on the Concorde and staying at posh hotels.

But the Hashemi brothers' dual sets of U.S. contacts—one the Carter administration and the other the Republicans—began to cross in March 1980. While staying at Washington's stately Mayflower Hotel, Jamshid said he was surprised by an unannounced visitor at his room: Roy Furmark knocked on the door. With Furmark, Jamshid claimed, was a tall, hunched man who spoke with a slurred New York accent. He was introduced as William Casey. By March 1980, Casey was director of Ronald Reagan's campaign for the Republican presidential nomination.

"Casey wanted to discuss political matters," Jamshid told us over the clicking of luncheon plates. "I cut him short. I said, 'I don't know who you are.' I called Cyrus and told him there was this gentleman here. Cyrus talked to Mr. Casey."

Jamshid said he thought little more about the Mayflower encounter until the summer. But in July, Cyrus confided to him that the relationship had taken another turn. "Cyrus asked me to bring Ayatollah[1] Mehdi Karrubi out of Iran for a meeting in Spain," Jamshid said. The brothers had known Karrubi, a hardline revolutionary mullah, and his brother, Hassan, in pre-revolutionary Iran, Jamshid said. To bring Mehdi Karrubi out, Jamshid said he arranged for the radical mullah to travel to Madrid. The Spanish capital was a favorite for the Iranians because no visas were required.

"The meeting took place at a hotel—the Ritz Hotel—at the end of

---

[1] Mehdi Karrubi's formal title is Hojjat El-Islam, one level below Ayatollah.

July," Jamshid said, claiming matter-of-factly that on the American side were William Casey and an active-duty CIA officer, Donald Gregg.[2] On the Iranian side, Karrubi came dressed in a turban and cloak, the traditional attire of an Islamic mullah. Jamshid and Cyrus attended to help with interpreting. But Jamshid expressed surprise that Casey was there.

"I remember saying, 'What the hell are you doing with Republicans?' " Jamshid told Ross and me. "My brother said the chance of Republicans getting to power was good and it was important to work with both sides."

Jamshid was sketchy about the dialogue at the meeting. He claimed the session began at about 11:00 a.m. and ended by late afternoon, with time out for sandwiches brought into the room for lunch. But Jamshid said that when Casey put his cards on the table, his desire was clear.

"The proposal was to hold the hostages until after the election, and then the Reagan administration would feel favorably towards Iran and release the FMS [foreign military sales] funds and the frozen assets and return to Iran what had already been purchased."

The already purchased supplies referred to $150 million in military hardware and spare parts bought by the shah from the United States but held back when Khomeini took power and the hostages were seized. Casey's offer also included F-14 spare parts, which were crucial to the maintenance of Iran's high-tech air force, Jamshid said.

As I scribbled in my notebook, which was perched at the edge of the dining table, Jamshid continued his story. He spoke deliberately, sometimes with hesitation. Occasionally he stopped in the midst of a detail to take a bite of food or answer the chirping of his cellular phone. Then he resumed the tale.

After the July meeting with Casey, Jamshid said, Karrubi returned to Tehran, where he consulted with Khomeini and the ayatollah's senior advisers. Two to three weeks later, Karrubi called and asked Jamshid for a second meeting. New arrangements were made, and that meeting, too, was held in Madrid at the Ritz. Casey and Gregg again represented the American side, and Karrubi was back for the Iranians. Jamshid said that throughout the two rounds, "Casey was running things," but Gregg "was giving

---

[2] Gregg later denied attending the Madrid meetings or even knowing Casey in 1980.

information that Casey didn't know or even we didn't know about, really inside-government information, like where the spare parts were."

At this second round, Karrubi again came dressed in full battle gear as an Iranian mullah. He "confirmed" Khomeini's agreement to release the hostages only after Reagan won power, Jamshid said. "Karrubi expressed acceptance of the proposal by Mr. Casey," Jamshid told us. "The hostages would be released after Carter's defeat."

As we finished with a light fruit dessert and delicious coffee at the Grosvenor House, I pressed Jamshid on one question in particular: Why was he talking now about events that he alleged happened a decade earlier? He answered that he was speaking from a sense of family responsibility over his younger brother's death. Jamshid rejected the medical finding of acute leukemia. "Cyrus passed a physical only a week before he died," Jamshid said. "The doctors found nothing wrong." Jamshid suspected that his brother had been murdered.

Jamshid said he hadn't told his story earlier because he felt it would destroy his business. Now, he said, he had made enough money to support himself and his family. Jamshid added that he also recognized that Cyrus's double-dealing would not make his late brother look good. But he wanted to know the truth about his brother's death. Talking about the October Surprise, he felt, was the only way to discover what really happened.

Though Jamshid held out the possibility of a fuller on-camera interview when he visited the United States around Thanksgiving, 1990, I felt little confidence that the dangled appointment would come to pass. Perhaps with less gentility than a Persian gentleman might expect, I kept returning to questions about the meetings in Madrid. Jamshid finally rose from the table. He needed to check, he said, on a silver tea set that he had ordered from the Grosvenor House gift shop.

We walked with him to the shop, which offered expensive objets d'art for sale. He talked briefly with the shopkeeper, made another call on his cellular phone, and led us out of the hotel to the waiting powder-blue Rolls Royce. He drove us back to his office near Victoria Station where we picked up our video gear. Our ploy for an on-camera interview had been a complete failure.

Before we parted, Jamshid offered to take us to some of his social clubs that night. Visions of roulette wheels and high-priced British call girls flashed briefly through my mind. But we declined, citing our scheduled flight home that afternoon. We left for Heathrow Airport, sensing that this might have been our only interview with Jamshid Hashemi.

Jamshid Hashemi's account of meetings in Madrid added a new complexity to the October Surprise story. We suddenly had another city, another set of meetings, a slightly different cast of characters, and an earlier timetable than before. Jamshid described meetings in July and August 1980 at the Ritz Hotel in Madrid, direct Republican-Iranian contacts starting as early as four months before the U.S. elections. Casey's alleged proposal was a release of the hostages after Ronald Reagan's election, with payment in both money and weapons.

The summer Madrid meetings would have preceded both the L'Enfant Plaza discussions in Washington and the mid-October 1980 contacts in Paris, outlined alternatively by Iran's ex-president Abolhassan Bani-Sadr, French arms dealer Nicholas Ignatiew, and the dubious duo of Oswald LeWinter and Richard Brenneke. Although the timing for the L'Enfant Plaza session was not clear, it apparently fell sometime in September or early October.

Ross and I had two fundamental problems in assessing these reported meetings. First, did the Madrid and Paris meetings happen at all? Considering the shakiness of the sources, this was the toughest issue to resolve. And second, if the three sets of meetings did occur, did they connect? Was Madrid a prelude to Paris? Was the L'Enfant Plaza discussion a separate initiative or somehow part of the bigger picture?

The only meeting we were sure happened was the one at the L'Enfant Plaza Hotel, near the Potomac River in Washington. Three prominent Republicans—Richard Allen, Laurence Silberman, and Robert McFarlane—confirmed that they had attended that meeting. But they could not recall with whom they met or what the date was, only that nothing came of the meeting. After the L'Enfant Plaza session was disclosed by the *Miami Herald*, Iranian arms dealer Houshang Lavi came forward to claim that he was the emissary and the date was October 2, 1980. But Lavi's credibility was almost as shaky as Brenneke's and LeWinter's.

As for Paris, the alleged meetings, as described, would have covered several days and possibly even several weeks. Bani-Sadr had put one meeting, at the Raphael Hotel, sometime before October 23, 1980. Brenneke and LeWinter cited the weekend of October 18–19, with Brenneke claiming that he may have stayed in Paris through October 20. Ignatiew was vaguer on the timing, but agreed that meetings did take place between October 19 and 22. All three mentioned several hotels, including the Raphael and the Waldorf-Florida. But the stories from Brenneke and LeWinter were suspect, to put it mildly. Bani-Sadr and Ignatiew also engendered little confidence. They both acknowledged that their information was, at best, second hand.

So Ross and I returned from our trip to Europe and the Middle East with more pieces of the puzzle, but no solution. Our original draft script had focused on a straightforward account about what various individuals had alleged about the October Surprise and an assessment of how questionable the evidence was. The original idea for the documentary also had envisioned lengthy sections on the history of U.S.-Iranian relations and on the secretly approved U.S. weapons flow to Iran in the early 1980s. On those points, Ross and I felt we were on firmer ground. But Jamshid Hashemi's Madrid tale led us deeper into the October Surprise fog—and it was getting denser.

8

AN ISRAELI TALE

Ari Ben-Menashe's trial was dragging through days of testimony about his alleged plot to ship three C-130 cargo planes to Iran. But life was looking up for the accused Israeli. The judge had decided that Ben-Menashe was not such a great threat to flee after all. The ex-intelligence man was released on bond.

Out of prison, Ben-Menashe was rejuvenated. His swagger and arrogance were back. After court, he spent hours pitching his stories to any number of journalists. One of his lawyers had even typed out a two-page list of media contacts—from the major American dailies to the television networks to Maury Povich and his tabloid TV show, *A Current Affair*.

Ben-Menashe would have been smarter to have selected a few serious journalists who could have checked out his claims methodically. But he opted for a public relations strategy that can only be described as promiscuous. It was a strategy guaranteed to diminish his reputation, like a high school girl determined to date the entire football team. Ben-Menashe was earning the kind of respect one gets from having a phone number written on a locker room wall.

At the request of the ABC News investigative unit, he submitted to a polygraph exam on his alleged contacts with Robert Gates, the former senior CIA man who had become President Bush's deputy national security adviser. The questions centered on Ben-Menashe's allegations that Gates had helped arm Iraq's Saddam Hussein during the 1980s. In fall

1990, the United States was nearing open warfare with Iraq over its August invasion of Kuwait. Ben-Menashe had been charging for months that the Reagan-Bush administrations had aided Saddam in his military build-up throughout the decade.

The White House had angrily denied Ben-Menashe's charges, and the allegations were widely disbelieved by the Washington press corps. Only a few news organizations, including *Frontline*, had noted the curious American hand in some Iraqi arms transactions. But Ben-Menashe's agreement to submit to an ABC-TV polygraph test didn't help him. Polygraphs are notoriously unreliable in determining if someone is telling the truth. But they are especially inaccurate when telling the truth can put the subject in greater danger than withholding the truth. To the extent the machines measure anything, they gauge a person's nervousness. The assumption is that a person is nervous when he lies and at ease when he tells the truth.

But in Ben-Menashe's case, assuming his story was true, he would be breaking his secrecy oath with the State of Israel. He would open himself to retaliation, criminal charges, possibly imprisonment. He would also be antagonizing the White House and the CIA. So whether he told the truth or lied, Ben-Menashe would feel nervous and conflicted, exactly what a polygraph would discern as "fluttering." But the cocky Ben-Menashe impetuously agreed to take the exam, which he flunked. The polygraph outcome undercut his already shaky credibility.

On October 30, 1990, after a few days of reacquainting myself with my family, I flew back to New York to interview Ben-Menashe about his claimed October Surprise knowledge. I hoped to get him on camera after one of his days in court. At least this would be a chance to talk to him outside prison. If Ben-Menashe lost his case, I might not have this opportunity again.

Late in the afternoon, I took a cab to the federal courthouse in lower Manhattan. The courthouse is next to MCC-New York, where I had talked to Ben-Menashe in jail. I wanted to catch a bit of the trial and then make contact with him, but a lawyer for Ben-Menashe's co-defendant had fallen ill, causing the trial to recess early. When I arrived, nobody was left in the courtroom. Cursing under my breath, I reversed course, departed the courthouse, and headed back uptown. After two months on this project, I had had my fill of chasing disreputable arms dealers around.

For this trip, I was staying at the funky Gramercy Park Hotel, near Greenwich Village. From my room, I called the home of one Ben-Menashe lawyer. An associate of the lawyer answered and told me that the Israeli was out. He was meeting with Mike Wallace of CBS's *60 Minutes*, the voice said with great self-importance. After that, Ben-Menashe had slated another interview with a reporter from the *Wall Street Journal*. Then he might find time for us.

By mid-evening Ross and I arrived at the lawyer's swank apartment on Central Park South. Ben-Menashe had finished with Mike Wallace, but was in another room expounding on his life's adventures to the *Wall Street Journal* reporter. At last he came into the dining room where Ross and I had been sitting with our video gear. Appearing exhausted, he apologized for the delay. I noticed, for the first time, that Ben-Menashe chainsmoked. During the prison interviews, he never had cigarettes, apparently a jail-house rule. His smoking fit the image of a life-on-the-edge spy. He favored Marlboros.

After a day in court and an evening of courting journalists, Ben-Menashe looked ragged when he finally sat down before our camera. He spoke even more hesitantly than usual, glancing away when answering many questions. Sometimes his voice was barely audible. I could sense from Ross's nervous twitching behind me that this interview was not looking good. But I thought it was worth at least letting Ben-Menashe explain how he saw the history that had led up to the mysterious events of 1980.

For two decades, Israel's quiet alliance with Iran had been the jewel in the Israeli strategy for countering pressure from neighboring Arab states, Ben-Menashe told us. The strategy was to build friendly ties to regional non-Arab nations. It was classic *Realpolitik*. Called the Periphery Doctrine, the idea was to establish discreet relations with Turkey, Ethiopia, and Iran—on the Arab world's periphery—to distract the Arab nations from concentrating all their military might against Israel. The Periphery Doctrine was deemed central to Israeli national security. The Jewish state would overlook unsavory behavior by these non-Arab allies if that was the price of maintaining the relationships.

Through the late 1960s and most of the 1970s, the Jerusalem-Tehran axis thrived. But the Israelis, who kept a close eye on events in Iran, grew worried about the staying power of the shah as the 1970s wore on. While American diplomats sent off reassuring cables to Washington, the Israelis were secretly predicting serious trouble for their longtime ally. But this prescience did the Israelis little good. When the shah fell to a popular uprising, the Israelis could only watch and hope that the new Iran would still have need for Israel's practical assistance. Iran's officer corps, after all, was staffed from top to bottom with men who had trained in Israel.

"There were a lot of Iranian officials, even today, who speak some Hebrew because from the times of the shah they were educated and trained in Israel," Ben-Menashe told us.

But Iran's new leader, Ayatollah Khomeini, was virulently anti-Israel. He denounced Israel as an enemy of Islam. Israel was the Little Satan, partner in blasphemy with the Great Satan, the U.S. government. Khomeini sought to purge both American and Israeli influence from his radical Islamic state. As revolution swept Iran, many of the shah's generals were jailed, exiled, or shot. But more practical Iranian officials understood the danger of cleansing the entire military. So, many of the second tier of officers were spared. The colonels survived, sometimes moving up into the top ranks to replace the deposed generals.

The wisdom of keeping a bridge open to Israel grew clearer as storm clouds built over Iran's disputed border with Iraq. The Iranians realized that their military defense would rest on their ability to keep their Western weapons in the field and in the air. Possibly, Ben-Menashe said, the worst problem was with the U.S.-supplied air force of F-4s and F-14s. With the hostage crisis continuing, the chances of obtaining new supplies from the Great Satan were almost nonexistent. So the Iranians turned to the Little Satan.

"Basically, the Israeli government was receiving informal requests in 1980 for help with military equipment to Iran," Ben-Menashe said, glancing at me and then looking away. "Here and there, there were rumors that the Iranians are interested in buying weapons."

For their part, the Israelis feared that Iranian instability played into the power-greedy hands of Iraq's Saddam Hussein, one of Israel's most dangerous Arab enemies. Perhaps the most charismatic Arab leader since the death of Nasser, Saddam based his popular appeal on Arab hatred of Israel and enthusiasm for the Palestinian cause. Saddam also had an eye on expanding his already vast oil reserves by grabbing Iran's oil-rich Khuzistan province just east of his long-disputed border with Iran.

"The first thing that clicked in various people's minds was the idea of the enemy of my enemy is my friend," Ben-Menashe recalled, picking up the pace of his commentary. "That was the concept. If these guys are well-equipped to go out to war with the Iraqis, Israel is off the hook for quite a while. And that theory proved true. In 1980, all kinds of former Iranian officials that had Israeli contacts from the times of the shah started asking them if it's possible to get some military equipment."

But the Carter administration was putting pressure on all its allies to choke off Iran from military equipment until the American hostages were freed. So Israel found itself caught between two powerful security interests: its vital alliance with the United States and its regional imperative to counter its Arab enemies. Meanwhile, President Carter seemed immobilized by the hostage crisis that was jeopardizing his re-election.

"Towards the middle of 1980, it was clear in the United States that the White House had turned into a hostage negotiation office," Ben-Menashe continued as cigarette smoke swirled around him. "It was completely paralyzed. The president and his advisers were only closed in on the issue of American hostages in Iran. People in Israel were looking for authorities to talk to in the United States.

"In 1980, everybody also says that the Carter administration is going to collapse. There will be no re-election for Mr. Carter. Reagan's campaign was very, very popular and very successful. Polls were showing that Reagan is going to become president of the United States. Already, in May, June, July, Israeli officials going to the United States first would go and visit Mr. Reagan or his people and not go see the Carter administration."

From the Reagan camp and from U.S. intelligence circles, Ben-Menashe said, the clearance came to open lines of communications to the Iranians: Find new ways to negotiate the hostage release. "The word came down to Israel, 'yes, we're willing to play ball. We think we can get the hostages out. We think that what the Carter administration is doing is very wrong,' which also the Israelis believed was very wrong."

One of the leading voices for that advice, Ben-Menashe claimed, was the GOP vice presidential candidate, George Bush. Ben-Menashe assessed Bush's sentiment as: "Play ball. I'll be the next vice president of the United States. Don't worry."

The rationale for the weapons sales would be for "creating a better atmosphere with the Iranians," the Israeli said. "We believed that with this atmosphere we will get the hostages out, which was a correct assessment. They did get the hostages out with the atmosphere that was created.

"I was sent because at the time I was one of the few people in the intelligence community that was thought to be a trustworthy person, educated in Middle Eastern studies. I spoke Persian. I spoke Arabic. I was thought to be one of the people to be sent to deal with these guys," the Iranian revolutionaries.

The Israelis informed the Iranians that willingness to supply weapons "is not coming from the White House, it's coming from the Reagan campaign headquarters," Ben-Menashe claimed. "We said that. They asked several times. They pointedly asked these questions. And they got straight answers from us."

"So what you were telling the Iranians," I asked skeptically, "was that the potential Reagan White House would favor making these deals with the Iranians?"

"Right," he responded, casually.

"While," I continued, "the Carter White House would not as long as the hostages were held?"

"The Carter administration was saying, 'No, period,' " Ben-Menashe answered, a touch of annoyance in his response to me. "They didn't say if. They said, 'We won't talk about anything before the hostages are out. Anything we do with the Iranians is going to be in the framework of a deal for bringing the hostages out.' The Reagan-Bush group were saying, 'Hey, Israelis, if you think you want to do something with the Iranians, we aren't that opposed to it.' "

Ben-Menashe went ahead with a cursory account of the supposed deal. He even claimed that he personally participated in meetings in Paris in 1980 with representatives of Iran and the Reagan-Bush campaign. But he was fading fast. Clearly we would need to schedule another interview when Ben-Menashe was better rested. We did have a sketchy version on tape, if this interview was the only time we would talk to him outside of prison. But first we needed to know more about this curious Israeli.

I arrived in Israel alone on November 8, 1990. Ross had diverted to Paris to film some of the hotels and other scenes connected to the October Surprise story. The plan was for me to get my bearings in Israel, a country I had never visited before. I had a list of names and phone numbers to try. I hoped to set up interviews to be shot when Ross arrived a few days later.

After collecting my luggage at Ben-Gurion Airport, I took a cab to Tel Aviv, a bustling, chaotic city on the Mediterranean Sea. The weather was mild, and the palm trees rustled in an offshore breeze. I checked into the Tel Aviv Hilton, a popular high-rise hotel that overlooks the Mediterranean and a white sandy beach. Throughout the year, the hotel is normally bustling with American tour groups. But in fall 1990, the hotel was nearly empty. The Middle East was in crisis over Iraq's invasion of oil-rich Kuwait.

Hundreds of thousands of U.S. troops were landing in Saudi Arabia to back up President Bush's demands for an unconditional Iraqi withdrawal. The State Department had cautioned American travelers about the dangers of terrorism. Plus, if full-scale war erupted, Israel would likely be a target of revenge for Saddam Hussein and Iraq's intermediate-range Scud missiles. Anticipating a possible chemical warfare attack, the Israeli government was distributing gas masks to civilians. It was not the best of times for tourism.

Though I had never been to Israel, I had long been fascinated by the country. In covering the Iran-contra affair and other national security issues, I had met a number of Israelis who worked in intelligence and military fields. I was impressed particularly with the older Israelis who had helped found the nation. These were single-minded individuals who had contributed to a feat unprecedented in history. They had returned an oppressed people to a historic homeland almost two millennia after their ancestors had been forcibly removed and scattered to the corners of the world. Israel's leaders accomplished this remarkable undertaking after the Jewish people had survived the most relentless genocide known to mankind.

The founders of the modern State of Israel had every reason to be proud of that achievement. But some of these remarkable individuals had grown concerned as well about what the Jewish people had sacrificed to secure their own homeland. There had been a hardening of the Jewish spirit, some of these Israelis felt. Out of necessity, the Israeli state had countenanced harsh acts to defend itself and to punish its enemies. Some of these attacks could be acknowledged, but others could not. To protect these secrets, the Israeli government had perfected the techniques of deception.

On day-to-day issues, Israel engaged in masterful public relations to burnish the nation's image and discredit Israel's critics. But these programs also meant that respect for truthful information, a hallmark of Jewish culture, sometimes was sacrificed to the practical demands of defending a modern state in a hostile environment. At times, some of these older Israelis worried that the country's national security needs diminished Israel's founding idealism. That was especially true when the nation was facing a direct threat, as it was in fall 1990.

As I went down my list of names and phone numbers to call, I found that many Israelis were unwilling to discuss either Ari Ben-Menashe or the events of 1980. Those who would talk curtly dismissed Ben-Menashe's claims.

"He is not a reliable person," said one Israeli who knew him. Official government spokesmen scoffed at Ben-Menashe's claims that he had personally represented Prime Minister Yitzhak Shamir on delicate operations in South America and the East Bloc from 1987 until 1989. As for his earlier work with the IDF's External Relations Department, Ben-Menashe was described as a translator who was wildly exaggerating his importance. A few Israeli officials even insisted that his letters of reference were bogus, though we had already ascertained that they were real.

Several Israelis compared Ben-Menashe to Victor Ostrovsky, the junior Mossad agent who had written a spy-and-tell book, entitled *By Way of Deception*. Ostrovsky had lambasted the Mossad as brutal, corrupt, and dishonest. He described poolside sex parties with young women recruits and violent assassination plots that indiscriminantly killed innocent bystanders. While the Israeli government denied many of Ostrovsky's allegations, the book had damaged the reputation of both the Mossad and the State of Israel. In a rare public relations bungle, the government worsened the predicament by seeking a court injunction to block the book's publication. The heavyhanded legal maneuver backfired. The publicity made Ostrovsky's book a bestseller.

"We can't stand another Ostrovsky" was how one Israeli intelligence man put it when discussing Ben-Menashe. Another was even harsher, calling Ben-Menashe a "traitor" who, like Ostrovsky, had divulged state secrets. One senior Israeli intelligence man called Ben-Menashe "our Ollie North," meaning that Ben-Menashe engaged in authorized clandestine operations, though he sometimes exceeded his orders.

But I had little success coaxing Israelis into on-camera interviews. I had intentionally bypassed the normal government-press channels, thinking that our chances for candid interviews were better if I approached people directly. I discovered, however, that even former government officials were leery about granting interviews without prior clearance from the government. Between my ignorance about how Israel worked and the touchiness of the time and topic, I struggled to reach the right people. When I did get through to key officials, I got my share of brush-offs.

Ross arrived with the camera equipment, but I had no formal interviews arranged. I finally called IDF spokesman Moshe Fogel. He told me that the press office had been aware of my presence in Israel and my inquiries. "We wondered when you'd get around to calling us," he chastised me. But he offered little help in arranging interviews on the twin subjects of Ben-Menashe and the October Surprise.

Despite my troubles with Israeli officialdom, I did track down Ben-Menashe's estranged wife, Ora. I talked to her twice over the phone before she hesitantly agreed to sit down with Ross and me for an off-camera chat about her indicted husband. She had little good to say about Ben-Menashe. But she sounded intriguing. Her voice on the telephone was soft as silk. I thought she might make a pleasant addition to the October Surprise cast. So I scheduled an appointment with Ora the next morning at 9:00 a.m. She suggested the Jerusalem Hilton, about a 45-minute drive from Tel Aviv.

The next morning, Ross and I were delayed leaving Tel Aviv because of a last-minute breakfast with a retired Israeli general. The general had been a figure in the Iranian arms pipeline during the 1980s and was worth meeting. But I was afraid the delay would foul up our interview with Ora.

When the breakfast ended, I hastily called the Jerusalem Hilton to leave a message advising Ora that we were running late. But I was nervous that she might not receive it.

Hopping into our rental car, Ross and I headed out of Tel Aviv and sped along the winding road that leads into the ancient hills around Jerusalem. We passed the burnt-out wrecks of armored vehicles destroyed in Israel's 1948 war of independence. The metal hulks, now painted a rust color, were left as visible reminders of Israel's fragile strategic position in the early years of its existence. The victories in 1948 and then in 1967 had allowed Israel to break out of its coastal positions and seize the West Bank, the Golan Heights, and the Suez peninsula. More than two decades after the 1967 war, only the Suez had been returned to Arab control, a concession to Egypt that was engineered by Jimmy Carter during the Camp David peace talks.

As we approached Jerusalem, we could see the Jerusalem Hilton, a towering modern hotel set on a hill near the Knesset in the city's western outskirts. To the east, the hotel commands a view of the historic city, which is visually striking because all the buildings—from the ancient walled city to the newest office complexes—are constructed with the same sand-colored stone. As Ross parked the car, I hurried into the Hilton to see if Ora was still there or if she at least had gotten our message. The hotel's reception desk assured me that she had been given the message and had indicated she would return at 10:00 a.m. So Ross and I waited for her in the spacious polished-stone lobby.

When Ora arrived, she looked cool and poised. It was obvious why Ben-Menashe had been taken by her. Her even features and large brown eyes were set off by a mid-length cut of shining dark hair. About 30 years old, she had a doe-like frame of more than average height. Ora wore a white silk blouse and dark skirt that looked both businesslike and sexy. Choosing a settee in a quiet corner of the Hilton's lounge, she sat with perfect posture, her knees and ankles together, leaning slightly forward to sip coffee.

Ora was an American-born Israeli who had lived in the suburbs outside Chicago. Like Ben-Menashe, she had moved to Israel in her youth. She also had been assigned to the Israeli Defense Forces External Relations Department. There she had met her future husband in the early 1980s. After leaving the military, she had entered a career in hotel management and public relations. Ben-Menashe was so smitten that he named his arms-exporting company after her, the ORA Group.

Ora had married Ben-Menashe in the mid-1980s when she was pregnant with their daughter, Shira. With Ben-Menashe frequently traveling abroad and later in jail, she was effectively a single parent to their three-year-old daughter. The little girl couldn't remember what her father looked like. Ora was openly bitter that Ben-Menashe was contributing no child support. She, quite bluntly, considered him a cad. But there had been better times, she said.

"We met when I was working at the External Relations Department in 1981," Ora told us. "Ari was quite dashing then."

In those days, Ora recalled, Ben-Menashe was often rushing off on assignments that seemed to come from orders above his superiors in the External Relations Department. But as a low-level staffer, she didn't really know for sure. "He seemed to have authority from somewhere else," she said. "He would just tell his ERD superiors that he had to go and he would go. They didn't seem to know where."

One mission, Ora remembered, took Ben-Menashe to communist Poland in the mid-1980s. They were dating at the time, and she talked with him by telephone from Warsaw. "The Polish authorities listened in on the conversations and later gave Ari tips about his love life," she laughed.

Ora's recollection of the Poland trip caught my attention. Her comments supplied the first corroboration of what had seemed like one of Ben-Menashe's most implausible stories. He had told me in one of our prison conversations that he had arranged the purchase of AK-47 assault rifles in Poland, something I found hard to believe. In the mid-1980s, Israel had tight restrictions on travel to communist countries, especially for government employees with access to secret information. But if true, Ben-Menashe's visits to the East Bloc would undercut the Israeli government's contention that Ben-Menashe was only a low-level translator bound to his tiny office.

For Ben-Menashe to have visited Poland without authorization and then to call his girlfriend on open phone lines would have been foolhardy. Even if the phone call had not been intercepted, Ora might have recounted the anecdote to friends in the military and intelligence communities. She had no hesitation in mentioning the visit to us. So an unauthorized trip to a communist country likely would have gotten back to Ben-Menashe's IDF superiors, putting him in very hot water. Ben-Menashe would have been subject to possible criminal charges upon his return home. But, in fact, he was never charged. That suggested either a glaring failure in Israel's highly regarded security—or that his Poland trip had been sanctioned. If his Poland trip had been sanctioned, then the Israeli government was still concealing its true relationship with Ben-Menashe.

Ben-Menashe's Poland story had made sense in another way. He described the Poland initiative as part of a secret strategy, ordered by Prime Minister Shamir, to open channels to the Soviet bloc. The strategic goals, Ben-Menashe said, were: first, to obtain light weaponry for sale to Iran, a tactical and financial priority, and second, to improve relations with Moscow so millions of Russian Jews would be permitted to emigrate to Israel. By gaining freedom for the Soviet Jews, Shamir believed, Israel could swell its manpower and expand settlements in the occupied West Bank. That would create a new reality on the ground, frustrating U.S. demands for Israel to relinquish those territories.

Another reason to take Ben-Menashe's Poland story seriously was the rich detail. In one prison interview, Ben-Menashe told me about a snowbound trip he took from Warsaw to Radun, a city about 70 miles south of the Polish capital. Along with him, he claimed, were two senior Polish military officers. They set out on the four-and-a-half-hour drive through a blinding snow storm in the winter of 1984–85.

"They brought out wood to warm up the diesel engine with fire," Ben-Menashe said. "When I asked if there were any kiosks for drinks, they looked at me and laughed, 'Where do you think you are, America?' "

When the little delegation reached Radun, the factory director was drunk, but the hospitable Poles had filled a conference room with food for their guest. "There was enough food to feed half the town, huge sausages, hot dogs," Ben-Menashe said. "Everybody but one production director got drunk. At the factory, when everybody was drunk, the two of us clinched a deal for 100,000 AK-47s at $81 each, with two magazines, cleaning kit, and sling. It was $4 below the production cost.

"This guy [the sober production director] got $80,000 in a bank in Vienna. This was the first load that went to the Iranians from Poland. We sold them to the Iranians for $125 apiece. We gave it to them cheap."

Though rich in detail and color, the story had struck me as fanciful. But Ora had confirmed that Ben-Menashe, in that time frame, had operated out of Poland. Ora also seemed to have no fondness for her wayward husband in fall 1990. Yet, she did believe that he had been carrying out assignments for the government. Those special assignments, Ora said, dated back to the early 1980s.

Ora's memories matched, generally, with Ben-Menashe's claim that starting in December 1980, he had been assigned to a special task force to implement Israel's covert program to supply Iran's war machine. Ben-Menashe said the six-member committee contained representatives from the key intelligence services, the Mossad and Aman, as well as officials from the prime minister's office and the defense ministry.

At first, Israeli officials denied the existence of any such committee. But General Yehoshua Saguy, ex-chief of the Aman, told me that Israeli intelligence coverage of Iran did change after the Islamic revolution in 1979. Before the revolution, the Mossad handled the covert but friendly relations with the shah. But after Ayatollah Khomeini seized power and began rattling sabres against Israel, the Aman asserted its responsibility to protect against armed threats. The result, Saguy said, was a shared intelligence responsibility between Mossad and Aman, much as Ben-Menashe described. An inter-agency "working group," consisting of 10 to 12 officials, met once a month to coordinate intelligence on Iran, Saguy acknowledged.

Ben-Menashe claimed he had fallen into the Iran operation in 1980 partly from luck and partly from his personal history. Like many Israelis, Ben-Menashe had a remarkable tale about his family's return from the Diaspora to the Biblical homeland. But unlike European Jews, many of whom faced the horrors of Adolf Hitler and the Holocaust, Ben-Menashe's family history was rooted in Iraq. That background gave Ben-Menashe a more personal understanding of the Muslim world than many Israelis possessed. But Ben-Menashe's family was not unfamiliar with the struggles that had forged the modern State of Israel.

Ben-Menashe's father, Gourdji, grew up in Baghdad. Then, as a young man, he went to France for his education and often visited Paris in the days before World War II. When war descended upon Europe, Gourdji

moved to Palestine, where the seeds of a Zionist independence movement were being planted. According to the family, Gourdji joined the
violent struggle for Israeli independence, working with the Lehi underground, a band of radical Zionists better known as the Stern Gang. The
Stern Gang was led by a young zealot, Yitzhak Shamir, the future prime
minister of Israel.

The group's terrorist attacks against British forces soon earned Gourdji
a place on a wanted list. He fled Palestine for Russia and India, where he
earned a living as a salesman. He later returned to Baghdad and married an
Iraqi-Jewish woman named Khatoun. The couple then moved to Iran, and
Gourdji took over a Mercedes-Benz spare parts dealership. The business
thrived and boosted the family into Iran's upper-middle class.

In Tehran, on December 4, 1951, a son, Ariel, was born to Gourdji and
Khatoun. Ari was a bright, energetic lad, who grew up with a strong Jewish
identification and powerful sympathies toward Israel. Ari attended the
American Community School in Tehran, where he studied English. At
home, he mastered Arabic, Hebrew, and Persian.

In his mid-teens, Ari Ben-Menashe was the first member of his family to
return to Israel, arriving in 1966 and later graduating from Bar Ilan
University. In 1974 he entered compulsory military service, where he
worked in a signals intelligence unit. Three years later, as a civilian, he
joined the Israel Defense Forces' External Relations Department, a wing
of Israeli military intelligence responsible for liaison with foreign militaries.

With the upheavals in Iran in 1979 and 1980, Ben-Menashe claimed, he
was dispatched back to Iran to exploit his childhood contacts. Israel was
trying to rebuild its decimated intelligence network, and Ben-Menashe's
personnel profile—his background, age, and language skills—made him a
prime candidate.

But was Ben-Menashe part of this intelligence initiative on Iran as he
described? Or was the Israeli government telling the truth—that Ben-
Menashe had fantasized an important role for himself as an Israeli spy? As
we left Israel, after a mostly frustrating week, Ross and I still didn't know
for sure.

9

A PARIS RENDEZVOUS?

Ari Ben-Menashe was celebrating. He had endured 11 months in prison and a draining trial. On November 28, 1990, he was acquitted by a 12-member federal jury. The jurors concluded that the government's case simply had too many holes. Apparently, they also believed Ben-Menashe's defense that he had remained an Israeli intelligence operative even after leaving the IDF's External Relations Department in 1987.

Ben-Menashe considered the turning point in his trial the introduction of a letter that prosecutor Baruch Weiss had sent to Israel. The letter asked about the three letters of reference that Ben-Menashe's mother had sent me and that *Newsweek* had corroborated. Weiss's letter suggested that the three letters of reference must be forgeries since the Israeli government had initially denied that Ben-Menashe had worked for military intelligence. But the Israeli government finally verified Ben-Menashe's employment. Defense lawyer Tom Dunn had managed to put part of Weiss's letter—and the Israeli reversal—into evidence.

Another key moment in Ben-Menashe's trial victory was the testimony of former *Time* magazine correspondent Raji Samghabadi. The journalist recalled that in mid-1986, when the Reagan administration's Iran-contra arms-for-hostage deals with Iran were a deep secret, Ben-Menashe approached him and tried to leak the story. The Reagan administration denied the story, and *Time* could not confirm the account of U.S. officials flying off on secret missions to Tehran. But the story broke several months later in a Beirut weekly, *Al-Shiraa*.

Samghabadi also testified that Ben-Menashe had told him then that the history of Reagan administration arms deals with Iran dated back to 1980. Again, Ben-Menashe's intimate knowledge of highly secret information—and his worldwide contacts with journalists and arms dealers—did not fit the Israeli story of a Walter Mitty character closeted away in a translator's office dreaming of international adventure. But the mainstream Washington press remained leery of Ben-Menashe's many tales of intrigue and espionage. The Israeli government, alarmed at his disclosures, was also stepping up its campaign to discredit him.

After Ben-Menashe's acquittal, when I was back in New York, Ben-Menashe invited me to join him at the Windows on the World restaurant at the top of the World Trade Center. He was celebrating the verdict with a woman friend. I took a cab from Ross's production studio in Soho through lower Manhattan to the Trade Center's twin towers. A high-speed elevator took me to the restaurant on one of the top floors. The lights of New York and suburban New Jersey sparkled far below. I found Ben-Menashe and his friend seated at a table in the cocktail lounge. Ben-Menashe had selected a table that overlooked the Statue of Liberty in New York Harbor. The choice seemed fitting.

By the time I arrived, Ben-Menashe had downed a large volume of champagne and was slurring his words as he recounted the high points of his trial. He credited my discovery that his letters of reference were genuine as an important step toward his acquittal.

"When Baruch Weiss said they were forgeries, that changed everything," he spoke loosely. "The jury didn't believe him after that." As he talked, he waved his arms as if embracing his freedom. To my discomfort, he kept calling me, "My friend, Bob Parry." Suddenly, he decided that he wanted to dance with his woman friend. Unsteadily he rose from his chair. Balanced against his date, he headed toward the dance floor.

Though not particularly handsome, Ben-Menashe had a knack for finding women wherever he went. Maybe it was his self-assurance or his gift for gab or the adventurous life he led. Certainly, he was worldly, having traveled to many corners of the globe—from Sri Lanka to Paris, from New York to Tehran, from London to Sydney. But in his late 30s, his hair thinning, his waistline thickening, his cologne a touch too strong, he struck more the image of a Middle Eastern traveling salesman than a dashing spy cut from the James Bond mold.

On the other hand, most of the women he had relationships with couldn't match the looks of his estranged wife, Ora. Some became obsessively devoted to him, at least during the early stages of romance. Sometimes, they would travel long distances to be with him. But invariably, he would treat them badly. He would get them to act as his secretary, placing calls and running little errands. He would use their telephones and run up exorbitant phone bills with his constant calling to cities around the world.

Most of the women quickly tired of his overbearing ways, or he would tire of them. Ben-Menashe once explained to me his primal urge about romance. "I like new sex," he said succinctly. Some of the women, left behind like wreckage in his wake, would have few flattering things to say about him and his behavior.

When he staggered back from the dance floor during his night of celebration, I reminded him that he had promised to lend me the originals of his passports which he had gotten back after the trial. Ross planned to make copies for possible use in the documentary if we decided to include Ben-Menashe. The passports, covering 1985 until his arrest in 1989, showed dozens of foreign trips to Europe, the United States, Central America, and South America. Ben-Menashe had been on the road for weeks on end. The passport stamps further undercut the Israeli government's story about a lowly translator who never traveled on government business. Ben-Menashe clumsily fished the passports out of a manila envelope and handed them to me.

"You know, I don't drink," he said as his words grew more and more indistinct. "I may have other vices, but I don't drink." Clearly, he had developed little tolerance for the stuff. He slumped back in his chair. I suggested that it might be time for him to call it a night and head back to New Rochelle, where he was staying with his friend. Ross and I would stop by later to do a full interview when he was better rested.

*   *   *

A week later, Ross and I wound our way from Manhattan through the early dark of a late fall evening to the suburban setting of New Rochelle. Ben-Menashe's friend lived in a pleasant split-level home. When we rang the bell, her teen-age children invited us in. Their mother and Ben-Menashe arrived home several minutes later.

Ben-Menashe looked relaxed and refreshed. He sat down with us in the living room and asked his friend to bring us some homemade pie and coffee. He was excited that his acquittal had been picked up in newspapers not only in America but back in Israel. He showed us some of the articles in Hebrew. Most were highly critical of him and accepted the government's continued denunciations of Ben-Menashe as an impostor who falsely claimed to have worked for the prime minister's office from 1987 until his arrest. Ben-Menashe appeared to relish publicity, no matter how negative.

But the sentiment about him inside the Israeli intelligence community was mixed, he insisted. He said he was still in touch with some old allies in Tel Aviv and Jerusalem. "I still have friends in Israel, you know," he said. "You may not think that, but it's true. I still talk to old friends in Israel." Some criticized his decision to speak out publicly, he acknowledged. But he claimed others faulted the government for disowning one of its operatives who was caught in a tight fix.

In New Rochelle, Ben-Menashe was less hesitant than when I questioned him in prison or at his lawyer's apartment. The acquittal had been a tonic for him. He looked relaxed. He was fresh-shaven and well-scrubbed—a contrast to the fidgety fellow with a five o'clock shadow whom we had found in previous interviews. This time Ben-Menashe was more vivid in his descriptions and more animated in his speech. With greater detail, he set the scene in 1979–80.

"There were Israeli intelligence estimates at the time that if the Iraqis were to invade Iran, it would take them three to four weeks to take all of Khuzistan and bring down the Khomeini regime," Ben-Menashe said, as he sat at a table with a box of Marlboros within easy reach. "There was one particular estimate that said if the Khomeini regime doesn't pull its act together and get consolidated quickly and put its military forces together quickly, they're going to fall apart."

Paradoxically, it was the seizure of the American hostages on November 4, 1979, and the outside world's condemnation that unified the splintered political factions inside Iran. The Iranians saw the external pressure as further evidence of the West's imperial designs. "People were identifying with something: the U.S. hate. 'Our problems are because of the U.S.' From the point of view of the Iranian regime, the takeover of the U.S. embassy was probably one of the smartest moves that Khomeini could have done in the early period after the revolution," the Israeli said.

As the Khomeini regime gained its political footing with the hostage seizure, Tehran began to address its pressing military worries. "Sometime in March of 1980, the first moves to put back together the military were being taken," Ben-Menashe continued. "There were some inquiries for military equipment to various Israelis that the Iranians thought would have contacts with the ministry of defense or the government or intelligence services. The Iranians' biggest worry was the Air Force; by that time, all the pilots were imprisoned. Plus, they had no tires. Their F-4s, and I believe there were some F-5s at the time, too, had flight tires that were not in good condition. They were looking for spare parts on tires and wheel bases. These were their first inquiries."

Ben-Menashe claimed that one longtime Iranian contact forwarded a purchase request to him. "One of these inquiries came to my own hands," the Israeli said, with a sly smile. "I was, like, lucky, as if we could call it lucky to be the first person in Israel after the revolution to actually do a military equipment deal with the Iranians. I take credit for that."

Soon his proposed F-4 tire sale rose to the top of the stack, he said. "All these things were piled up. And an approval came from the prime minister's office—it went all the way to the prime minister's office for the inquiry that I got, and they were the tires." With a casual shrug of his shoulders and an amused lilt in his voice, Ben-Menashe continued, "And so we sold them the tires."

The modest sale of about 300 tires to Iran, Ben-Menashe recalled, did not sit well with President Carter, who had demanded that American allies join in a tough trade embargo. Ben-Menashe said Carter personally complained to Prime Minister Menachem Begin about the tire sale and demanded that all deals must stop. Growing bitter over Carter's constant lecturing, Begin privately became a rooter for a Reagan victory.

"The Israelis were interested in developing a relationship with the new Iranian regime," Ben-Menashe explained. "Iran was very important to us. And by that time, Begin was completely impatient with Carter."

Begin's annoyance with Carter stretched beyond Iran to the tense negotiations at Camp David, where Begin had been pressured into surrendering the Sinai in exchange for a peace agreement with Egypt. The Israelis were also disappointed that another longtime friend, Nicaragua's dictator Anastasio Somoza Debayle, had been abandoned during the Sandinista revolution. But Ben-Menashe contended that for Israel, it was the prospect of Iraqi gains in oil-rich Khuzistan province that pushed Begin over the edge.

"The Iraqis could not take over Khuzistan, southern Iran," Ben-Menashe said. "It was like inviting a big national security threat to Israel. Begin was obsessed by this matter. In August 1980, the final decision comes down that we are going along with the Reagan campaign. We have to get closer to the Iranians and deal with the Iranians for several reasons. First of all, it was perceived as an Israeli national interest. Secondly, by then, the Reagan/Bush campaign was seen to be the next legal government of the United States, so we have to get along with them. Let's work with them.

"But everybody in Israel was very careful and it was not hindsight. The matter was then perceived that if there's ever going to be any scandal, the Israeli government will be held responsible by Congress and the U.S. public that it participated in subversion of legal government of the United States."

I stopped Ben-Menashe there. "Well, that is an awfully big risk," I said, amazed at the scope of his allegations. "Why did Israel take it?"

"What were the options?" Ben-Menashe responded, matter-of-factly. "Reagan/Bush were going to take over so we had to please them. We had to . . ."

"You didn't have to please them," I interjected, with a mixture of impatience and disbelief.

"Yeah, well, they believed that," Ben-Menashe shot back. "And Reagan was perceived to be a good president for Israel. He was a good president for Israel. He is going along with the Israeli perception of Iran, meaning we have to deal with these guys. We have to strengthen their hand against the Iraqis. We have to stabilize them. Basically, the Reagan campaign was seeing eye to eye with Begin about Iran. So, let's go with them.

"It was a tremendous risk, yes. But Begin took it. He took it upon himself. He made a decision in August, Begin and his closed cabinet. This went down from the highest level in the Israeli government. And remember, at the time, Begin was very powerful, extremely powerful over his cabinet. He was extremely popular. He had support. He made the decision and it came down from there."

The account of Begin's supposed decision to throw his lot in with the Republican campaign was vintage Ben-Menashe. His story sounded unbelievable on its face and was certain to draw angry denials from anyone in Israel who held a position of power at the time. Yet, Ben-Menashe was correct in describing the private feelings of Begin's inner circle. Besides strategic differences over Iran, Begin deemed Carter and his human-rights-driven sympathy for the Palestinians a threat to Israel.

I found these Israeli concerns expressed bluntly by David Kimche, the urbane Israeli diplomat/intelligence officer, in his book on Mideast tensions, *The Last Option*. Kimche, a senior Mossad official who shifted over to the Foreign Ministry, described bitterly how Carter pressured Israel to surrender territory to the Arabs. To the Israelis, Carter and his top advisers had tilted to the Palestinian side.

"Begin was being set up for diplomatic slaughter by the master butchers in Washington, while Israel was being taken to the cleaners by the experts of the National Security Council and the Middle East specialists of the State Department," Kimche wrote. "They had, moreover, the apparent blessing of the two presidents, Carter and [Egyptian President Anwar] Sadat, for this bizarre and clumsy attempt at collusion designed to force Israel to abandon her refusal to withdraw from territories occupied in 1967, including Jerusalem, and to agree to the establishment of a Palestinian state. This plan—prepared behind Israel's back and without her knowledge—must rank as a unique attempt in United States's diplomatic history of short-changing a friend and ally by deceit and manipulation."[1]

The normally soft-spoken Kimche denied that this was a case of Israeli government paranoia over Carter's intentions. Begin and his government reasonably viewed the prospect of a second Carter term with dread.

"Unbeknown to the Israeli negotiators, the Egyptians held an ace up their sleeves, and they were waiting to play it," Kimche recalled. "The card was President Carter's tacit agreement that after the American presidential elections in November 1980, when Carter expected to be re-elected

---

[1] David Kimche, *The Last Option* (London: Weidenfeld and Nicolson, 1991), p. 92.

for a second term, he would be free to compel Israel to accept a settlement of the Palestinian problem on his and Egyptian terms, without having to fear the backlash of the American Jewish lobby."

So, as bizarre as Ben-Menashe's account of Begin siding with Reagan might seem, there was at least the plausibility of motive. Begin saw Carter's second term as a major national security threat to Israel. Begin, too, was a political leader who did not shy from risky strategies when he considered them vital to Israel's national interests.

An Eastern European Jew, Begin had lost his parents and brother to the Nazi extermination campaigns. He escaped to British-ruled Palestine, where he joined the violent underground movement determined to fulfill the Zionist dream of a Jewish state. Trusting in bold action, armed struggle, and a zealous defense of Jewish rights, Begin despised negotiations and concessions.

As a leader of the Irgun Zvai Leumi, or National Military Organization, Begin targeted British forces for violent attacks, even when those actions resulted in the killing of large numbers of civilians. The Irgun's most notorious operation was the 1946 bombing of the King David Hotel in Jerusalem, which housed the British administrators for Palestine. Nearly 100 people, both British and Jewish, died.

When the British executed Irgun members charged with terrorism, Begin's organization retaliated by hanging two British soldiers. In 1948, an Irgun-led assault slaughtered 200 Arab men, women, and children in the village of Deir Yassin. The attack embittered Arabs throughout the region and set the tone for the eye-for-an-eye vengeance that would bloody and blind Israeli-Arab relations for decades to come.

But even with Begin's personal history, Ben-Menashe's contention that the Israeli prime minister would conspire with the Republican campaign to undermine a sitting president and his chances for re-election seemed beyond belief. Even if Israel's hardline leaders saw Carter as a dire threat to Israeli security, Begin would need some assurance that any secret GOP-Israeli alliance could be kept hidden. Protection of that secret would remain a top priority for the Israeli government for years to come.

Yet, Ben-Menashe's story would go further. To my surprise, Ben-Menashe claimed to know about the sessions in Madrid that Jamshid Hashemi had described. The Israelis, Ben-Menashe said, heard about these meetings both from contacts inside the Republican inner circles and from Israel's own sources inside Iran.

"The information was there," Ben-Menashe continued in the interview. "It was hard. It was that Casey was meeting high Iranian officials from the ruling council, a member of the Supreme Council at the time. It was Hojjat El-Islam Karrubi in Spain and there were rumors that there was going to be a final meeting in October."

The Israeli said meetings between Republicans and Iranians in Madrid dated back even earlier, to March 1980. Ben-Menashe thought Jamshid Hashemi's claim of meetings with Casey in July and August sounded too late, but could be right.

"The Americans agreed to release money and make promises for the future when Reagan/Bush take over to make relations better and the Iranians promised to release the hostages," Ben-Menashe said, fingering his packet of cigarettes. "And the Americans also promised to allow arm shipments to Iran, indirect arms shipments to Iran. And this is why Israel is brought in."

The Israelis were asked to assist in the operation by Casey himself, Ben-Menashe claimed, with direct contacts between the Republican campaign director and Yehoshua Saguy, then chief of Israeli military intelligence, the Aman. Other details were ironed out between lower-level CIA officials and their Israeli counterparts, Ben-Menashe said.[2]

According to Ben-Menashe's story, the Israelis initially believed that the Republican-Iranian meetings in Madrid and the proposed weapons swap were sanctioned by the CIA as an authorized program for winning the hostages' freedom. But from the start, he said, the Israelis were suspicious.

"At this time, did the Israelis have any inkling that there was anything more to this than an effort to get the hostages out right away?" I asked.

"They didn't know and they didn't want to think," Ben-Menashe answered. "There's a saying in Israel when you don't want to know, you

---

[2] Saguy denied to me that Casey made any such overtures, although acknowledging a close relationship with Reagan's campaign director. Another Israeli intelligence officer confirmed that there were "out-of-channel contacts" during this period between U.S. and Israeli intelligence officers about the hostage issue. But this officer said he did not know how far those contacts had gone.

don't look for anything. You try to play the 'small head.' We wanted to believe that this is authorized by the Central Intelligence Agency. But in the back of our minds, the Israelis are extremely sensitive to this."

When a follow-up meeting was scheduled in Paris in October, Ben-Menashe claimed the Israelis sent representatives, but still kept some distance. "The Israelis did not send a high-level delegation to Paris. They sent relatively junior people, except one senior intelligence officer. The rest were relatively junior."

Ben-Menashe claimed that he was part of this six-member Israeli team that prepared the Iranians for the approach by the Americans.

Ben-Menashe's Paris tale came replete with rich detail, just as his story about Poland had. "The Israelis flew in at the official invitation through phone calls by Casey himself to the intelligence chiefs," Ben-Menashe said. But the Israeli goal was to expedite an end to the hostage crisis, not prolong it. The Israelis still were looking to clear the obstacles blocking resumed Israeli military shipments to Iran—and the hostages were the biggest impediment.

"At that point, it was still not clinched in Israel who's going to do what. We were still what we call in our diapers on the subject," Ben-Menashe continued. "My job, basically, was to compile a telephone book from the Iranians. I was suppose to just listen to the Americans but keep away, not make any promises to the Iranians, but compile a telephone book from the Iranians—telephone numbers, addresses, positions, how we can contact them in the future. And I did that very well."

For the Paris meetings in mid-October, Ben-Menashe said he and two lower-ranking Israelis stayed at the Tour Eiffel Hilton, and their Iranian counterparts checked into the Hotel Montaigne, a pleasant hotel on the tree-lined Rue Montaigne. Ben-Menashe refused to give the names of the other Israelis.

Besides exchanging phone numbers, Ben-Menashe said the Israelis and the Iranians got chummy. "I became friendly with them," he said. "I was supposed to get friendly with them, try to take them out to dinner or lunch. I spoke their language. They were impressed by that." The Israelis also exposed the Islamic fundamentalists to the worldly side of Paris nightlife. "I took two Iranians to the Pigalle," Paris's strip-joint district, Ben-Menashe said, with a short laugh.

For the American side for the Paris meetings, the Iranians were demanding at least one high-ranking Republican, Ben-Menashe said. "They were not sure if Casey is going to be a member of the future administration, but they were sure that Bush would be because he had an official position at the time. Casey was, for all they knew, not to be part of the new government. They were guessing that he might be secretary of state. But Bush, they knew, is going to be vice president."

Ben-Menashe's account of the supposed Paris meeting was filled with anecdotes and some plausible elements. But it also had serious credibility problems. Vague stories about a Paris get-together had long circulated, and Ben-Menashe could have pieced together enough details to build his account. Most troubling was his stubborn insistence that vice presidential candidate George Bush attended a round of meetings in Paris. Ben-Menashe compounded his believability problem by maintaining that Robert Gates, who in 1980 was executive assistant to Jimmy Carter's CIA director Stansfield Turner, also joined the meetings. Ben-Menashe said he knew these two men were present in Paris because he had seen them firsthand.

The top Americans arrived several days after the Israeli delegation, Ben-Menashe insisted. During the early afternoon of one of those days, Ben-Menashe claimed to have seen Bush and Casey go into a meeting with cleric Mehdi Karrubi at the Ritz Hotel, an expensive but discreet hotel in downtown Paris. The Israeli said he did not attend that meeting, but saw the Americans and the mullah shake hands before a door was closed.

At other sessions with lower-level Americans, Ben-Menashe claimed to have listened but not talked. The Americans "were basically saying to the Iranians that if we work out a deal on the hostages to be released on a certain date, we will accommodate you."

But Ben-Menashe said he heard no explicit instructions to hold the hostages until after the November election or until Ronald Reagan took office. "The Americans were not saying that, not in so many words," Ben-Menashe maintained. "But they made it clear that 1981, the 19th or 20th of January is the time."

The Iranians, he added, were eager to unload the hostages as soon as possible: "The Iranians were basically saying, 'Okay, enough is enough, they can have their guys. Let's get the money, we need the money.' The Americans were saying, 'we cannot release the Iranian money so quickly.' They did not come and tell them, 'keep the hostages until January.' They were basically saying, 'well, it will take time to release the money. Let's set a date in January for the release.' The Iranians were saying, 'Just give us the money and you can get your guys.' The Iranians were saying basically that."

Ben-Menashe's tale of the Paris meetings suffered some serious shortcomings besides the unequivocal denials of Bush, Gates, and senior Israelis. Ben-Menashe, with his characteristic self-assurance, said he was certain that he had arrived on a Tuesday in mid-October, most likely the 14th. He said he believed the top Americans, including Casey and Bush, arrived on Thursday, presumably the 16th. The account was classic Ben-Menashe, insisting that he recalled the precise day of the week when events occurred a decade earlier. He was unshaken by conclusive proof to the contrary.

"You know, in that week Bush was campaigning," I noted. We had checked newspaper articles and videotape of the Republican vice presidential candidate jumping from city to city in the Midwest before stops in Pennsylvania and New Jersey at week's end.

"I believe it was the Thursday that he came in, yes," said Ben-Menashe unmoved by the evidence.

"Well, when did you see him?" I asked, aware that Ben-Menashe had a tendency to incorporate what he might have heard into his definitive stories.

"I saw him with Casey, yes."

"And you saw them, are you sure it was that early in the week?" I pressed. "Could it have been over the weekend?"

"No, Thursday, they were there," Ben-Menashe said, crossing his arms as he dug in his heels. "I believe it was a Thursday. It was before the weekend, if I remember correctly. I would believe it was before the weekend, yes."

"You mean, they stayed for several days?" I asked, incredulously.

"Talking. By Sunday, the major ones left." But he said he saw Bush and Casey only once. The rest of his information about their itinerary, he acknowledged, was secondhand.

When I asked Ben-Menashe how he could remember something as

obscure as the day of the week from a decade earlier, he said he recalled going to the synagogue the following night. His assumption was, he said, that he had attended weekly services on Friday night, meaning that his encounter with Bush would have been the day earlier, on Thursday. I again told him that our research had proven conclusively that Bush was campaigning in public that day and could not possibly have slipped away to a meeting in Paris.

The obstinate Ben-Menashe continued to insist that his memory was clear, though he acknowledged there might have been another reason for him to attend synagogue. He suggested that the Jewish holiday of Succoth might have fallen during that time frame, causing him to go to synagogue on a day other than Friday. In 1980, however, Succoth fell in September, not October.

Overall, Ben-Menashe's unwavering declaration that he had seen Bush and Casey brush by him and into a meeting with Karrubi devastated the Israeli's personal credibility. Even though many of his specific claims about other events—his role in Iranian weapons shipments, his trips to Poland, his curious activities in South America and his attempts to leak the Iran-contra arms-for-hostage scheme—checked out, it was "Bush in Paris" that underscored his unbelievability. Not only could Bush not have traveled to Paris on any Thursday in mid-October since he was on the campaign trail, his whereabouts on other days were recorded by the Secret Service, which had the candidate under round-the-clock protection.

Indeed, there was only one time period when Bush was out of the public eye long enough to have flown to Paris, attended a brief meeting, and returned. A flight by private jet to and from Paris alone would have taken about 15 hours, a car ride into Paris and back another two hours, and then an hour or so for a meeting. The only hole that large in Bush's pre-election schedule was a 20-hour-plus rest stop beginning Saturday night at 10:00 p.m., October 18, when the vice-presidential candidate returned to Washington from a campaign swing, until Sunday evening, at 7:00 p.m., October 19, when Bush spoke to the Zionist Organization of America at the Capital Hilton in Washington.

Earlier, I had obtained Secret Service records covering this period under the Freedom of Information Act. Though heavily censored, the notations indicated that Bush's detail left the candidate's Washington residence in mid-morning on October 19. The Secret Service detail went to the Chevy Chase Country Club in suburban Maryland, arriving at 10:29 a.m. and departing an hour and a half later, at 11:56 a.m. I had been told the records recounted a second trip in the afternoon to a personal residence, but that entry had been censored for reasons of personal privacy. The sheet contained no notations of exactly who went on the trip to the country club, stating only: "10:29 a.m. - Arr. Chevy Chase Country Club; 11:56 a.m. - Dep above via motorcade, same assignments as above."

I had hoped to bolster the Secret Service document with an interview with one or more of the agents on duty. But the Secret Service refused to provide anyone, even a spokesman, who would vouch publicly for the accuracy of the reports. When I tracked down three of the Bush agents independently, all three cited secrecy rules and refused to confirm or deny taking Bush to the country club. Country club officials were equally unhelpful, saying they had no memory of Bush visiting the club during that time frame.

One club official had suggested to a congressional investigator earlier in 1990 that Bush might have been a guest of then Supreme Court Justice Potter Stewart, a club member and close friend. But Stewart had died in 1985. So again, the account could not be crosschecked with an eyewitness. Plus, Robert Ross's examination of Justice Stewart's personal calendars at the archives of Yale University showed no entry for that Sunday in mid-October 1980.

Though Ross and I gave great weight to the Secret Service records, we had failed to find anyone who would confirm seeing Bush in Washington that fall Sunday, prior to his evening appearance at the Zionist Organization's dinner. On the other hand, there were two other individuals who claimed they might have seen Bush in Paris during this time period. But by comparison, they made Ben-Menashe look like a rock of reliability.

One was Heinrich Rupp, the pilot friend of Oregon arms dealer Richard Brenneke. Rupp claimed that he had served in the German air force at the end of World War II and remained an admirer of Adolf Hitler's Nazi Party. In addition, he was a felon convicted of participating in a bank fraud scheme in Colorado. Rupp claimed to have flown Casey from Washington to Paris in October 1980. He also asserted that he saw a man he believed to have been George Bush on the tarmac at LeBourget Airport. Rupp said that he had used a Saudi-owned BAC-111 jet for the flight, leaving late one rainy October night from Washington's National Airport. We confirmed that Rupp had flown for the Saudi royal family, but Rupp would supply no documentation about his flights during the last half of 1980. These months were missing from records that he had turned over to his attorney earlier.

The other supposed Bush sighter was Oswald LeWinter, a.k.a. "Mr. Razine," the ex-literature professor and admitted disinformationist. LeWinter claimed that on October 19, 1980, he had seen a limousine parked near the U.S. embassy in Paris with a man who looked like Bush sitting in the back seat. But like Rupp, LeWinter could supply no documentary evidence supporting his own presence in Paris, let alone Bush's.

As for another questionable part of Ben-Menashe's story—his claim that Israeli military shipments to Iran began in early 1980—that, too, raised strong doubts about his credibility. Gary Sick, who had worked in Carter's National Security Council staff on Iran, had heard of no tire sale as described by Ben-Menashe, nor did Sick know about a complaint from Carter to Begin, as the Israeli claimed.

But our view on that point was different. In an earlier interview we had been told by Jody Powell, Carter's press secretary and close confidante, that Carter had clashed with Begin in spring 1980 over violations of the U.S. arms embargo.

"There had been a rather tense discussion between President Carter and Prime Minister Begin in the spring of 1980 in which the president made clear that the Israelis had to stop that, and that we knew that they were doing it, and that we would not allow it to continue, at least not allow it to continue privately and without the knowledge of the American people," Powell told us. "And it was stopped."

We doublechecked Ben-Menashe's story with a senior American diplomat who was in a position to know whether such an exchange had occurred. The diplomat confirmed that Carter had lodged a protest with Begin over Israeli violations of the anti-Iran embargo. The diplomat recalled that the complaint had been contained in a private letter delivered to Begin in early 1980.

10

MOSCOW EAST

Ari Ben-Menashe was galling. Jamshid Hashemi was slippery. But these two new witnesses in the October Surprise mystery could not be as summarily dismissed as some of the earlier ones. They had worked for intelligence agencies for two of the countries allegedly involved in the negotiations.

For all the problems with his testimony, Ben-Menashe had a documented relationship with a unit of Israeli intelligence. Though Israeli spokesmen insisted his position was low-level and non-operational, Ben-Menashe did have access to secrets about the U.S. arms-for-hostage trades in 1986 and tried to leak the information to American reporters. It was conceivable that he got hold of similar second-hand information six years earlier—about Republican-Iranian contacts in Madrid and Paris.

Jamshid Hashemi had acted as an agent for the CIA in 1980. He and his brother, Cyrus, had funneled covert CIA cash to the presidential campaign of their friend, Admiral Ahmad Madani. In 1980 Cyrus also had been in touch with personal friends of William Casey and had worked with them again in 1985 at the start of the Iran-contra scandal. While one might distrust Jamshid and his story of summer meetings in Madrid, he was in a position to know what the CIA and Casey's associates were doing.

Yet we still had no hard evidence that either set of meetings occurred. Outside of the witnesses' claims, there was no proof that Republicans met with Iranians either in Madrid in July and August or in Paris in October.

There was only one certain contact in 1980 between senior Republicans and an Iranian emissary. It was the curious get-together at the L'Enfant Plaza Hotel, a modern luxury hotel situated between the Smithsonian museums and the Potomac River in Washington.

But even that meeting was a mystery. The location was certain. The three Republican participants confirmed that. But little else was known for sure. Not the date. Not the identity of the Iranian emissary. Not even his nationality or title.

All that had been nailed down was a sketchy outline of the emissary's offer to free the hostages to candidate Ronald Reagan, the location at the L'Enfant Plaza Hotel lobby, and the names of the three Republicans: Richard Allen, candidate Reagan's chief foreign policy consultant; Laurence Silberman, another campaign adviser; and Robert McFarlane, a member of Senator John Tower's Republican staff on the Senate Armed Services Committee and later Reagan's national security adviser who played a major part in the Iran-contra affair.

It was like a Clue® mystery game. You knew in which room the fictional murder was committed, but not the murder weapon or the killer. There were many questions without adequate answers: Why had these three Republicans consented to this meeting in the first place? Wouldn't they have checked out the Iranian emissary before agreeing to meet him? How could they all have forgotten everything about him—even what he looked like? Was this just one information-seeking meeting in a political campaign obsessed by the hostage crisis? Or was there something more? Were these three Republicans hiding something?

The only one who agreed to our interview request was Richard Allen, a tough, combative veteran of Washington political battles. Sharp-tongued and impeccably tailored, Allen was a classic foreign policy lobbyist and periodic presidential adviser. His chief clients were rightist governments, most notably South Korea and Taiwan.

Though politically well-connected, Allen had taken his bureaucratic lumps. He was aced out of the Nixon administration by Henry Kissinger, who considered Allen too doctrinaire. Then Allen tied his political fortunes to Ronald Reagan in the 1970s. It was a smart move. While the Establishment Republicans like Kissinger foundered before the conservative Reagan tidal wave, Allen rode the surge back to the White House.

Allen was named the new administration's first national security adviser in 1981.

But Allen's government career itself ran aground several months later amid a mini-scandal in which Allen accepted a $1,000 payment and the gift of two Seiko watches from Japanese journalists. They were thank-you presents for arranging an interview with Nancy Reagan. Although Allen was cleared of any criminal wrongdoing, and the $1,000 had been left in a White House safe, the controversy gave ammunition to Allen's powerful enemies in moderate Republican circles.

Sensing the kill, his opponents tossed the wounded Allen to the political sharks—and he was ripped to shreds in an ugly journalistic feeding frenzy. An excited press corps circled Allen's front lawn for days on end as Allen was left dangling like political red meat. Allen would complain bitterly that some reporters even climbed up trees to peer into his house to check if he was home.

The nasty experience had reminded Allen about the viciousness of Washington. And in the intervening years, he had sharpened his own aggressiveness whenever confronting an inquisitive press. Though we weren't looking for a confrontation, Allen saw no reason to avoid one. Interviewing him at his well-appointed office only a few blocks from the White House, we asked him to start off with a routine statement that he had consented to a filmed interview for a *Frontline* documentary.

"I know that I'm being filmed by WGBH *Frontline*, a.k.a. Radio Moscow or Television Moscow East, and I understand that I am to give my consent," Allen said unsmilingly into the camera. "Your KGB has been very effective."

When Allen had finished putting us in our place, he described how he had helped William Casey clamber to the post of campaign chairman in March 1980, over the political corpse of Reagan's first chairman, John Sears. In the early months of the 1980 campaign, Sears ousted many members of Reagan's inner circle of Californians, including Michael Deaver, Martin Anderson, and Lyn Nofziger. The last of the old insiders, Edwin Meese and Allen, were battling to hold onto their campaign jobs.

"Fortunately, I had read and understood Lenin a lot better than maybe some of the others," Allen said in explaining his survival. "We came to the conclusion that a change had to be made." With the efficiency of a

Bolshevik purge, Allen and his forces plotted a countercoup against Sears. The plan was to bring in Casey, a Long Island politician and former Nixon administration official. Allen had worked with Casey on the 1968 Nixon campaign—and respected the tough and crafty old spymaster.

In 1980, Reagan was stunned by a loss to George Bush in the opening Iowa caucuses. Although Reagan's prospects were looking up in New Hampshire, the candidate agreed that it was time for a change.

A week later, on the day of the New Hampshire primary, which Reagan would win, the putsch was completed. Sears and his crowd were ousted, and Bill Casey was appointed the new campaign chairman. "I feel very strongly that this country is in trouble, that it needs to be turned around and I have felt for over a year that Governor Reagan is the only man in America who's ever turned a government around," Casey said after his formal appointment.

Casey worked hard organizing a staff as conservative and savvy as he was. Reagan was soon rolling to victory in primary after primary, routing the Republican field and dispatching finally his last rival, George Bush. At the GOP convention, Bush was brought on board as the vice presidential nominee. Many of the ex-CIA men in Bush's camp came with him.

As the general election campaign began, Reagan held a comfortable lead in the polls, but Carter began closing the gap. A break in the hostage crisis or some other good news could seemingly have pushed Carter into the lead. By late October, the polls were showing a neck-and-neck race between Carter and Reagan.

But in our interview, Allen argued that not even the hostages' freedom could have salvaged Carter's re-election. "The Reagan campaign was a juggernaut, and Carter could not have saved himself even with the release of the hostages," Allen maintained.

Yet Allen admitted that he and other senior campaign advisers acted almost obsessively when they picked up tidbits of news about hostage developments. "Of course, we watched for the possibility of some dramatic impact," Allen said. "We're not foolish. Of course, it was incumbent on us as running an election, to be aware of what might happen to derail or to dent in any way the kind of juggernaut victory that we expected to turn in."

Even scraps of news about the hostages were rushed to the campaign hierarchy. Allen recalled one urgent memo he wrote when he was told by a journalist that Secretary of State Edmund Muskie had floated the possibility of a swap of military spare parts for the hostages. Like a scene in a bad spy novel, Allen coded the journalist as "ABC" and Muskie as "XYZ" and slapped together a quick memo on the hot news. "I breathlessly sent this out to the campaign, to Casey, to Wirthlin, to Meese, I think [to] the president and maybe [to] George Bush," Allen told us.

But, recalling his insistence that Reagan was headed for a landslide victory, I asked, "why did anyone care?"

"It's a fact," Allen responded, with clear annoyance in his voice: "It's an important fact that they were willing to trade, were willing to say, 'all right, we will sell you parts if you'll release the hostages.' That's a major fact about United States policy. And our job was to know what United States policy would be, especially about that subject. We cared. Of course, we cared a great deal."

"You also felt that it would not affect the . . ."

Allen cut me off, "I felt it would not affect the election. But I had to know about it. I wasn't going to ignore it. Don't make a mountain out of a molehill. Of course, I'm going to be intrigued by it. So would you, were you sitting in my shoes."

"But I'm not sure why you'd be that concerned about getting it immediately to the candidate and to Casey and the others," I said.

"Gee, that's too bad that you're not certain about that," Allen snapped. "I'm sorry that your inadequacies prevent you from seeing it from the standpoint of a person who has the responsibility to report information to his candidate and his colleagues quickly. After all, allow me my own sense of urgency and don't try to impose a priority from without. Yeah."

Allen also took notes about a call on October 13, 1980, from Angelo Codevilla, a Republican staffer on the Senate Intelligence Committee. According to Allen's scribblings, Codevilla volunteered that highly sensitive "admin. embargoed intelligence" showed the hostages purportedly being returned to the embassy. In our interview, however, Allen dismissed the note's significance.

That message meant, he said, "nothing more than the fact that my logs were filled with volunteered information of that type. It would have meant that Angelo would have said this to me or he'd heard this and I would have written it down. As you can see, there was no outgoing memorandum."

Allen was equally testy when asked about the meeting at the L'Enfant

Plaza Hotel. When I asked for his "recollection" of the get-together, he snapped again: "No, it's not my recollection; it's what happened. What happened was that Bud McFarlane called me several times in an attempt to get me to meet with someone about the Iranian problem."

Allen said his alarm bells went off because he had witnessed a minor election scandal years earlier when the 1968 Nixon campaign was accused of plotting to undermine the Vietnam peace talks. Nixon emissaries had urged South Vietnamese president Nguyen Van Thieu to resist President Lyndon Johnson's plan to start peace talks with the North Vietnamese. The Nixon team feared the negotiations could catapult Hubert Humphrey to victory and, once more, deny Nixon the presidency. In effect, Johnson's proposed Vietnam peace conference was seen as an October Surprise for 1968.[1]

Thieu did block the negotiations, but Allen maintained that the interference by Nixon activists was the unauthorized work of "self-starters." Nixon hung on to win a narrow victory. The Vietnam War continued for four more years. Tens of thousands of American soldiers died, as did hundreds of thousands of Indochinese. Years later, the Nixon peace talk gambit had come to light and generated some criticism of Republican tactics.

So when McFarlane proposed the meeting with an Iranian emissary, Allen said, "I wasn't keen to do that at all. Knowing what I'd been through in 1968 on this very problem, I was highly reluctant to do it. But McFarlane was working for John Tower; John Tower was a friend of mine; McFarlane is not a particular friend, an acquaintance, nothing more than that. He was quite insistent that I do this."

Reluctantly, Allen agreed. Allen said that after a foreign policy advisory group meeting in Washington, he asked one of those advisers, Laurence Silberman, to join him for the meeting. "McFarlane wants me to meet somebody concerning the Iranian hostage business," Allen recalled telling Silberman. "But I want a witness in this meeting because I don't want it to turn into anything that could run against us. And I won't meet in this office. I will not have anybody say that he came to my office. I've said to McFarlane, 'I'll meet you in the L'Enfant Plaza Hotel, but only in the lobby where there's plenty of people out there. We're not going to have any meetings in a room.'

---

[1] Hersh, *op. cit.*, pp. 21–22.

"So Larry Silberman and I got on the subway and we went down to the L'Enfant Plaza Hotel where I met McFarlane and there were many people milling about. We sat at a table in the lobby. It was around the lunch hour. I was introduced to this very obscure character whose name I cannot recall. Eventually, I'll find the memorandum that I wrote on this meeting, but I haven't been able to find it yet.

"The individual who was either an Egyptian or an Iranian or could have been an Iranian living in Egypt—and his idea was that he had the capacity to intervene, to deliver the hostages to the Reagan forces. Now, I took that at first to mean that he was able to deliver the hostages to Ronald Reagan, candidate for the presidency of the United States, which was absolutely lunatic. And I said so. I believe I said, or Larry did, 'we have one president at a time. That's the way it is.'

"So this fellow continued with his conversation. I was incredulous that McFarlane would have ever brought a guy like this or placed any credibility in a guy like this. Just absolutely incredulous, and so was Larry Silberman. This meeting lasted maybe 20 minutes, 25 minutes. So that's it. There's no need to continue this meeting. I'm not interested in this. I didn't even say I'll get back to you or anything of that nature. Silberman and I walked out. And I remember Larry saying, 'Boy, you better write a memorandum about this. This is really spaceship stuff.' And it, of course, set my opinion very firmly about Bud McFarlane for having brought that person to me in the first place."

Allen described the emissary as "stocky and swarthy, dark-complected," but otherwise "non-descript." The man, Allen said, looked like a "person from somewhere on the Mediterranean littoral. How about that?" Allen said this Egyptian or Iranian "must have given a name at the time, must have." But Allen couldn't recall it. He also said he made no effort to check out the man's position or background before the meeting.

"Bud McFarlane, understand, was no one associated with our campaign. You do understand that? He had no role, zero role in the campaign. He was working for Senator Tower."

"But did you ask McFarlane, who is this guy?" I asked.

"I don't recall having asked him, no," Allen answered.

"I guess I don't understand why you wouldn't say, 'Is this guy an Iranian, is he someone you've known for a while?' " I pressed.

"Well, gee, I'm sorry that you don't understand," Allen chastised me.

"I really feel badly for you. It's really too bad you don't understand. But that's your problem, not mine."

"But wouldn't you normally ask that kind of background question?"

Allen: "Not necessarily. McFarlane wanted me to meet a guy and this guy was going to talk about the hostages. I met plenty of people during that period of time who wanted to talk to me about the hostages. Dozens and dozens of people. This was no different from anybody else I would meet on this subject."

"It obviously turned out to be different from most people you've met on the subject," I noted.

Allen: "Oh, it turned out to be because this guy is the centerpiece of some sort of great conspiracy web that has been spun."

"Well, were there many people who offered to deliver the hostages to Ronald Reagan?"

Allen: "No, this one was particularly different, but I didn't know that before I went to the meeting, you understand."

"Did you ask McFarlane what on earth this guy was going to propose?"

Allen: "I don't think I did in advance, no"

Allen said he believed he included the man's name in his memo to the file, but had since forgotten both the name and where the memo went. "I have tons of papers through which I'm not going to go even for this purpose," he added. "But I'll get there eventually. I will find a copy. It will show up someplace."

Beyond what Allen and Silberman did do, however, was what they didn't do. Though Allen acknowledged that he and Silberman recognized the sensitivity of the approach, neither of candidate Reagan's foreign policy advisers thought to contact the Carter administration. Notifying the incumbent administration would have protected them from a possible accusation of a back-channel contact with a hostile foreign government. Allen had been so cognizant of that possibility that he had scheduled the meeting for a hotel lobby.

More importantly, the emissary might have been able to help the U.S. government solve the impasse with Iran. Allen might have been right that the supposed emissary lacked any substance. But Robert McFarlane must have felt differently. After all, he had gone to the trouble of pestering Allen into agreeing to the meeting.

Allen's account of the L'Enfant Plaza meeting left a host of other questions. How did this emissary find his way into McFarlane's office on the minority side of the Senate Armed Services Committee? Why wouldn't the foreigner have gone to the Senate Foreign Relations Committee, a more likely contact point for a diplomatic overture? Why would as savvy a political operative as Allen agree to meet a foreign national, purporting to represent a hostile state, without first determining exactly who the man was and what he planned to propose? Why was everyone so fuzzy about even basic facts such as: What was the name of the Iranian representative? What was his title or company affiliation? Was he a government official? What day did the meeting occur?

Though the meeting apparently occurred in September or early October 1980, none of the American participants offered a precise date. Although Allen divulged the meeting to a reporter three years before our interview, he had made little or no effort to reconstruct the facts. More recently, Silberman and McFarlane had joined Allen in claiming they have no idea whom they met with, an assertion that was especially hard to believe coming from McFarlane, who supposedly arranged the meeting in the first place. For his part, McFarlane refused to talk with us.

Iranian arms dealer Houshang Lavi did come forward after Allen's initial comments in 1987 and claimed that he was the mysterious emissary. Government documents show that Lavi had made a similar approach to the independent presidential campaign of John Anderson. But unlike Allen and the Reagan campaign, the Anderson campaign promptly brought Lavi's initiative to the attention of the CIA and State Department, which held a series of inconclusive meetings with Lavi.

Lavi claimed the L'Enfant Plaza session occurred on October 2, 1980, and his account generally meshed with the three Republicans' stories. But the three Republicans did not believe Lavi was the man whom they encountered. Silberman insisted he was not even in Washington on the date that Lavi recalled. But Silberman, who was a federal appeals court judge in 1990, refused to say what dates he was in the capital.

The defensiveness of Allen and his colleagues only added to our suspicions about what had happened in 1980. If nothing had happened between the Republicans and the Iranians, why was everyone so unwilling to answer simple questions?

11

LAVI'S LABYRINTH

I spotted Houshang Lavi as he stepped off the plane at Kennedy International Airport. It was hard to miss him. He was dressed in a green Alpine outfit that looked ludicrous against his dark Middle Eastern complexion and jet-black hair. I greeted him, and we crossed through the airport terminal to a conference room where Robert Ross had set up the camera for the interview. Lavi had agreed to talk with us during a stopover at Kennedy while en route from Los Angeles to Vienna, Austria, in November 1990.

Lavi had lost weight since I had first interviewed him in April 1989. Then, he had reminded me of the blubbery *Star Wars* creature Jabba the Hut. Like Jabba, Lavi had a multiplicity of double chins and a tendency to mumble his words. Though thinner than he was in 1989, Lavi looked pale. He seemed less alert, as if his health were failing. He still chain-smoked.

While the Republicans disputed Lavi's claim that he was the L'Enfant Plaza emissary, there was no doubt that Lavi was a well-connected Iranian arms dealer. Lavi had played a middleman role, funneling weapons to Iran, both before and after the Islamic revolution. He had brokered the Grumman sale of $2 billion in F-14s to the shah of Iran, the only foreign sale of that advanced American aircraft.

After the shah's overthrow, he went back into business, exploiting his contacts with the Bani-Sadr wing of the new Iranian government. In the United States, he approached the CIA and the State Department and promoted himself as an intermediary during the hostage crisis in 1980. Then, at the start of the Reagan administration, Lavi, an Iranian-born Jew, worked with Israeli arms dealers shipping weapons to Iran.

Yet many of the details about his 1980 activities were murky. Lavi's only documentary support for his L'Enfant Plaza claim was a handwritten note referring to the meeting with the three Republicans. He had given the note to researchers looking into the October Surprise question. The scrawled writing on the lined piece of paper read: "Oct 2, 80. Eastern Shuttle to D.C. E.Plaza Hotel. . . . To meet Silberman, Allen, Bob McFar. 40 page document F14 parts already paid for in rtun of hostages. Swap in Karachi. Charter 707."

But the note could have been a fabrication. Even the date—October 2, 1980—clashed with the imprecise recollections of the Republicans. The note also conflicted with Allen's claim that Silberman was a last-minute addition to the meeting. In Lavi's note, Silberman was one of the three expected participants.

So again Ross and I were confronted with a problem of whom to believe—and again the Republicans were lucky that Lavi was no choirboy. He was an arms dealer who lived on the edge. The personal fortune, which he had amassed and squandered, rested on his careful use and possible misuse of information. Lavi had fallen into bitter legal disputes in the mid-1980s over his claim that he was cheated by an Israeli-connected arms company over his fees for weapons sales to Iran. The company, in turn, alleged that Lavi had lied about a delivery.

After sitting down in front of Ross's camera and lighting a cigarette, Lavi told us that he turned to the Republicans in 1980 only after other doors at CIA and the State Department were closed to him. The Republicans "listened to what I had to say over the telephone, a number of times," Lavi said as cigarette smoke swirled around his deeply creased face. He claimed the Republicans eventually referred him to Silberman. It was Silberman who proposed the meeting in Washington that eventually occurred at the L'Enfant Plaza Hotel, Lavi maintained.

"Silberman wanted me to go down to Washington and talk about the American hostage situation," Lavi said. Lavi claimed that the meeting was in a lobby of a Washington hotel near the Potomac River, a description that would fit the L'Enfant Plaza. "It was an expansive lobby," he said.

"This was a big lobby." The L'Enfant Plaza Hotel does, indeed, have a large lobby.

"I waited for Mr. Silberman to arrive," Lavi said. "He arrived and he was accompanied by two other gentlemen." One of the men was identified as McFarlane, but Lavi did not recall whether Richard Allen was the third individual.

"Who did most of the talking on their side?" I asked.

"Silberman," Lavi claimed. "I believe he is the one who told me that 'Mr. Lavi, we have one government at a time.' I took it that they do not want to interfere, but it turned out to be, I found out later on, that that's not the case. The Reagan-Bush campaign made a deal with the Iranians together with the help of the Israelis for the supply of arms to Iran."

For Lavi, the only outgrowth of the L'Enfant Plaza meeting was a call from Cyrus Hashemi, the Iranian financier who was in touch with both the Carter administration and the Republicans. "Yes, somewhere around these times, I was contacted by the late Dr. Hashemi. He was a banker. I did not know him, but he contacted me and he knew me as an arms dealer. He invited me to go to London and then on to Paris because of the requirements of the Islamic Republic of Iran going into the international market to purchase arms. I went to London, then we, Hashemi and I, both, we went to Paris. To tell you the truth, I don't remember the dates, sir."

I reminded Lavi that when I had interviewed him 18 months earlier, he had recalled the dates as around October 20, 1980. "I don't remember," he said. "Right now, I don't remember." But Lavi claimed that he and Cyrus Hashemi stayed at the Raphael Hotel in Paris for a few days while Hashemi engaged in rounds of meetings with arms dealers.

"I could see that Mr. Hashemi had a number of meetings with some of his Iranian colleagues, as well as some Americans, as well as some French and Germans and what have you—and Israelis," Lavi said. "But I did not interfere in any of those meetings."

Though outside the meetings, Lavi said Hashemi was keeping him abreast of events. "He told me that he wants to make a deal in order to get the release of the hostages from Khomeini in return of supply arms to the government of Iran," Lavi said about Hashemi. "He was very adamant and confident that he can achieve this."

"Did he say who he was dealing with in Paris?" I asked.

"I believe he was in contact with a gentleman by the name of Shaheen, if I'm not mistaken."

"Could it be John Shaheen?" I asked, thinking of Casey's close friend and former OSS veteran.

"Maybe," Lavi responded. "He was talking with a number of Iranians. I believe [Khomeini in-law Sadeq] Tabatabai was in that meeting, too, if I'm not mistaken. And there were a bunch of Americans. I don't know who exactly, but I do know that he was talking to Shaheen because I remember I heard that name when I was in Paris with him and a number of Israelis."

"Did he mention any members of the Reagan-Bush campaign to you?"

"No sir."

"He did not mention the name of Mr. Casey?"

"I don't remember," Lavi responded vaguely. "Right now, I don't remember." In the earlier interview, Lavi had claimed that Hashemi had mentioned a plan to see Casey. But 18 months later, Lavi insisted he had no recollection.

"Do you recall Hashemi saying anything about Casey desiring that the hostages be released only after the election of President Reagan?"

"No sir," Lavi answered. "That's a mystery to me, sir. I do know that by the time that the election was over, Iranians could have very easily released the hostages because then the Israelis started shipping arms to Iran. I could never understand why the hostages were kept in Tehran for another 76 days more."

But what about Lavi's story could we verify? According to U.S. government documents, in September 1980 Lavi did approach his lawyer, Mitchell Rogovin, a former CIA counsel and then a senior adviser to the independent presidential campaign of John Anderson. Lavi brought with him a plan for freeing the hostages in exchange for military spare parts. The scheme resembled in general terms the proposal described in Lavi's handwritten note about the "E.Plaza Hotel" meeting. So Lavi was peddling a plan to swap arms for hostages in fall 1980.

Lavi also was telling the truth about his access to Iran's President Abolhassan Bani-Sadr. In Rogovin's presence, Lavi called directly to

Tehran and got Bani-Sadr immediately on the phone. Rogovin was so impressed with Lavi's genuine connection to Bani-Sadr that the street-smart lawyer arranged a meeting for Lavi with the CIA and later with State Department officials.

According to a partially censored CIA memorandum about the Lavi meeting, Rogovin hosted the discussion between Lavi and a CIA officer at Rogovin's law offices in Washington. The meeting was on October 2, 1980—the same day that Lavi claimed the L'Enfant Plaza get-together occurred. The CIA-Lavi discussion began at 10:30 a.m. and ended at 11:25 a.m., according to the CIA memo.

Lavi "wished to arrange the delivery to Iran of $8 million to $10 million of F-14 spare parts" as part of a swap for the 52 American hostages then being held in Tehran, the memo said. "If the USG [U.S. government] would also agree to Khomeini's three terms: unfreeze Iranian assets in the U.S.; drop all claims against Iran; [and accept] noninterference in Iranian internal affairs, [Lavi] would arrange a swap of all the hostages upon delivery of the spare parts."

The unidentified CIA man, however, was clearly dubious about Lavi. "Oddly," the CIA memo said, Lavi "remarked that his two children were in the U.S., with the implication that the children were our hostages, also guaranteeing his good faith. . . . There was also a bit of mumbling [deleted] about the possibility of an Israeli escort for the plane carrying the spare parts, but the thought trailed away."

The memo concluded with the comment, "It looks like [Lavi] is trying to get an offer from us for the 'purchase' of the hostages, which he would then broker with unnamed Iranian contacts. He gave no other indication that he had anything else to sell than his, in effect, 'good' offices."

If Lavi's handwritten "E.Plaza Hotel" note was correct, the Iranian arms dealer would have gone to the L'Enfant Plaza meeting with the Republicans later the same day. Again, Lavi would have outlined his proposal to drop off arms for Iran and pick up the hostages. Only this time, he would have pitched the plan to the Republicans—Allen, McFarlane, and Silberman.

But Rogovin, the ex-CIA counsel, raised doubts about the second meeting on October 2. He told Ross and me that Lavi never mentioned the L'Enfant Plaza meeting, reporting only vaguely that he had made independent contact with some Republicans. Lavi also hadn't talked about any trip to Paris, Rogovin said.

Ross and I interviewed Rogovin at his office in the high-priced Washington law firm that had been founded by William ("Wild Bill") Donovan, the American spymaster who had been William Casey's boss at the OSS during World War II. Rogovin was surprisingly eager to help, in contrast to the hostile reception our October Surprise inquiries encountered from most Washington insiders.

Voluntarily, Rogovin pulled down his large bound notebooks from 1980 and read from his handwritten notes. Rogovin's contemporaneous accounts of his talks with Lavi established Lavi's preoccupation with the hostage crisis and his solid connections to President Bani-Sadr and other senior Iranians. The notes also revealed Lavi's interest in the U.S. presidential race and the political impact of the hostage crisis. But the notes contained no evidence that Lavi had gone to the L'Enfant Plaza meeting or to Paris with Cyrus Hashemi in October 1980.

"Lavi talked to Bani-Sadr, interested in who would win election," said one Rogovin notation dated October 13. "Lavi said Iranians not willing to deal with Carter," read another note on October 16. "Lavi received call from Bani-Sadr," said another on October 17. "They [the Iranians] stressed to Lavi that they didn't want to deal with the Carter administration but did want to do a swap."

As for Lavi's contention that he traveled to Europe in October 1980, Rogovin doubted that Lavi could have gone to Paris around October 20 because he arrived at Rogovin's office at 9:30 a.m. that morning. Lavi, however, did have some unusual news for his lawyer the next day.

According to Rogovin's handwritten notes for October 21, there was the following cryptic message from Lavi: "Foreign agent in Paris sold documents endangering U.S. and Israeli—Involved in war with Iraq—48 hours Iranian agent coming—No release to anyone before election—Want to talk to Bush."

When I asked Rogovin what the reference to Bush meant, he seemed nonplussed and responded hesitantly, "Yes, I don't know what that . . ."

"Don't know what he's talking about?"

Rogovin: "No."

On October 24, Lavi again returned to the issue of the hostage release.

Rogovin wrote: "Lavi—will not happen before Nov. 4 and we will be in on it." November 4 was Election Day 1980. But Lavi expected quick action after the election. On October 29, Lavi had more hot news: "Lavi—Iran will send delegation to wrap up. Nov. 5–10."

At Kennedy airport, I asked Lavi what the Bush reference meant in Rogovin's October 20 notation. He answered in his singsong voice: "I do know, sir, for a fact that Mr. Mitch Rogovin is a very good friend of President Bush. That I know because he has told me so."

But like Rogovin, Lavi could not—or would not—put the reference to then vice presidential candidate George Bush in any context. The note suggested that someone may have tried to contact Bush about the hostage issue. However, the curious notation would dangle like so many other loose ends of the October Surprise investigation.[1]

After the 1980 election, Lavi did join the long line of arms dealers feeding the Iranian war machine. An Israeli weapons dealer in Europe once handed me an original telex detailing Lavi's work on purchasing thousands of mortar rounds, tens of thousands of grenades and grenade launchers, and millions of rounds of machine gun ammunition. The telex, dated March 23, 1982, said the military supplies were to move through Lisbon, Portugal, and listed the destination as South America. But the Israeli weapons broker said the real buyer was Iran. The original telex was hard evidence that in the early years of the Reagan administration, Lavi had jumped back into the arms business. He was exploiting his dual contacts in Israel and Iran.

During the interview at Kennedy airport, I presented the telex to Lavi for identification. The telex was addressed to "H. Lavi," referred in the

---

[1] One last note about Lavi's contention that he left for London and then traveled to Paris with Cyrus Hashemi in October 1980. Lavi's wife, Debbie, told reporter David Marks that she took Lavi to LaGuardia Airport once during that time period and was surprised when he called her a day later from Paris. But Cyrus definitely was not in Paris on October 20, 1980. FBI wiretaps placed Cyrus in New York on that day. Cyrus did travel to London and Paris on October 28, a week later, according to FBI records. That left open the possibility that Lavi and Cyrus had met in London, as Lavi alleged, and then flown on to Paris a week later than Lavi's admittedly vague recollection.

text to "Houchang Lavi" [*sic*] and was signed "P. Lavi," apparently for Parvis Lavi, Houshang's brother and business associate. Houshang Lavi grew flustered.

Showing him the telex and its weapons lists, I said, "Is this a proposed deal? Was it a deal that was completed?"

"What does it say, sir?" Lavi hesitated. "I don't know. I gotta put my glasses on. I broke my glasses."

"Well, let me read it then," I offered. "This was on a telex at the Sheraton Hotel in Tel Aviv. Dated 23 March 1982. It says, 'please pass this message to Mr. H. Lavi, Room 410. Dear Mr. Lavi: Very, very urgent." I then read through the first section of the message listing various arms for sales. Finally, he interrupted me.

"That's not related to me, sir," Lavi said. "That is not related to my operation with the Iranians. I believe I know what that is. That belongs to some other guy. His name is also Lavi." He finally agreed that the telex was from his brother Parvis. But Houshang Lavi continued to insist that he was not part of that operation.

Yet Lavi freely admitted that he did work on other shipments to Iran. "The most important items on the list of the Iranians were some F-14 parts, as well as electron tubes for the HAWK missile batteries," he said.

"How did they get those?"

"The Israelis shipped them. This is right after the election. The F-14 parts, sir, were not that important to the Iranians. They were important but they wanted the HAWK missile batteries operational, and for that, these electron tubes were essential. It was of utmost importance that they have these things in their hands."

Lavi said a retired Israeli general arranged the deal through Americans for the parts, which were shipped from the Israeli inventory and later were replenished by the Reagan administration. Lavi claimed that the Israeli operatives also arranged transfers of other military supplies from NATO.

"What the Israelis are doing, they took it upon themselves to ship arms to Iran, and then they went through every stockpile of every NATO nation and they just shipped anything they wanted to the Islamic Republic of Iran, without any hesitation of any sort," Lavi claimed. "Anything that they could not supply from Israel, they would supply from Belgium. The Iranians would come there. They would be taken to NATO bases, partic-

ularly the bases in the border in between Belgium and Germany and they
would pick whatever they want and the Belgians would ship it to Iran."

"Like a shopping expedition?" I asked quizzically.

"That's correct," he responded.

"Well, would they just say, 'we want that electron tube over there'?"

"Yes, sir, believe you me, sir, I swear to God, I've seen this with my
own eyes."

"Well, how would these things be arranged?" I asked. "I mean, you
can't just have Iranians going into NATO bases and taking out equipment.
You have to have someone with some authority taking out the equipment."

My skepticism did not faze Lavi. "Exactly, sir," he answered. "They
had the blessing of the Belgian government and the German government.
Everything went through Malta, the island of Malta. I call it the Maltese
Operation. Cargo planes would come to Malta, the Belgians would ship it
to Malta, and it was gone to Tehran."

Lavi maintained that the Israelis and the Belgians who handled these
transactions made huge profits, partly by bartering the weapons for Iranian
oil which was then sold on the world market at Rotterdam for more than
double the price. He claimed that one $120 million deal led to the oil being
resold for $320 million.

"So the Iranian government ended up paying through oil much more
than it should have?" I asked.

"Oh, definitely, yes, sir," Lavi responded. "Out of being in need of the
arms and out of desperation and as well as stupidity, of course."

But Lavi clammed up when I asked what Americans participated in
these schemes.

"If I would know, I wouldn't tell you," Lavi said.

"Why not?" I asked.

"I'm afraid," he answered.

"Were these people from the CIA? Were these people from the State
Department or the Pentagon?"

"I think I've already said enough, Bob."

Lavi's claim that NATO warehouses had been raided to arm Iran struck me
as one more implausible assertion in a sea of bizarre stories. But another

October Surprise witness had given a similar account, an American arms dealer named William Herrmann. I had first interviewed Herrmann in November 1988 when he was in a federal prison at Loretto, Pennsylvania. Herrmann had been convicted in London on charges of possessing counterfeit U.S. currency and was completing his sentence in the United States under an exchange treaty that permits prisoners to transfer to prisons in their home countries.

Herrmann, a German-born American citizen, was in his 50s, He was average height and had thinning white hair. A reserved yet personable fellow, he spoke with a slight New Jersey accent. According to his police record, he had been in prison before. One of his past convictions was for a felony motor vehicle theft. But he had also acted as a reliable federal informant, according to internal FBI cables that Herrmann had obtained for his defense in the counterfeiting case.[2]

After his release from prison, Herrmann started a construction business in New Jersey. He also agreed to be reinterviewed for the *Frontline* program at Ross's loft/studio in Soho. His account in 1990 matched closely with what he had told me in 1988.

In both interviews, Herrmann claimed to know about a pre-Iran-contra set of U.S.-sanctioned arms sales to Iran, transactions dating back to 1980. That information, he insisted, came to him through his work supplying light weaponry to Iran's Revolutionary Guards and his business relationship with Hamid Naqashan, a principal arms procurer for Iran's radicals. Herrmann said Naqashan told him that the U.S. arms shipments grew out of Republican commitments predating the 1980 election. Herrmann's October Surprise story went as follows:

---

[2] Herrmann was arrested on May 17, 1985, in London for possessing $3 million in counterfeit American currency. But he argued, with some truth, that he had alerted the FBI to the activities of the counterfeiting ring a week earlier. The FBI teletypes showed that Herrmann was in contact with two federal agents—one in New Jersey and another at the U.S. Embassy in London—about the counterfeit money in the days before his arrest. Both FBI men asserted, however, that they instructed Herrmann not to accept any counterfeit money until he received specific instructions. But Herrmann said that when the counterfeiters dropped off a supply of bills at his hotel room, he saw no choice but to accept the phony currency. Scotland Yard arrived shortly afterwards and arrested Herrmann. Herrmann got a five-year sentence.

"Hamid Naqashan, at the time, was a deputy minister of the Revolutionary Guard," Herrmann told me. "I came back here to the United States and made arrangements for a Brazilian company to sell some small arms. We both went to Brazil to make the arrangements with the factories over there. That was in the early part of December 1980. We were in Brazil for about 10 days and made the necessary purchases. He went back to Europe and I went back to the United States."

For those first months in late 1980, Naqashan remained guarded about sharing information. But "during the Christmas holidays of 1980, we did conclude our first transaction. From that time on, the man showed confidence and trust in the relationship with me. In January 1981, I was invited to Tehran to meet with the minister of defense."

That is when Herrmann claimed he heard about Republican contacts with the Khomeini regime. "I was summoned and issued a visa by the Iranian government on a piece of paper, to go to Tehran to discuss arms sales to Iran. And our discussion lasted for three days. During the time of the Inauguration of President Reagan, I was in Tehran."

"The 21st of January 1981, this was a day before I came back to Europe. Naqashan met me at the hotel and we went out to dinner. We discussed the release of the hostages and what transpired prior to the release of the hostages with the negotiations that were made by different people. Naqashan told me that a deal was struck by the Reagan administration in October of 1980, before the election, not to release the hostages until after Reagan was sworn in.

"I believe the information that Naqashan told me is correct. Naqashan had no reason to lie. He had been very fair with me, quite honest as far as his information is concerned. I believe that he was telling the truth, due to the fact that at that time, he had nothing to lose or nothing to gain. The hostages were gone and whatever transpired prior to the release apparently was immaterial to the Iranians."

The key meeting was "in Paris in October, toward the end of October 1980." Herrmann said. The most important Americans whom Naqashan mentioned in connection with the Republican-Iranian talks were William Casey, George Bush, Richard Allen, and Robert McFarlane. But Herrmann said Naqashan did not spell out exactly who was in attendance at the Paris meetings.

"Naqashan indicated that 'we received a lot of materials from the United States, shortly after Mr. Reagan became president,' " Herrmann said. "Later, through my own sources, I found out that NATO stocks had been shipped to Iran from various areas from Europe. Most of the materials were shipped from Belgium and Holland, using different methods of transportation, by air and sea. How much was shipped? Nobody really knows."

The NATO stocks were "mostly spare parts for aircraft: F-4s, the Phantoms, which Germany had in ample supplies; tank parts; tank engines; and things of that nature," Herrmann said. "The HAWK part shipments, they all came from Israel." Herrmann claimed the NATO equipment, including 155mm ammunition and 104mm recoilless rifles, would be declared surplus and then be released to a friendly country where middlemen would take over the transaction and transfer the weapons to Iran. "The German government was behind it. The Belgian government was behind it. The Dutch were behind it."

The hungry Iranian war machine was well-fed by the surplus NATO stockpiles, Herrmann told me. But the stores eventually were drawn down to dangerously low levels and the NATO shipments stopped.

Herrmann's account about Naqashan fit with another story that one of Martin Kilian's colleagues at *Der Spiegel* heard in Switzerland. The *Spiegel* reporter was told by Karl Heinz Ottershagen, a German arms dealer, that Iranian arms buyer Hamid Naqashan had meetings with senior Republicans in Zurich in September 1980. The topic allegedly was an exchange of U.S. arms for the American hostages.

Ottershagen added that Naqashan took part in a later series of meetings in Paris that were held to arrange the logistics for the weapons shipments. Besides obtaining arms for Iran, the German said, Naqashan had described the purpose of the deal as "socking it to the people around Jimmy Carter and Iranian president Bani-Sadr," who was despised by many Islamic radicals. Though not firsthand witnesses, Herrmann and Ottershagen supplied at least hearsay testimony that Iranian arms procurers, such as Naqashan, were in touch with Republicans during the 1980 campaign.

*   *   *

Less than two months after we interviewed Lavi at Kennedy Airport, I received a call at home from Lavi's wife, Debbie. I had never talked with her before and the news she brought was startling. Houshang Lavi had died of a heart attack. He had been suffering from heart problems for years, yet he had continued to smoke and work under the pressures of international trade. So his death was not entirely unexpected, Mrs. Lavi said. But she was calling because he had told the family about his videotaped interview with us. She was wondering when it would air. A date had not yet been set. But I promised that we would notify the family when the schedule firmed up.

Weeks later, when I passed the word of Lavi's death to the Israeli arms broker in Europe who had dealt with Lavi, the Israeli refused to believe it. The Israeli thought that Lavi was deceptive enough to fake his own death. I told the Israeli that I had spoken with the widow, and by then, Lavi's brother and Lavi's son. All agreed that Houshang Lavi was dead.

The Israeli was still suspicious. He demanded that I get documented proof of Lavi's death. So *Frontline* obtained a copy of Lavi's death certificate from the local authorities in Santa Monica, California. I sent it to the Israeli. His suspicions seemed assuaged.

12

THE SANE MAN

As we plodded along the October Surprise trail through the United States, Europe, and the Middle East, Robert Ross and I had entered a maze, and an exit was nowhere in sight. So far, there had been no tape-recorded admissions, no pristine witness who stepped forward with an unassailable account, no "smoking gun" as reporters like to say. There was a body of testimony—some of it conflicting, some of it corroborative, some of it unbelievable. But the "witnesses" who alleged that a deal was done were just too questionable to justify a solid judgment.

Yet the "respectable" people were little better. Robert McFarlane, President Reagan's third national security adviser, had pleaded guilty to lying about the Iran-contra scandal. Reagan himself was caught lying when he insisted first that the stories of 1986 arms trading with Iran were false and then a second time when he denied that the Iran-contra deals had included any arms-for-hostage swap. Vice President George Bush claimed, falsely, that he had been "out of the loop" on Irangate, though it turned out he had been a participant in many of the key meetings. CIA director William Casey escaped prosecution for his Iran-contra lies only because he collapsed and died of brain cancer in 1987.

Despite our concern over the available sources, Ross and I favored pressing ahead with the documentary. No matter how unpleasant, the

October Surprise issue deserved a serious examination. The American people had a right to hear the controversy, even if there was no neat ending or solid judgment. By lying so repeatedly about its dealings with Iran during the mid-1980s, the White House had no right to be sanctimonious now when allegations surfaced about other deceptions dating back to 1980.

The Republican record for honest campaigning was certainly not pristine, either. In 1968, GOP activists sabotaged Vietnam peace talks for political advantage. In 1972, there was Watergate and the Nixon campaign's bottomless bag of dirty tricks. So what was so fantastic about suspecting more foul play in 1980? Jeopardizing the lives of American servicemen in Vietnam by torpedoing the 1968 peace talks was no less cynical and sinister than interfering with hostage negotiations in 1980. Further, some of the foreign policy professionals did not share the American public's dewy-eyed sentimentality about the hostages. As CIA veteran Miles Copeland told us: "There was very little sympathy for the hostages. We all have served abroad. . . . It's a chance you take."

Plus, the federal government had tipped the balance. A federal prosecutor sought to disprove the October Surprise allegations in the Brenneke trial—and failed. The government had literally made a federal case out of the controversy. The trial put the suspicions firmly onto the public record. That reality could not be ignored.

But we knew that our reasoning would not spare us a merciless trashing by those in Washington who wanted the October Surprise story kept outside the boundaries of acceptable debate. The October Surprise allegations had too long been dismissed by "responsible" journalists and their official sources in Washington.

The executives at *Frontline* were supportive but nervous. Like Ross and me, they wanted conclusive evidence that would settle the question one way or the other. We had been unable to bring them that. But rather than pulling back, the *Frontline* senior producers decided to sharpen the show's focus. They junked our initial approach for a program that took a historical look at U.S.-Iranian relations with the October Surprise included as a central question.

David Fanning, *Frontline*'s executive producer, ordered the show recut to give it a "political spine," one that would follow the course of the 1980 presidential election rather than the crisis in U.S.-Iranian relations. It was the right editorial prescription, but it meant locating new footage and more delays. Fanning also wanted us to build up the role of Gary Sick, the respected naval intelligence officer who had worked on President Carter's White House staff.

For years, Sick—a scholarly and cautious man—had dismissed the October Surprise allegations as fanciful. His book on the hostage crisis, *All Fall Down*, had ignored the controversy entirely. But as he researched a book on the early days of the Iran-contra scandal, Sick gradually changed his mind. The number of arms dealers, intelligence operatives, and Iranian officials claiming Republican interference had reached a critical mass in his thinking. His careful analytical mind was like a scale in which grains of sand kept mounting on one side until they finally outweighed the pile of doubts on the other. Slowly at first and then more decisively, Sick's thinking had tipped over from the side of disbelief to the side of believing in a Republican obstruction.

Though I respected Sick—for his deliberative scholarship, his graceful writing and his straightforward Middle American decency—we had never exactly hit it off. He was a little too serious, not quite irreverent enough. Sick and Ross were more soul mates, enjoying discussions about the Middle East where both had personal experiences. Similarly, Kilian and Sick shared the same optimistic view of the world that held that by acting honestly and honorably, a person would prevail in the end. I had seen too much chicanery in my years reporting about Washington.

But Ross and I agreed that the interview with Sick could help pull an otherwise complicated story together. As a dramatic device, the Sick interview would reflect the Carter administration's naivete and confusion. Sick's struggle with his own doubts also mirrored our own uncertainties, although he had reached a conclusion that we had not. Sick now believed that Casey and the Republicans had manipulated the hostage issue.

For the Sick interview at his upper West Side apartment in New York City, Ross splurged. He hired a two-person crew, using a Beta-format camera that produces a richer image than the Hi-8. But the Beta camera also is heavier and requires extra lighting. When I arrived, Sick's compact living room had become an impromptu set with lights carefully positioned and white cardboard reflectors lined up along the mantle. Two chairs were sitting in the middle of the room for the interview. Ross had the luxury of acting only as the producer/director, rather than the cameraman, too.

But the elaborate set-up backfired. One of the cardboard reflectors buckled from the heat and toppled a hand-made vase off the mantle. The vase landed on a delicate side-table, breaking off one of the table legs. The vase itself shattered into a half-dozen pieces. Sick was visibly annoyed by the damage to his personal art works but soldiered on with the interview.

A Kansas native, Sick looked and sounded a lot like actor Gary Cooper. Tall and slow-spoken, Sick conveyed a sense of honesty and seriousness. Wearing a dark sports jacket and tie, Sick was also a welcome relief from the strangely dressed sorts that we had found ourselves interviewing. A jacket and tie convey credibility to the television audience.

Sick recalled the embassy takeover and the hostage seizure on November 4, 1979, as "a shocking event. That a major government, not a small two-bit banana republic, but Iran's a big country and an important country, could capture a group of American diplomats and hold them for a significant period of time was really unthinkable."

From Sick's seat on the NSC staff, he watched the crisis grip President Carter, as it did the country. "This became the central, dominant feature of the Carter administration from the day it happened on November 4, 1979, until the day they were released, on the day that Jimmy Carter quit being president. It was the one thing that drove everything else in the White House. That probably was a mistake, but that's the way it was."

The initial Carter strategy was to isolate Iran as a pariah state and make the price for holding the hostages so high the Islamic government would let them go. "I think that our strategy on that," Sick said, "though it didn't work, wasn't bad in the sense that there are very few countries in the world that would have taken the kind of beating that Iran took between November of '79 and January of 1981 to make a political point. But Iran was a revolutionary society and revolutionary societies are slightly crazy and Iran was slightly crazy at that time. The idea of humiliating the Great Satan was more important to them than trade or economics or military development."

Though the public rallied behind the president during the first months of the crisis, White House insiders feared that the support would evaporate if the crisis dragged on. Pictures were beamed back to the United States daily showing Iranians using the American flag to haul garbage or the radical students parading blindfolded Americans in front of the cameras. The image of an irresolute America humiliated by Islamic fundamentalists did, over time, erode Jimmy Carter's public standing.

As the Carter administration fished for the right strategy in early 1980, the Iranian conditions for freeing the hostages continued to harden. Initial hopes for a quick resolution had faded by February. "In early March, Khomeini, in effect, said that he was going to entertain no ideas for the release of the hostages until a Majlis, a new parliament, was elected," Sick said. "At that point, the program of persuasion was pretty much dead."

Hopes for a peaceful settlement faded further in April. So Carter ordered a military rescue mission on April 24, 1980. But the daring plan ended in ignominious failure when three helicopters developed mechanical problems and one crashed into a refueling plane at a staging area known as Desert One. Eight American servicemen died, and Iran rejoiced at the defeat of the Great Satan.

"There was a long dry spell after the rescue mission failed—from the end of April really until the end of August," Sick recalled. In August, the administration renewed its appeals to Iran for a settlement. Whether in response to those initiatives or for their own reasons, the Iranians proposed a resolution of the hostage impasse in early September.

The Germans relayed a message to the Carter administration from Sadeq Tabatabai, a son-in-law of Ayatollah Khomeini. Tabatabai carried "a set of conditions for ending the crisis that were really much gentler than anything Iran had offered before," Sick recalled.

The Iranian proposal boiled down to unfreezing its assets in the United States, giving them access to the shah's overseas fortune, no retaliation against Iran, and an American agreement to refrain from future interference in Iran's internal affairs. They were no longer demanding the shah's return—a moot point since he died in July—nor a formal apology from the United States for past violations of Iran's sovereignty.

* * *

While in Europe, Ross and I had located Sadeq Tabatabai and persuaded him to meet with us at the Düsseldorf Hilton. That was the same hotel and the same night for our interview with admitted disinformationist Oswald LeWinter. Shortly after we had finished with LeWinter, Tabatabai arrived at the hotel lobby wearing a stylish checkered sports jacket. He was self-assured and handsome in an Atlantic City sort of way. Both in facial appearance and in his slick mannerisms, he resembled casino-and-real-estate mogul Donald Trump. Though Tabatabai refused to go on camera, he did talk with us, through a German interpreter, for two hours.[1]

Tabatabai had feared that the prolonged hostage crisis was hurting Iran, particularly as Iraq began moving troops closer to the disputed border. As an in-law to Khomeini, Tabatabai had intimate access to the Islamic leader. He used those connections to plea for a resolution of the hostage impasse. Tabatabai said he appealed to Khomeini by putting the pro-settlement arguments on tape casettes. Tabatabai knew that Khomeini enjoyed walking in his garden and listening to a Sony Walkman tape player. Through the tapes, Tabatabai said he persuaded Khomeini to reopen channels to Washington.

"I realized there were many ways to resolve the crisis," Tabatabai told us. "But if parliament were to solve the problem, it would take a very long time." However, Tabatabai noted, time was running short, with war clouds building over the disputed Iran-Iraq border and with the U.S.-imposed isolation sapping Iran's strength.

Tabatabai's proposal focused on release of frozen Iranian funds and a commitment against further U.S. intervention. "The Imam [Khomeini] said that was what he pretty much had in mind," Tabatabai said. "I asked if it wouldn't take much too long for the parliament to make these formulations and suggested that he might want to put these words in the mouths of the legislature. The Imam suggested that we test this out with the Americans first."

After consulting with Khomeini's son, Ahmad, and with Ali Akbar Hashemi Rafsanjani, the new speaker of the parliament, Tabatabai said he got in touch with the Americans. President Bani-Sadr was bypassed

---

[1] German is one of the languages that Ross does not speak, and Ross felt that his Persian was too rusty to risk relying on it for an important interview.

entirely, Tabatabai told us. The overture to Washington went through the Germans, who had remained on good terms with Tehran despite the revolution. The messenger was Hans-Dietrich Genscher, West Germany's foreign minister.

"The answer came fairly quickly," Tabatabai recalled. "Genscher said the mood in the United States would be receptive." A direct meeting between Tabatabai and an American delegation representing President Carter was arranged. The meeting took place in Bonn, West Germany, and the framework for an agreement was speedily hammered out.

"I was very optimistic at the time," Tabatabai said about the three rounds of talks lasting between 12 and 14 hours. "Mr. Carter had accepted the conditions set by the Iranians. I sent an encrypted message to the Imam, saying I would be back the next day."

But Tabatabai's return flight was delayed. The long-simmering dispute with Iraq's Saddam Hussein finally boiled over into full-scale war. "My plane could not take off," Tabatabai said. "The airport in Tehran was being bombed by Iraqi forces. As a result, I had to stay for another two weeks in Germany before I could travel back to Iran by military jet."

The outbreak of war with Iraq would be only the first of a series of delays hindering the revived hostage talks. Though Rafsanjani would put the proposal before the parliament, the radical forces in the Majlis repeatedly blocked action. "Every time it was to be taken up by parliament, some of the radical members left the parliament to prevent a quorum from being present," Tabatabai said.

The radical mullahs seemed determined to block any hostage settlement that might benefit Jimmy Carter. "One radical was quoted as saying, 'what difference does it make if Carter wins the election or if Reagan wins the election,' " Tabatabai said.

The legislative delays continued up to literally the eve of the American presidential election, when Majlis agreement was finally granted. But the vote was too late to bring the Americans home before Carter went down to defeat.

In our interview, Tabatabai flatly denied playing any double game, though acknowledging that he had heard accounts of other Iranian officials meeting with Republicans. "I heard lots of rumors that Republicans had met with important people in Europe and that Republicans made promises to Iranians living abroad," he said. "I also read that I was assumed to have conducted talks with Republicans in Paris and in Geneva. A source in the United States said I was in Paris from October 18th to 21st with Ahmed [Khomeini's son]. I wish to deny this categorically."

As for the broader question of Republican and Iranian government contacts, Tabatabai said he considered it "highly unlikely that there were direct talks, but there might have been some indirect contacts between Republicans and Iranians representing themselves as having contacts." He said his suspicions were raised by the coordination of the radical members of the Majlis in blocking a settlement. "One-third of the assembly would leave the room when key votes were taken" on the hostage matter, he said. But he added hastily: "I don't accuse all of them of collaboration in this. They were not all influenced or bought by the Republicans."

The picture that Tabatabai sketched was one where competing Iranian groups sought to turn the hostage issue to their own advantage. Khomeini's son-in-law believed Iranian radicals were in touch with the Republican campaign. His faction, supposedly with Khomeini's and Rafsanjani's support, was negotiating with Carter's administration. Lavi's initiative with President Bani-Sadr's backing may have represented a third grouping.[2]

Though Tabatabai refused to tell his story on camera, Ross was prepared. He hired a German photographer to wait outside the hotel until the interview was over. As Tabatabai left the Düsseldorf Hilton, the photographer snapped a dozen shots of the Iranian as he moved toward his car. Tabatabai offered a strained smile and I'm sure some Persian curses for us under his breath.

While the Islamic radicals were blocking final action on a hostage deal, the Carter administration was hoping against hope that the crisis could finally

---

[2] But as complicated as this competition might seem, the reality could have been even more convoluted. Ross and I heard another story from an Iranian who participated directly in the events of 1980. This Iranian said Tabatabai was indeed playing a double game. Inside senior Iranian government councils, this Iranian defense official said Tabatabai aggressively pushed for a policy of pitting one American political group against another, the Democrats against the Republicans, with the idea of extracting the best possible deal for Iran.

be resolved and the hostages freed. In the October 28th debate with Ronald Reagan, President Carter stated that if the hostages were released safely, he was prepared to return all the $150 million in frozen military equipment that belonged to Iran.

But the delays inside the Majlis hurt. "Everything was strung out," Sick said, "delayed from day to day to day, and the reports coming back to the United States from a variety of sources were that there was a lot of internal debate. Having started out in early September saying 'we want to resolve this whole issue very quickly,' all of a sudden it was just strung out indefinitely with absolutely no action at all. They weren't coming back and asking us for new positions. They weren't in contact with us. They were just going about it in their own way, and nothing was happening in Tehran, from mid-October on."

For years, Sick had given little thought to Iran's indecision. It could be explained, he felt, as a combination of confusion surrounding a new revolutionary government and the chaos caused by the war with Iraq. As the days were crossed off the political calendar, President Carter's hopes of freeing the hostages and winning re-election disappeared, too.

"Obviously, from the point of view of the White House and President Carter, it would have been beneficial for him, there's no question about that, if the hostages had suddenly returned home just before the election," Sick acknowledged. "But that was not to be."

Carter's October Surprise, the eleventh-hour hostage release that William Casey had so feared, never happened. The hostages' captivity continued. But would their release have saved Carter's failing political fortunes in any event? Amid high inflation, high unemployment, high interest rates, Sick agreed that Carter might still have lost.

But he noted, "the polls in that month of October, as most people forget now, were running pretty close to neck and neck. Two or three days before the election, the papers were saying it was too close to call. What happened is in the last day or two of the election, all of the undecideds, instead of dividing evenly, all went to Reagan and the fact that the election took place on the same day as the hostages were taken the year before—November 4th, twelve months to the day, every one of the news media carried full-scale space about the hostage crisis."

After the election, Carter and his negotiators entered a bitter-sweet transition period. The State Department team headed by Warren Christopher finally achieved the breakthrough on the hostage talks that had long eluded them. Some frozen Iranian money was released, and an arbitration mechanism was established for resolving other financial disputes, including possible recovery of the shah's family assets. The military hardware that had been purchased by the shah remained in U.S. government warehouses, pending further negotiations.

Though the crisis was over, the national catharsis that came with release of the hostages would redound not to Carter's favor but to Reagan's. The Iranians would wait until Carter's presidency was officially extinguished before ending the ordeal. A frustrated Carter team would immediately begin to suspect foul play on the part of the Republicans.

"There was talk about this quite openly when the hostages were released just 30 minutes after Ronald Reagan became president," Sick remembered. "The timing seemed peculiar. And we had reports later on that the people holding the hostages in fact were standing with watches waiting at the airport to make sure that the time had passed, that Carter was no longer president before releasing the hostages.

"Again, that could have been explained simply on the grounds that they detested Jimmy Carter, that he had been the symbol of the Great Satan for them all the way through, and that this was just one more turn of the knife and conceivably so. But it did strike many, many people as peculiar—the timing of the thing, and the way the Iranians worked it out. And a lot of people suspected right then that some kind of a deal had been done between the Reagan people and the Iranians. That this was not a coincidence. So the stories began to evolve then."

But Sick gave the conspiracy suspicions little mind. "I wrote a book about this period and I didn't mention those stories at all," Sick said. "I didn't give them any credit. I felt that American politics really doesn't get played that way, and I felt again that you could explain these peculiarities because of the revolutionary situation in Iran, the conflict with Jimmy Carter, and so forth."

Sick said his analysis started changing when he set out to write a book about the Reagan administration's relations with Iran. Like an explorer searching for the source of a river, Sick traced the flow of the Iran-contra weapons deals back in time. He came to believe that the fountainhead of the Reagan team's association with Iran could be found in the campaign days of 1980.

"Slowly, as I got into this process, I began to do some interviewing myself," Sick told me. "I began to do some more reading, and as I went further and further, what surprised me was that this testimony did not go off in fifteen different directions. What I discovered as time went on, as I built up a chronology and began to work on the issue, was that there was a sort of nucleus. Then I began to have multiple sources that were saying the same thing. So it was really only in 1989 that I finally came to the conclusion that it was more difficult to explain why all these people were lying to me than it was to conclude that, in fact, something happened."

Despite the story's complexities, Sick had begun building a framework for understanding what happened. That structure went as follows: "My working hypothesis at this point, based on conversations with a number of people, is that William Casey made contact with Cyrus Hashemi, this Iranian guy who had developed a relationship with the U.S. government and who was acting as an intermediary about things that were going on with the hostage negotiations. So he was technically associated with the U.S. government [the Carter administration]. But in the early stages of 1980, he established a contact with Bill Casey, who was the campaign manager for the Reagan campaign, to talk about what was going on in Iran, and that that contact blossomed over time without the knowledge of the U.S. government.

"So, in effect, we had this man who, well, I think you could say without stretching the term that he was a double agent; that he was working for the U.S. government, but he was providing information on the side to the Reagan campaign.

"I've been told that in July and August, the initial meetings took place in which a senior Iranian official was brought out of Iran to Madrid and there met with Casey and perhaps some others. There was a preliminary meeting to talk about whether they could do a deal; a second meeting in which it was mostly decided that a deal could be done; and then there were a series of implementing discussions and meetings that took place in the later part of that period and that contacts went on, culminating in some meetings in Paris in mid-October of 1980 in which Iranians, Israelis, Americans, and some others were represented in which we are told by a number of people that a decision was taken to delay the release of the hostages until after the U.S. elections to ensure that Ronald Reagan would be elected and that Jimmy Carter would be defeated."

Sick recognized that the principal sources were a "mixed bag" of dubious characters—"money-movers, arms dealers, low-level intelligence operatives, people who work undercover and who, for one reason or another, are now dissatisfied with their lot and are prepared to talk about some of what they knew, perhaps with considerable exaggeration." But the sources came from a variety of different countries and represented diverse points of view. How likely was it that these dozen or so individuals would concoct such a politically sensitive story and why?

"That's a difficult conspiracy theory itself to construct why all of these people are inventing this story and telling me about it, in terms that are not precisely the same, as if they had prepared a story, but as if they were getting one little perspective here and another dimension there, and putting it together, but in which there is a core of persuasive evidence that is very difficult to just dismiss out of hand," Sick said.

Yet the possiblity that politicians would disrupt negotiations for the freedom of 52 Americans to win an election would challenge the cynicism of even the dourest skeptic. Sick appreciated that fact. "I didn't want to believe that American politics could or would be played that way, that people would play these kinds of games with American electoral politics. Curiously enough, I've had the same thing said to me by any number of non-Americans that I've talked to, that they found it hard to believe that something like this could happen in the United States. But if it did, it's sad. It's a very, very sad reflection on our system, and that makes me sad."

13

A LOVER OF DECEPTION

The Victorian Gothic mansion on the quiet Long Island cove had a stately spookiness that Bill Casey must have loved. Set back from the road, behind a stone wall and a circular driveway, the house was shaded by large deciduous and evergreen trees. Its walled front entrance was marked by a discreet sign giving the estate's name, Mayknoll, and that of its owner, "Wm. J. Casey." The mansion that Bill Casey bought in 1948, three years after the end of World War II, seemed to capture the spirit of the man who owned it. Mayknoll was a house of many gables, with a seemingly endless number of angles.

As a reporter covering national security, I had followed Casey's government career, but mostly from a distance. I first saw him in January 1981, grabbing a take-out breakfast at a coffee shop on M Street near the Reagan transition office in downtown Washington. When Casey was under attack for ethical questions after taking over at the CIA, I watched his tall stooped figure fend off reporters at a hallway news conference in a Senate office building. Despite his business indiscretions, he escaped with his job and the backhanded congressional endorsement that he was "not unfit to serve" as CIA director.

In 1982 I was one of several reporters invited for breakfast with the director at CIA headquarters in Langley, Virginia. Casey spoke only as a "senior administration official," but his main message was that Bill Casey was doing a great job running the CIA. He was obstreperous as well as confident. He tongue-lashed a *New York Times* reporter who was sitting next to me for some critical reporting on the CIA. After the breakfast, Casey's press aide, a man drawn from the covert operations section, asked the reporters to stay behind so he could correct some of Casey's misstatements.

I last saw Casey departing from the restricted elevator at the U.S. Capitol which goes only to the secure offices of the House Intelligence Committee on the building's fourth floor. It was October 1984, and he had been summoned to answer questions about the so-called CIA assassination manual which counseled Nicaraguan contras to apply the "selective use of violence" to "neutralize" Sandinista civilian officials. He had been furious with the story that I had written for the Associated Press about the booklet. It was crazy, he argued, to equate the word "neutralize" with "assassinate."

Casey would return to the Congress again in November 1986 to testify about the Iran arms sales, his last and greatest scandal at the CIA. He collapsed from brain cancer a month later. He died at home at Mayknoll on May 6, 1987, as the congressional Iran-contra hearings were getting under way.

Traveling to Mayknoll to speak twice with Casey's widow Sophia did help fill in my sketchy picture of this historic character. Inside, the mansion's rooms had a musty odor of old books, which lined many of the walls from floor to ceiling. The books, along with dozens of pictures of Casey and world dignitaries, were the dominant features of the spacious and elegant downstairs rooms. Like Casey, the house seemed more rumpled than formal, though still stately and imposing.

For the documentary, Ross and I interviewed both Mrs. Casey and Casey's daughter, Bernadette, in a sitting room lit by a large bay window. Both were fiercely loyal to Casey's memory and tried to defend his reputation. As noble and even touching as that was, I could not help thinking that Casey probably would have relished his posthumous image as a mysterious and even devious figure.

For those who admired him, those who despised him—or even for those who simply distrusted him—William Casey had been larger-than-life, a man who strode history's stage, influencing the events of his age. But his role had a sinister Shakespearean quality to it. Influencing Reagan administration decisions from the shadows of the CIA, Casey was the clever hero/villain who manipulated those around him in pursuit of his personal and political goals.

Casey and his love for intrigue would rest at the center of the October Surprise mystery. He was the chief suspect, the common element in virtually all the allegations. But what was real and what might be the covenient scapegoating of someone no longer around to defend himself? Without doubt, Casey feared that President Carter might manipulate the hostage issue for political gain in the final weeks of the campaign. Casey did put in place an apparatus for monitoring hostage developments, literally around the clock. He received intelligence reports gleaned from a federal bureaucracy which grew more and more hostile to Carter's presidency as the election neared. In case the hostages were freed, Casey even ordered his favorite campaign advertising man, Peter Dailey, to ready a barrage of television attack ads that would rake Carter's domestic record and divert attention from the happy homecomings.

But still, would Casey go so far as to interfere with President Carter's pre-election efforts to free 52 American hostages? Wouldn't that be a line that no loyal American would cross? Or did Casey regard Carter's re-election as so dangerous to the nation that it must be prevented at all costs? Or was it that Casey was so sure Carter couldn't get the hostages out that arranging their freedom on January 20, 1981, was the earliest practical date? That way, at least, the crisis would not spill over into the new administration and force a military confrontation with an important nation in the Islamic world.

On one of our visits to Mayknoll, Sophia Casey gave me an unpublished paper containing Casey's personal reflections on the 1980 campaign. Though the report focused on campaign mechanics, it did stress Casey's dread at the prospect of four more years under Jimmy Carter. Casey saw that in the darkest of hues. "In 1980, everyone [in Reagan's camp] agreed that Jimmy Carter had to be removed from office in order to save the nation from economic ruin and international humiliation," Casey wrote. To spare the country, the Reagan-Bush campaign consciously highlighted Carter's floundering over the hostages. "The Iranian hostage crisis was the focal point of the failure of Carter's foreign policy," Casey wrote. That focal point could have shifted quickly from failure to success if the hostages had suddenly come home.

William Casey was a man of rich contradictions and great complexity. He possessed a strong intellect, yet garbled speech. He loved books and could absorb diverse points of view, but he was still a man who saw the world in blacks and whites. He had survived the dirty and cold-hearted demands of wartime intelligence. No doubt in World War II he had to send men to their deaths in pursuit of tiny scraps of knowledge, truthful information about Nazi activities. He also understood the power of propaganda and disinformation, two important tools in the tradecraft of the professional intelligence operative.

In a speech that Casey once gave about his World War II experiences as a spymaster, Casey praised the skillful use of deceit. "It is better and more effective to use stealth and deception than brute force," Casey quoted Winston Churchill advising his military men. "In order to outfox the enemy and to harass him at every twist and turn of the road, [Churchill] practiced the clandestine arts on a scale unprecedented in history." Casey credited deception for the very survival of the Allied beachhead at Normandy, as Hitler held back his crack Panzer divisions, fearing a second Allied landing near Calais.

That speech also revealed another side of Casey's personality—a man who loved action and hated timidity and rules. As for World War II, he lamented that the role of intelligence consistently was underappreciated and obstructed by powerful bureaucratic forces. He described the OSS during the war as "embattled" and its founder, William Donovan, as fighting for resources and respect.

"It is no exaggeration to say that Donovan created OSS against the fiercest kind of opposition from everybody—the Army, Navy, and State Department, the Joint Chiefs of Staff, regular Army brass, the whole Pentagon bureaucracy and, perhaps most devastatingly, the White House staff," Casey complained.

The experience of his mentor, Bill Donovan, shaped Casey's own attitude toward finicky bureaucracies with their endless caution and regulations. "It was the kind of grinding opposition that would have worn down anyone with imagination and lust for action, such as Donovan had," Casey said. "But he survived all this, sustained, I suppose, by his vision of the role intelligence, subversion and irregular warfare had to play in a successful American war effort."

Casey's contempt for bureaucratic interference would remain a hallmark of his adult life. Like his hero Donovan, Casey believed that political niceties were obstacles to the larger goal. But did Casey's fondness for bold action and his contempt for timidity lead him into unorthodox strategies in 1980? To understand Casey's mindset in 1980, Robert Ross and I sought out Casey's friends and associates. We talked to one longtime friend, Albert Jolis, at a cluttered office in midtown Manhattan. Jolis, who knew Casey when both served in the OSS, said a driving force in Casey's life was "an abiding concern about the threat of communism. We'd fought in the war together as a battle against totalitarianism. And we both felt that we'd only done half the job, because the repression and the violence that was being perpetrated on people under communist rule was, in our view, just as bad as what Hitler had been doing."

Jolis shared Casey's alarm in the late 1970s when American international power appeared on the wane. "The mood was that the Soviets were advancing and the West was passive and inactive," Jolis said. "And the United States was not taking any steps to protect its own national interest, in terms of its global responsibilities and its trade interests. Casey was fully aware of that and very worried about it."

In spring 1980, concerned about Ronald Reagan's image in Europe as a "trigger-happy cowboy," Jolis urged Casey to send Reagan to the Continent to counter that negative perception. Casey rebuffed the advice, citing Reagan's busy schedule. But Casey agreed to go himself, taking along Reagan's chief foreign policy adviser, Richard Allen. The trip was planned for several days at the end of June and the start of July. In London, Casey and Allen met with British Prime Minister Margaret Thatcher, a newly elected European conservative strongly in favor of Ronald Reagan's candidacy.

"They were talking about the campaign and talking about the prospects of Reagan's victory, and what the new administration might be like," Jolis recalled. "It was a very general conversation, and there was obviously a lot of warmth and friendliness on Margaret Thatcher's part for Ronald Reagan."

Throughout the European swing, Casey encountered European and American conservatives distraught about Iran's humbling of America. "Everybody was upset," Jolis said. "Everybody was hoping that the situation could turn around. The feeling was one of almost despair, 'what's happening to our country?' We were being pushed around by these tin-pot dictators and not reacting, not responding and floundering. It was a very depressing period. And the Reagan campaign was hailed as a savior."

In Paris, Casey insisted on a private get-together with Count Alexandre deMarenches, another veteran of World War II intelligence operations and then head of the French secret service, the *Service de Documentation Exterieur et de Contre-Espionage*, the French equivalent of the CIA.

"You know, Casey's over there on a three-day visit and it was all compressed into a highly concentrated three days," Jolis said. "There wasn't much sleeping going on. And he said, 'I've got to see Marenches.' And he went off and saw Marenches. I don't know where he saw him."

Besides their common background in World War II, Casey and deMarenches saw eye to eye on the need to stop Soviet advances and to back old allies like the shah of Iran. "DeMarenches felt strongly that the West was failing to stand up for its historical values and traditions, and was allowing itself to be simply smothered by this communist Soviet expansionism," Jolis said.

DeMarenches was an imperious aristocrat who coveted the possession of secrets like other men might hoard gold. The spymaster had a full French face, a graying mustache, thinning hair, and dark eyebrows that seemed to perch over his eyes in a look of inquisitiveness or disdain. His physique reminded many of the portly actor, Sidney Greenstreet.

By 1980, deMarenches had been director of French intelligence for a decade. A devout believer in the secular religion of clandestine operations, he wanted the Western alliance to enter a crusade against its enemies on the "battlefield of the mind." There, he believed, an enemy could be confused and defeated through stealth and deception, rather than through force alone.

"I believe in *la raison d'état* which may outweigh any conventional morality," deMarenches would write. "As one of the longest-standing leaders of Western intelligence, I have learned that there are two sorts of history. There is the history we see and hear, the official history; and there is the secret history—the things that happen behind the scenes, in the dark, that go bump in the night. . . . As a player in the first and a manipulator in the second, I have attempted to bring to my work the kind of understanding of both aspects of history."[1]

DeMarenches and his intelligence service would figure in the allegations of a secret October meeting in Paris between Republicans and Iranians. Although not direct proof of those assertions, the existence of a close relationship between Casey and deMarenche at least made a discreet October meeting, with French intelligence officers handling security, feasible.

Like deMarenches, Casey also had a motive to act. Casey saw the future of his conservative faith and the Free World at stake in the 1980 election. "Casey was spiritually, emotionally, and physically dedicated to what he conceived as the preservation of Western civilization," his friend, Jolis, told us. "He was Catholic. And he saw that all of this was crumbling under a massive onslaught from the Soviet world on one hand and internal rot in the democracies."

And Casey, the old spymaster, still felt that lasting contempt for bureaucratic strictures. "He wasn't a wild man as he's sometimes painted," said Jolis. "But he was a risk taker. He would act on his hunches. He was a political animal, don't forget. And he understood how politics work. He had a very sharp mind, very quick. And he could see through the fog and cut right through. He had an enormous capacity for work. He wanted to make things happen, no doubt about that. And the way to make things happen was, if you knew the right person who could help you make things happen. And getting to the right person was part of his nature.

"You know, there's been a lot of propaganda about Bill Casey. People haven't liked him because of his policies. Because of that they have sought to picture him as a corner cutter and a fellow who would maybe not be too fussy about the ethics of the issue or things like that. That's just sour grapes as far as I'm concerned. This wasn't so. He was an honorable man, highly honorable, ethical, principled. But getting things done meant either

---

[1] Count Alexandre deMarenches and David A. Andelman, *The Fourth World War* (New York: William Morrow, 1992), p. 33.

getting around the red tape, or cutting through it, or ignoring it. But he couldn't stand the red tape."

Other Casey admirers remembered his love for intrigue and espionage. Robert Garrick, a senior Reagan-Bush campaign aide, was awed by Casey's commanding presence and amused by his conspiratorial bent. Casey had assigned Garrick, a retired admiral, to monitor last-minute hostage developments in the 1980 campaign. When we interviewed Garrick in Los Angeles, I had expected a gruff, take-charge guy. But Garrick turned out to be a friendly, garrulous sort whose background had been in Navy public relations, not in commanding fleets. His weathered face was more likely creased by the southern California sun than the icy winds of the North Atlantic.

"Bill Casey struck me as a man totally in control of himself and the situation at all times, almost relaxed," Garrick marveled. "I sort of wished I could be something like him."

I asked Garrick about the plausibility of Casey's having snuck off to Europe for talks with Iranians. "Yes, he could have," answered Garrick. "If we had scheduled a meeting on Sunday, maybe he didn't show. My mind would have presumed he went to mass. He and Ed Meese would leave and be gone for three and four days. They'd catch up with the airplanes and travel with the candidate for a while. I don't say it's impossible.

"I must say Bill Casey, to me, was sort of a mystery man. You know, he was here, he was there, he was around. He had his own driver, and the car would whip away. The driver brought him to these meetings when he showed up and that was it."

But Garrick sometimes found Casey's passion for secrecy a bit ludicrous. When Garrick was called to testify before the 1983 congressional probe into the theft of Jimmy Carter's debate briefing book, the mild-mannered admiral encountered Casey during a visit to the White House. At the time, Casey was a prime suspect in the never-resolved mystery of how the 1980 Reagan campaign got a purloined copy of Carter's preparation papers for a pivotal presidential debate.

"I went inside to go up to see Meese, when Bill's car arrives," Garrick remembered. "He greets me, very friendly, and we both step into the men's room, to answer a call. And I'm saying to Bill, 'You know, I'm before this Albosta committee and, Bill, I'm just telling the truth, and I don't know what they're after.' We're both standing at the urinal, and he starts to say something. He stops, gets down on his hands and knees and looks at all the commodes, and then continues the conversation."

For some reason, Garrick considered that point the appropriate place to end his anecdote. After waiting expectantly for more of the conversation, I finally asked, "So what did he say?"

"Well, in essence, he said, 'Now we can talk.' And I thought what a sight! Here's the head of the CIA, this great Bill Casey, down on his hands and knees, checking all the commodes to see if anybody's occupying them."

"Well, did he say anything worth recording?" I pressed.

"No, I just remember the sight of him down there," Garrick said, refusing to discuss the incident further. Even after Casey's death, his friends were not willing to violate his confidences.

As President Reagan's CIA director, Casey would prove again and again how much of a "mystery man" he could be and how much he hated red tape. In his six years in the job, Casey would earn the image as a modern-day swashbuckler. He was the captain of Reagan's gunboat diplomacy. His spy agency mined the harbors of Nicaragua, threatening international commerce and drawing the censure of the World Court. He joined forces with "counter-terrorists" in the Middle East who were as bloodthirsty as the killers and kidnapers they sought to counter. His CIA-sponsored "freedom-fighters" in Central America, Africa, and Asia became better known for their human rights atrocities and drug trafficking than for their love of democracy.

Despite legal prohibitions against the CIA influencing domestic politics, Casey did not confine his anticommunist activism to foreign countries. When his pet CIA projects were threatened, he directly intervened in the national debate. He tried to intimidate members of Congress by bandying about classified reports suggesting that they were communist dupes. He personally supported a domestic "public diplomacy" apparatus run out of the National Security Council. Using propaganda experts from the CIA and the military, the operation targeted domestic opponents of Casey's overseas operations and planted pro-administration propaganda in the nation's press.[2] Even inside the CIA, professional analysts complained that Casey slanted intelligence reports to justify his desired actions. In line with deMarenches, Casey believed that national security could "outweigh conventional morality."

But Casey's brazen style would finally undo him in the Iran-contra scandal. His dream of an extra-legal "off-the-shelf" intelligence apparatus was exposed along with an arms-for-hostage scheme that contradicted some of the administration's most solemnly stated policies. President Reagan's tough talk, vowing never to negotiate with terrorists, was exposed as hollow rhetoric.

But what Ross and I wanted to know was whether Casey's swashbuckling had begun in 1980. Had he made secret contacts with Iranian government representatives about the hostages? On that point, neither his widow, Sophia, nor his daughter, Bernadette, could establish his whereabouts on the key dates when he was alleged to have been in Europe. They were certain, though, that he had not traveled to Europe during the last months of the campaign.

"If he were taking a trip, I would know about it because I would fix his bags for him," said Sophia Casey, a smallish woman whose New York accent reminded me of Casey's. As for overseas trips during the campaign, she was certain that he could not have gone, due to his responsibilities for running the campaign headquarters in Arlington, Virginia. "He just couldn't leave the job because he was afraid something would go wrong."

Sophia Casey's repeated defense against the October Surprise suspicions was the illogic of her husband traveling to Europe at key moments of the campaign. "I'm sure he wasn't at this October meeting," she said. "He never would leave six weeks before the election."

"Well, what about July or August?" I asked.

"I don't know anything about that," she answered. "I wish I could tell you something about it, but I never heard it before."

When I asked her about the early July trip to London and Paris, she could not recall it without Bernadette's reminder. Nor did she remember

---

[2] For details, see Part 2 of my earlier book, *Fooling America* (New York: Morrow, 1992).

him talking about meeting Prime Minister Thatcher or any other luminaries on the trip. Clearly, Bill Casey was not a man who confided to his
wife about his professional activities nor always counted on her to pack his
bags.

But Sophia agreed that her husband might have met with Iranians
during the campaign, out of curiosity or to get information. "Oh, he would
talk to Iranians, sure," she said. "He had no reason not to."

"But do you know if he did or did not talk to Iranians during this
period?" I inquired.

"I don't know," she responded. "I really don't know, but I say he would
do it, I'm sure. I'm just saying, my own opinion, he would do it for
information. How would he get it? He'd want to know what the other
fellows knew, about the Iranians, or the situation there or what was gonna
happen."

But Mrs. Casey was sure he would not have taken any action to delay the
hostages' release. "I know for certain he would never do a thing like that,"
she said. "He had great compassion for the hostages, and he would not
delay their getting out of that terrible situation for one minute. He would
never do that. He would find that very, very wrong."

14

"READ MACHIAVELLI"

For the October Surprise documentary, *Frontline* senior producer Martin Smith arranged for us to use footage from an interview that a Bill Moyers team had done with Nicholas Veliotes, the Reagan administration's assistant secretary of state for the Middle East. As we worked in Ross's Soho loft, Smith slid the tape into the VCR. Veliotes's long, thin face flickered on the screen. His voice was a throaty whisper.

Veliotes diagnosed the "germs" of the Iran-contra arms-for-hostage scandal, tracing the sickness back to an Israeli weapons flight shot down over the Soviet Union on July 18, 1981. The chartered Argentine CL-44 turboprop had strayed off course over Soviet territory on its third mission to deliver American military supplies from Israel to Iran via Larnaca, Cyprus.

"We received a press report from Tass [the official Soviet news agency] that an Argentinian plane had crashed," Veliotes said. "According to the documents . . . this was chartered by Israel and it was carrying American military equipment to Iran. Obviously, I was interested in that because we had a very firm policy [against arms trade with Iran]. I don't need to tell you that Ronald Reagan was no friend of the ayatollah, and we [were] all still scarred by the hostage crisis.

"Here we are a few months later. So I did what you usually do under those circumstances, I tried to get to the bottom of it. And it was clear to me after my conversations with people on high that indeed we had agreed that the Israelis could transship to Iran some American-origin military equipment. Now this was not a covert operation in the classic sense, for which probably you could get legal justification for it. As it stood, I believe it was the initiative of a few people [who] gave the Israelis the go-ahead. The net result was a violation of American law."

For the flight that crashed in the Soviet Union and other Israeli shipments, no formal notification was given to Congress—as required by the Arms Export Control Act. The reason was obvious: evidence that the Reagan administration had authorized arms shipments to the hated Ayatollah Khomeini would have ignited a political firestorm.

The former assistant secretary of state claimed to have objected to deceptive wording in the official State Department "press guidance" about the Tass report. But the Washington press corps was easily mollified. No one caught on to the misleading language which asserted U.S. ignorance about the arms flow. The arms-to-Iran project, Veliotes believed, was "very small and informally done. But of course, you couldn't do it informally. That's what the laws were about. But I think you see here certain germs of the later Iran-contra."

According to Veliotes, the Reagan camp's dealings with Khomeini's radical Islamic regime might have gone back even further to before the 1980 election. "The actual timing on when the Americans got involved with the Israelis in an effort to reach out to the post-shah government, different people date it at different times," Veliotes said. "But it seems to have started in earnest in the period probably prior to the election of 1980, as the Israelis had identified who would become the new players in the national security area in the Reagan administration. And I understand some contacts were made at that time."

Q: "Between?"

Veliotes: "Between Israelis and these new players."

Veliotes's account pricked my ears. The first witness who had claimed pre-election contacts between the Israelis and the Reagan campaign had been ex-Israeli intelligence man Ari Ben-Menashe. I had given that claim little credence. But here was a senior Reagan administration official tracing Israel's arms shipments to Iran to similar pre-election discussions between Israeli government officials and GOP national security advisers.

In the early 1980s, senior Israelis also pointed to Reagan administration approval for their shipments to Iran. Defense Minister Ariel Sharon told the *Washington Post* in May 1982 that U.S. officials had acquiesced to the Israeli shipments to Iran. "We discussed this months ago with our American colleagues," Sharon said in the interview. "We said that notwithstanding the tyranny of Khomeini which we all hate, we have to leave a small window open to this country, a tiny small bridge to this country."

Israel was volunteering to be this bridge, keeping open avenues into the Iranian military in case it decided to oust Khomeini at some point. Sharon termed the Israeli arms sales "a symbolic supply" cleared with the United States. "We gave them the lists," he said. "They knew exactly." Later in 1982, Moshe Arens, then Israeli ambassador to the United States, made a similar claim in an interview with the *Boston Globe*. Arens, who later became Israeli defense minister, said the arms shipments to Iran had been arranged with U.S. consent "at almost the highest levels."[1]

In my work on the Iran-contra scandal, I had also obtained a classified summary of the testimony of a mid-level State Department official, David Satterfield. He gave congressional investigators a slightly different account of how the U.S. clearance had occurred.

"Satterfield believed that Israel maintained a persistent military relationship with Iran, based on the Israeli assumption that Iran was a non-Arab state which always constituted a potential ally in the Middle East," the summary read. "There was evidence that Israel resumed providing arms to Iran in 1980."[2]

A Mideast counter-terrorism expert, Satterfield offered no explanation for the Israeli-backed arms shipments in 1980 or in summer

---

[1] Bob Woodward and Walter Pincus, "Israeli Sale Said Allowed by Haig in '81," *Washington Post*, November 29, 1986, p. A1.

[2] Despite Carter's arms embargo against Iran and the President's strong protests to Prime Minister Begin, an October 1980 shipment went forward. As Gary Sick recounted, a cargo plane, belonging to a French company called Aerotour, left Paris in the pre-dawn hours of October 23. After a brief stop at an airfield in northern Corsica, a French island in the Mediterranean, the plane left for Tel Aviv where it was loaded with 250 F-4 tires and then returned to France, where the tires were transferred to a DC-8 cargo plane along with spare parts for M-60 tanks and other military equipment. On October 24, despite American objections, the shipment flew to Tehran. (Gary Sick, *October Surprise* (New York: Times Books, 1991), pp. 165–7. Gary Sick, "The Election Story of the Decade," *New York Times*, April 15, 1991.

1981. But he did describe Sharon's approach to Haig in December 1981.

"Sharon approached Secretary Haig and stated that Israel was in contact with key Iranian officials and wanted to engage in some arms transactions involving United States weapons in order to develop these contacts," the Satterfield summary said. "Haig told Israel that 'in principle' this was okay, but only for limited F-4 spare parts. Haig told Israel that these had to be commercial, rather than FMS [foreign military sales], transactions. Haig also insisted that the United States had to approve in advance specific lists of parts to be sold by Israel to Iran.

"Between January and March 1982, it became clear to the United States that Israel had not gotten the message, because they sent proposed lists of weapons which went beyond the agreed-upon limited list of F-4 spare parts. By March of 1982, the Central Intelligence Agency opposed any further agreement on this matter based upon new knowledge concerning the identity of the supposed Iranian middlemen and contacts. The Central Intelligence Agency doubted the credibility and power of Israel's channel. Satterfield did not know the specific names."

In 1982, the Reagan administration's covert policy in the Middle East was shifting again. Iran, sustained by its pipeline of Western weapons, had gained the upper hand over Iraq in their bloody border war. CIA Director William Casey and other key administration officials decided that it was time to tilt toward Iraq.

In the meantime, however, "Satterfield stated that approximately $53 million in weapons and parts had been sent to Iran, most of which were not within the agreed-upon guidelines." Satterfield, who by 1990 had been promoted to Secretary of State James Baker's staff, refused our request for an interview.

Satterfield's account represented an official document, a rarity in our investigation that had so many spoken words from hazy characters. But it offered only a sliver of the total picture. A senior Israeli intelligence officer in Europe told me that $246 million in U.S. military hardware had been shipped in the early days of the Iran pipeline. Israel supplied F-4 spare parts, M-48 tank parts, and parts for M-113 armored personnel carriers, he said. The F-4 parts were pulled from the German air force. Private dealers shipped other equipment from the United States, the Israeli added.

The Israeli intelligence officer claimed that these deals grew from "a verbal agreement" between Sharon and Haig. Ya'acov Nimrodi, a close friend of Sharon's, worked his longstanding arms contacts in Tehran to pave the way for the sales. "Sharon was a strong pioneer to sell items to Iran because he looked into the face of Iraq, not Iran," the Israeli told me. "After the Iranians released the hostages, I believe Israel started the deals in the first half of '81." But the Israeli said he did not know if the Republican clearance for the sales predated Reagan's electoral victory.

Ari Ben-Menashe described even larger arms deals. He put the total size of the Israeli arms pipeline to Iran in the tens of billions of dollars for the entire eight years of the Iran-Iraq war. Though we could fix no particular dollar amount to the shipments, our investigation found an Israeli hand in the brokering of dozens of "private" arms deals through Brussels, Paris, Madrid, and Lisbon. The Israeli government seemed to have played a worldwide coordinating role for Iran's arms procurement.

On January 9, 1991, Ross and I set up our video gear in Alexander Haig's spacious Washington office. Haig was much in demand for comment because of the deepening crisis in the Persian Gulf. President Bush's deadline for Iraqi withdrawal from Kuwait was less than a week away. But Haig found time to entertain our questions about an earlier American crisis in the Middle East. The former secretary of state and four-star general sat in a dark-leather, straight-back chair that tilted forward and back, forcing Ross constantly to adjust the camera's focus.

Haig looked like he had been sent from central casting for a movie role as a retired general. He had silver hair and rugged good looks, a trim build, and a clipped way of talking that often ended in a tense smile. His tightly wound personality could be unnerving, as it was to the nation when he declared after the 1981 assassination attempt on President Reagan that he, Haig, was "in charge" at the White House. Sometimes he got a peculiar Strangelovian look in his eye.

During the 1980 presidential campaign, Haig reminded us, he had been running United Technologies, a leading defense contractor based in Hartford, Connecticut, not working on the Reagan campaign. His contact with the hostage negotiations only came later, he said, during the transition period, when President Carter's negotiators were trying to finish up work on the deal.

"At that time, of course, the great concern of the Carter administration was that the deadline would run out before Inauguration and, in political terms, that whatever the outcome after that, the other party would get the credit," Haig said. He was suggesting that it was the Carter side that was being crassly political. But he hastened to add: "That's very natural and I'm not being critical about it. That's what American politics is all about." Haig finished his jab at the Democrats with a short laugh.

The Iranians, Haig insisted, were afraid that they would get harsher treatment if they dilly-dallied and the talks dragged on into the Reagan administration. "We had a new president whose reputation was one of a great deal of courage if not hawkishness," Haig said. "I talked to President-elect Reagan and urged him to make it very clear that as of Inaugural Day in January, it was a whole new ball game.

"It was clear that Tehran was getting increasingly nervous that Ronald Reagan would immediately change the rules of the game. And as a result, we had a rather harried period just as the President was being inaugurated. At 12:30 p.m., the planes had not taken off. We stayed relatively calm and I think five or ten minutes later they indeed took off. So the bluff, if that's what it was, worked. And it worked because the Iranians concluded that Ronald Reagan would take drastic and if necessary military action in the face of this crisis."

Haig was giving us the full-scale Reagan-scared-the-heck-out-of-'em version of events. In the days before the inauguration, the story of the Iranians quaking in their turbans circulated widely in Washington. Though popular among Reagan's supporters, the image was not true. The final obstacles to the hostage release had been cleared away hours before the inauguration. Whether the final delay was to insult Jimmy Carter one last time or to curry favor with the new president or to accommodate air traffic concerns, the post-inauguration release did not result from a sudden collapse of Iranian nerve.

As for the Israeli military shipments in 1981–82, Haig insisted they were sent without his permission. "This issue did come to my attention in a very forceful way during my first visit to the Middle East after the inauguration," he recalled. "It was the spring of '81 when my old friend who was then defense minister, Ariel Sharon, accosted me in the King David Hotel in Jerusalem. He made a very strong plea for Israel's ability to transship some spare parts to Iran. These involved some F-4 equipment. And I said at that time, 'Mr. Minister, whatever my views are is irrelevant. If it is a U.S.-supplied piece of equipment, it is illegal for such transshipment to occur.' Well, he got very outraged."

Haig's account didn't square with either Sharon's later claims or Veliotes's discoveries after the chartered Argentinian plane was shot down over the Soviet Union in July 1981. As for Veliotes's suggestion that Haig protected the Israelis on the plane crash, Haig insisted that he was "not even aware of the incident" and then added, "I've never ceased to be astonished by things I hear from former bureau fellows, including Nick Veliotes. If that indeed happened, I wonder why he didn't bring it to my attention because I saw him regularly and my position was clear."

Haig insisted that he rejected another Israeli proposition to ship arms to Iran in late 1981. "I made that point very forcefully again as Christmas approached in 1981 and it was finally raised with me shortly before my resignation in the spring of 1982," Haig said. "On every occasion, I was very adamant in refusing permission. I forbade it, and I had the right to."

But Haig did not rule out that American arms had found their way to Iran via Israel. "Now subsequently, I've heard that despite those positions that I took—and I think my constituents in the State Department took when they were approached—some equipment may have actually been shipped that was U.S.-supplied to Israel and then transshipped to Iran," he said. But he pointed his finger in another direction.

"If that happened, it happened through the good offices of somebody in the White House staff and I don't discount that could have happened because I ran into countless episodes where I had an approved position from the president and was pursuing it, and members of the White House staff were pursuing precisely the opposite."

"Any suspects?"

"Well, it's immaterial now," Haig responded. "What was important was that there was a total lack of discipline, not only in policy-making but in policy-implementing in the Reagan administration that ultimately led to my resignation."

Asked again who might have authorized the Israeli shipments, Haig returned to his theme of an out-of-control team around President Reagan. "I have a sneaking suspicion that somebody in the White House winked," Haig said almost gleefully.

But what about the public reports that Israel had defied his instructions? "Did you ever sit down and say, 'I want to get to the bottom of this? I want to know'?" I asked.

"Yes, yes, of course," Haig responded. "I've said it to Sharon. I said, 'I have a report of this' and all he said was 'no' . . ."

"He said they didn't ship?" I interjected.

"No," Haig said, indicating he had gotten a flat denial from Sharon.

"But later, he and Arens both claimed that there were shipments by Israel, with American approval," I noted.

"Well, it wasn't my approval, and it wasn't the secretary of state's approval when I was secretary of state. But I've already drawn for you a picture that would suggest there was nothing unusual about that."

"But doesn't that upset you a bit, that here's a man, Sharon, that you've dealt with and you have a friendship with and he would mislead you on something as important as whether or not . . ."

"Oh, no, no, no, no," boomed Haig, shaking his head in disgust at my naïveté. "On that kind of thing? No. Come on. Jesus! God! You know, you'd better get out and read Machiavelli or somebody else because I think you're living in a dream world! People do what their national interest tells them to do and if it means lying to a friendly nation, they're going to lie through their teeth."

I was momentarily stunned by Haig's bluntness. But I managed to recover enough to ask whether informal approval of the Israeli arms deals dated back to the 1980 Reagan campaign as Veliotes suspected?

"It wouldn't surprise me," Haig answered, his voice registering his old frustration with his lost bureaucratic battles in 1982. "By the time I was brought to resign, it was because I had concluded that we had a bureaucratic zoo in that period, which I think carried through to the Iran scandal, where we had the NSC acting as free agents."

"So it would not have surprised you that there may have been some pre-inauguration contacts about what to do in Iran?" I asked.

"Not a bit! Not a bit! There was a lot of freewheeling going on between

Dick Allen and the Koreans and other governments with whom we did business, the West Germans, for instance. But that's not unusual and there's nothing scandalous about it because I found that with every administration I've worked." Yet, Haig found President Reagan's team a little more byzantine than most. "There were wheels within wheels in the Reagan administration," he nearly chortled.

Haig also said he would not have been surprised if William Casey had met with Iranian emissaries. "After all, Bill Casey was leading the campaign for Ronald Reagan," Haig noted. "One of the main campaign issues was the Iranian hostage crisis and the perception that the Carter administration just totally goofed up in dealing with it. Therefore, it was high on the administration's agenda as something that had to be solved and hopefully, before Ronald Reagan had to deal with it and get his hands dirty with it. So it wouldn't surprise me a bit and as I say, this is business as usual in American politics."

A devoted practitioner of *Realpolitik*, Haig even saw merit in Casey's contacting the Iranians, "I wouldn't be critical of it," Haig said. "If Bill Casey could have worked out a deal which would have opened a lot of doors promptly in the event that President Reagan was elected, I don't consider that either wrong, morally or practically. That's the American system and it ain't very savory sometimes, but it's nonetheless better than most." Haig ended his comment with a good-natured laugh.

Haig was telling us that the idea of William Casey contacting Iranians behind Jimmy Carter's back wasn't as outlandish as many people had argued. But Haig claimed not to know what actually had happened. Ross and I sought Haig's help on one other point, the allegations that we had received about NATO stockpiles being drawn down so military supplies could be diverted to Iran from Europe. We thought that as former NATO commander, Haig could lay these stories to rest.

"So reports about Iranian representatives going in with people from these various warehouses and making sure that certain equipment's there, which is going to be shipped to Iran, would on its face be preposterous to you?" I asked, only to be surprised by the answer.

"Well, no," answered Haig. "It wouldn't be preposterous if a nation, Germany, for example, decided to let some of their NATO stockpiles be diverted to Iran. They'd have total control over such a decision." But he added, "It would surprise me very much if American-controlled equipment were transshipped from Europe to Iran. I would be very surprised."

In January 1991, Ross and I had scheduled one more interview with a convicted Iranian arms dealer about the early days of the U.S.-Israel-Iran arms pipeline. We had both been tempted to cancel it. We had talked to enough arms dealers and other individuals of dubious character to last us a lifetime. But we decided to go ahead and drove up Interstate 684 from New York City to the Federal Correctional Institution in Danbury, Connecticut. After arriving, we submitted to the now numbingly familiar procedure: forms to fill out, pockets to empty, metal detectors to pass through.

The inmate, Arif Durrani, was escorted to the interview room. He was dressed in a bright orange prison jumpsuit. Then in his early 40s, the Pakistani-born arms dealer wore his hair puffed up on his head in a style reminiscent of the late TV star Michael Landon. A soft-spoken man, Durrani called himself the only person sentenced to hard jail time—ten years—for a role in the Iran-contra scandal.

Like nearly everyone in jail, Durrani had a tale to tell. Only Durrani's was more interesting than most. It was a story of international intrigue and double-cross. Durrani claimed he was locating some of the components for Oliver North's shipments of HAWK missiles to Iran in 1985–86 when he ran afoul of U.S. Customs. But Durrani's defense that he was part of the bigger scandal, not just a freelancer out to make a buck, failed to convince a jury. Durrani was found guilty.

After his conviction, Durrani continued to insist on his innocence and began providing more and more details about his work for the Iranian government as far back as 1981. During those years, he was scouring Europe looking for military equipment and vital spare parts as well as running a military manufacturing plant in California. Durrani claimed top-level contacts inside Iran's Revolutionary Guards and with Ayatollah Khomeini's family.

Durrani's description of the Iranian arms supply network was generally accurate. He knew how the weapons flowed through Lisbon, Madrid, and other European cities. He would drop the names of key middlemen who had worked with both Israel and Iran. Iranian arms procurement officials also confirmed to us that Durrani was one of their suppliers.

Ross and I had hoped Durrani could add to our information about weapons pulled from NATO stockpiles for Iran. We were surprised, however, when he claimed inside knowledge about contacts by one Iranian operative, Hamid Naqashan, who had allegedly been in touch with Reagan campaign figures in Europe. Both American weapons broker William Herrmann and German arms dealer Karl Heinz Ottershagen had described conversations with Naqashan about Republican-Iranian contacts at the time of the hostage crisis. Durrani claimed that Naqashan had talked directly with William Casey and other senior Republicans.

"This all started in summer 1980—July, August—and became very active in September and October 1980," Durrani said. "I was told that it's inevitable that the Iranians would be making some sort of adjustment or arrangement with the United States government to release the hostages in exchange for other considerations. The follow-on was there were feelers sent through what you call the Reagan people. Subsequently, the negotiations shifted to those people."

When I asked if high-ranking cleric Mehdi Karrubi had played any role in these negotiations, Durrani said Karrubi had been a principal emissary. "Whenever there is any contact overseas or with foreign governments, he is like a nominated official by the inner group of the Iranians that they send in to negotiate. Karrubi knows Naqashan really well, and Naqashan is actually the person who brought Karrubi into these negotiations."

Without further prompting, Durrani then volunteered another surprising assertion. "Karrubi also had meetings in Spain," the arms dealer said. "That is from where all these contacts started with."

"Do you remember when those were?" I asked.

"I do not recall the exact dates."

"And you were told this by whom?"

"By Mohsen Rafiqdoust and the Revolutionary Guard officials."

"Did they say who the meetings in Spain were with?"

"I have been told they were directly with Director Casey at one time."

Ross and I were surprised that Durrani knew about the Casey-Karrubi-Madrid allegation, because it had yet to be made public. He might have picked it up from someone who had been questioned by us or by Gary Sick, who was also exploring this claim by Jamshid Hashemi. But Durrani insisted that he had heard the allegation from the Revolutionary Guard officials back in Tehran. There was, of course, no way to be sure.

By now, Ross and I had compiled a long list of individuals who had stated on-the-record that the Reagan campaign had sought independent contacts with the Iranians about the hostages. It was just too bad that none of the witnesses was Mother Theresa.

Still, a lot of people would have to be lying for the October Surprise allegations to be total nonsense. Even discounting Richard Brenneke and Oswald LeWinter, the list included: the ex-president of Iran, Abolhassan Bani-Sadr; a former Iranian/CIA operative, Jamshid Hashemi; an ex-Israeli intelligence official, Ari Ben-Menashe; a French arms dealer with confirmed intelligence ties, Nicholas Ignatiew; a former American arms dealer and federal informant, William Herrmann; an Iranian arms merchant and CIA collaborator, Houshang Lavi; pilot Heinrich Rupp; senior PLO official Bassam Abu Sharif; and Durrani.

Others had indicated to us a general awareness of GOP-Iranian contacts: Khomeini son-in-law Sadeq Tabatabai said he believed some of the radical mullahs had been paid to block a hostage settlement, and veteran CIA officer Miles Copeland told us that CIA/Republican operators had "word back" from the Iranian "devil" that the hostages would be freed as soon as Reagan took office.

Even Casey supporters, such as Alexander Haig and Sophia Casey, had declared that Casey would see nothing wrong with talking to Iranians about the hostage impasse. Mitchell Rogovin's notes from October 1980 showed Lavi recounting the Iranian government's desire to do a hostage swap, but "not willing to deal with Carter."

There were other sources who had been interviewed by other reporters and who had added their own claims, like tiles to a complex mosaic. Iran's acting foreign minister Sadegh Ghotbzadeh told Agence France-Presse in September 1980 that the Republicans were "trying to block a solution" to the hostage crisis, but his claim drew little attention at the time.

Michael Riconosciuto, a mysterious figure in allegations that the U.S. government stole valuable computer software, claimed he went to Iran in 1980 for the Reagan campaign to deposit bribes into the bank accounts of radical mullahs. *Der Spiegel* reporters interviewed two other witnesses: Ottershagen, the German arms dealer who alleged that Republicans met Iranians in Switzerland, and a senior French intelligence official who claimed that October Surprise meetings in Paris did occur.

But we recognized the possibility that somehow the witnesses might have coordinated their stories as part of a grand trick. Some, I knew, had crossed paths before. French arms dealer Nicholas Ignatiew had known Oregon businessman Richard Brenneke, who also worked with a mutual business associate of Israeli intelligence man Ari Ben-Menashe.

Yet, the possibility of coordinated lying by all the witnesses suffered from logical as well as logistical difficulties. Even among the characters who shared some mutual background, there were sharp differences in their accounts. Ignatiew and Ben-Menashe, for instance, told us that they thought Brenneke was lying about his presence at the Paris meetings. If they were in cahoots, why wouldn't their stories mesh? Why would they be so eager to cast aspersions on each other?

In January 1991, Gary Sick had planned to write an opinion piece for the *New York Times* describing his new certainty that the Reagan administration had interfered with the hostage release. The timing was linked to the tenth anniversary of the hostages' freedom. But the Persian Gulf War had exploded those plans. In April, Sick saw the approaching air date for the *Frontline* broadcast as another news peg for his opinion article, which he wrote and submitted.

Sick's article appeared on Monday, April 15, 1991, and covered nearly two-thirds of the *Times*'s Op-Ed page. It outlined how Sick had progressed to his conclusion that the Republicans had struck a secret hostage deal. Sick also argued that the gravity of the longstanding suspicions demanded a more thorough investigation than a handful of journalists and scholars could muster. Besides raising questions about the susceptibility of U.S. leaders to blackmail if these meetings had happened, Sick wrote, "it implies a willingness to pursue private, high-risk foreign policy adventures out of sight of the electorate. That may be *Realpolitik*. Its practioners may indeed win big. But it is profoundly antidemocratic."[3]

When the *Frontline* documentary aired the next day, on April 16, 1991, we struck a neutral stance on whether Republican-Iranian contacts had, in fact, occurred. We repeated several times that conclusive proof of any deal was lacking. But because we recounted the allegations in a reasonably respectful way, some Reagan supporters complained that *Frontline* gave inordinate weight to the claims of dubious characters who inhabited a netherworld of gunrunning and intelligence gamesplaying.

We also came under criticism from Carter sympathizers for the muddled closing line of the show, which went: "The 1980 hostage mystery might never be solved. After 10 years, no smoking gun has been found proving that the Reagan campaign struck a deal with the Khomeini regime, yet the corroborative accounts of so many people make the allegations difficult to explain." The two sentences of inelegant prose had been the product of hours of discussion within *Frontline*. The closing was meant to convey both our skepticism about Washington's political system getting to the bottom of anything and our doubts about the witnesses who were at the center of Gary Sick's change of heart.

But editorials and articles praising the documentary outweighed the criticism. Martin Kilian poked fun at my earlier nervousness, my expectation of a ferocious reaction that would simply not permit the story to be taken seriously. Delighted that Congress might finally enter the fray and find the truth, Kilian noted that even *Newsweek*, that editorial bastion of conventional wisdom, was taking a second look. The magazine, not known for its investigative reporting, had begun putting together a special team to examine the issue.

I had been paranoid, Kilian told me. Maybe, I thought, but I still felt uneasy.

---

[3] Gary Sick, "The Election Story of the Decade," *New York Times*, April 15, 1991.

15

MORE QUESTIONS ABOUT ARI

After winning acquittal, ex-Israeli intelligence man Ari Ben-Menashe left New York. His woman friend in New Rochelle must have tired of his overbearing personality and his hogging the telephone. Ben-Menashe also needed to recover whatever money he could from his days in the arms business. So the Israeli moved from the urban/suburban tracts of New York to the rolling hills of horse country in Lexington, Kentucky. There, in the city's neat and orderly downtown, he rented a two-bedroom apartment where he stayed with his elderly mother who had flown over from Israel.

In Lexington, Ben-Menashe was conniving with some curious friends in a scheme to gain access to money that he said he had stashed in bank accounts around the world. The money, he had said earlier, belonged to the Israeli government. But he now added, with a grin: "During the trial, they said it wasn't theirs. So it must be mine."

Even though work on the *Frontline* documentary was over, I was still trying to assess what Ben-Menashe really knew and what he only pretended to know. If he were telling the truth, he could be the key to unlocking not only the October Surprise mystery, but other important stories. He claimed insights into the Reagan-Bush policy of coddling Iraq's Saddam Hussein prior to Saddam's invasion of Kuwait. He put Israel's use of American spy Jonathan Pollard in the context of a larger espionage operation. Ben-Menashe even claimed that Prime Minister Yitzhak Shamir had launched his own détente with the Soviet Union.

In early 1991, Ben-Menashe asked me to fly to Lexington, promising more details about his life inside Israeli intelligence. I agreed to listen one more time.

Ben-Menashe met me at the small airport in Lexington. He was in the company of a new lady friend, an attractive older woman with a trim figure and a dyed-blonde bouffant hairstyle. A youthful grandmother still looking for some excitement in life, she drove a luxury model four-wheel-drive all-terrain vehicle that sported a power antenna, power windows, a pricy sound system, and plush seats. Her second car was a white Jaguar. She also owned a pie shop, and frequent trips there showed on Ben-Menashe's waistline. After we left the airport, he insisted we stop in for some morning pie before doing anything else.

As Ben-Menashe's new friend drove us around Lexington later in the day, past the long wooden fences and prancing thoroughbreds, we talked about the October Surprise investigation. From the back seat, I mentioned in passing that the old CIA man, Miles Copeland, who had volunteered a plan for freeing the hostages in 1980, had died in England. Ben-Menashe whirled around in his front seat to look at me. His concern seemed genuine.

"Oh no," he exclaimed. "That's terrible."

"You knew Miles Copeland?" I responded with surprise.

"Oh, yes," answered Ben-Menashe. "You know, he was the conceptual father of all of this." To my amazement, Ben-Menashe claimed he had first met the CIA man in Washington during the 1980 hostage crisis and that Copeland had brokered Republican cooperation with Israel. "You know, I really liked him," Ben-Menashe said.

I would take note of this claimed contact, though it seemed just one more farfetched story from Ari Ben-Menashe, who acted like a man determined to undermine his own credibility. Copeland had been one of the CIA's most committed Arabists. He had been a behind-the-scenes adviser to Egypt's nationalist president Gamal Abdul Nasser, Israel's chief nemesis in the 1950s. Copeland had even joined others in the Eisenhower administration arguing that the United States should break with its traditional allies, England, France, and Israel, and side with Egypt during the 1956 Suez crisis.

Copeland was an unlikely "conceptual father" for collaboration between the Reagan campaign and Israel in 1980. But I recalled that there was that reference in Copeland's autobiography, "The Game Player," about lunch with former CIA counterintelligence chief James Angleton and an unnamed Mossad official. Copeland described the topic of the luncheon conversation as the embassy takeover and the resulting hostage crisis.[1] But Copeland mentioned no other contacts with Israelis on the issue.

Yet, I was interested in following leads about Copeland's role because I still suspected that his CIA old boys' rescue plan might have been the seed from which later Republican efforts sprouted.

After returning to Washington, I wrote to Copeland's widow, first to express my sympathy at the passing of her husband, a truly engaging human being; second to ask coldheartedly for access to his diaries and notes from 1980; and third to test Ben-Menashe's claim that Copeland had met with Israelis in 1980. If nothing else, I thought, I could use a response to challenge Ben-Menashe again about his truthfulness, which had become a regular and blunt point in our conversations.

The return letter from Lorraine Copeland arrived a couple of weeks later. Miles Copeland's files, she said, had been shipped away and would not be available to me. But in response to my comments about an Israeli speaking highly of her late husband, Mrs. Copeland expressed surprise, "given Miles' well-known pro-Arab stance." But then she added: "With regard to Miles' relationship with the Israelis, he did have a brief honeymoon period with them around that time," 1980. She knew of at least one other meeting with an Israeli intelligence officer in the Middle East that year. So, as unlikely as it might have seemed, there was, at least, some plausibility to Ben-Menashe's assertion.

Despite all the doubts about Ben-Menashe's truthfulness, the Israeli did have some pluses in his credibility column. I had confirmed that Ben-Menashe did work for an office in Israeli military intelligence from 1977–87. Clearly, he did have accurate insights into Israel's dealings with Iran. He had tried to leak the story of U.S. arms sales to Iran in mid-1986, months before they became public.

---

[1] Copeland, *op cit.*, p. 256.

After one interview for the *Frontline* documentary, Iran's former defense minister Ahmad Madani, the presidential candidate whose campaign received CIA money via the Hashemi brothers, startled me with another confirmation about Ben-Menashe. I had been commenting about some of the peculiar characters we had encountered in our investigation. When I mentioned Ben-Menashe by name, Madani lit up. Madani, who had been governor-general of strategic Khuzistan province, claimed that he had dealt personally with Ben-Menashe on Iranian issues after the Islamic revolution.

"Ben-Menashe was well known around Iran," Madani said. "He was known as an Israeli intelligence officer." I was almost speechless and called for Ross to come into the room to hear this.

"Was he an important player?" I asked Madani after recovering from the surprise.

"With the Israelis, the person who seems least important can be the most important," the distinguished-looking Madani responded with a slight smile on his face.

"Would you say Ben-Menashe was high-level, low-level, or mid-level?" I asked, thinking of the repeated Israeli description of Ben-Menashe as a "low-level translator."

After pausing for a moment, the ex-defense minister answered carefully: "I would say mid-level." That Ben-Menashe would have dealt directly with the Iranian official responsible for Khuzistan province on the frontlines in the crisis with Iraq further established the Israeli as a genuine player. But still what to make of his overall credibility and his bizarre claim about seeing George Bush in Paris?

During one of our conversations, Ben-Menashe startled me again by offering a new take on another October Surprise mystery, the curious meeting at the L'Enfant Plaza Hotel. Ben-Menashe began insisting that the L'Enfant Plaza meeting with Richard Allen, Robert McFarlane, and Laurence Silberman was more than just a freelance attempt by Iranian arms broker Houshang Lavi to resolve the hostage crisis. Ben-Menashe claimed that the Israeli government was behind that initiative, too.

According to Ben-Menashe's new interpretation, Lavi had been assigned by Israeli intelligence to handle the logistics for the talk. Lavi was instructed to work through Senator John Tower, who, Ben-Menashe said, had been approached earlier by senior Israeli intelligence officials. Tower's staff aide, McFarlane, was assigned to coordinate the details and bring along the other two Republicans: Allen and Silberman.

"Sometime in September 1980, some Israeli intelligence officers worked out a plan to get American hostages out with some Iranian officials in Europe," Ben-Menashe told me as I interviewed him in spring 1991 in my Arlington home. "Then, the director of military intelligence at the time, Yehoshua Saguy, communicated the plan to Casey."

"It was set up through two people," Ben-Menashe continued. "Rafi Eitan, who was then counter-terrorism adviser to Israel's prime minister, sets it up with McFarlane and through an Israeli agent, an Iranian Jew that was living in the United States at the time, Houshang Lavi. He also contacts McFarlane and makes sure the technical affairs are taken care of."[2]

But Ben-Menashe claimed the Republicans were hesitant. "The Americans still procrastinate and they say we would like an Iranian official to come to Washington and tell us this officially," he said.

According to Ben-Menashe, the Israeli proposal sought "a swap in Karachi, Pakistan, where the hostages would be flown in by the Iranians and the Americans would pick them up there." Ben-Menashe's description of the deal matched the handwritten notation on Houshang Lavi's lined paper about the "E. Plaza Hotel" meeting on October 2, 1980 with "Silberman, Allen, Bob McFar." The note referred to the hostages being flown to Karachi, where a Boeing 707 jetliner would arrive with military spare parts to Iran and then leave with the 52 Americans.

But Ben-Menashe's biggest shock about the L'Enfant Plaza meeting was his claim that he personally attended it. When he told me this, I shook my head in amazement and disbelief. Ben-Menashe, however, was unfazed, and pressed ahead with his story.

For the L'Enfant Plaza meeting, Ben-Menashe said, he brought to Washington an Iranian named Abolhassam Omshei, a former French

---

[2] Rafi Eitan gained notoriety in the United States in 1985 for overseeing the work of Jonathan Pollard, a U.S. Navy official who was spying on the U.S. government for Israel.

literature professor with strong revolutionary credentials. Ben-Menashe described Omshei as an aide to Iran's minister of defense and a close associate of radical cleric Mehdi Karrubi, the alleged emissary to the Madrid meetings.

Ben-Menashe said he and Omshei took a Pan Am flight from Frankfurt, West Germany, to New York. Ben-Menashe had no personal recollection of the date. But based on Lavi's note, Ben-Menashe believed the flight would have arrived October 2, 1980. Ben-Menashe recalled landing at Kennedy International Airport in New York at around lunchtime. He and Omshei then grabbed a cab to LaGuardia Airport about 20 minutes away and met Lavi for the Eastern Airlines shuttle flight to Washington's National Airport. After a short cab ride across the Potomac River, they arrived at the L'Enfant Plaza Hotel, the Israeli said.

Ben-Menashe remembered the time of the meeting as shortly after the lunch hour. He said he shooed Lavi off to the sidelines, a slight that upset the arms dealer, who had wanted to play a more prominent role. As for the Republicans, McFarlane arrived first, Ben-Menashe said, followed by Allen and Silberman, who arrived together. According to Ben-Menashe, Omshei spoke in his limited English and outlined the hopes for a fast settlement.

"Dr. Omshei talked about the fact that our two peoples are friends and we have to resolve this issue," Ben-Menashe said. "He gave details to McFarlane about how this deal should be carried out. And McFarlane's answer was—which we didn't understand—'I'll report back to my superiors.' We didn't understand who his superiors were. But that was his reaction."

After that, according to Ben-Menashe's account, the meeting ended. Omshei stayed in Washington to visit his son, who lived in suburban Maryland. Ben-Menashe said he headed back to National Airport for a return flight to New York with Lavi. Ben-Menashe and Lavi separated at LaGuardia. Ben-Menashe rented a car and drove north to a relative's house in suburban New York to spend the night. The next day, he flew back to Israel, where, he said, the Republican response to the L'Enfant Plaza overture was read as an unwillingness to resolve the hostage crisis quickly.

"Within 20 hours or so, I was in Israel and my superiors were told by the Reagan campaign team that 'we have already worked out a meeting in

Paris for mid-October. We're going to go forward with it.' But this in Israel was seen as plain procrastination. And at that time, we realized that nothing is going to be done by these people before the election."

As implausible as I found this story, it did have some charm. Ben-Menashe's L'Enfant Plaza account incorporated what looked like an anomalous meeting into the comprehensive October Surprise mystery. Instead of the L'Enfant Plaza get-together being an inexplicable encounter between a few Republicans and a mysterious Iranian emissary, it would be part of the fluid back-and-forth of the three-cornered contacts involving the Iranians, the Israelis, and the Republicans. The curious loss of memory by the three Republicans would also appear in a new light. Their forgetfulness would make sense because the meeting would have been an outgrowth of secret Republican-Iranian negotiations that could not now be acknowledged.

Ben-Menashe's story also had some plausible elements. Lavi, an Iranian Jew, was close to the Israelis in those years. The contact, through Senator John Tower's staff, suggested political savvy, since Tower was an important second-level figure in the Reagan-Bush campaign entourage. Better than any other foreigners, the Israelis knew the lay of the Washington political landscape. They would have understood Tower's importance as a powerful Republican from George Bush's adopted home state of Texas. On the other hand, the Republican story that the L'Enfant Plaza contact resulted from a walk-in by the Iranian emissary to the Senate Armed Services Committee minority staff never made much sense. So there was an appealing logic to Ben-Menashe's account of the L'Enfant Plaza meeting as an Israeli initiative to resolve the crisis in a politically neutral way.

But as with many of Ben-Menashe's tales, there were serious problems. According to Pan Am's regular flight schedules for October 2, 1980, the earliest plane from Frankfurt would have arrived in New York at about 2:30 p.m., not around 12:30 p.m. as Ben-Menashe recalled. Considering the time it would take to clear customs, collect luggage, find a cab for the ride to LaGuardia and fly to Washington, the earliest one could reach the L'Enfant Plaza Hotel would be late afternoon, not shortly after the lunch hour as Ben-Menashe claimed. Richard Allen, too, had placed the meeting near the lunch hour.

And there was Houshang Lavi's earlier meeting that morning, October

2, with a CIA representative in Mitchell Rogovin's Washington office. For Ben-Menashe's story to work, Lavi would have had to leave that meeting, rush to National Airport, and catch a shuttle flight to New York. Lavi would then meet Ben-Menashe and Omshei at LaGuardia, catch another shuttle and fly back to Washington for the L'Enfant Plaza meeting. The earliest that roundtrip could finish would be late afternoon, not lunchtime.

Ben-Menashe's story suffered another credibility problem. He hadn't told it to me until after Lavi had died, so there was no way to crosscheck the information with Lavi. In addition, Lavi had not mentioned Ben-Menashe or Omshei when he was alive. Lavi had told me once that other individuals—besides the Republicans—did have a hand in the L'Enfant Plaza meeting. But he gave no names nor did he specify what exactly these other people did.

While the three Republicans were suspiciously fuzzy about the man they met, they certainly had not described a delegation to us. Richard Allen had consistently recalled meeting with one man, possibly an Iranian or an Egyptian. Silberman had disputed the possibility that Lavi was the emissary because he thought he would have remembered a Jewish name. McFarlane also had insisted he had no idea of the identity of the emissary, even though he, McFarlane, had arranged the meeting.

The other possibility was to locate Dr. Omshei. But Ben-Menashe said he had heard that the academic-turned-government-emissary, too, had died. Another conveniently uncheckable source, I thought. But I found a phone number in Tehran for an "A. Omshei" among Ben-Menashe's personal papers that I had collected from his mother and his lawyer.

Ross, using his Persian-language skills, put a call through to the number and found a living-and-breathing Dr. Omshei on the other end of the line. When Ross outlined his question about whether Omshei participated in a meeting in Washington in 1980 about the American hostages, Omshei answered, "I recall something like that." But he would not elaborate over the phone. He did, however, agree to meet with us, possibly in Europe or in Iran at some later date.

Omshei's reaction gave me pause. I decided to suspend judgment about Ben-Menashe's unlikely L'Enfant Plaza tale until Ross and I had a chance to interview Omshei more closely.

16

WHERE WAS BILL?

The White House press corps was ushered into the Oval Office on May 3, 1991, for a routine photo opportunity. It was a common ritual for the reporters and photographers who cover the president. Venezuela's President Carlos Andres Pérez was visiting President Bush, and the topic of the day was inter-American relations. But as often happens, the reporters did not confine their questions to the prescribed topic that the two heads of state were addressing in their private discussions. The three-week-old controversy over Gary Sick's *New York Times* opinion piece and the *Frontline* documentary was still in the air. One reporter took the occasion to ask President Bush if he had gone to Paris in October 1980.

"Was I ever in Paris in October 1980?" a clearly annoyed president responded, repeating the questions through pursed lips. "Definitively, definitely, no."

Five days later, Bush's anger had not subsided. "I can only say categorically that the allegations about me are grossly untrue, factually incorrect, bald-faced lies," he fairly seethed. Bush emphatically denied "this little word-of-mouth ugly rumor." President Bush was taking the allegations of a few marginal characters very personally.

Knight-Ridder's White House correspondent Owen Ullmann called me in early May. He wondered how I had gotten myself into such a bizarre story. Ullmann, an old friend during our days at the Associated Press in the early 1980s, said he intended to write an article establishing, once and for all, that George Bush had not gone to Paris in October 1980.

I encouraged Ullmann to try, but noted that we had hoped to put that issue to rest, too. We found clarifying the point more difficult than we had expected. Censored Secret Service records, which we had obtained under the Freedom of Information Act, did show Bush's detail going to the Chevy Chase Country Club on the morning of Sunday, October 19. We put the records on the screen to buttress the president's denial of a Paris trip. But we had found no independent corroboration.

Ullmann, an experienced reporter, also got conflicting accounts of Bush's activities that day. A former Bush campaign aide, David Q. Bates, thought he had played tennis with Bush that day at the Chevy Chase club. But a White House aide told Ullmann that Bush had spent the entire Sunday at home preparing for his speech that night to the Zionist Organization of America. Bush's press secretary, Peter Teeley, said he could not recall what Bush was doing, but knew he wasn't in Paris. The president, Ullmann noted in his article for the Knight-Ridder newspapers, "has not detailed his activities on the October weekend in question." So instead of solving the mystery, the Knight-Ridder article only added to it.

But there was help on the way for President Bush and his Chevy Chase alibi. Later in May, *Wall Street Journal* reporter Gordon Crovitz wrote on the newspaper's staunchly pro-Republican opinion page that "it can now be told" about Bush's activities that Sunday. Crovitz asserted that Bush had lunch at the Chevy Chase Country Club with Justice and Mrs. Potter Stewart. But Crovitz did not explain why this could not have been told earlier, nor did the article cite a single source for the information.

Justice Stewart died in 1985 and Mrs. Stewart had apparently not been questioned. She was supposedly very ill. So it wasn't clear how Crovitz could know with such certainty what had happened that day. Despite the thinness of the sourcing, the Crovitz article was quickly cited by Republicans as more conclusive proof against the Bush allegations.

I already knew that Secret Service shift supervisor Leonard Tanis had told congressional investigators that Mr. and Mrs. Bush had joined the Stewarts for Sunday brunch. But his account could have been influenced by the questioning from a congressional investigator. The investigator had told Tanis about speculation by the club's restaurant maitre d' that the

Stewarts, who were club members, might have hosted their friends, the Bushes. But Tanis would not return my phone calls or agree to be interviewed about his recollection.

Then, after the Ullmann and Crovitz articles, I discovered that there might yet be a source who could confirm the Chevy Chase story. I learned from another old AP friend that the reports of Mrs. Stewart's poor health were wildly exaggerated. She was even dating my friend's widower father. So I called Mrs. Stewart and left a message. When she called back, I found her to be bright and chipper on the phone. I asked about the possible October 1980 brunch with George and Barbara Bush.

"It was our custom to have lunch together at the Bushes' home on Sunday mornings when we were all in town," Mrs. Stewart answered cheerfully. When the Supreme Court was in session, as it would have been in October, she and her late husband often would walk over to the Bushes' house on Lowell Street in the quiet Washington neighborhood for a leisurely brunch. "But I don't know for sure if we did that weekend."

"Well, what about the Chevy Chase Country Club?" I asked.

"What about it?" she responded.

"Well, the story is that you and your husband had brunch at the Chevy Chase Country Club with the Bushes."

"I don't remember anything about the Chevy Chase Country Club," Mrs. Stewart answered, sounding honestly baffled. But she then admonished me, "You should believe whatever the president tells you."

But the president hadn't told me anything. He was only denying going to Paris. He didn't say where he did spend the Sunday in question. Again, though, a possible corroborating witness for Bush's presence at the Chevy Chase club for Sunday brunch had no memory of the event.

Further undermining the likelihood that Mrs. Stewart had brunch with her husband and George Bush on the morning of October 19 is the evidence that Mrs. Bush did not. *Frontline* had filed another Freedom of Information Act request for Mrs. Bush's Secret Service logs. According to her records, Mrs. Bush's detail left the Lowell Street residence at 10:00 a.m. and went to the C&O Canal jogging path. Her Secret Service detail returned to the residence at 11:00 a.m., where it stayed until an afternoon trip to a location deleted from the document.

Since the Bushes and the Stewarts were friends, it seemed peculiar that

Mrs. Bush would have gone jogging if Justice and Mrs. Stewart were hosting George Bush at the Chevy Chase club. According to his records, Bush's detail left the residence at 10:18 a.m., arriving at the Chevy Chase Country Club at 10:29 a.m. and departing at 11:56 a.m. The two Secret Service details then joined up at 1:35 p.m. for the afternoon trip to a still undisclosed location, presumably the home of a family friend.

On a Saturday evening in mid-June 1991, I tuned in to the network news. I had been called by Martin Kilian and alerted to a likely October Surprise story. The lead item on the news showed Ronald Reagan and George Bush playing a public round of golf in Palm Springs, California. One reporter shouted an October Surprise question—and Reagan responded curiously. The aging ex-president turned to the row of reporters and denied there was a deal to delay the hostages' freedom. But with golf ball in hand, Reagan added:

"I did some things the other way, to try and be of help getting those hostages. I felt sorry for them . . . and this whole thing that I was worried about that as a campaign thing is absolute fiction. I did some things to try the other way."

When reporters pressed him to clarify his answer, Reagan only muddied the waters more.

"Every effort on my part was directed towards bringing them home," Reagan said.

"Does that mean contacts with the Iranian government?" a reporter asked.

"Not by me, no," the former president said.

"By your campaign, perhaps?"

"Well, I can't get into details," Reagan responded good-naturedly. "Some of these things are still classified."

As he strolled toward the next tee, it was impossible to know exactly what ex-President Reagan was driving at. He refused to elaborate further. But actions by his campaign staff could not be classified secret because his subordinates, at the time, were not part of the official government.

But Reagan took one step toward seeking an answer to Casey's elusive whereabouts. The ex-president ordered his presidential library staff to examine the 1980 campaign records to see if there was any evidence that Casey held secret meetings on the hostages. Despite doubts about its central credibility, the October Surprise story was gaining a critical mass.

On June 20, 1991, a few days after Reagan's golf course comments, ABC's *Nightline* joined the controversy with a detailed half-hour report on Jamshid Hashemi's October Surprise claims. *Nightline*'s talented and gutsy producer, Tara Sonenshine, had coaxed Jamshid into a lengthy one-on-one interview with *Nightline* host Ted Koppel. Jamshid elaborated on the story he had previously told Sick, Ross, and me about two rounds of meetings at Madrid's Ritz Hotel, first during late July and then in August. But Jamshid still had no precise dates for the meetings and remained camera shy, refusing again to submit to a filmed interview.

Jamshid's most important add-on was his assertion that the first Karrubi-Casey meeting in Madrid stretched over two days in late July. The opening session, Jamshid said, was dominated by Iranian cleric Mehdi Karrubi's vitriolic denunciations against the United States and especially against the incumbent president, Jimmy Carter.

During Karrubi's first day's diatribe, Jamshid told Koppel, Casey was "silent, very cool, not reacting to the other man's anger. . . . When Casey did raise the subject of the hostages, Hashemi remembers, there was no suggestion that their release be delayed. Indeed, Casey simply asked what Iran's intentions were toward the hostages and what it would take to get them out as quickly as possible. Karrubi said nothing could be done without the explicit approval of the Ayatollah Khomeini."

Prior to that second day's session, Jamshid told Koppel, Karrubi seemed "a little befuddled" about the purpose of the first meeting and asked curiously, "what did Casey want?"

Jamshid claimed that Karrubi posed just that question at the start of the second round the next morning: "What was Casey authorized to say on the subject of the hostages and the release of Iran's frozen assets. . . . Karrubi acknowledged that it might be difficult to arrange for the release of those weapons, since the Republicans were, after all, not in power, but he wanted to know if weapons could somehow be transferred through a third country."

It was then Casey suggested a post-election hostage release: "Casey had some questions. Was Iran ready to deal with the Republicans and hand over the hostages? Was Karrubi empowered to confirm a deal on Khomeini's behalf? Could he give assurances that the hostages would be well-treated? And would they be released to President-elect Reagan after the election?

"If that happened, said Casey, the Republicans would be grateful, and would arrange for the release of Iran's frozen assets and the military equipment that had been held up. Karrubi said he would need time to get specific confirmation from Khomeini. Then, in an aside to the other Iranians in the room, a comment that was not translated into English, Karrubi said: 'I think we are now opening a new era and we are now dealing with someone who knows how to do business.' "

Karrubi then returned to Tehran, where he consulted with Khomeini and his senior advisers. Jamshid claimed that two to three weeks later, Karrubi called him and asked for another meeting. It, too, was held in Madrid at the Ritz, with Casey and the CIA officer representing the American side and Karrubi back for the Iranians. Karrubi expressed Khomeini's acceptance of Casey's proposal, according to Jamshid.

The ABC *Nightline* team had found circumstantial evidence to support Jamshid Hashemi's claims for at least his presence in Spain during the key time periods. Working jointly with the *Financial Times* of London, *Nightline* investigators had gained access to records at the Plaza Hotel in Madrid. They found names used by the Hashemi brothers for the two periods—one from July 25 to 29 and the second from August 8 to 13—roughly the periods when Jamshid claimed the Madrid meetings happened.

Yet the Casey family and Reagan foreign policy adviser Richard Allen vigorously protested that Casey had not left the country at all after the Republican convention in mid-July. His last trip abroad, they were sure, was his three-day swing through London and Paris before the July Fourth weekend. After that, Casey's supporters said, he was far too busy to leave on a foreign trip.

But *Nightline* cited an old article in the *New York Times* that said otherwise. The article, buried way inside the newspaper's Metro section, discussed a planned peace-making conference between the Reagan

campaign and anti-abortion groups critical of the vice presidential nominee. George Bush then was considered pro-choice on abortion. The article
quoted a Reagan spokesman as saying Casey would chair those negotiations "when he returns today from a trip abroad." The date of the article
was July 30, 1980.[1]

The article established that Casey had left the country in late July.
Contrary to the assurances of his family and friends, he had not been too
busy to travel. But there was no hint where he had gone or why.

Nightline asked Casey's secretary, Barbara Hayward, to review her
calendar. It mentioned no overseas trip. But a one-line note in her calendar
suggested that Casey was in Washington on Saturday, July 26. Proving that
reality is sometimes more bizarre than fiction, Casey had scheduled dinner
with George Bush at the Alibi Club in Washington on the night of July 30.
The club is famous as a reclusive hideaway for the capital's great and
powerful who are ducking inquisitive spouses or avoiding telephone calls.

But the combination of the sketchy note in the secretary's calendar
about July 26 and the *Times*'s report that Casey was returning from abroad
on Wednesday, July 30, set off a scramble among journalists to figure out
where he had been over those four days.

The first break in the mystery of Casey's whereabouts came when
historian Robert Dallek, a professor at UCLA, called Congress. Dallek
had watched *Nightline* and knew where Casey had been for part of that
time. Dallek was put in touch with the chief counsel for the House Foreign
Affairs Committee, R. Spencer Oliver. Dallek told Oliver that Casey
had attended a historical conference at the Imperial War Museum in
London. The conference began on Monday, July 28, and ended on Thursday, July 31.

But it was not clear when Casey was in attendance. He did pose for a
photograph with Dallek and some other historians at a Monday evening
reception after the first day of the conference. Casey gave his talk, in praise
of World War II deception tactics, during the morning of the second day,
Tuesday, July 29. He apparently left the conference for good that afternoon. But exactly when did he arrive in London and when did he depart?

---

[1] Maurice Carroll, "Right to Life Leaders Say Choice of Bush Bars Backing of Reagan,"
New York Times, July 30, 1980, p. B6.

After Dallek's call, Spencer Oliver contacted *Nightline* to inform the ABC team about the new information. *Nightline* checked the material out and then broadcast an update to its original report. The brief update, at the end of a regular program, noted that Casey had gone to London. But Koppel added that Casey still would have had time to travel first to Madrid and then make the 90-minute flight to London for the conference.

However, Jamshid said the meetings had covered parts of two days. So the possible time for the Madrid meetings was growing tight. If Casey's secretary was right about his presence in Washington on Saturday, July 26, then the first meeting presumably would have been held on Sunday, July 27, and the second session on the morning of Monday, July 28. Casey would have then needed to fly immediately to London to arrive at the conference late Monday afternoon.

At *Frontline*, executive producer David Fanning ordered renewed research on the October Surprise controversy, with an eye toward a possible update. Working out of *Frontline*'s Boston office, producer Jim Gilmore reached 23 of the several dozen historians who had attended the conference. Their memories, understandably, tended to be fuzzy. But piece by piece, Gilmore put together the sometimes conflicting accounts about Casey and the conference.

A couple of participants thought Casey was introduced at a reception on the Sunday night before the conference. But the host of that get-together said the event occurred on Monday night. The head of the American delegation, Arthur Funk, told Gilmore that he believed Casey arrived at the conference late in the day on Monday, July 28. So did three other members of the American delegation, two of whom were housed with Casey and Funk at the Royal Army Medical College in London. If they were right, Casey would have had time to conduct the meetings in Madrid and jet to London.

But the investigation took another turn when Jonathan Chadwick, the Imperial War Museum's director, dug into his files and pulled out the decade-old records of the conference. Chadwick, a finicky British bureaucrat, had kept detailed planning records for the meeting. He listed the 50 expected participants and which speeches they planned to attend.

Chadwick's hand-drawn charts showed the names of the participants in a left-hand column and the different sessions listed across the top. He then placed x's in the boxes when a participant was not expected to attend and check marks when a person was scheduled to be there. For Casey, on the crucial first day, there were pencil-mark x's covered later with ink-mark checks. For the afternoon session, there was a line through the box and the notation, "came at 4 p.m."

When first contacted by *Frontline*'s Gilmore, Chadwick was at a loss to explain the Casey entries. Based on other documents, he recalled he had been informed by Professor Funk that Casey was not planning to attend the first day's session, which explained the x's in pencil.

But as for the inked checks, Chadwick said they meant either that Casey arrived unexpectedly on Monday morning or that someone told Chadwick that Casey had changed his mind and was planning to attend. But in that scenario, Casey might not have actually arrived until the afternoon. That might explain the "came at 4 p.m." notation.

As for Casey's day-to-day whereabouts in 1980, even investigators ordered by President Reagan to examine campaign records were having trouble finding a trace of the mysterious campaign director. Reagan library director Ralph Bledsoe oversaw a review of the million-and-a-half pages of 1980 campaign archives, which had been moved to the new Reagan presidential library in southern California.

After an 18-day search, Bledsoe reported finding no evidence that Casey or any other member of the campaign had met with Iranians. But what Bledsoe, a mild-mannered bureaucrat, didn't highlight was that the search could pin Casey down for only a couple of days for the entire campaign.

"Did you find any records pertaining to Mr. Casey's whereabouts, his travel, airplane tickets, hotel receipts?" I asked Bledsoe in an interview about his investigation. "You know, anything of that sort?"

"No, there were a few references to him in different kinds of activities that he was engaged in, but none related to the specific search request that President Reagan asked us to make," Bledsoe answered.

"Obviously, Mr. Casey's whereabouts would be important in either establishing or debunking these allegations," I continued. "So if he, for instance, is in the United States on certain days when some people place him elsewhere, it would be very relevant."

"It's hard to tell exactly where he is on certain days," Bledsoe said, looking uncomfortable before Robert Ross's camera. "We did not find, as I recall, any kind of materials that were dated during the period of time we were searching for, that would place him in one particular place. That's why I'm saying the search really didn't show much."

"But just a summary," I added, "there were no expense records for Mr. Casey?"

"We found none."

"There were no travel records for Mr. Casey?"

"We found no travel records, yes."

"There was no calendar for Mr. Casey?"

"We found no calendar for him."

"And except for a handful of dates, you cannot establish his whereabouts anywhere over that several months period from the convention to the general election?"

"That's correct."

17

"SIMPLY THE BEST"

I had taken the two-hour flight from Washington to Miami many times before. It was almost a regular commute when I was working on stories about the Nicaraguan contras and Oliver North's secret network. But this time I was checking out another witness who had popped onto the October Surprise radar screen. The witness was Richard Babayan, an Iranian who had crossed paths with Israeli Ari Ben-Menashe, both as youngsters in Tehran and as intelligence operatives in the 1980s.

As flight attendants offered drinks and snacks to the passengers with me in coach class, I flipped through the notes and papers I had collected on Richard Babayan. With relish, Ben-Menashe had once described to me his greeting from Babayan when the two got reacquainted at Babayan's business office outside Washington in 1984.

"I get this majestic hug as I enter," Ben-Menashe said, smiling broadly and imitating Babayan by holding his arms outstretched. "Girls start to run all over. Babayan says, 'Welcome, my friend. We have big things to do together. Fate has big things in store for us.' I said to myself, 'Uh oh.'"

Babayan's idea was to interest Ben-Menashe and his Israeli associates in arming Iraq's Saddam Hussein as a means of ridding Iran of Ayatollah Khomeini and his Islamic fundamentalists. The strategy, of course, went nowhere, since the Israelis had, years earlier, thrown in their lot with Iran versus Iraq. But Ben-Menashe said he and Babayan had stayed in touch after that, partly because the Israelis were interested in learning about Saddam's arms network.

While searching through Ben-Menashe's personal papers, I also had found repeated references to Richard Babayan. According to business cards, Babayan was associated with some companies based in Rosslyn, a business section of Arlington, Virginia, directly across the Potomac River from Georgetown. One of Babayan's firms was Commonwealth Telephone of Virginia; another business card listed a company called International Defense Systems. I thought Babayan might shed more light on the mysterious Ben-Menashe.

Through corporate records in Richmond, Virginia, I could find the names of some officials of the Babayan companies, but the firms had been shut down. My calls led to a dead end. However, several weeks later, I received a tip that I might find Richard Babayan after all. He had been arrested somewhere in Florida for a securities fraud scheme relating to telephones. After calls to Florida, I discovered that a Richard Babayan was locked up in the county jail in West Palm Beach, Florida, on charges that his company, Commonwealth Telephone of Virginia, had sold far more pay phones than the company could deliver. All these characters seem to end up in jail sometime, I thought to myself. I sent off a telegram to West Palm Beach County jail, and Richard Babayan called back collect.

As youngsters, Babayan and Ben-Menashe had both attended the American Community School in Tehran. Babayan said he remembered Ben-Menashe, though Ben-Menashe said he had only a vague childhood recollection of Babayan, who was several years younger. Both had been privileged young men in Tehran, but the Babayans were higher on the social ladder. Babayan's father owned a major shipping line in Iran and had direct access to the shah's inner circle. He had been part of Iran's élite business class.

But the Iranian revolution in 1979 drastically altered the Babayans' personal fortunes. Babayan's parents fled into exile in France. They left behind in Iran their luxurious home and the shipping firm's assets. As working professionals in France, they adopted a much more modest lifestyle, living in a small apartment in a Paris suburb. Richard Babayan, who had worked for his father's shipping company in Washington, saw his prospects turn downward, too. Like many young men who had thrived under the shah's rule, he gravitated to the exile political groups and their dreams of getting back what they had lost.

After landing in Miami, I rented a subcompact and drove north to West Palm Beach, the exclusive and stuffy resort for America's old-monied wealth. Another prison interview, I grumbled to myself as I arrived at the courthouse. But at least Babayan had been transferred to a comfortable conference room off a judge's chambers. Two prison guards had been assigned to sit through the entire interview. But Babayan seemed to speak freely.

Babayan was chubby with a stubbly beard. He was dressed in a beige prison jumpsuit and spoke in a low, soft voice. His English was impeccable, and his style was that of a well-educated man. He looked to be in his mid-30s.

"My family owned a shipping company in Iran by the name of Cargo and Shipping, S.A.," Babayan began. "My father was the chief maritime adviser to the Iranian Ministry of War. Cargo and Shipping had the exclusive contract from 1973 to the time of the Islamic revolution to transport all of the Iranian military purchases from the United States and Great Britain to Iran."

Babayan claimed he was recruited into Iran's military intelligence unit, G-2, while still a teenager. His father's firm, he said, had worked closely with the CIA and also had served as the agent for Israeli companies doing business in Iran. The firm's strategic role as the shah's chief military shipper gave the Babayans access to a wealth of information about covert as well as overt deliveries.

Babayan's connections brought him into touch with American intelligence. His principal CIA contact, he said, was Arthur Callahan, a respected station chief in Tehran in the 1970s. Babayan also told me that he knew former CIA director Richard Helms personally from Helms's days as ambassador to Iran. Babayan claimed that one of his lower-life connections to U.S. intelligence was renegade CIA officer Edwin Wilson, who was convicted of supplying explosives to Libya's Muammar Qaddafi.

Babayan said he had turned to his CIA contacts when the Islamic revolution forced the shah from the Peacock Throne in 1979. Babayan was in Paris staying with his parents and wanted to know what could be done to block the Islamic radicals. "I contacted Callahan, and he said that there wasn't much that could happen at that time," Babayan told me. "The dust had to settle. And he put me in touch with one of their operatives in Europe who was going by the name of M.K. Moss." The idea was to look toward a longer-term strategy.

Babayan said Callahan described Moss as one of the CIA's top operatives in Switzerland. Moss, a Saudi, owned a company in Geneva called Diwan. "Moss was in the finance business," Babayan said. "He would fund certain covert activities for the agency. He was very well connected." Babayan said Moss also helped the CIA through his management of money for some of the world's richest despots, from the Saudi royal family to the Marcoses of the Philippines.

"He was very closely involved in the Philippines," Babayan said. "I met President Marcos and Imelda once when they were in Switzerland; he was handling a lot of the personal finances of the Philippines. He was one of the agency's primary contacts in the Philippines. That was his claim to fame."

At Callahan's instructions, Babayan said, he placed a call to Moss and was told to go to Geneva. The time frame, Babayan recalled, was mid-to-late 1979, sometime prior to the seizure of the U.S. embassy in Tehran on November 4. But there was already interest in organizing exile groups into political and possibly military cadres to challenge the Islamic fundamentalists coming to power in Tehran.

Arriving at Moss's Geneva office in the early afternoon, Babayan said, he was surprised to see Robert Gates of the CIA finishing a meeting with Moss. But Babayan said he did not speak with Gates then and wasn't sure what Moss and Gates had been discussing.[1] On Moss's orders, Babayan said, he went to work in Paris recruiting former Iranian military officers for anti-Khomeini exile groups.

Babayan claimed that in August 1980, while working with the exiles, he had been contacted in Paris by an Iranian friend who worked for Kho-

---

[1] During Senate confirmation hearings in 1991 to become CIA director, Gates denied knowing Moss or Babayan, and the Senate Intelligence Committee concluded that "no credible evidence has been presented . . . to support these allegations."

meini's intelligence service. The friend said Republican and Iranian emissaries had met in Madrid that summer, Babayan told me. At that session in Spain, Casey had made promises of military help to the Iranians once the Republicans took power, Babayan said. But he refused to identify his Iranian contact, citing safety concerns.[2]

"The approach that was made to the Islamic government was when Reagan comes in, you will be getting a trickle of spare parts. That's the primary reason why the hostages were released at the time of the Reagan administration officially coming into power. This offer came through Mr. Casey, directly. The Islamic government had no other choice and they went for it."

Babayan insisted that the hostage initiative was spearheaded by "an inner core in the CIA of people who are career intelligence officers as opposed to political appointees. They would do a lot of things on their own, or without permission of the hierarchy. Things that they were doing would be routine and necessary and required to be done."

"But having contacts with the Iranians, using the Reagan campaign, would not be routine," I protested.

"No, it wouldn't be routine," Babayan admitted. "But I know that there was a lot of inside talk that obviously Casey would get the job of director of Central Intelligence, and based on that a lot of people were in contact with him, because he was respected at the agency."

The two prison guards who had been patiently sitting through the two-hour interview told me my time was up. I shook Babayan's hand and told him that I hoped we could talk again. Babayan returned to his cellblock. I headed back to Miami to catch a flight to Washington. Babayan was one more witness added to our growing list of questionable sources claiming to know about Republican contacts with Iran in 1980.

When I returned home, I called both Callahan and Helms. Both acknowledged knowing Babayan but insisted that the contacts were only social. Two U.S. government sources told me that Moss, also known as Mustafa el-Kastaui, had moved money for the CIA, but the CIA officially denied any connection to Moss.

---

[2] Babayan would later identify his Iranian contact as an intelligence official named Mohsen Baranriz.

On the other hand, Babayan's descriptions of the Western arms flow to Iraq, using arms manufacturers in Chile and South Africa, proved to be on target. And his family members confirmed that Babayan was recruited by Iranian intelligence while still in high school. But Babayan, like Ben-Menashe, was badly tainted in the eyes of official Washington. He was a foreigner with a secretive past. Plus, he was facing fraud charges and was speaking from jail.

In late June 1991, Robert Ross and I were finishing a four-day visit to Israel. I'd had better luck this time than during my first trip to Israel seven months earlier. Then, in the midst of the Persian Gulf crisis, I'd failed to coax a single Israeli into an on-camera interview. But with the war over, the mood in Israel was more relaxed. The American tourists again filled the rooms of the Tel Aviv Hilton.

Working through the government press office, we found most of our interview requests accepted. Our *Frontline* topic this time was less sensitive. It was whether the United States should allow American defense contractors to rearm the Middle East, a prospect that Israel was eager to discourage. Ross and I also were asking questions for a special broadcast that *Frontline* was preparing on Robert Gates's controversial nomination to head the CIA. But whenever the opportunity arose, we would slip in a question about Ben-Menashe and the events of 1980.

The official government line was still that Ben-Menashe was just a lowly translator working on the Hebrew/English translating desk. His job, the government now acknowledged, did require his handling some classified material, including messages transmitted from Jerusalem to Washington. But he never traveled on government business. His only overseas trips were for vacation, for personal medical attention or for family emergencies, government spokesmen told us.

The spokesmen said they had no idea how Ben-Menashe could have traveled for weeks on end throughout Europe and Latin America, going to many countries far beyond his announced itinerary. Yet Ben-Menashe had made no secret about most of these trips. They showed up on his passport, which he presented to Israeli immigration authorities whenever he flew into or out of Ben-Gurion airport. Indeed, two of Ben-Menashe's personal passports, introduced into evidence at his trial, show 47 international trips between April 1985 and September 1987, to the United Kingdom, Guatemala, El Salvador, France, Australia, Germany, the United States, and Canada. These, Ben-Menashe said, were only the trips he did not take on his diplomatic passport. But the Israeli government denied that Ben-Menashe ever possessed a diplomatic passport.

The Israeli government's latest explanation of Ben-Menashe's globe-straddling activities was that maybe he was moonlighting in the arms trafficking business while holding down his day job as a government translator. But that story amounted to an admission that Jerusalem's vaunted security apparatus had suffered a major breach. It would mean that an employee with access to sensitive information had wandered the world, undetected, making unauthorized contacts with foreign nationals, arranging arms shipments, and disclosing government secrets.

On our last morning in Israel, the Israeli Defense Forces' spokesmen took one more crack at convincing us that we should believe the government story about Ben-Menashe. An IDF spokeswoman asked us to stop by IDF headquarters in Tel Aviv for a high-level briefing.

Returning from an interview in Jerusalem only a few hours before our plane's scheduled departure, Ross and I hurried to the IDF's no-frills building in downtown Tel Aviv. There we were greeted by the spokeswoman, who was an attractive blonde with a short punk hairstyle. The combination of her "wet look" hair and her crisp khaki uniform was stunning. She offered us some bad-tasting instant coffee.

As we sipped the coffee, the spokeswoman handed me a faxed copy of an article that *Time* magazine had just published about Ben-Menashe. The two-page spread in *Time* was Ben-Menashe's introduction into big-time media. The photo showed him standing, arms crossed, in front of his lawyer, Tom Dunn. But the story was not what a public relationist would have planned. Summing up the key question about the Israeli, *Time* entitled the article "Con Man or Key to a Mystery?" Although the article offered evidence on both sides, the newsmagazine laid its money on the former, not the latter.

The *Time* article acknowledged that Ben-Menashe did have access to some sensitive information. The Israeli intelligence man had been "among the first to leak the details of secret U.S. arms sales to Iran back in 1986,"

Time reported. The magazine knew that because one of the recipients had been *Time* correspondent Raji Samghabadi.

Though Ben-Menashe had been right in 1986, it won him no good will five years later. *Time* attacked Ben-Menashe for his allegations linking Robert Gates, then President Bush's nominee to head the CIA, to the October Surprise controversy and to the misguided policy to arm Saddam Hussein's Iraq. Ben-Menashe's claimed meetings with Gates, *Time* said, had not shown up in Gates's travel records and work logs. The magazine even suggested that Ben-Menashe threw Gates into the story only after Bush nominated Gates to be CIA director.

"Ben-Menashe now belatedly portrays Gates as a central figure in the secret arms deals," *Time* said. But at least on that point the magazine was wrong. Months before Gates's CIA nomination, Ben-Menashe had been alleging a Gates role in the October Surprise and in arming Iraq. We had Ben-Menashe on videotape pointing the finger at Gates as early as August 1990, when Gates was a little-known deputy national security adviser at the White House.

But, right or wrong, *Time* magazine set what quickly became Washington's conventional wisdom about Ben-Menashe. "Ben-Menashe, on balance, appears to be a practiced poseur," the magazine concluded. Considering our own frustrations with the annoying Israeli, it was hard to disagree entirely with *Time*'s conclusion.

As I skimmed the *Time* article, a senior IDF intelligence officer strode in to the cramped room. He was tall and moved with crisp military bearing. His khaki uniform was neatly pressed, and he held his military beret under one arm. He spoke in a warm, friendly style, more like a skilled diplomat than a military officer.

The IDF officer told Ross and me that he knew Ben-Menashe personally and liked him. The officer immediately acknowledged that Ben-Menashe's letters of reference were real, not forgeries, as some Israeli government officials were still claiming. But he insisted the lavish praise in the letters about Ben-Menashe's important assignments was just puffery. The wording, he said, had been drafted by Ben-Menashe himself.

But why, I asked, would a low-level translator propose language about his executive skills and creativity when his chances for future employment in his field would depend more on precision and dependability? Why was there not a single reference in the letters to Ben-Menashe's language skills? Why would IDF officers sign misleading letters?

Ben-Menashe was well-liked, the officer responded, and his friends wanted to help him out, even if the comments weren't accurate. Maybe, the officer added, Ben-Menashe wanted to change fields and thus needed to stress his executive abilities even if they were irrelevant to the government job he had performed for a decade.

"But one thing I don't understand is how Ben-Menashe could have traveled to Poland apparently to buy arms while working in Israeli intelligence," I said. "Poland was a communist country."

The IDF officer looked at me coolly and answered: "We can confirm Poland." I was startled. I had been expecting a flat denial or at least a claim of ignorance.

"You can confirm Poland?" I stammered. "But why would a low-level translator who never traveled on government business be working in Poland?" At that question, the officer only shrugged.

"Wouldn't that be a serious breach of Israeli security?" I asked.

The officer thought for a moment and then agreed. "Yes," he said opaquely, "I suppose it would be." But he volunteered no explanation. The intelligence officer had done little to clear up the Ben-Menashe mystery.

After leaving Israel for Europe, Robert Ross and I took a side trip to Geneva to track down the Saudi financier, M.K. Moss. I wasn't sure what we would find, but the trip felt necessary to me. Maybe it would lead nowhere, but my hunch was that Moss was a link between CIA and Saudi finances.

When we landed in Switzerland in early July, Geneva was at its postcard best. The Rhone River, which divides the city north and south, glistened in the early summer sun. Geneva's *jet d'eau* spouted a stream of water high into the air. The streets bustled and the sidewalk cafes were busy.

For decades, Geneva had thrived as an international crossroads for money and secrets. As clean and pretty as it was on the surface, Geneva was dirty and craven at a deeper level. The city lived by the convenient ethics of the bankers and financiers who were the community's economic bedrock.

The city, too, was a natural home for spies. Its elegant hotels, secretive banks, and historic neutrality made it a perfect waystation for espionage. Geneva was convenient to central as well as western Europe and was a favorite second home for Middle Eastern millionaires. The CIA maintained a large station in Geneva for managing the spy agency's worldwide finances.

Even the amateurs around Oliver North and the Iran-contra scandal turned to a Geneva bank, Credit Suisse, to hide their millions of Iranian arms profits. Quaint Lisbon was a favorite city for CIA arms transfers to the Middle East; sunny Miami was a hotbed for covert plots in Latin America; but elegant Geneva was still the city of choice for the trafficking in illicit dollars.

Ross and I had been told by a Moss associate that he would not see us. So we chose the direct approach. With our video equipment in hand, we trooped over to Moss's office on the Cours de Rive, a street a couple of blocks south of the waterfront. In a modest-looking building, we found the name Diwan printed on a mailbox inside the front door. A directory said the firm was located on the top floor of the seven-story building. So we entered a cramped elevator and headed up. When we reached the top floor, Ross and I found ourselves on a small landing with a door at each of the four corners. With Ross filming, I knocked on the door for Diwan. No answer.

Undeterred, we left messages for M.K. Moss in his office door and mailbox. Before heading back to our hotel, Ross filmed the front of the building, Diwan's mailbox, and anything else he could think of. Our hope was that by making our presence obvious, we might convince Moss to respond. After coming up empty at the office building, we went to an apartment that had been listed in a Swiss business directory as his residence. Again, no answer. But we made a point to talk with his neighbors and left another message in his door. We asked him to contact us at the Hotel du Rhone, a middle-priced businessman's hotel, where we were staying.

To my surprise, the ploy worked. That night, a fax message was slipped under my door at the hotel from M.K. Moss. But he was not a happy man.

"Thank you for having so generously been at one of our Geneva offices, filming the signs on the door as well as on the mail box. Not to mention the kind note you left at my downtown residence," Moss wrote sarcastically. "You did not have to go through all these troubles to get in touch with me, all that you had to do is just simply call and explain your mission. Most likely, I would have been delighted to host you and your colleague for a luncheon or a cocktail at your convenience."

Moss said he was not in Geneva, but suggested that I contact him two days later on July Fourth. By then, however, I was scheduled to be back in the United States. Moss finished his note with a flash of arrogance:

"You should not be surprised about how much I know about you, your visit to Geneva, your camera and your activities around town. After all— when you took on that job—you should have been told that you were simply dealing with the best." Ross and I promptly dubbed Mr. Moss, "STB," for "simply the best."

Though he may not have meant it, Moss did say that he was looking forward to hearing from me. So I wrote him a return fax, apologizing for any offense we had caused and requesting, in a more formal fashion, a meeting. I told him that although I was flying to the United States on July Fourth, I was planning to return to Europe a few days later with my wife for a previously scheduled trip to Germany. I offered to divert my travel plans to Geneva for the proffered opportunity for a talk and lunch.

Before I departed for the United States, another fax was slipped under my door. "May I suggest that you enjoy your July Fourth holiday," Moss wrote. "I have not suggested any meeting but rather disapproved of your approach. Let us all sleep on it for a while. I am sure the day will come that I will welcome your telephone call and maybe a meeting. In the meantime, it is my advice that you do not seek the secrets of Washington in the mountains of Switzerland." Just as we apparently had piqued M.K. Moss's interest enough for him to communicate with us, he had aroused our curiosity. I decided to continue pressing for a meeting.

A committed New Yorker, Ross disliked Geneva as the Big Apple's urban opposite. He couldn't stand the cleanliness, the efficiency, the storybook prettiness. But he agreed to stay a few extra days to finish some research on Moss while I tried to persuade Moss to reconsider his rejection of the interview. I left for Boston to spend a day working at *Frontline* on a script for a program we were preparing on the nomination of Robert Gates to direct the CIA. While in Boston, I finally reached Moss by telephone, and, after a surprisingly friendly chat, I convinced him to meet with Ross and me two days later. Moss agreed to a conversation but made clear he would not go on-camera.

Now, all I had to do was break the news to my wife that after an all-night flight from Washington to Frankfurt, we would have to board a train for a day-long trip to Geneva. By this point, after nearly a year tracking far-flung leads of the October Surprise story, I thought a train trip through the German mountains and Swiss Alps would fit right in. But for my wife Diane, it would be just a grueling experience with jet lag and discomfort.

So I felt enormously guilty as I dragged Diane from the Frankfurt airport into the German train system for the trip south. I made a mistake and ended up with second-class tickets. So we were sitting in an old non-airconditioned railroad car on a hot and humid day. But at least the window would open and we had the compartment to ourselves.

Diane was stretched out across the seat on the other side of the compartment, sleeping fitfully. As she rested, the train to Switzerland rolled through well-kept German towns and past tidy houses with burnt-orange or brown tile roofs. In the distance, the green hills looked gray in the summer haze. After a stop in the little town of Olten, we boarded another train that took us the rest of the way to Geneva.

At noon the next day, Ross and I left the Hotel du Rhone, crossed into Geneva's business district, and made our way back to the Cours de Rive. This time, when we reached the seventh floor and knocked on the door to the Diwan office, we were greeted by one of Moss's assistants, a tall blond man with an Italian last name. He led us into a small conference room which had two walls covered with photographs. They showed a short Middle Eastern man smiling with dozens of government officials and celebrities. Though many of the Third World potentates were unknown to me, some of the personalities couldn't be missed: former Texas Governor John Connally, ex-astronaut Frank Borman, former President Gerald Ford, Philippine first lady Imelda Marcos, and singer Tony Bennett.

Within a few minutes, the Middle Eastern man featured in the photographs entered the room. "Mr. Parry," he said shaking my hand. "I am Mr.

Moss." Moss looked to be about 50 years old. He had gray flecks in his mustache, and his hair was unruly. His suit was not as elegantly cut as one might expect of a Swiss-based financier. Perhaps his business had fallen off from the salad days of a decade earlier. In our background check of Moss we had learned that in 1978 he had purchased the 170.9-carat "Star of Peace" diamond for the Saudi royal family, a very wealthy clan to which Moss claimed to belong.

When Moss sat down, he was polite but blunt. "We have the capability of filming and recording everything that goes on in this room," Moss told us. "We are not. Is the same true of you?" We answered that we had left our camera at the hotel and were not surreptitiously tape-recording anything. I privately doubted that the same was true of him.

Moss told us he would be of very little help to us. But he wanted to know who had directed us to him. I told him that several people had mentioned his name, but that the first person was Richard Babayan. We were there, I said, because a *Frontline* program on Robert Gates's nomination might mention Moss's alleged role in connecting Babayan and Gates. Moss acknowledged knowing both men. But he wanted to know whose interests we were serving by damaging Gates. Throughout the conversation, Moss would refer to Gates simply as "Robert."

Moss informed us that he had obtained our October Surprise documentary that had aired in April. He said he had watched it and considered it "excellent." But he wanted to know who had funded it and why. We tried to explain the concept of public broadcasting, but I felt as if we were talking across a cultural or political chasm. Moss seemed to view all information as serving some political goal; news was put out only for a specific propaganda purpose. The idea of objective journalism seemed foreign to him.

As for our chances of solving the October Surprise story or nailing down the truth about Robert Gates's covert activities, Moss said, with a sly smile, "not in a hundred years will you or any organization come up with the hard evidence."

"The hard evidence for what?" I asked.

"Of anything," he answered. "Of course, these things are true, but it's not true if it can't be proven."

He reiterated that he would be no help. "You could put a gun to my head and I will not tell you," he said. "Would you deal with us if we talked about what we did?"

Moss did tell us that he often had served as an intelligence operative transferring money. "I have been asked by various intelligence services, including the United States, to help and I have helped," he said. "If we have done something for the Americans, it was in the interest of America."

Moss also admitted knowing former deputy CIA director Vernon Walters and William Herrmann, the American arms dealer who claimed to have learned about the October Surprise deal from Iranian arms procurer Hamid Naqashan on January 21, 1981. Herrmann had told me that he once met with Moss and Walters at CIA headquarters in Langley. Moss confirmed that he had talked with both men. However, the CIA denied any relationship with Moss.

During the two and a half hours with Moss, first in his office, then at a nearby restaurant for lunch, and then back at his office, he had sparred with us. Ross and I had gained a sense of the man, but we had landed no solid punches. He enjoyed bobbing and weaving, safely out of our reach. He was proving to us that he was indeed "simply the best." He also sought to dissuade us from mentioning him in the *Frontline* broadcast about Gates. At one point, he put his warning bluntly:

"As they say about me in Washington, I break the arms of those who point fingers at me." But he issued the warning with the same pleasant smile that had stayed on his face for most of the interview. Ross and I told him that he would most likely be mentioned in the Gates broadcast. Neither side having given or gained much ground, Ross and I left Moss's office and Geneva.

But our travels were not over. Soon after Ross and I returned home, we learned the Iranian government had finally approved our request for visas, clearing the way for a trip to Iran that we had first requested nearly a year earlier. Ross began brushing up on his Persian.

18

ISLAMIC
REVOLUTIONARY CHIC

I landed in Tehran in the dark of night, on September 18, 1991. The Austrian Airline flight arrived at 2:30 a.m. Tehran time. Women on the plane, who had been stylishly dressed and coiffed just minutes earlier, hastily pulled on chadors, the shapeless garments worn by women in Islamic countries to cover their heads and bodies. Many women on our plane clearly did not don the chadors by choice. They favored fashionable dresses while outside Iran and put on their chadors only as the plane landed. If the women didn't cover up, they could be punished under Iran's strict Islamic codes.

As we disembarked and walked toward the immigration desks, the more defiant women were adjusting colorful head scarves so some of their hair would show. Since the dress code is applied even to non-Islamic women, the Western airlines spare their female employees the degradation of compulsory cover-up by turning their planes around and immediately flying out of Iran. It felt like Austrian Airlines was abandoning the passengers to the world of Islamic fundamentalism.

American passports were still a rarity at Mehrabad airport. But after a 30-minute wait in line, I was waved through immigration with only a cursory examination of my papers. I collected my baggage and exited the airport without a hitch. Robert Ross, who had flown in three days earlier, met me after I cleared customs. In the early morning dark, we caught a cab and headed into the city, through Tehran's deserted streets.

As we settled uncomfortably into the cab's cramped back seat, Ross looked slightly dejected. "I have some bad news," he said. "I've talked with Omshei. He now says he knows nothing about L'Enfant Plaza. He has no memory of anything like that."

Abolhassam Omshei was the Iranian professor-turned-arms-dealer whom Ari Ben-Menashe had placed at the strange hostage talks with three Republicans at the L'Enfant Plaza Hotel in Washington. When Ross had called Omshei several months before, his original response had been that he "recalled something like that." If Omshei had stuck by that account, he could have been an important corroborating witness.

But now Ross and I were left with just another question: Had Omshei's initial reaction been correct and he simply had thought better of it? Or was he now telling the truth and his immediate answer had resulted from confusion over Ross's question? Whatever the case, Omshei's retraction was another blow to Ari Ben-Menashe's wobbly credibility.

As our cab passed from Tehran's outskirts into the poorly lit downtown, Ross said he had made arrangements for the two of us to talk directly with Omshei later that day. Ross also suggested that we stop by the Ministry of Islamic Guidance and renew our requests for interviews with government officials. The interview at the top of our list was for cleric Mehdi Karrubi, William Casey's alleged contact in Madrid and now the speaker of parliament.

The cab dropped us off at the old Intercontinental Hotel, where Ross had booked us rooms. The high-rise hotel was close to the city center and offered some measure of comfort. The air conditioning worked, at least sporadically. Before the revolution, the Intercontinental Hotel was owned by the U.S. airline, Pan American. But it soon was confiscated by the Khomeini government, and its name was changed to Laleh International, after the Persian word for tulip.

Everything else about the hotel looked old. Nothing had been refurbished since the revolution. The lobby was cavernous, dingy and dark. The rugs were badly worn, and the wallpaper was soiled and peeling. One post-revolution addition to the decor could be made out against the rear wall of the tea lounge. Next to a large photograph showing the stern visage of Ayatollah Khomeini were brown tiles that had been glued to the wall and read: "Down with USA."

On another wall was a map of the world with flags and digital clocks showing the times in major cities. To drive home the point about America's lingering unpopularity, red "x's" had been taped across the two American flags next to the times for the East and West coasts. In big ways and small, Iran still seemed angry after all these years.

I got to my room on one of the top floors at 4:00 o'clock in the morning. The room was spartan, except for a 26-inch "super color" TV encased in an ornate wood frame. It reminded me of the days in my youth when televisions were sold as distinctive pieces of furniture and given a prominent spot in the average American living room. For prayers by the Islamic faithful, a little card near the upper right corner of the window pointed out the direction of Mecca. Sunlight began pouring through that window a few restless hours later.

When I woke, I looked out onto the haze-covered downtown of Tehran. There seemed to be impressive mountains in the distance. But the smog and dust that choked the city left them as vague, brownish shapes. The view from my window of barren hills obscured by smog was reminiscent of Los Angeles during a summer drought.

But in a depressing contrast to that California metropolis, only half the population could enjoy the sun, work on their tans, or relax in swimsuits. Below my window, there was a bright blue hotel pool, but only men and boys were sunning themselves or swimming. Under strict Islamic law, women are forbidden to swim in public or in mixed company. Whenever out of the house, they are required to stay covered from head to toe.

Islamic prohibitions aside, Tehran looked like many other bustling Third World cities. Its undistinguished architecture was dominated by concrete, box-shaped buildings that captured the worst of the geometrical style popular in the United States in the 1960s. The eight-year war with Iraq and declining oil prices also had eroded Iran's standard of living. Only slowly was the country recovering from the devastating war.

Despite the hard life in Tehran, a modern infrastructure remained. The phone system functioned decently, the water ran, and, except for periodic outages, the electricity worked. A free market offered a variety of clothing, food, electronics gear, refrigerators, and other consumer goods. Food supplies were plentiful, with vendors displaying their colorful fruit and vegetables in open-air markets.

Always, however, memories of the revolution and the long war with Iraq were near. Parts of Tehran had been damaged by Scud missile attacks, and the city's population had swelled with war refugees. But on a more personal level, many shopkeepers would display in their stores the framed photographs of their dead sons.

My first afternoon in Iran, Ross and I stopped by the Ministry of Islamic Guidance. It was housed in one of the many nondescript buildings that face onto Vali-ye-Asr Street, the thoroughfare that runs north and south through Tehran. From the ministry's name, I expected government officials in turbans and robes. Instead, the ministry was staffed with young men wearing white shirts and showing little religious fervor.

The chief spokesmen had the unenviable task of trying to make modern Iran look reasonable to Western journalists. But they also knew that the reporters were almost certain to file critical stories about Iran: its chadored women, its human rights violations, and its theocracy. Nagged on one side by journalists who demanded entree to senior levels of the government and berated on the other by officials who found those encounters predictably unpleasant, these men couldn't win. Neither side would be happy, and both would blame the middlemen at the Ministry of Islamic Guidance. The ministry's bureaucrats also complained privately that they weren't paid enough.

Without much enthusiasm, the ministry officials agreed to submit our list of interview requests. Some of the requests, such as former United Nations ambassador Sa'id Rajaie-Khorasani, were possible, the officials told us. But they expressed surprise at other names. Our list included little-known leaders of the Revolutionary Guards and senior officials at the Ministry of Defense. But our most unlikely interview request was the one for Mehdi Karrubi.

The senior ministry official said our chances of convincing the speaker of parliament to accept an interview with American journalists were almost nil within our week-long stay in Iran. "Write out your questions for Karrubi in advance," the official advised us. The anti-Western cleric normally avoided American journalists, but maybe our questions would persuade him to make an exception. Our list included general inquiries about U.S.-Iran relations as well as one about Jamshid Hashemi's allegation placing Karrubi at two summer 1980 meetings with William Casey in Madrid. The ministry official was bemused by the question, but agreed to translate the letter into Persian and pass it on.

Our next stop was the interview with Omshei. His offices were in a business district, not far from the old U.S. embassy in downtown Tehran. The cabdriver located the address, and we found the name of Omshei's import-export company, Guilsar, on the directory. After taking a small elevator up to the offices, we were greeted at the door by a woman receptionist in a black chador. She led us into an airy, sparsely furnished office. There a small man with white hair, a white mustache and a deeply lined face introduced himself as Professor Omshei. Speaking elegant French and a little English, he offered us tea and a bowl of dried lemons as a snack.

At the time of the Islamic revolution in 1979, Omshei had been head of the Faculty of Letters at the University of Tehran, where he taught the French language and literature. Omshei also maintained an apartment in Paris and spent a good deal of time in Europe. When Iranian president Bani-Sadr shut the universities in 1980, Omshei resigned his post and established Guilsar. In that export-import business he was aided by former students, including a young friend who was highly placed in the Revolutionary Guards. Omshei's new career and his European contacts quickly put him into the lucrative arms trade.

An Omshei associate, a Mr. Reza'i, joined the meeting. Reza'i—about 30, stocky, with a stubbly beard and an arm crippled in the Iran-Iraq war—was Omshei's young friend, the weapons procurer for the Revolutionary Guards. In the 1980s, he said, he had been in business with Omshei scouring the European arms bazaars for military equipment. Since the war's end in 1989, the two men had shifted their commercial interests to less explosive—and less profitable—commodities. During the meeting, Omshei took a few telephone calls to discuss a deal to purchase chemicals for the Iranian petroleum industry.

When we asked Omshei about his alleged participation in the L'Enfant Plaza meeting, he repeated the denial that he had given to Ross earlier.

Omshei insisted that he had participated in no meetings in the United States in 1980. He had not been in the United States during that period, he said. But he did visit Washington a few years later because his son, a computer specialist, had settled there. Omshei claimed his earlier ambiguous answer had resulted from a misunderstanding over the question.

Ross asked him if he had ever met Houshang Lavi. Omshei thought for a moment and responded that the name was vaguely familiar, but he could not remember exactly where the two might have met. But when we mentioned the name "Ari Ben-Menashe," Omshei brightened. "Yes, Ben-Menashe," Omshei said with a smile suggesting that he did indeed know the sometimes charming, sometimes infuriating Israeli. "I do know Ben-Menashe."

Omshei said Ben-Menashe had been well known in Tehran in the early 1980s. The ex-literature professor said a friend had put him in touch with the Israeli about purchasing weapons some years ago. Their first conversation was over the phone, Omshei recalled. Ben-Menashe had spoken to Omshei in English until Omshei realized that Ben-Menashe spoke Persian. Omshei had found Ben-Menashe's preference for English—which forced Omshei to struggle with a language he spoke poorly—impolite since both he and Ben-Menashe had grown up speaking Persian.

Omshei recalled that he had negotiated arms deals with Ben-Menashe in Paris and Zurich in 1985. In Paris, the elderly Iranian said, he had lunch with Ben-Menashe at the Bar du Theatre, next to the Hotel Montaigne located on a fashionable tree-lined avenue. Ben-Menashe was accompanied by a man identified as an Israeli colonel. Omshei also remembered that Ben-Menashe always paid for his expenses in cash, never using a credit card, to avoid a paper trail. Ben-Menashe was "very talkative and full of stories," but secretive about his business dealings, Omshei said.

Reza'i, Omshei's Revolutionary Guard associate, also nodded that he knew Ben-Menashe. But, more close-mouthed than Omshei, Reza'i was unwilling to discuss his contacts with either the Great Satan (the United States) or the Little Satan (Israel). He did add that he had visited the United States on Iranian government business during the 1980s. His trip, he said, included a special guided tour of the White House, a story that reminded me of the Iran-contra tale about Oliver North showing Iranian radicals around the Oval Office in 1986. But when I asked

Reza'i if he had ever met North, he chastised me for my indiscreet questioning and refused to answer.

As with my first trip to Israel, I felt a sense of futility trying to convince people from a starkly different culture and in a risky political environment to open up and tell me what they knew. For the next several days in Tehran, we also had trouble contacting the Iranian defense and intelligence officials who might actually know about any contacts with Republicans in 1980. But we finally had a breakthrough. An American businessman with ties to the late CIA director William Casey had slipped me the phone number for an Iranian ex-student radical. I was able to reach him at his home.

The former student had helped storm the U.S. embassy in 1979, establishing his revolutionary credentials. The Casey associate said the man was now an influential member of Iran's secretive intelligence apparatus, enjoying close personal ties to the brother of Iran's President Ali Akbar Hashemi Rafsanjani. When I reached the ex-student by phone, he sounded excited to talk with someone who knew his American friend. He invited Ross and me to dinner, offering to pick us up at our hotel that evening.

The ex-student arrived about 20 minutes late and was effusively apologetic. Pulling up to the front door, he bounded out of his white Mercedes sedan. His arms outstretched, his head shaking from side to side, he expressed how sorry he was. The traffic, the Tehran traffic, he shrugged. Ross and I had just finished filming some scenes at an open-air bazaar and had been caught in the evening traffic gridlock as well. No apologies were necessary.

Our host treated us with traditional Iranian courtesy, politely ushering us into the leather seats of his well-appointed sedan. He pulled out of the hotel driveway and headed north toward the exclusive section of the city and a Japanese restaurant that appeared to be a favorite of Westerners. The clientele was mostly European businessmen hoping to profit from Iran's post-war reconstruction.

During dinner, the Iranian described how he and other radical students had seized the American embassy. "I had been very active in the revolution," said the former radical, his voice low, his tone modest, his manner almost bashful. With his bearded face and round glasses, he still looked like the student activist that he had been more than a decade earlier as the dramatic events of November 1979 unfolded.

"So when some of my friends said there was to be an important meeting at the university, of course, I went. The classroom was crowded and there were three blackboards that had been turned toward the wall. We were told that the mission would be important for the revolution and had the support of the Imam," the religious term for the Ayatollah Ruhollah Khomeini.

"They said it would be dangerous and that anyone who didn't want to take part could leave now. But no one left. Then, they turned around the blackboards. There were three buildings drawn on the blackboards. They were the buildings of the U.S. embassy."

But the target of the raid was not the embassy personnel, the ex-student explained. "We had believed that the U.S. government had been manipulating affairs inside Iran and we wanted to prove it," he told me over the buzz at the crowded restaurant. "We thought if we could get into the embassy, we could get the documents that would prove this. We hadn't thought about hostages. We all went to the embassy. We had wire cutters to cut through the fence. We started climbing over the fences. We had expected more resistance. When we got inside, we saw the Americans runnings and we chased them. We chased one man into a building and caught him."

Marine guards set off tear gas in a futile attempt to control the mob, but held their fire to avoid bloodshed. Suddenly, maybe unexpectedly, the militant students had on their hands dozens of American hostages—and an international crisis.

"I stayed in the embassy for a few days," our dinner companion continued. "But then I left to get back to my studies." He seemed proud of his participation in an historic event, but sensitive to his story's possible offense to an American. My personal reaction to this tale of unintended consequences was a mixture of revulsion and fascination. Remembering the images of blindfolded American diplomats and trash being carried in American flags, I had assumed that the students were something less than human.

Yet this Iranian participant, who was politely sipping his Japanese soup and picking at the shrimp tempura at our table, appeared not at all the heinous criminal that one might have expected. He seemed chagrined by the outcome of the embassy takeover and apologetic to an American whose nation was humiliated by the event.

But he was also confident about the rightness of the cause that he had embraced during those tumultuous days of his youth: the overthrow of the corrupt Pahlavi dynasty. In his mind and that of his classmates, the U.S. government had meddled brutally in their national life, and their seizure of the embassy exacted only a small measure of revenge for the quarter century of tyranny under the U.S.-imposed shah.

After listening to his story, I broached the other subject: Had the Republicans negotiated secretly with Iran in 1980? I outlined the allegations that we had heard, particularly the assertion that Mehdi Karrubi had acted as a middleman in the talks. But as casual as I was in posing the question, our Iranian host looked stricken, as if I had unintentionally violated some obscure Islamic custom. He paused and thought before answering.

His voice dropped even lower to only slightly above a whisper. "Yes," he said, "a deal did happen. But I do not know about it directly. Others know more. But it is difficult to talk about. We could talk about it if it involved only Karrubi on our side. But it involves many others and they cannot let it be known that they dealt with the Americans."

Our host agreed to check on what could be told to us and to help us locate some other Iranian militants on our list of requested interview subjects. Because of his days as a student radical, he knew many senior military officials. Storming the U.S. embassy, it seemed, had been a credentialing experience for the new Iranian élite, like attending the right prep school or Ivy League college in the United States.

The cream of this radical élite had come to enjoy the spoils of the Islamic victory. They held important jobs or won lucrative trade concessions, some, ironically, serving as commercial representatives for Western companies. These privileged ex-students stood out when moving around Tehran because they drove sparkling new white Mercedes sedans. The rest of Tehran made do with cheaply built Peykans, which looked like Ramblers in Third World disguise. The battered and smoky Peykans clogged the streets and contributed to the choking haze over the city.

After dinner, our companion apologized that he did not have time to drive us back to our hotel. He found us a cab and waved as we pulled away. Then he climbed into his white Mercedes and left.

Inside the U.S. embassy in November 1979, the Islamic students had captured hundreds of secret U.S. documents. Over many months, the papers were painstakingly analyzed and assembled for publication in a series of more than 50 booklets. Some documents, which had been hastily run through shredding machines by panicky embassy staffers, were first glued back together, a process akin to solving dozens of giant, black-and-white jigsaw puzzles with the pieces all mixed together.

Teams of Iranian students took to the task with revolutionary zeal and reconstructed dozens of those papers into readable form. But most of the sensitive papers did not require such patient sorting and pasting. By the drawerful, documents were seized intact by the students as they rifled through embassy files in their pursuit of an evidentiary trail of U.S. misdeeds.

The resulting book series was called "Documents from the U.S. Espionage Den," published by the "Muslim Students Following the Line of the Imam." At a bookstore located at the front gate of the old U.S. embassy, Ross and I bought a dozen or so volumes that were still in print. The books carried catchy titles like "America: Supporter of the Usurpers of the Qods"[1] or "Leaders of the Arabian Peninsula: Puppets of the Great Satan." That volume—number 35 in the series—showed that after the overthrow of the shah, the Saudi royal family fretted about its own security, just as the old CIA man, Miles Copeland, had told us a year earlier.

"Developments in Iran . . . could be seen as an example of U.S. seeming indifference or impotence," Saudi Prince Fahd complained to visiting Carter administration officials. "Instead of pressuring the shah into bringing his thoughts and actions up to date so as to pull the rug out from under the communist agitators, you let him go." According to the secret State Department cable, the crown prince then warned of imminent communist advances in the Middle East that would threaten Saudi Arabia and the other Persian Gulf sheikhdoms.

---

[1] "Usurpers of the Qods" is a reference to Israel; Qods, or Holy Place, means Jerusalem.

"Shortly, perhaps within a few months, Khomeini will be out and Iran will become another Ethiopia, ruled by communists placed there by Moscow," Fahd predicted alarmingly. The cable continued: "The crown prince regretted that the United States did nothing to counter the communist threats in the region. Fahd further noted that Iran was threatening Bahrain, Kuwait, and other Arab countries of the Gulf. There had, however, not been a word of caution to Iran from President Carter to reassure not only weak countries, like Bahrain, but also America's other friends in the area and around the world."

In effect, Fahd was calling due the post-World War II American commitment to protect the security of the Persian Gulf sheikhdoms in exchange for reasonably priced oil. One secret State Department cable, dated July 5, 1979, bluntly explained the point: "Oil for security is still the essence of the special relationship" with the Saudis.

The secret documents seemed relevant to our historical research a decade later. They showed that even before the American hostages were seized, the conservative monarchies of the oil-rich Middle East were angry about Jimmy Carter and nervous about their own fate before a wave of Islamic fervor—and imagined communist expansion.

19

ONE ANGRY MULLAH

A call rang through to Robert Ross's hotel room. The bureaucrats from the Ministry of Islamic Guidance had gotten word back on our interview requests. We would be permitted to interview Sa'id Rajaie-Khorasani, the former U.N. ambassador who was now chairman of the Majlis committee on foreign relations. But there was a bigger surprise. We would also be granted an audience with the speaker of the Iranian parliament, Mehdi Karrubi. Even the blasé bureaucrats at the Ministry of Islamic Guidance were impressed.

When we arrived at the Majlis, the parliament building, security was tight though reasonably good natured. The security men confiscated our wallets, keys, pens, even my plastic comb. The guards said only pens with see-through casings were permitted. After a careful frisking, the Revolutionary Guards permitted us to enter the Majlis, a modernesque building with the architectural flavor of the Kennedy Center in Washington.

We were directed to a cramped press office to wait. The black-and-white television, tuned to Iranian national TV, was showing a concert by the uniformed North Korean military orchestra and chorus. After the full chorus performed a patriotic number or two, a North Korean army trio began strumming guitars and singing in a country-and-western style. Just as the show was getting interesting, we were pulled away and escorted upstairs.

Behind a desk in a corner of a spacious conference room sat Rajaie-Khorasani, a man with a warm smile and a prominently beaked nose. After finishing a phone call, Rajaie-Khorasani greeted us in excellent English, a language he had mastered during his tour as Iran's ambassador to the United Nations. The ex-ambassador was dressed in a distinctly Iranian style, white shirt buttoned to the top, with a dark jacket but no tie. Iranian officials shunned the Western business suits favored in the Persian Gulf sheikhdoms.

A pragmatist linked to President Rafsanjani's more moderate political faction, Rajaie-Khorasani was known as a man who liked to talk and felt secure enough in his relationship with the ruling hierarchy to speak his mind. As I explained our interest in the October Surprise issue, Rajaie-Khorasani seemed to relish Mehdi Karrubi's predicament. The ex-ambassador also volunteered that he considered a Republican-Iranian deal in 1980 quite likely.

"This is very, very reasonable to be the case," said Rajaie-Khorasani about the October Surprise allegations. "Probably the Carter administration wanted to exploit the situation for its own internal interests, and on the other side, the Reagan administration did not wish to miss any chance which was available and therefore they decided to make their own contacts and send their own mediators. Thus, the whole argument seems to be extremely reasonable, although I am not in a position to comment on the specifics of this case, because actually I don't know who sent what and what kind of messages the supporters of Reagan sent to Iran or whom they approached."

As for Mehdi Karrubi's alleged contact with William Casey in Madrid, Rajaie-Khorasani again said he had no direct knowledge, only an observation: "If someone like Mr. Karrubi has had any contact of this nature, it is most reasonable to assume that he prefers to keep the news of that contact secret and undisclosed.

"I don't think that if you go to Mr. Karrubi now and asked him about the date and the content of those meetings, that he would be very pleased. I think he would be absolutely embarrassed to say 'yes or no.' He would say, 'no, I don't remember,' or something, if he has had any contact. If he did not have any contact, then he says, 'no, absolutely wrong.' But I think Mr. Karrubi did have trips to outside Iran in those days, on many occasions. Once when I was in New York, he came to London because there was a religious ceremony by the Iranian Moslems in London."

Not only would Karrubi be loathe to discuss talks with any Republicans. But Rajaie-Khorasani believed the time was not ripe for the government to supply any official confirmation if indeed any meetings had occurred.

"Suppose that such a thing did happen and Mr. Karrubi did go to Madrid and did have these conversations with Mr. Casey and others—and that he came back to Iran and passed the message to the office of the Imam [Khomeini]," Rajaie-Khorasani continued. "Mr. Karrubi, with the revolutionary platform that he is holding now, is in a very embarrassing situation to say, 'yes, we all did it.' "

Rajaie-Khorasani pleaded for our understanding. "What should we do?" he asked, smiling about the dilemma. "It is true that it is very important for the American people to know all these things, but it is also at this moment very important for the Iranian people not to know all these things, because of the political platforms that, for instance, Mr. Karrubi and also some friends around him are holding. Therefore, it's very difficult at the present juncture to get access to the right information.

"When the present fervor is over, later on, this information becomes not relevant to the immediate political affairs of the different political rings of Iran. But now, I don't think that it would be very likely. It's exactly like expecting Mr. Casey in those days to come to the American people and tell them what he did in Madrid. And definitely Mr. Casey would not say anything. And our Mr. Casey is not going to say anything now."

There was another reason for the Iranian government to tread softly around the issue of secret U.S.-Iranian contacts. Iran's political forces were on the verge of a battle between the "Second" and "Third Lines." The more pragmatic Second Line had coalesced around President Rafsanjani. Mehdi Karrubi was a leading spokesman for Iran's ultra-radical Third Line.

The word around Tehran political circles was that the more moderate Second Line was plotting a government-wide purge that would eliminate the hardline Third Liners. The First Line, the moderates who had favored a non-sectarian Iranian government after the 1979 revolution, was long gone. Many First-Liners had faced firing squads in the early years of Khomeini's reign.

A similar fate could await losers of the current power struggle. Already, Rafsanjani's allies were making life hard for Karrubi. His brother, Hassan, an opportunistic intelligence figure who had played a role in the Iran-contra scandal in 1985 and 1986, had been thrown into jail. The unspecified charges apparently related to corruption, either financial or moral. No one seemed to know—or would say—for sure.

When we returned to the Majlis after lunch for our interview with Karrubi, I remembered to bring a see-through Bic pen, so it wouldn't be confiscated. But I still lost my comb, wallet and keys. Our greeting at the Majlis press office was not as casual as it had been in the morning visit. One of the government press functionaries ran up to us as we arrived. He scolded us in Persian for being late, even though we were there nearly a half hour before our appointment with Karrubi.

Hastily, we were led to an ornate sitting room with a coffee table surrounded by three chairs, one resembling a throne. Already, two government cameras were set up to film us filming Karrubi. I knew immediately that any slim hope we had of getting the radical cleric to talk freely was shot. While we had succeeded in drawing Rajaie-Khorasani into a candid conversation about the realities of Iranian politics, the formality of this arrangement would permit only set-piece questions and answers.

As Ross unpacked our video camera, Karrubi's personal translator arrived, and another functionary brought in garlands of flowers to place on the coffee table. For additional decoration, the table sported two photographs, one of Khomeini and the other his successor as religious leader, Mohammed Ali Khamenei.

Accompanied by several aides, Karrubi then swept into the chamber. He wore the flowing white robes and turban of a mullah and stopped as he approached the throne-chair to rearrange the pictures on the table. He moved Khomeini's picture into a more prominent position and partly obscured the photo of Khamenei, a political gesture, I presumed.

By this point, late in our week-long visit to Iran, I had met a few dozen Iranians and found them to be a friendly, polite people. Karrubi was unlike any other Iranian I had encountered. He would look away for minutes at a time, as if I weren't there, and then swing his head toward me, his hand curled under his white beard, and fix me with a sly smile.

Since we had obtained the interview with promises to ask about a range of U.S.-Iran relations, I was obliged to run through our list of pre-submitted questions, only one of which was about Karrubi's alleged meeting with Casey. I began by asking him to summarize the two nation's troubled bilateral history. Karrubi was clearly a man who still harbored a grudge against America.

"For a period of 25 years, from the fall of the Mossadegh government in 1953 to the 1979 Iranian revolution, the government in power, the shah, exerted all kinds of pressure on the people of Iran," Karrubi said through his interpreter. "Groups of people were executed at that time and many uprisings of the people were suppressed very brutally. And the supporter of the Shah's regime was the United States government. The U.S. endorsed everything that the shah's regime did during this period."

On one very sore point, Karrubi blamed Americans for Khomeini's forced exile in 1964. "They are the cause of the exile of our leader, a leader that was both a political and also a religious leader for the people of this country," the mullah said. "And we have documents to prove this."

Karrubi promised to be "very brief," but he was working himself into a diatribe. "Even after the 1979 Islamic revolution, the United States did not stop its conspiracies against this people," he continued. "And they have direct links with those who caused these disturbances inside this country, and the Americans provided these conspirators with guidance and assistance. The U.S. has not done anything since that time in order to make up for these things that it has done during all these years."

Although President Carter came under harsh criticism in the United States for weakness in not backing the shah in a bloody suppression of the revolution, Karrubi found Carter's policy just more of the same American interference. "We didn't see anything new from the United States," he said. "The United States continued the same approach as it did before."

After listening to his complaints for a reasonable length of time, I asked the October Surprise question. "There have been some questions raised about whether or not there were additional contacts [on the hostage crisis] that came from Republicans, from candidate Reagan's campaign, with officials of the government in Tehran," I said, pointedly excluding any mention of Karrubi from this first question. "Are you familiar with any of these contacts?"

When my query was translated, Karrubi seemed flustered. "Is this the question about me?" he asked his translator in Persian. The translator responded that the question referred to no one specifically.

"Regarding the contacts by the Republican Party," Karrubi answered, "there is no document, there is nothing pointing to this matter. I deny such a thing. I think it's a baseless rumor. And for us, what difference does it make, whether Mr. Carter is in power or Mr. Reagan is in power. There was no contact from the Reagan election organizations with the Iranian officials."

"But," I continued, "some of the statements that have been made by people from Iran as well as from other countries are that there were meetings in Madrid, Spain, in July and August 1980 and that you, Speaker Karrubi, were asked to meet with William Casey and that the question of U.S.-Iran relations was discussed at that time. Is that at least true, that there were discussions about future U.S.-Iran relations?"

Karrubi: "These things on numerous occasions, I have heard about them, about such meetings, but I want to say here that they are pure lies. There is no truth to them. And it is interesting to note that I have never been to France and Spain, the countries that have been mentioned."

Throughout this response, Karrubi was remarkably cool. As his translator was giving the speaker's answers in English, Karrubi would turn to look at me, nod his head for emphasis and smile. Though it was clear that Karrubi was issuing a categorical denial, I recounted Jamshid Hashemi's claim that Karrubi did meet with Casey in Madrid.

"Do you know that Jamshid Hashemi, who was originally a lower-level official with the revolution, has made these statements? We also have talked to others, from other countries, including an Israeli official and a person who was helping the Iranian government obtain weapons, who have also made these statements. Are they all making this up for some reason?"

Karrubi: "I have never been involved in any of this. I have no information about these matters. I don't know Mr. Hashemi and I have never paid a visit to those countries. And as far as my information allows, I have no knowledge of other officials being involved in such matters."

However, Karrubi did leave open the possibility that other Iranian leaders from competing factions might have had dealings with the Republicans. "The government, during 1980, was in the hands of Bani-Sadr and his group, the liberal government," Karrubi said, his voice registering some contempt.

"I don't have any information about their contacts and these other persons. But what I know is the present government and the people that are working here now in the government, I don't have any information indicating that there ever have been such contacts between the present people that are in the government and the Republicans."

"Do you know why the hostages, the American hostages, were released on January 20, 1981, shortly after President Reagan was sworn in as president?" I asked. "Some of President Reagan's supporters suggest that Iran was frightened of President Reagan and that Iran released the hostages out of fear that he would retaliate if the hostages were not out by the time he came into office. Is that true?"

Karrubi bristled at my continued questioning about the hostages. "My comments to your questions are all impromptu because I did not know that you were going to concentrate your questions on this issue," he snapped. "But regarding your question, the decision of the parliament to free the hostages was made during Carter's administration, not the Reagan administration. And the Islamic Republic of Iran and the late Imam [Khomeini] had shown that they are not afraid of such things."

If not out of fear, I wondered, was the inauguration day release "an effort to show goodwill?" Karrubi responded, "Many things take place accidentally. I think this was a pure coincidence."

Karrubi was showing impatience with the length of the interview. But I took one more shot at learning more about the October Surprise allegations. Following up on Karrubi's claim that no documents had been found proving Iran's complicity in a deal with the Reagan campaign, I asked if there had been "a thorough examination of what the record might show."

Karrubi: "We have carried out such an investigation, but no, nothing has been found. We have questioned people that we thought may have had some contacts, but no results. Investigations have been made in this connection because at that time, the climate of the country, the political atmosphere, was very free, there might have been some contacts. But we investigated and found nothing."

"You are categorically denying any knowledge of any contact?" I asked in a closing question. "Yes," Karrubi said, emphatically.

On our last full day in Tehran, our dinner acquaintance from the Japanese restaurant called us with a phone number for an arms procurer for the Revolutionary Guards, Hamid Naqashan. We had been looking for Naqashan for more than a year. He had been cited by three October Surprise witnesses as a key figure in secret negotiations with Republicans. American arms dealer William Herrmann had told me that on the day after Ronald Reagan's inauguration in 1981, Naqashan had talked about a Republican-Iranian deal to release the hostages. Pakistani arms broker Arif Durrani had also mentioned Naqashan as a participant in GOP-Iranian talks. A reporter from *Der Spiegel* had spoken with Karl Heinz Ottershagen, a German arms merchant in Switzerland who claimed to have been with Naqashan in September 1980 when the Iranian was ferrying between meetings with Republicans.

Other numbers we had gotten for Naqashan hadn't worked. But this one did. Ross was able to reach Naqashan and his business associate, Hamid Zarga. The pair were commercial representatives for Hankar Machinery, the Iranian dealership for the U.S.-owned Caterpillar earth-moving equipment company. Zarga was sales manager and Naqashan was chairman of the board. After some hesitation, they agreed to meet with us that night.

We were picked up at our hotel by Zarga, a small, bearded, fast-talking man. Driving a white Mercedes, he took us to Naqashan's office in a modern residential-style apartment building. Out of the elevator, Zarga led us into a conference room and offered us tea and cookies. Zarga chattered non-stop about the high quality of Caterpillar equipment and the cutthroat competition from the Japanese firm, Kaimatsu. He also was curious how we had located them. We told him that we had gotten numbers for Naqashan from a variety of people, which was true.

A few minutes later Naqashan entered. A heavy-set man with a closely cropped beard, he could have passed for a Mafia don or a villain from a James Bond movie. Though only in his 30s, he moved with the confidence and girth of a man accustomed to power. He was cordial and cautious, letting Zarga do most of the talking.

Though Naqashan seemed to be the one in charge, Zarga barely let him get a word in edgewise. It was as if Zarga feared Naqashan might tell us something that could harm their business. When we did penetrate Zarga's verbal defenses, Naqashan fended off our questions about 1980 with a shrug of his shoulders or a short dismissive remark. Then Zarga would jump back in with more chatter.

Naqashan looked annoyed when I asked about the statement by Herrmann. "Yes, I know Herrmann," Naqashan said. "We did a little business together through Brazil in the early '80s. It was not very much. But I never talked with him in Tehran. I talked with him in Frankfurt. And I never told him anything about a hostage deal."

When we pressed Naqashan more about the hostages, Zarga cut in, turning the conversation to less controversial matters. The shadow-boxing went on for an hour as Ross and I tried to gain Naqashan's confidence. He seemed to know more than he was saying. Finally, Naqashan noted that the hour was getting late and proposed that we go with them to an Iranian restaurant for chelo-kebabs, a traditional spicy meat dish.

For the trip to the restaurant, Naqashan ordered us into his sparkling new four-by-four "all terrain vehicle." As he drove through the darkened streets, Naqashan spoke cryptically about a meeting in 1980 between Jamshid Hashemi, the brother of President Carter's intermediary Cyrus Hashemi, and Hassan Karrubi, the brother of cleric Mehdi Karrubi. I tried to scribble notes in the back seat as the car bounced over the uneven streets. But between the darkness and the jostling, my handwriting was a barely legible scrawl.

Naqashan said the Jamshid-Hassan meeting occurred in Dubayy, a dusty Persian Gulf port city known as a center for smuggling. The purpose of the meeting, Naqashan claimed, was to arrange arms shipments. Some Americans were also involved. But Naqashan would not explain the significance of this meeting or supply other details. Again Zarga interrupted, cutting off Naqashan's brief comments with more talk about the success of their Caterpillar franchise.

We parked in a quiet, low-rise neighborhood and entered the restaurant, where Naqashan was greeted warmly as a regular customer. The chelo-kebab restaurant was brightly lit and garishly decorated with glass chandeliers and formica tables. The conversation through dinner was more of the same. We pressed Naqashan to talk about his activities in 1980, and Zarga steered the discussion elsewhere. From Zarga's description of their business, it was clear that the two men were getting very rich from the sale of American earthmoving equipment.

Finally, toward the end of the meal, Naqashan told Zarga to find a quiet corner of the restaurant for his evening prayers. "Go pray," he said bluntly. "This is a good Islamic restaurant. There must be some place for prayers."

I thought Naqashan might be getting ready to tell us something. But even without Zarga's chattering presence, Naqashan chose his words carefully. He continued to deny any personal involvement in the October Surprise negotiations. But he added, "There were discussions within the inner circle around Khomeini about the benefit of playing the Republicans against the Democrats, but I do not know the outcome of those discussions." He would say no more. Soon Zarga was back and the dinner was over.

As Naqashan drove us back toward our hotel, Ross and I continued to ask questions about U.S.-Iranian arms deals. At one point, Zarga turned to look at us in the back seat. He had lost his patience.

"This is not the United States," he scolded. "There are no golden parachutes here. One day, you can be making big money. The next day you can be running a chelo-kebab stand." Then, his voice turned threatening: "The questions that you ask could be very dangerous for you."

"Well," I responded, tired from the frustrating evening conversation, "we're leaving tomorrow anyway."

Naqashan and Zarga clearly did not want to find new jobs cooking chelo-kebabs.

20

A LIAR EXPOSED

On October 25, 1991, a gray and misty day, Robert Ross and I found ourselves on the Connecticut Turnpike heading east. We were driving from New York City to Madison, Connecticut, a small suburban town about 17 miles east of New Haven. We had finally persuaded a book researcher named Peggy Robohm to let us examine documents from the personal files of Oregon money-launderer/arms dealer Richard Brenneke.

Robohm had started collaborating on a book with Brenneke early in the year. She offered to help Brenneke write his autobiography that was to describe his role in a range of intelligence activities and the October Surprise. But she discovered instead that Brenneke's personal financial records showed that he indeed had been lying about key moments in his career, including his supposed trip to Paris in October 1980 to participate in secret meetings with William Casey and assorted arms dealers.

Brenneke's undoing dated to his victory celebration in May 1990, after he was acquitted on perjury charges for claiming to have witnessed an October Surprise negotiation in Paris. He vowed to tell his story in a book. "Just read my book because, ladies and gentlemen, there's going to be one," Brenneke announced on the courthouse steps in Portland, Oregon.

But Brenneke spent much of the next year struggling with his health and his finances. He lost his Lake Oswego home in his personal bankruptcy, and he was kept on medication for his heart problems. Then, in early 1991,

Peggy Robohm arrived on Brenneke's doorstep. She professed to be an admirer who wanted to help him bring some order to his voluminous files.

Robohm had a background in writing children's books and a fascination with U.S. intelligence activities. She had made a hobby of studying Yale University's traditional role as a breeding ground for CIA recruits. Robohm also became a specialist on Yale's secret campus organizations, such as Skull and Bones, whose most prominent member was George Herbert Walker Bush. Robohm would boast that she knew when the secret societies would conduct their clandestine initiation rites and which rooftops offered the best view of the nighttime ceremonies. Her interest in Yale's intelligence ties, she said, had brought her into contact with a number of former CIA men.

For a time in early 1991, Robohm moved in with Brenneke and his wife in Oregon. But eventually she convinced Brenneke to pack up his files and drive with her to Connecticut. There, she told him, they would be closer to New York publishing houses and could get to work on his autobiography. Brenneke told associates that he was leaving his wife and hoped to marry Robohm.

In a rented van loaded with Brenneke's files, the couple headed east. Brenneke moved into Robohm's modest suburban home in Madison, where she lived with her husband. But as Robohm assisted Brenneke on his book outline, she began to grow suspicious. Key details in the story kept changing as Brenneke's claimed role in the October Surprise kept expanding. Brenneke soon decided to return to his wife in Oregon.

In mid-May 1991, a month after the *Frontline* documentary had aired, Brenneke visited Washington, and I met with him along with Martin Kilian and Gary Sick. All three of us had been deeply suspicious of Brenneke's Paris tale.[1] But in spring 1991, Brenneke told an even stranger story. The money-launderer told Kilian, Sick, and me that he had partici-

---

[1] In the *Frontline* documentary, we summarized the story of Brenneke's perjury trial. We noted that the federal prosecutor failed to convince a single juror that Brenneke had lied about the Paris meetings. But the documentary added that the money-launderer's credibility remained suspect and that his acquittal did not mean that any of his assertions about Paris were true.

pated in not just the Paris meetings but the Madrid meetings as well. Yet Brenneke had never mentioned Madrid to any of us before Iranian arms dealer Jamshid Hashemi had described the Madrid meetings publicly. Brenneke now insisted that he was in Madrid in the summer of 1980 and saw a number of Republican luminaries at an outdoor plaza near the Ritz Hotel. They were there for the secret meetings, Brenneke claimed.

To bolster his revised tale, Brenneke turned over a list of names, people who he claimed had joined the Madrid meetings. He insisted that he had possessed the list since 1980. But he was lying. The list, we knew, was identical to one compiled by the ABC-*Financial Times* investigators for the *Nightline* program. They had written down all the non-Spanish surnames from the registry at the Plaza Hotel, and clearly not all those people were part of the alleged meetings. Later, Kilian learned that Brenneke had gotten the list from a friend in Israel who apparently had been questioned about the names by ABC-*Financial Times* reporters.

Brenneke was on a one-way course toward self-destruction. His earlier stories had been clumsy and implausible. But now he was telling tales that could do nothing but shred what little credibility he had left.

Turning over his personal records to Peggy Robohm proved even dumber for Brenneke. After the falling-out with his researcher, Brenneke left his cache of records behind. Robohm said that only then did she begin looking through Brenneke's old financial records. Poring through those files, she discovered credit card and other records for the calendar year 1980. She also located Brenneke's daily calendars. The documents proved that Brenneke had not gone to Paris over the weekend of October 18–19, 1980, as he had claimed in his sworn court testimony. He had been attending a martial arts tournament in Seattle, Washington.

On the key date of Sunday, October 19, when Brenneke claimed to be settling in at the Waldorf-Florida Hotel in Paris, his records showed that he really was staying at a low-rent motel in Seattle. Brenneke checked out late in the morning, got his car washed, and then drove home. He had dinner at Mazzi's, an Italian restaurant in Portland, according to another receipt.

By summer 1991, Robohm had turned her research over to ex-CIA officer Frank Snepp, who was writing investigative stories for New York's *Village Voice* newspaper. For several years, Snepp had been promoting Brenneke to other journalists as a credible source, and the spy-turned-reporter had testified in Brenneke's defense at the Oregon man's 1990 perjury trial.

But after confronting Brenneke with copies of the documents and getting no satisfactory explanation, Snepp wrote an article debunking the small-time arms dealer. Dated September 10, 1991, the article was entitled "Brenneke Exposed" and established what many had suspected, but what federal prosecutor Thomas O'Rourke had failed to prove: Richard Brenneke had lied about his presence in Paris.

As we began work on a follow-up program about the October Surprise, *Frontline* sought access to these Brenneke files. Initially Robohm and Snepp balked at sharing the papers with other investigators, but eventually Robohm agreed to let us see some of the documents that she had pulled from Brenneke's personal files.

When Ross and I reached Robohm's ranch-style house in a quiet woodsy neighborhood, the book researcher greeted us at the door. Peggy Robohm looked to be in her late 40s, with a trim figure, short dark hair, and large glasses. She moved and talked quickly, as if nervous around strangers. Bookshelves in her living room were filled with children's books, and the furniture was cluttered with stuffed animals. Though she lived in the house alone with her husband, she explained that the stuffed animals were a leftover from her work as a writer of children fiction.

Robohm said she was on edge because she feared Brenneke might retaliate against her for publicizing his records. She noted that Brenneke once had asked for his personal files back and promised to send "some friends from New York to pick them up." Robohm said she knew what he meant by "some friends from New York—the Mafia." With a twitching smile, she told Ross and me that she had installed a burglar alarm in her house and had moved the documents to the offices of a private investigator for safekeeping. We would have to drive there to see the papers.

Ross and I followed Robohm as she drove toward town. She pulled into a parking lot of a two-story frame building. The three of us climbed the outdoor wooden staircase to the private investigator's second-floor office, where a tall man in shirtsleeves let us in. He wore a holster and revolver on his hip. I glanced at Ross, who was as startled as I was. Apparently, we would be allowed to examine Brenneke's financial records only under armed guard.

After some small talk, the private investigator began removing the documents from a safe. Each receipt or monthly billing statement was in its own manila folder. Ross and I were allowed to inspect and film the documents one at a time. Each was put back in its manila folder and returned to the safe before another was taken out and handed to us. The receipts for the hotel and charge-card slips, faded with age, looked genuine. The motel receipt was marked by a time stamp showing an 11:23 a.m. checkout on Sunday, October 19, 1980.

When we were shown Brenneke's 1980 calendar, Robohm opened it to the weekend of October 18–19. The notation for the weekend reflected plans to attend a kendo tournament, a type of martial art in which the combatants fence with staves. But when I tried to flip the pages to see other dates, Robohm objected and reached for the calendar.

"Who said you could turn the page," she interjected testily. "You said you only wanted to see the October dates. You didn't say anything about other dates."

"I never said any such thing," I responded, surprised by the intensity of her objection. "I said we wanted to review Brenneke's documents for 1980. Anyway, I just want to see how he makes his entries."

After a few minutes of discussion, Robohm relented. I flipped through some other pages which showed occasional entries, some apparently listing dosages of medication that Brenneke was taking. There was no indication of any overseas trips in July and August.

In an interview on camera, Robohm said she had first become suspicious as Brenneke changed his chronology of his career. She then discovered other inconsistencies. When she brought the problems to Brenneke's attention, she said he instructed her to compare his written recollections with his documentary records.

"He commented that I had the files," Robohm told us. "If I wanted to check his career against his writings, why didn't I look in the files. So then I looked in more of the files."

"So Mr. Brenneke says to you, 'go back and read my records'?" I asked.

"That's right," she responded.

" 'If you think I'm wrong on these things, you've got the files, go check them'?" I summarized.

"Correct."

"So you go check them?"

"I started reading various files and found credit card receipts," Robohm said.

"Isn't that a little dumb to ask someone to go check files that have information that would contradict what you say?" I asked.

"I was surprised, yes," Robohm responded.

"Why do you think he did that?"

"He may not remember what's in his files," she answered.

"It does seem monumentally stupid to be preparing a book to talk about a life that you did not lead, but to bring documentation that would show you to be not telling the truth, does it not?"

Robohm smiled slightly. "I would say careless," she responded.

Robohm traced some of that carelessness to Brenneke's heart ailment and the confusion that had surrounded his bankruptcy and foreclosure on his house. But it still seemed strange that Brenneke would have forgotten that he had fabricated a personal role in the October Surprise meetings.

Though the documents found by Robohm appeared conclusive in proving that Brenneke had lied about his presence in Paris, the question remained, why had he lied? What was his motive? What had driven Brenneke not only to spin a yarn about his personal participation, but to repeat his assertions, under oath before a federal judge at an unrelated sentencing hearing for his friend, pilot Heinrich Rupp? Then, why did Brenneke stick by his story even after he was indicted and the prosecutor offered him a generous plea bargain deal that simply called for Brenneke to admit that he had lied? He had, after all, endured medical collapse and personal bankruptcy instead of making a simple admission.

Also perplexing was his more recent behavior. In May 1991, as congressional interest grew about launching a formal October Surprise investigation, why did Brenneke re-emerge with new and even more ludicrous tales of his own adventures? Why did he leave incriminating documents in the hands of a researcher? Why did he urge her to check them?

For his part, Brenneke continued to insist through his lawyers that he was in Paris. He claimed that Robohm's documents were created in 1980

In this murky tangle, the author seems unaware of Barbara Honnegger's discovery of the Snepp-Robohm forgeries to debunk Brenneke (see Rosebomb).

as a cover for his trip to Europe. But he could supply no evidence to back up that excuse. He also refused to be re-interviewed or to return my phone calls.

Explaining Brenneke's actions is not easy. His behavior could be a case of bizarre psychological disfunction, a kind of Zelig-complex. Like the Woody Allen character, Brenneke might see himself on the screen of history as part of every important event. Conceivably, he could have picked up some rumors about Republican-Iranian contacts from his arms trafficking associates in Europe and simply painted himself into the picture. Or he could have harbored implausible dreams of somehow cashing in on his fantastic stories. But it seems preposterous that he would have thought he had a chance of getting a book contract when he had reneged on an earlier one without repaying the advance.

There was also the possibility that Brenneke was in cahoots with Oswald LeWinter, the mysterious Mr. Razine. Two months before the 1988 presidential election, Mr. Razine began calling reporters with false leads about the October Surprise allegations. It was Mr. Razine who first put Brenneke into the story by claiming that the Oregon money-launderer had participated in the Paris meetings. After being contacted about Mr. Razine's claim, Brenneke promptly corroborated the account. Unless there was some coordination, how could Mr. Razine have known that Brenneke would endorse the story?

When Mr. Razine's falsehoods were discovered and his real identity as Oswald LeWinter unmasked, LeWinter told us that he had been paid to insert the lies so the entire October Surprise investigation would be discredited. One of those lies turned out to be Brenneke's eyewitness role at the Paris meetings.

After Brenneke's lies were exposed in summer 1991, LeWinter told Martin Kilian that Brenneke had figured out one more way to earn money from the unidentified intelligence men. LeWinter asserted that Brenneke had been paid to destroy his own credibility and derail, once more, the October Surprise investigation. But the latest assertion from LeWinter, a confessed disinformationist, could be taken no more seriously than his earlier ones. There were no easy answers in the October Surprise mystery.

21

MYTH MATCHED

We had been hearing for weeks that there would be a new round of attacks on the October Surprise story. This time, they would come from the *New Republic*, a neoconservative political journal, and from *Newsweek*, where a special team had been formed to examine the issue in spring 1991. By early November, the two magazines were racing to be first to print the definitive debunking. October Surprise was not a mystery, they had decided. It was a myth.

The *New Republic* was first out of the starting block, with a long article that denounced the witnesses as frauds, impostors, and liars.[1] The magazine hit Ari Ben-Menashe the hardest. To research the article, writer Steven Emerson flew to Israel. There he received special briefings from the Israeli government, which was still trying to discredit its renegade intelligence man.

Emerson, known for his closeness to Israeli sources, claimed that he was even given access to Ben-Menashe's private personnel file. In it, he said, he spotted a description of Ben-Menashe as "delusional." Though providing no context for the characterization, Emerson cited it as conclusive proof that the events Ben-Menashe described never happened.

The *New Republic* did acknowledge, however, that Ben-Menashe did travel to the United States in 1986 and did leak real secrets about the

---

[1] Steven Emerson and Jesse Furman, "The Conspiracy That Wasn't," *New Republic*, November 18, 1991.

Reagan administration's arms sales to Iran. That would seem to contradict the "delusional" theory, but the magazine had a ready answer: Ben-Menashe had routinely handled "a report in 1986 prepared for the United States discussing Israel's request to replenish weapons that it supplied to Iran as part of the Iran-contra operations." But even if that were true, why would a "delusional" office-bound translator travel to the United States—presumably at his own expense—contact American journalists, and risk his job by discussing Washington's secret arms pipeline to Tehran? These were questions left unanswered.

The article also disparaged reporters who had worked on the October Surprise investigation as "entrepreneurial journalists." That was to suggest, presumably, that Robert Ross, Martin Kilian, and I had latched onto this project in order to profit from it.

I was assigned the role of Jamshid Hashemi's "supporter." The article said that I believed, along with radical attorney William Kunstler, "that Cyrus [Hashemi] was murdered to shut him up about what he knew about the October Surprise and that the U.S. government has covered up the murder." This was all news to me. I had never believed or said that Cyrus Hashemi was murdered. It had never crossed my mind that the motive for Cyrus's death, even if he had been murdered, would have been the October Surprise. Nor had I ever thought that the U.S. government was covering up Cyrus's presumed murder. The Iranian banker, after all, had died in London.

The *New Republic* also attacked Gary Sick for gullibly accepting the word of liars, ABC's Ted Koppel for airing Jamshid Hashemi's account of Madrid meetings, and investigative reporter Seymour Hersh for quoting Ari Ben-Menashe as a source in a book about Israel's nuclear program, *The Samson Option*. But when the layers of character assassination were stripped away, there was only one new argument. Based on the magazine's analysis of records for the London historical conference on World War II, the article concluded that Casey could not have traveled to Madrid in late July 1980, as Jamshid Hashemi had claimed.

Casey's schedule, the article argued, did not have a two-day gap that would have permitted two consecutive morning meetings in late July. The reasoning went as follows: Jamshid recalled that the Madrid meetings took place on two consecutive mornings. ABC *Nightline* reported that a Hashemi alias was registered at Madrid's Plaza Hotel starting Friday, July 25. Casey's secretary, Barbara Hayward, told *Nightline* that her calendar put Casey in Washington on Saturday, July 26. Since Casey gave his conference speech on the morning of July 29, a Tuesday, and returned to Washington by July 30, a Wednesday, those two days were also ruled out. So the Madrid meetings must have occurred on Sunday, July 27, and Monday, July 28.

But the *New Republic* argued that Casey could not have been in Madrid for meetings that covered those two mornings because he arrived in London on Sunday night, July 27, and was at the historical conference in London on the morning of July 28. "Casey is . . . accounted for . . . the night of July 27 and all day except for a brief absence, on July 28," the *New Republic* said. "This makes Jamshid's story of two consecutive days of meetings impossible."

The *New Republic* ridiculed ABC *Nightline* for failing "to find out that Casey was not in Madrid, but in London." The magazine also mocked Ted Koppel for his *Nightline* update, which noted that Madrid was only 90 minutes from London by air and that Casey still might have had time to go to Madrid. "*Nightline* was wrong again," the magazine gloated.

To match the *New Republic* on the newsstands on the first weekend in November, *Newsweek* slapped together its own debunking article, also concluding the historical conference documents proved, beyond any doubt, that "Casey did not go to Madrid" and that, in effect, Jamshid was a liar.

"Casey's whereabouts are convincingly established by contemporary records at the Imperial War Museum in London," Newsweek wrote. "Casey, it turns out, took a three-day breather from the campaign to participate in the Anglo-American Conference on the History of the Second World War."[2]

New Republic and *Newsweek* both splashed their findings on their covers—and the articles left no doubts about the conclusion: There had been no October Surprise contacts between Casey and the Iranians. The allegations were a "myth." The witnesses were liars. And anyone who gave them credence was a dupe. The October Surprise story was "a

---

[2] "Making of a Myth," *Newsweek*, November 11, 1991. p. 18.

conspiracy theory run wild." Republicans in Congress quickly seized on the findings to argue that no official investigation was needed.

But how good were the debunkings? Did the crucial records in London prove categorically that Jamshid Hashemi lied about the meeting between Casey and Karrubi? Or were the *New Republic* and *Newsweek* rushing to judgment—in effect denying even the possibility of an October Surprise scenario before Congress could get around to investigating?

Inside *Newsweek*, reporter Craig Unger had disagreed with the magazine's October Surprise conclusions. Hired by *Newsweek* to work on this investigation, Unger strenuously objected to the decision to frame the late July "window" on Casey's whereabouts by using the dates July 27 through 29. Unger complained that the magazine did no original work to determine how certain Casey's presence in Washington was on Saturday, July 26.

"They knew the window was not real," Unger said of his superiors. "It was clear, they were not doing the whole window." But the magazine brushed aside the internal concern that the debunking rested on an uncritical acceptance of the secretary's calendar notation, a document that *Newsweek* had not seen.

"It was the most dishonest thing that I've been through in my life in journalism," said Unger, who had been a reporter for 20 years. Unger left *Newsweek* after the "myth" cover and was promptly denigrated by *Newsweek* editors as an "October Surprise true-believer."

But how objective had the two magazines been? Was there any way that Casey could have met with Karrubi in Madrid on two consecutive mornings in late July? The key questions remained: When did Casey show up at the conference and what did the conference planning records prove about Casey's whereabouts on the morning of Monday, July 28? The *New Republic* and *Newsweek* "debunkings" rested heavily on records maintained by Jonathan Chadwick, the Imperial War Museum's director.

When *Frontline* first contacted Chadwick in the summer of 1991, he had no recollection when Casey arrived. But as he spoke with more reporters, Chadwick began insisting that Casey had, indeed, arrived on the morning of July 28. Chadwick started interpreting his records to mean that Casey attended the morning session that Monday and then left for several hours over lunch, returning late in the afternoon. There was a notation in the

afternoon box for Casey that read: "came at 4 p.m." *Newsweek* and the
New Republic concluded that the several hours over the long lunch would
not give Casey enough time to fly to Madrid and return. So it was the
certainty that Casey had attended the morning session that was crucial to
the October Surprise debunkings.

Yet, when *Frontline* producer Jim Gilmore interviewed 23 of the conference participants, he discovered uncertainty about Casey's presence on
that first morning. Sir William Deacon, the British chairman of the conference, recalled Casey arriving for the first time on late Monday afternoon.
The head of the American delegation, Arthur Funk, also told Gilmore that
he believed Casey arrived late in the day on Monday. So did three other
members of the American delegation. If they were right, Casey would
have had time to conduct the second meeting in Madrid on Monday
morning and then jet to London.

Whom to believe? Jonathan Chadwick and his checks or some of the
conference's participants and their decade-old memories?

So Robert Ross and I retained doubts about the meaning of Chadwick's
records when we hauled our video gear back across the Atlantic in mid-
December 1991 to get Chadwick's account on tape. The weather was
bitterly cold, and the late-fall sun never rose very high into the London sky.
The several-story Imperial War Museum stood, austerely, alone on a small
hill overlooking London. The old brick building had once housed an
insane asylum. Now it was filled with relics from Britain's past wars,
particularly weapons from World Wars I and II. The museum's entrance
was dominated by two huge cannons from a British warship.

Ross and I were led to Chadwick's cluttered office, where the museum
director greeted us cheerfully. He seemed to have gotten into the spirit of
this little historical drama and was eager to play a deciding part. He took us
into the same conference room where Casey had mumbled through his
historical paper a decade earlier. Amid portraits of British warriors in
battle, Chadwick sat at the long conference table and unfolded his now-
famous charts.

Though a relief from the unsavory characters who had filled our investigation, Chadwick looked like a satirist's idea of a British academic.

Dressed in a dark suit, bespectacled, with rather prominent ears and a slightly eccentric style, he plunged into a lively dissertation on the meaning of his charts and their various x's and checks, which the British call "ticks." Because the sessions were held in a modest-sized conference room with only 50 chairs, Chadwick explained, he needed to keep close track of who was expected at each speech to avert an overflow.

As Ross began filming, I asked Chadwick to say "as conclusively or as inconclusively" as he felt about where Casey was during the days of the conference.

"To address myself to the question you've just asked, where Mr. Casey was concerned, my best information, to begin with, was simply that he was going to attend the conference," Chadwick began. "Now on my chart, I see I have marked that on 16th July 1980, Professor Arthur Funk, who was chairman of the American delegation, telephoned me to say that Mr. Casey would not be coming on the 27th or 28th July after all. But we could expect him to arrive on the 29th, and I marked my chart to show that information." Chadwick had penciled in x's to show that Casey was not anticipated on the first day. But the plans apparently changed.

"When Mr. Casey appeared on the morning of 28th July, I was naturally taken by surprise because my last information was that he wasn't going to be here until the next morning," Chadwick told us. "Anyway, I was glad enough to see him and it looked as if rather presumptuously, I assumed he was going to be here all day and transported ink ticks for him right through the day thinking, 'Right, we got Mr. Casey in after all, today.' " That was why, Chadwick said, the ink check marks were over the penciled x's.

Yet at other points in the interview, Chadwick acknowledged that his memory of that first day was not as precise as he was now leading us to believe. "My recollection—and all recollections—are inherently unreliable eleven years later," he stipulated. "But my recollection is that on that morning of 28th of July, Casey arrived with the other Americans, in a sort of bunch."

There was also the peculiar notation—"came at 4 p.m."—to explain. On that point, Chadwick spoke as if his memory were again crystal clear. "In the afternoon, for the session on Russia after lunch, I looked around the room from my desk and saw Mr. Casey wasn't there," Chadwick said. "An empty chair. So I put a check through that, marking him absent. And then he reappeared at four o'clock, which was around the time when we would have been breaking up to have tea. I just annotated the chart, 'came at 4 p.m.' Now that evening, he attended the reception given by the trustees and there's a photograph of him which has been published."

On the next day, Tuesday, July 29, Casey was marked in attendance the whole day. He gave his paper, on the value of intelligence operations and wartime deception, in the morning. "He simply read the paper through in a deep voice that was rather difficult to hear from where I was sitting," Chadwick recalled. "I had hoped we might get a little more new material and that it might even be more audible." Sometime on July 30, Chadwick said, he was informed that Casey had left the conference for good.

But how reliable was Chadwick's interpretation of his charts? His memory had been enhanced—and possibly influenced—by the press interviews that he had done in the months since the ABC *Nightline* report. Chadwick initially had no clear recollection of Casey on the first day. Now Chadwick could picture Casey and the other Americans arriving "in sort of a bunch."

Yet, *Frontline* producer Gilmore had found one of the Americans with a particularly strong recollection about Casey. That historian was UCLA professor Robert Dallek, who had first notified Congress that Casey had attended the London conference. Dallek was scheduled to give one of the morning talks on the first day of the conference, Monday, July 28. Dallek recognized Casey's importance in the 1980 campaign and wanted Casey to hear his speech. Dallek had been on the lookout for Casey that first morning. After returning from London, Ross and I scheduled an interview with Professor Dallek in New York City.

"I was on the program the first morning, that Monday morning," Dallek told Ross and me. "And I have a very strong memory of not seeing Mr. Casey at the conference that morning, because I was giving my talk at 11:30 in the morning and I looked for him in the room. I remember looking for him in the room. I knew he was a prominent figure. I was interested to know whether he was going to be there or not. And the room wasn't that crowded. And it wasn't as if it were an audience that you looked out at, but there was a long table and people sitting around the table and people sitting on the sides of the room."

Dallek said Casey did not arrive until late that first day. "I remember meeting him late that afternoon, because we walked around the Imperial War Museum together and Arthur Funk was there and that's when that famous photograph was taken of Arthur Funk and myself and Casey," said Dallek, speaking in a slight Brooklyn accent. "And I believe that was sometime around six o'clock in the afternoon." The next morning, Casey joined Dallek for breakfast at the Royal Army Medical College before going to the second day of the conference. Casey gave his talk that morning. "And I would say that by Tuesday afternoon, he disappears from my radar scope," Dallek said.

Dallek's memory, which conformed to the recollections of the other Americans we interviewed, also matched Chadwick's curious note: "came at 4 p.m." In Dallek's version, that would have been when Casey first arrived at the conference, not when he returned from lunch.

But what about Chadwick's check marks for the morning of the first day? Dallek had one other recollection that could help explain them. The American historian remembered that someone had remarked on the first morning that Casey was on his way to the conference, but had been delayed because "he had to see people or something to that effect."

When I called Chadwick to see if Dallek's memory of an announcement might explain the check marks, Chadwick said he had no recollection of any announcement. But he said if one had been made, it would have been "very feasible" that he would have put check marks across Casey's line for the whole day. If Casey had then shown up at 4 p.m., that arrival time would fit with both Chadwick's note and the Americans' recollections.

So the *Newsweek-New Republic* certainty seemed misplaced in two ways. First, Chadwick's notations did not provide conclusive proof that Casey sat through the morning session on July 28. Several witnesses, including a distinguished historian with a clear memory, were stating that Casey was not there—and there was a feasible explanation for Chadwick's check marks for the morning. He could have been expecting Casey, following the announcement that Dallek recalled, and then noted on the records the time of the GOP campaign chief's actual arrival: 4:00 p.m.

If Casey were missing on the morning and afternoon of July 28, he would have had adequate time to fly to and from Madrid. So the possibility of two meetings on consecutive mornings could not be ruled out for July 27 and 28.

Another hole in the magazines' logic was their unquestioned reliance on the notation in the calendar belonging to Casey's secretary. As Craig Unger argued, the uncorroborated notation about Casey being in Washington on July 26 could not be judged definitive evidence either. The secretary's calendar had other obvious gaps: it had made no mention of Casey's trip to London for the historical conference. So there was room for doubt. The secretary, Barbara Hayward, refused our repeated requests for an interview.

While not proof that Casey had gone to Madrid, the absence of definitive evidence on his whereabouts for those days in late July prevented an ironclad conclusion that Jamshid Hashemi was a liar—or that the October Surprise allegations were, without doubt, a myth.

Though the big question remained "Where was Bill?" our investigation stumbled over a footnote to another question that we thought had been safely discarded: "Where was George?" As Ross and I worked on the *Frontline* update, I received a copy of a recent letter sent to Congress by a former State Department foreign service officer named David Henderson. In 1980, Henderson was stationed in Washington and recalled a strange conversation with a journalist.

This journalist came to his house on October 18, 1980, according to Henderson, and asked about a hot tip—that the Republican vice presidential candidate George Bush was on his way to Paris to meet with Iranian representatives about the hostages. Years later, the weekend of October 18–19, of course, would be the commonly cited date for the alleged Paris meetings. Henderson said he did not remember the name of the journalist, but did recall that he worked for the *Chicago Tribune*.

"It was almost as though he was saying something was so hot, he was excited because he had this piece of information or intelligence that something was about to happen right then," Henderson told a *Frontline* reporter in fall 1991. "He blurted out excitedly that George Bush was going to Paris, or was on his way, or was essentially there already. It was clear to me that it was an imminent thing that was about to happen right that weekend, to meet with the Iranians to talk about the release of the American hostages."

The Henderson lead was hard to take seriously. Here was a supposedly contemporaneous account of a rumor that George Bush was flying to the same city on the same day for the same purpose as October Surprise figures would allege years later. I presumed that Henderson was a kook.

"This probably doesn't mean anything," I told *Frontline* senior producer Martin Smith, "but if you're looking for leads to run down, maybe it's worth a few calls." Smith turned over the Henderson information to producer Jim Gilmore, who was proving himself a diligent and tenacious investigator. Gilmore came through again. Through a process of elimination, he determined that the *Chicago Tribune* reporter who had talked with Henderson must be John Maclean, who had worked in the paper's Washington bureau in 1980 but had since returned to Chicago.

Maclean initially had no recollection of the meeting with Henderson. But the journalist later confirmed that he had spoken to the State Department officer in that time frame about a rumored Bush trip to Paris. Ross and I decided that we should get Maclean's account on tape. So we flew to Chicago and arranged for an interview with the veteran reporter. Maclean was a tall man with graying hair. He wore a neatly trimmed goatee and a dark business suit. He was the son of noted author Norman Maclean, whose best known work was *A River Runs Through It*.

"I was told by someone who was in a secondary position in Republican circles—I suppose that's a decent way to describe it—where he would have access to information of this kind, that Bush was planning or was on his way to Paris to discuss the hostage situation," Maclean remembered.

But when Maclean checked out the lead, the Bush campaign flatly denied it. "I know I took some steps to check it out," Maclean recalled. "I can't remember who responded to me from official circles. I can't remember that. I know I got a response. I mean it was a dismissive one." With that, the reporter concluded that he had gotten a bum tip and dropped the story.

At our request, Maclean went back to his original source, whose name he refused to divulge. Maclean said the Republican insider claimed to have no recollection of a Bush trip or even of telling Maclean about one.

But the Henderson-Maclean story did establish one important point: rumors about an October Surprise meeting and even Bush's participation did not start years later. They dated back to 1980 and to the heat of the Reagan-Carter presidential campaign. That suggested that if the later October Surprise witnesses were lying, they were at least drawing from stories that pre-dated their own dubious arrivals on the scene.

22

WHEELING AND DEALING

Federal Express brought a large box to my front door. The package, sent by *Frontline*, contained FBI records of the bureau's four-year investigation of Cyrus Hashemi, the Iranian financial wheeler-dealer and alleged Reagan-Carter double agent. The thousands of pages of documents, loosely bound in about 15 volumes, had been released under a Freedom of Information Act request.

I opened the box, took a look inside at the piles of heavily censored pages, and sighed. Besides interviews in prisons, one of my least favorite tasks is reading raw government files which contain blacked-out text.

During the Iran-contra affair, many of the records that raised hopes of answering vexing questions had been so heavily "redacted"—as the lawyers say—that the documents were more frustrating than helpful. Sometimes they were even dangerous, because they might lead a reporter to suspect something that the censored portion would disprove. But contemporaneous documents have obvious advantages over witnesses. Documents do not suffer memory lapses, nor can the knowledge of one particular moment be embroidered with details from a later time.

In summer 1980, suspicious that Cyrus Hashemi was financing Iranian terrorists in the United States, the FBI had used new counter-terrorism laws to obtain court permission to bug Cyrus's New York office. The FBI planted listening devices in his office at 9 West 57th Street in midtown Manhattan in early September 1980. The FBI also monitored his telephone calls.

The FBI eavesdropping found no evidence that Cyrus was a paymaster for terrorists. Nor did the intercepts settle the issue of William Casey's Madrid meetings which allegedly took place in late July and mid-August before the bugs were installed. But the wiretaps did reveal Cyrus's activities as an intermediary for the Carter administration and his secret work arranging military shipments to Iran. It was that later discovery that prompted a separate FBI probe into Hashemi's possible violation of the Arms Export Control Act.

But more important to our investigation, the documents shed new light on Cyrus's shadowy financial world. From the FBI documents, Cyrus Hashemi seemed to be at the nexus of major international financial intrigue in 1980. He also was knotting his business ties with personal friends of Reagan-Bush campaign chief William Casey. The most important Hashemi entrée to Casey's inner circle was John Shaheen, Casey's old OSS chum and longtime alter ego. I had known that Cyrus and Shaheen had crossed paths in 1980, but I didn't know if their association was casual or close.

According to a *Wall Street Journal* article dated October 21, 1980, Cyrus had stepped forward with a $45 million bail-out deal that would have continued Shaheen family control over a bankrupt oil refinery that Shaheen had built on a rugged ocean cove at Come-by-Chance, Newfoundland. Cyrus's $45 million package would have allowed Shaheen's son, Bradford, to buy the refinery. Explaining the offer, Cyrus told the *Journal* that he wanted to expand his oil investments and "other satisfactory financing relationships" with the elder Shaheen.

But the Hashemi bail-out scheme did not save the refinery. The shoddily designed plant never produced a drop of gasoline and led to Canada's largest bankruptcy, leaving behind $600 million in debts. The Canadian taxpayers lost millions in investment guarantees, and angry Newfoundland authorities were investigating possible fraud in Shaheen's construction of the refinery. So Cyrus's bail-out offer was rejected by a Newfoundland bankruptcy court unwilling to gamble again on John Shaheen and his oil refinery pipe dream. But as the dispute wore on, the refinery's bankruptcy pushed Shaheen closer to the brink of financial ruin.

The FBI intercepts picked up conversations about the Come-by-Chance deal and a cryptic connection to the CIA. "On October 16, 1980," an FBI cable read, "Cyrus Hashemi with [two unidentified Americans] discussed the purchase of a refinery in Newfoundland in concert with [one line deleted]. Discussion was centered on legal points to be directed to CIA if he took the stand in defense of an applicant to be presented before a judge on the financial status of Hashemi and [unidentified American] group." A CIA spokesman told me that he had no idea what the "legal points" might have been.

Cyrus had other curious business schemes under way in fall 1980. Most centered around the First Gulf Bank and Trust Company, a merchant bank that was the flagship of his financial network. Cyrus took pains to shield those activities from official oversight. First Gulf was incorporated as an offshore bank in the Netherlands Antilles, though its offices were in New York and London. He also circumvented New York State legal requirements that he register First Gulf as a bank in New York.

Cyrus saw himself as a well-connected mover and shaker who could flout the rules. According to FBI intercepts, Cyrus boasted of interlocking relationships between two of his companies, First Gulf and Yorkhouse Trading Company, and two high-flying Middle Eastern financial institutions: the Arabian Overseas Corporation and the Bank of Credit and Commerce International. In 1980, with strong backing from the Persian Gulf royal families and the chiefs of Saudi intelligence, BCCI already was emerging as a leading bank in the Islamic world. BCCI also was expanding into Great Britain and the United States. BCCI's modus operandi was to buy influence and assist sensitive Western intelligence operations by funneling money. The bank collapsed in a messy financial-political scandal in July 1991.

The FBI also found that, by fall 1980, Cyrus's complex business interests had merged with his responsibilities brokering an end to the embassy hostage crisis. One of Cyrus's assignments from Iran's Islamic government, the FBI discovered, was to track down the hidden wealth of the late shah of Iran and his royal family. Cyrus considered the recovery of this money vital to the settlement of the hostage crisis. "The key issue [in the hostage impasse] seems to be the U.S. willingness to assist Iran in identifying and returning the shah's assets," Cyrus was recorded as saying in one intercepted communication. Meanwhile, John Shaheen, Cyrus's business associate and Casey's pal, was known to be a close friend of Princess Ashraf, the twin sister of Iran's deposed shah.

Even earlier in our investigation, I had come to suspect that Cyrus's business relationship with Casey's chum John Shaheen might rest at the heart of Cyrus's alleged doubledealing. If he did have a number of "satisfactory financing relationships" with Shaheen—as Cyrus had told the *Wall Street Journal*—could these business deals have captured Cyrus's personal loyalty? Could money explain Cyrus's reputed betrayal of the Carter White House as alleged by his older brother, Jamshid?

So as *Frontline*'s follow-up program on the October Surprise was nearing completion, I was on the lookout for associates of John Shaheen who could shed some light on the shadowy business schemes between Shaheen and Cyrus Hashemi. My first break came when *Frontline* received a call from a Canadian businessman who had operated on the fringes of Shaheen's financial world. He put me in touch with two close associates of John Shaheen, and they agreed to meet me.

I caught the shuttle again to New York and took a cab to the Union Club on Park Avenue. Entering the club's spacious lobby, I checked my coat and asked directions to the lounge. The Union Club is a place of hushed tones, high ceilings, and tuxedoed waiters. It is a woody bastion of Republican privilege and power. Portraits of all the GOP presidents hang from the walls of the stately receiving rooms. One side room is filled with elaborate displays of painted toy soldiers massed for historical battles.

In a quiet lounge off the restaurant I was greeted by two of John Shaheen's closest associates. They had agreed to meet me for lunch as long as I would not mention their names publicly. Over drinks, we talked about the October Surprise controversy. Both thought the theory that Casey and Shaheen secretly negotiated with Iranians was fully in character for the two OSS veterans.

"But they would have been trying to get the hostages out," the First

Associate said. "They would have wanted to show up Carter." After all, Casey and Shaheen had excelled in the ruthless espionage game of World War II. Casey operated in London and ran spies behind Nazi lines in Europe. Shaheen had headed a secret mission that persuaded Italy's naval high command to surrender.[1]

"They never stopped being spies," the First Associate said. "Those were the formative days of their lives."

Shaheen and Casey stayed close over the decades that followed. Unlike many OSS officers who were recruited from Ivy League schools and who sported aristocratic pedigrees, Casey and Shaheen came from modest backgrounds. Shaheen was an immigrant from Lebanon, and Casey's father had been a Tammany Hall bureaucrat. After World War II, Shaheen and Casey relied on their OSS connections the way other ambitious men would count on their prep school ties to get ahead. The OSS experience opened doors for Casey and Shaheen into the world of high finance and power politics.

In the late 1960s and early 1970s, both Casey and Shaheen worked for the Nixon administration and were proud to claim President Nixon as a personal friend. The Second Associate said a week would never go by without Casey and Shaheen exchanging views on a wide range of topics, either in person or over the phone. Those conversations continued through the election year of 1980 and included discussions about the ongoing Iranian hostage crisis, the Second Associate said.

In private life, as in wartime, Casey and Shaheen also had much in common. As freewheeling businessmen, the pair shared an interest in oil and chancy investments. They were entrepreneurs ready to take gambles and cut corners. Both men had made and lost fortunes in the oil business. Shaheen, particularly, loved the oil trade's fast money and back-room deals. A favorite Shaheen saying was: "Have oil, will travel."

But Shaheen achieved his first business coup after World War II with the mass-marketing of airplane flight insurance. Shaheen first sewed up exclusive contracts at airports around the country and then persuaded Mutual of Omaha to step in as his partner. To boost profits, Shaheen urged the home

---

[1] William Casey, *The Secret War Against Hitler* (New York: Berkley Books, 1989), p. 76.

office to dress insurance saleswomen in low-cut blouses, the First Associate said. "He wanted the boobs to show."

Flight insurance made Shaheen a millionaire, but he was eager to branch out into oil and other more lucrative investments. When Shaheen decided to sell his share in the flight insurance business to Mutual of Omaha, he gave the assignment to one of his bookkeepers, Roy Furmark. It would be Furmark's moment to shine. Furmark negotiated a higher price than Shaheen had expected. Returning to New York, the bookkeeper earned a gold star pasted on his office mailbox—and a position of greater responsibility in Shaheen's enterprises. Through Shaheen, Furmark would also become a personal friend of William Casey and later a figure in the Iran-contra scandal.

Shaheen's biggest dream was to build an oil refinery in Canada, a move that would enhance his reputation in the fast-money oil world. The politically well-connected Shaheen convinced the provincial government of Newfoundland to back the refinery project with loan guarantees. Casey assisted the project as a trusted Shaheen adviser and legal counsel. In the 1970s, Casey even traveled with Shaheen to Kuwait to negotiate a source of oil for the refinery.

But the refinery was an engineering disaster. The chemical process for refining the oil never worked properly. Shaheen rented the Queen Elizabeth II luxury liner for a gala opening off the windswept rocky shore of Newfoundland. But the celebration was the refinery's high point. It soon became clear that the project was a white elephant.

A furious Canadian government struck back, trying to recover some of its massive losses. By the late 1970s, the refinery was in bankruptcy court, and an investigation had started into possible fraud. Canada froze Shaheen's bank accounts. "There were restraining orders everywhere," recalled the Second Associate. But Shaheen was not a man to take misfortune lying down.

In early 1980, Shaheen fast-talked his way through the luxury hotels of Paris and London. He wined and dined Arab oil sheikhs, worked his worldwide Rolodex of rich contacts, and never let on that he was nearly broke. During this same period of Shaheen's financial duress over the Newfoundland bankruptcy, Cyrus Hashemi entered the picture as an important Shaheen partner. "Suddenly, Cyrus was on the scene," the

Second Associate recalled over another round of drinks at the Union Club.[2]

By spring 1980, Cyrus and Shaheen were already close, so close that in early June, Cyrus was hard at work trying to save Shaheen's financial skin. Shaheen sent a personal assistant to London with a power of attorney to arrange a desperately needed loan, the Second Associate said. Shaheen told the assistant to contact Cyrus Hashemi, who took the assistant to the London offices of BCCI and Marine Midland Bank seeking $3 million. Cyrus negotiated the loan for Shaheen on his second try at Marine Midland. Channeled through a front company, the money enabled Shaheen to pay his short-term bills and stay afloat, the Second Associate said.

After examining some of the FBI documents that I had brought along, the associates filled in an important missing link for understanding the documents. "Mid Ocean," a firm listed in the FBI intercepts as doing business with Hashemi's First Gulf Bank and Trust, was, in fact, a Bermuda-based front company controlled by Shaheen.[3] The FBI documents showed a $2.5 million deposit from "Mid Ocean" into Cyrus's bank in summer 1980, possibly the Marine Midland loan minus $500,000 to pay business expenses. Several months later, the FBI intercepts showed, Mid Ocean and First Gulf, "as partners, intend to open a bank in the United Kingdom with capital investment of $10 million with $5 million from each partner."

So Shaheen and Cyrus Hashemi were not just casual business acquaintances. By mid-1980, Shaheen so trusted Hashemi—or was so desperate—that he sought Cyrus's help in circumventing the Canadian court orders that had frozen Shaheen's bank accounts. It was Cyrus Hashemi who tossed the $3 million life preserver that kept Shaheen's head above water.

Neither the refinery bail-out nor the European bank worked out. But

---

[2] Another Shaheen friend told me that the Hashemi-Shaheen relationship dated back to 1979. This friend said Shaheen even introduced Cyrus Hashemi to the CIA, a contact that contributed to Hashemi's recruitment as a financial conduit to funnel CIA money to the U.S.-favored candidate in the 1980 Iranian presidential election.

[3] Bermuda's corporate records are unavailable to the public. But two other sources close to Shaheen confirmed that Mid Ocean was a Shaheen company.

Hashemi and Shaheen redirected their efforts toward the establishment of another bank, with Philippine interests. An FBI intercept discovered that in mid-October 1980, Hashemi deposited "a large sum of money" in a Philippine bank and planned to meet with Philippine representatives in Europe. The topic of the meeting: the creation of a new bank, possibly in the Caribbean. In late 1980, Shaheen also was negotiating with Filipinos about founding a bank in Hong Kong.

But where did Cyrus and Shaheen get this money for their wheeling-and-dealing? What happened to the millions that Cyrus had put into the refinery bail-out that Canada had rejected? And how might these high-roller schemes connect to the October Surprise mystery?

On a later trip to New York, I located a third Shaheen associate who I thought might hold some answers. This longtime business adviser admired Shaheen as a man of action who had great contacts and could get things done, just like Casey. "Here was a guy [Shaheen] who, because he was in the OSS, knew everybody," especially in the oil-rich Middle East, the Third Associate said. "John was staying in Paris in 1980 and always meeting with Arabs."

Shaheen's financial troubles were exacerbated by the oil embargo against Iran and the resulting disruptions in the world's energy markets. So Shaheen sounded out Arab leaders about ideas for ending the Iranian impasse. Shaheen also talked with Casey about the hostage crisis, and the two ex-spies plotted strategies to show up President Carter, the Third Associate said. But the pair's goal was not to delay the hostages' release.

"They wouldn't have done that in a million years," the Third Associate said. "Shaheen was trying to get those guys out. That's what John was talking about. He loved this clandestine stuff. He ate it up. These guys [Casey and Shaheen] were real patriots. They would have been involved in it under the table, over the table, and on the side of the table. But they would have done it."

While talking up plans with Casey to resolve the Iranian hostage crisis and possibly reopen access to Iranian crude, Shaheen also was maneuvering to escape his worsening financial crunch. In late 1980, as a spin-off from his negotiations with Cyrus Hashemi, Shaheen worked out arrangements to open a bank in Hong Kong. His partner was Herminio Disini, an in-law of the Philippines' First Lady Imelda Marcos. Disini was known as a top moneyman for President Ferdinand Marcos.[4]

Called the Hong Kong Deposit and Guaranty Company, the bank came into existence on January 22, 1981, with $20 million in capital funneled through Jean A. Patry, a Rockefeller-connected attorney in Geneva, Switzerland. The actual investor was unnamed in the formal transactions.

After the bank opened, Disini flew with Shaheen to the Philippines to meet directly with Marcos, the Third Associate told me. "Everybody knew that Disini was Marcos's bag man and that Marcos was in charge," the Third Associate said. "John had no doubt that he was meeting his new partner. For Marcos, the bank was a way to get his hands on some of the Arabs' Euro-petrodollars that were going to start moving out to the Far East."

Soon, Hong Kong Deposit and Guaranty, along with its sister financial institution, Tetra Finance, were attracting prominent Arabs to their boards of directors. Some of the Arabs had connections to BCCI. One director was Ghanim Al-Mazrouie, secretary-general of the Abu Dhabi Investment Authority, who simultaneously served on the board of BCCI and controlled 10 percent of BCCI's shares.

Another Hong Kong Deposit and Guaranty director was Hassan Yassin, a Saudi businessman who is a cousin of financier Adnan Khashoggi and was a consultant to Shaheen on the ill-fated Newfoundland refinery. Yassin was also identified by former Saudi intelligence chief Kamal Adham as the person who recommended in 1979 that Financial General Bankshares, then owned by President Carter's first budget director, Bert Lance, would be a good target for a BCCI takeover.

During its two-year existence, the Hong Kong bank took in tens of

---

[4] In the mid-1980's, Disini was accused of accepting kickbacks on construction of a $2 billion nuclear reactor in the Philippines. According to Philippine government documents, Disini deposited into a Swiss bank $11 million in commissions from the Westinghouse reactor deal. When dictator Ferdinand Marcos was ousted in 1986, Disini fled to Europe, where he reportedly moved into a castle outside of Vienna. Curiously, a principal U.S. government proponent of the Philippine nuclear reactor was William Casey when he served as president of the Export-Import Bank in 1975. (Raymond Bonner, *Waltzing with a Dictator*, [New York: Vintage Books, 1988], p. 267; "Manila Out to Prove U.S. Firms Paid Bribes," *Chicago Tribune*, April 8, 1986, p. C1.)

millions in Arab oil money, which either passed on to other banks or was shuffled around a host of shell companies before disappearing. The Third Associate said large sums were routinely funneled into accounts belonging to a shadowy American named Mel Gordy. "This money was just disappearing," the Third Associate told me. "There was no collateral or nothing. Shaheen never fully understood what Gordy was doing." Much of the bank's money disappeared into movie projects and mining deals involving Gordy, while other funds ended up in the Philippines, the Third Associate said.

In 1983, Hong Kong Deposit and Guaranty, Tetra Finance, and other affiliated companies collapsed amid allegations of fraud. The initial $20 million investment vanished, as did many of the other deposits. The bankruptcy trustees sued John Shaheen, seeking $24 million. The trustees also sought repayment of a $1.8 million loan made to Shaheen's son shortly after the bank opened in January 1981. The total losses from the bank's collapse exceeded $100 million.

The Marcos connection, revealed in the Hong Kong bank, was an intriguing subplot to the October Surprise mystery. When Marcos's 21-year reign tottered in 1986, President Reagan dispatched Sen. Paul Laxalt to Manila to advise the dictator. Laxalt, a Nevada Republican and longtime Reagan political ally, had served as chairman of Reagan's 1980 presidential campaign. He may have had that history in mind during discussions about Marcos's shaky future.

After Marcos's ouster in March 1986, political opponents ransacked the files of the deposed dictator and his cronies. The anti-Marcos forces claimed to discover one letter, allegedly written by Marcos's executive assistant Victor Nituda. It described Laxalt's negotiations over the terms of Marcos's exile and a purported White House demand that sensitive Filipino files be turned over to the Reagan administration.

Laxalt "expects all documents checklisted during his last visit or the deal is off," the letter read. One of the files cited was entitled "1980 SEC-014, Funds to Casey." Another was "1980 SEC-015, Reagan Funds Not Used."[5]

---

[5] Gary Thompson and Steve Kanighar, "Huge Hoard Funds Secret U.S. Operations," *Las Vegas Sun*, April 4, 1993. It was not clear what the file name "SEC" meant, but the other language suggested that Marcos had supplied secret funds to the 1980 Reagan-Bush campaign.

While the authenticity of the letter could not be confirmed, and Laxalt denied that destruction of documents was part of his mission, Marcos allegedly told confidantes during his exile in Hawaii that he had made $4 million contributions to Ronald Reagan's 1980 campaign. Lawyer Richard Hirschfeld secretly taperecorded Marcos boasting about his assistance to Reagan. Hirschfeld said Marcos also recounted how the CIA helped him ship his personal gold reserves out of the Philippines.[6]

The possibility that Marcos had supplied Casey with a secret slush fund in 1980 could explain Casey's stubborn support for the dictator during the early-to-mid 1980s, as Marcos turned increasingly brutal in suppressing dissent. Still, despite the Reagan administration's sympathies, a "people's power" uprising finally overthrew Marcos and installed Corazon Aquino as president. Marcos fled the Philippines for Hawaii, where he died in 1989.

But could Casey have made use of Marcos's alleged largesse in 1980 to finance undercover political operations? Could the Marcos money have gone into overseas bank accounts to bribe influential Iranian mullahs? Was the Hong Kong bank a means of paying Marcos back?

The allegation of Republican payoffs to the mullahs had surfaced occasionally during our investigation. For one, Ayatollah Khomeini's son-in-law Sadeq Tabatabai told Robert Ross and me in 1990 that he suspected that some radicals had been bribed to obstruct settlement of the hostage crisis. But Tabatabai quickly added, "I don't accuse all of them of collaboration in this. They were not all influenced or bought by the Republicans."

The strange connections tying Shaheen and Cyrus Hashemi into banking deals with Filipinos in late 1980 and early 1981 added new strands to the web of suspicion. Once the Hong Kong Deposit and Guaranty was in operation, Marcos and his cronies extracted tens of millions of dollars. But according to court records from the bankruptcy case, the Marcos group never invested any of its own money. Most deposits came from the Middle East, and the original $20 million investment arrived through the Swiss attorney Jean Patry. But Patry was only a front man for that money. Who was the silent partner? Why had elaborate safeguards been taken to protect the investor's confidentiality? Would knowing the answer resolve some of the October Surprise questions?

---

6 William Scott Malone, "The Golden Fleece," *Regardie's*, October 1988.

Hong Kong Deposit and Guaranty's original $20 million, it seemed, had its own intriguing history. The Third Associate told me that the $20 million used to capitalize the bank was part of the earlier $45 million package that Cyrus Hashemi had offered in the failed bail-out deal for Shaheen's Newfoundland refinery. It was also the same money that Hashemi and Shaheen had planned to invest in a joint bank in Europe.

But where did this money come from? Why was Shaheen, who was broke in June 1980, suddenly flush with mysterious backing through Cyrus Hashemi in September and October? Who was the unnamed benefactor?

The Third Associate was hesitant to talk about this secret. "I really can't say," he told me with a gleam in his eye that left no doubt this was a detail worth knowing. After a great deal of hemming and hawing, he finally relented. "The $20 million came from Princess Ashraf, the shah's sister." The money was part of the Pahlavi family fortune.

I was startled by this disclosure, but I was even more puzzled. My mind couldn't compute how this new fact might add to the complex equation. Why would the strong-willed deposed princess of Iran be investing $20 million in schemes with John Shaheen and Cyrus Hashemi? The Third Associate didn't have a very good answer. "It was funny money," he said with a shrug. It was, he believed, money that the Islamic revolutionary government was claiming as its own.

Later, I located a fourth Shaheen associate who confirmed that Princess Ashraf was indeed the mysterious investor in the Hong Kong bank.[7] This Fourth Associate said Shaheen and Ashraf had long been neighbors on fashionable Park Avenue in New York City. But Shaheen would say little about her. The Fourth Associate said Shaheen jealously guarded the princess's privacy and his financial relationship with her. "When it comes to Ashraf, I'm a cemetery," Shaheen once told the Fourth Associate.

But what was most striking about the Ashraf money and the Shaheen connection was the conflict of interest that it created for Cyrus Hashemi. In October 1980, while President Carter was desperately trying to

---

[7] All told, I confirmed Princess Ashraf's role as the Shaheen benefactor with a half-dozen sources. In a call to Geneva, I asked Jean Patry, the Rockefeller-connected lawyer who handled the investment, if he could confirm that Princess Ashraf had invested $20 million in the bank. He answered succinctly in a way that precluded a follow-up: "You are talking to a Swiss lawyer," Patry said. "Our professional rules are very, very strict."

break the hostage impasse, one of his key middlemen was entering into lucrative financial schemes with William Casey's best friend, John Shaheen. During this period, Casey also met with David Rockefeller, a Pahlavi financial adviser. On September 11, visitor logs showed Rockefeller arriving at Casey's office with three aides, including Archibald Roosevelt, the CIA veteran who helped Miles Copeland draft a never-implemented hostage-rescue plan in March.

The Ashraf millions had another implication. Cyrus Hashemi was the man assigned by Iran's Islamic government to locate the shah's family money. The recovery of that money was regarded as crucial to the resolution of the hostage crisis. The shah's fortune was one of the last sticking points in the hostage negotiations. Now we were told that Cyrus Hashemi had gotten his hands on some of the money. But instead of pressing for its return to Iran, he and Shaheen eagerly sought to invest it for themselves. The new evidence established a simple motive for Cyrus Hashemi to betray Jimmy Carter—greed.

Although Cyrus Hashemi's name did not show up in the Hong Kong bank's records, the Iranian financier continued his multi-million-dollar investments with Shaheen into the early 1980s. Hashemi's Gulf Trust bank lent Shaheen's Mid Ocean front company $3.5 million on January 7, 1981, just as negotiations for creating the Hong Kong bank were nearing completion, according to Shaheen's personal business records.

There was also the question: Why would the deposed Iranian royal family risk $20 million in such chancy investments as a bankrupt oil refinery or a fly-by-night bank? Neither could have looked very promising or safe. But one possible explanation was that the princess was putting up protection money for the rest of her fortune, a treasure estimated in the hundreds of millions—possibly billions—of dollars. Shaheen and Hashemi could play with the $20 million if they helped ensure that the Iranian mullahs didn't get the rest. A decade later, after the elections of Presidents Reagan and Bush, the bulk of the shah's money had not been returned to Iran.

The Shaheen-Hashemi business relationship also added some credibility to Jamshid Hashemi's story about Madrid meetings. Jamshid said he first met Casey at Washington's Mayflower Hotel in March 1980. Jamshid claimed that Casey was accompanied by Roy Furmark, Shaheen's long-time assistant. Jamshid told us at our lunch in London that by spring 1980, he knew Furmark through Cyrus's business dealings with Shaheen.

Yet, Jamshid's Furmark line clashed with Furmark's earlier testimony to the Iran-contra congressional investigators in 1987. Then Furmark claimed that he had not met Cyrus Hashemi until 1983. If that were true, Jamshid's link to Furmark through Cyrus in 1980 would have been impossible.

But when I tracked down Furmark at his home in Vermont in early 1992, he told a different story. Furmark now recalled meeting Cyrus Hashemi not in 1983 but four years earlier, in 1979, on an oil deal in the Bahamas. Furmark's revised story was that in 1980, he and Cyrus were working together on real estate and oil transactions. "We tried a number of financial things—an oil company in Oklahoma, real estate in New York—but we weren't successful in those years," Furmark told me.

Furmark, a Scandinavian by both heritage and temperament, turned distant and vague when I asked about Jamshid Hashemi's claim of meeting Casey at the Mayflower Hotel in March 1980. "Jamshid has his own view of things," Furmark answered opaquely. When I pressed the issue, Furmark responded, "I met him [Jamshid], but much later." Furmark did not say exactly how much later. He then cut off the telephone interview. But I could not forget that Furmark had given the Iran-contra investigators a later date for meeting Cyrus than he was now admitting to me.

Without doubt, John Shaheen was one of Casey's true confidantes. Shaheen may even have helped rally Casey to Ronald Reagan's banner. According to the Fourth Shaheen Associate, Casey and Shaheen once engaged in a frank political debate about the pluses and minuses of the competing GOP candidates in late 1979. Over dinner at the swank 21 Club in New York, Shaheen objected to Casey's early preference for ex-Texas Governor John Connally. Shaheen argued that Connally's perceived pro-Arab tilt in the Arab-Israeli dispute would be a hard sell politically.

Shaheen and Casey then went down the list of possible Republican candidates. "They settled on Reagan by a process of elimination," the Fourth Associate said. "But Shaheen had also known Reagan from childhood in Tampico, Illinois. Shaheen called him 'Dutch.' Reagan used to beat Shaheen up when they were kids. So they became friends."[8] Shaheen helped win Bill Casey to Ronald Reagan's cause.

There was a nagging question that undercut suspicions that Cyrus Hashemi had secretly aided Shaheen and Casey on any hostage initiative: If Cyrus had been the double-agent that his brother Jamshid alleged, wouldn't Cyrus have revealed the October Surprise secret when he came under FBI investigation again in the early 1980s? We could find no direct evidence that Cyrus blackmailed Casey over October Surprise—a point against believing in the conspiracy. But Cyrus did succeed in avoiding prosecution for arms smuggling. Indeed, the Iranian financier seemed to benefit from a string of actions under the Reagan administration.

In February 1981, the new Justice Department ordered the wiretaps yanked from Cyrus Hashemi's office. At the time, some FBI agents complained that Cyrus was scouting the U.S. market for missiles that could be used by the Iranian air force. At least a few wanted to listen in. But the field office was ordered to terminate its electronic surveillance. Though losing the wiretaps, the FBI vowed to "vigorously pursue prosecution in view of the wealth of information obtained that subject and others have and are in conspiracy to sell military armaments to Iran which are obtained from United States suppliers."

But obstacles soon appeared. A New York FBI proposal for a search warrant to seize documents from Hashemi's office got lost in a blizzard of technical objections. In April 1981, the Justice Department questioned the value of the case, doubting that a conviction would lead to jail time. "A fine will give Hashemi an aura of respectability," one cable argued implausibly.

According to a January 29, 1982, internal FBI memo, a review of the evidence by senior professional staff at the Justice Department "determined that there is a strong case for prosecution against Cyrus Hashemi." But Reagan's first Attorney General, William French Smith, withheld

---

[8] Though several of Shaheen's associates claimed that Shaheen had known Reagan for decades (since Reagan was a boy in Dixon, Illinois), Reagan would deny to congressional investigators having any recollection of ever meeting Shaheen.

approval, and the grand jury was postponed "because of national security considerations," an FBI memo said. The heavily censored document did not spell out what those "national security considerations" were.

But even two years later, as the wheels of justice turned slowly toward formally charging Cyrus Hashemi and others, the gears would jam again. On May 16, 1984, the FBI field agents complained that their hope of nabbing Cyrus when he returned to the United States was blocked by another Justice Department intervention. Cyrus had been scheduled to fly from London to New York on that day. He would be arrested on May 17. Those plans, however, went awry when the Justice Department insisted on alerting the target of the long probe.

"For information FBIHQ, Cyrus Hashemi cancelled his Concorde flight reservations to New York on May 16, 1984, at last minute," the New York FBI office reported. "Hashemis now obviously aware of prosecution plans due to exposure when DOJ deputy attorney general Lowell Jensen ordered USA, SDNY [U.S. attorney, southern district of New York] to discuss evidence and prosecution because he made such a commitment to Hashemi's attorney, former Attorney General Elliot Richardson, who obviously had Cyrus Hashemi notified."

The FBI agents noted sarcastically that other targets of the probe "will also receive the above DOJ-sponsored courtesy. . . . Obviously the arrests will not be announced if they do not occur which in final analysis is not likely. This case began on July 18, 1980 and because of above, results of a positive nature do not appear forthcoming despite the mammoth investigative effort put forth thus far."

But the headaches for the "mammoth investigative effort" were not over. Only a few days before the long-overdue indictments were scheduled, the FBI's terrorism section discovered that two wiretap tape recordings had disappeared. The loss of the tapes weakened the case and prevented the indictment of Hashemi's lawyer, Stanley Pottinger, a former Justice Department official during the Nixon and Ford administrations who collaborated with Cyrus on his Iran activities. But Cyrus Hashemi was finally indicted on July 18, 1984, a full four years after the case commenced.

The indictment also charged another brother, Reza, and several associates with conspiracy to ship military equipment to Iran in violation of U.S.

arms export control laws. The illegally shipped items included night vision equipment, military field communication wire, military rafts, outboard engines, radar electronics, and spare parts for aircraft. Jamshid Hashemi was later added to the indictment. Several of Cyrus's subordinates, including brother Reza, pled guilty and received brief jail terms. But Cyrus and Jamshid, alerted to the pending legal action and safely out of the country, escaped prosecution.

To clear up his legal problems, Cyrus stressed his past assistance to the CIA on Iran and again offered his services to the U.S. government. According to records uncovered by the Iran-contra investigations, Cyrus did convey, through Shaheen to Casey, an offer to help spring the U.S. hostages in Lebanon. Cyrus proposed bartering his influence with Tehran in exchange for dropping the charges against him. Subsequently, Cyrus did work with Shaheen and Furmark in early 1985 on the Lebanon hostage crisis. Another participant in those early Iran-contra schemes was Iranian emissary Hassan Karrubi, the brother of radical cleric Mehdi Karrubi.

Cyrus eventually avoided prosecution by acting as an undercover agent in the sting operation that netted 17 alleged arms dealers from Europe, the United States, and Israel in April 1986—the so-called "merchants of death" case. It was the same sting which angered Israel's conservative leaders and, according to Ari Ben-Menashe, led to his efforts to leak the Iran arms story to the American press. At least in that way, the October Surprise mystery had blended with the Iran-contra affair.

Cyrus died on July 21, 1986, from what was diagnosed as acute leukemia. But even earlier, his American partner, the freewheeling ex-spy John Shaheen, had passed from the scene. Beset by financial calamity and still trying to salvage his bankrupt refinery, Shaheen succumbed to a battle against liver cancer on November 1, 1985. William Casey was one of the mourners at Shaheen's funeral.

23

No Exit

Robert Ross and I were making what we hoped would be our last trip to MCC-New York. It was late December 1991, almost two years since I had entered the same prison and gone through the same screening procedures to meet with Ari Ben-Menashe. We had located one more witness who claimed to hold one more piece of the puzzle.

The new witness was a South African arms dealer named Dirk Stoffberg. He, like some others in the October Surprise story, had been caught in an entrapment net dropped by the ever-trawling U.S. Customs Service. Stoffberg had been charged with trying to sell silver-plated ceremonial automatic pistols to Chile. At the time of the attempted sale, the military government of Chile was on the U.S. arms embargo list.

Stoffberg protested his innocence and complained it was unfair to arrest a South African for violating a U.S. foreign policy initiative. But he was nabbed in Germany and extradited to New York. Like Ben-Menashe, Stoffberg was a foreign national denied bail because he was considered a high risk to flee.

Told of Ben-Menashe's success in beating the federal charges against him, Stoffberg retained the same attorney, Tom Dunn. A low-key lawyer whose practice relied heavily on court referrals, Dunn recommended to Stoffberg that he cooperate with authorities and accept a plea bargain. Dunn recognized that if Stoffberg chose to go to trial, he would face a year in prison awaiting his day in court and still run the risk of losing. If he entered a guilty plea, he would likely be out in three or four months counting his time already served. Not surprisingly, Stoffberg was willing to plead guilty.

But Stoffberg was also ready to talk about the October Surprise—or at least the little portion he claimed to know. Stoffberg said he had new information about William Casey's whereabouts in 1980. Dunn suggested that Stoffberg talk to us and to congressional investigators.

Lugging the camera, tripod, and sound equipment, we were led to a small common room in the prison. Because we were filming an interview rather than just talking to an inmate, the prison put us in a larger room than the one where I first met Ben-Menashe. Hand-made Christmas decorations—green paper cut-out Christmas trees—were taped to the wall in a pathetic attempt to capture the holiday spirit. As in the small rooms, the acoustics were terrible. Every sound reverberated off the concrete walls, and the radiators would rumble on and off.

Stoffberg was led in through a door from the cellblock. He was a slight, wiry man with a close-cropped white beard and graying hair. He carried himself with military bearing and spoke in a clipped fashion. Between his South African accent and the poor acoustics, he was hard to understand. His story, too, was vague on dates and other details.

"It was during the summer of 1980. Some colleagues of mine were instrumental in assisting the release of three British hostages," Stoffberg said. "We used the kind offices of the Swedish Embassy and had to deliver various arms to the Iranians. As a result of this, I was contacted by the Brits. I went to London in the summer of 1980. I was booked into the Carlton Tower Hotel. I stayed for about a day or two and I was told [by British intelligence] I must leave. I was taken by a British official to the Capital Hotel in Knightsbridge."

Both the Carlton Tower Hotel and the Capital Hotel are upscale hotels in the stylish Knightsbridge section of London. The Capital is known for its excellent French restaurant and is located within a short walk of Harrods, the pricy British department store. Stoffberg said he was told to stay at the Capital and wait for a call. The call came several days later, the South African remembered. The British officials brought over a tall, blond-haired German who was introduced as Reiner Jacobi. Jacobi was supposedly assisting U.S. intelligence on the hostage issue.

Jacobi wanted to know if the South Africans could help in freeing the American embassy hostages in Tehran, Stoffberg said. The South African responded positively, and the two men discussed the matter for awhile. Jacobi suggested that there might be a follow-up meeting with an important American.

"Reiner came to pick me up the next evening and took me to the Churchill Hotel," Stoffberg then said. "It was about 8:30 and he introduced me there to a man whom he called Mr. Casey—a tall man, balding and slightly stooped. He was sitting at a table alone. I joined him. We had dinner. It lasted about three hours."

Stoffberg said Casey wanted to know about the South African contacts inside Iran. "I said, 'Certainly, we'll talk to the people concerned and give whatever cooperation we could.' " Stoffberg claimed Casey's goal seemed to be to arrange as early a release of the 52 American hostages as possible. Casey specifically asked about South Africa's G-5 and G-6 cannons, which would have been attractive for Iran's military needs, Stoffberg said.

"And Mr. Casey was looking for a way to get the hostages out, not keep them in?" I asked.

"Most definitely," Stoffberg answered. "He wanted them released. We had to use whatever methods we could with the Iranians, and the Iranians wanted weapons."

While Stoffberg could not supply a date for the meeting, his lawyer gave us hotel receipts showing that Stoffberg had stayed at the Carlton Tower from August 11 to 14, 1980. Stoffberg claimed he did not have a bill from the Capital because that expense was paid by the British. Stoffberg's passports also revealed an entry at London's Heathrow Airport for August 11. But there was no stamp for his departure. There was also no entry stamp giving the date when he returned to South Africa. I found a boarding pass for a regularly scheduled return flight to Johannesburg, but it, too, revealed no date of departure.

Based on his account and the Carlton Tower receipt, the date of the Casey meeting presumably would have been on or about August 17 or 18. But I could not verify that Stoffberg had stayed in London after August 14, when he checked out of the Carlton Tower. None of the business telexes I was given by Stoffberg's lawyer had any date later than August 14. But one handwritten note suggested that August 14 was the day that the South African planned to leave London. The note referred to the flight to Johannesburg and the date August 14. Stoffberg could, of course, have delayed his departure because of the requested meeting, but I saw no hard evidence that he did.

As I sorted through Stoffberg's papers, I also got a phone number for Reiner Jacobi, who allegedly had picked up Stoffberg at the Capital Hotel. Jacobi was living in Hong Kong and was facing extradition to the United States on federal charges that he had leaked sensitive police information to drug traffickers. A freelance intelligence operative for several nations, including the Philippines and Australia, Jacobi had been assisting the U.S. government on a major marijuana-smuggling case when the Drug Enforcement Administration received allegations that Jacobi also was back-channeling government information to the smugglers. The U.S. Attorney in Miami obtained his indictment.

Though a man with a checkered and mysterious past, Jacobi had worked for the democratically elected Philippine government in its attempts to trace and recover Ferdinand Marcos's personal fortune. Jacobi achieved some notoriety in Europe for trying to break into Swiss bank computers to locate Marcos's gold bullion accounts. His activities landed Jacobi in legal trouble in Switzerland and Germany, two countries where high-finance computer hacking is not appreciated.[1]

When I reached Jacobi by telephone at his hotel in Hong Kong, he was polite but standoffish. He said he was not willing to say much about the events of 1980, but he agreed to discuss Stoffberg's allegations. "A meeting did take place between Mr. Casey and Mr. Stoffberg," Jacobi said with a slight German accent. "I picked him up at the Capital Hotel. Stoffberg had dealt with the Iranians and said he could deal with them again. All I will tell you is that a meeting did take place, period."

But as we talked, Jacobi added more details. He claimed that by 1980, he had known William Casey for a number of years. They had met through

---

[1] In summer 1992, a Hong Kong judge heard and rejected the U.S. motion for Jacobi's extradition. The judge ruled that the United States had presented insufficient evidence of Jacobi's guilt. Jacobi then returned to the Philippines and his work tracking down the Marcos fortune.

conservative European intelligence circles. Jacobi described himself as a
protege of Reinhardt Gehlen, Hitler's spymaster, who had later become
head of West Germany's CIA, the *Bundesnachrichtdienst*. Gehlen had
known Casey since the early 1970s when they met at an OSS convention in
Germany.

"Mr. Casey was a game player and always was," Jacobi said, claiming
that Casey had long kept a hand in intelligence matters even when a private
businessman.[2]

Jacobi said he "was contacted by Bill himself" to handle some security
work for the 1980 campaign and to help on the hostage issue. "I did it for
friendship," Jacobi told me. "I have helped in the past with other hostage
crises, but always behind the scenes." The new assignment, he said,
brought him from South Korea to London in mid-August 1980 to check out
the qualifications of a South African arms dealer named Stoffberg. Jacobi
said Casey sent a Saudi-owned BAC-111 private jet to pick him up.

Stoffberg was known to have good connections inside Iran through
family relations and the Swedish embassy. But Jacobi said the Americans
were not aware of Stoffberg's work on the British hostage question, as
Stoffberg believed. While the two men's accounts contained minor differences, Jacobi corroborated the central points of Stoffberg's tale.

"When I met Mr. Stoffberg at the Capital Hotel, I was not very impressed," Jacobi said in a dignified voice. "I recommended to Mr. Casey
that he not bother to meet with him. But Mr. Casey wanted to evaluate
every possible channel to Iran himself."

So, Jacobi claimed, he was sent back to the Capital Hotel to pick up
Stoffberg and bring the South African to have dinner with Casey. Jacobi
recalled the dinner taking place at the Grosvenor House or another hotel
that faced Hyde Park, not at the Churchill, which is nearby but not directly
on the park.

"I left the two of them to talk and I went for a walk in Hyde Park,"
Jacobi recalled. "I returned a couple of hours later and took Mr. Stoffberg

---

[2] A former CIA security officer told me that William Casey, while in private life, served as
a CIA-approved tax consultant for the spy agency's front companies and for undercover
agents. This CIA veteran also claimed that in the summer of 1980, he encountered Reiner
Jacobi at Casey's office in the Reagan-Bush campaign headquarters in Arlington, Virginia.

back to his hotel." Jacobi put the date for the London meeting on or about August 17.

But Jacobi's story had another new wrinkle. The intelligence freelancer said the trip to London was his second of that summer. The first had occurred several weeks earlier. Jacobi said he met Casey one evening in late July while Casey was attending the World War II historical conference at the Imperial War Museum.

Jacobi recalled Casey complaining about some Iranians he had met earlier on the same trip. "He got upset about the Iranians lying," Jacobi said. "Mr. Casey didn't believe he could trust the Iranian representatives with whom he had been dealing." But Jacobi added that Casey joked about what a wonderful cover the conference had given him. "I had the impression that Mr. Casey had just flown in from either Brussels or Madrid." But Jacobi offered no documentary support for his account.

Both Jacobi and Stoffberg agreed that Casey's initiative in the summer was aimed at freeing the hostages, not prolonging their captivity. Still, in the absence of better documentary evidence, Ross and I remained suspicious of the Stoffberg-Jacobi story. Though we knew that in Europe Stoffberg had been claiming for years some knowledge about the October Surprise story, he had not divulged any details until after his arrest on arms trafficking charges. Jacobi, too, was in legal hot water.

When congressional investigators interviewed Stoffberg, they insisted that he sign a sworn affidavit outlining his allegations. The South African did. In response to Stoffberg's affidavit, R. Spencer Oliver, chief counsel for the House Foreign Affairs Committee, expressed appreciation in a letter that was introduced by lawyer Tom Dunn at Stoffberg's sentencing hearing. The letter persuaded Stoffberg's judge to shave a few months off the South African's sentence. That move drew angry protests from the federal prosecutors. It also made Stoffberg the first October Surprise witness to benefit directly from his testimony.

Although our investigation continued to inch forward, the climate for examining the October Surprise questions had changed. The double-dip "debunking" by the *New Republic* and *Newsweek* emboldened Republicans to demand that all further congressional inquiry be dropped.

Republicans denounced the Democratic congressional staff and any member of the news media who still dared considered the possibility of a GOP-Iranian deal in 1980.

The *New Republic* had cast a cloud not only over the story with its personal attacks on witnesses—Ari Ben-Menashe, in particular—but also over the investigators, from Gary Sick to me. The nastiness scared away many who were examining the issue. To continue an honest inquiry opened journalists and government officials to ridicule sufficient to put a person's career at risk.

In the Senate, Republicans stepped up their attacks, filibustering a bill that would have authorized an official investigation. When the Democrats tried to break the filibuster, Senate Minority Leader Bob Dole invoked strict party discipline. Dole demanded that all Republicans oppose the Democratic attempt to force an up-or-down vote. President Bush personally joined in the legislative strategy meetings to kill the investigation. The Republican filibuster succeeded when the Democrats could muster only 51 votes, nine short of the 60-vote super-majority needed for cloture. The Democrats then withdrew the resolution.

Despite the Republicans' floor victory, an informal investigation was started by the Senate Foreign Relations subcommittee on the Middle East. The panel's Democratic chairman, Terry Sanford of North Carolina, and the ranking Republican, Jim Jeffords of Vermont, agreed that the October Surprise allegations should be settled, one way or the other. They used modest funds available to the panel to hire an outside counsel to do a limited investigation.

On February 5, 1992, the political fight shifted to the Democratic-controlled House, where partisan battling had long ago left the institution divided into two bitter camps. On one side was a strident band of Republicans, led by the likes of Minority Whip Newt Gingrich, and on the other, Establishment Democrats under the timid leadership of House Speaker Thomas Foley. For the October Surprise floor battle, the Republicans planned to take no prisoners. One after another, the GOP members rose to rail against a wasteful investigation into a discredited conspiracy theory. They armed themselves with posterboards highlighting the articles from *Newsweek* and the *New Republic*.

"This is about as smelly as it gets around here," complained Rep. Bob

McEwen, the Ohio Republican who got the assignment to lead his party's charge. "What we are going to do is another political effort to do a very partisan act in violation of all basic common principles and decency."

McEwen saw the real target of the probe as President Bush, who faced re-election in November and was slipping in the polls because of a stubborn recession. "Suppose they find out something. What do they intend to do with it?" McEwen asked rhetorically. "This select committee cannot legislate, and so it is a platform established for the partisan purpose: to smear George Bush so they can take every incompetent impostor and fraud, and let me quote the *New Republic*, the key sources, on whose word their story rests, are documented frauds and impostors representing themselves as intelligence operatives."

Taking aim at one of the Democratic staffers who had worked on the preliminary factfinding, the House Republicans opened fire on Spencer Oliver, who had written the letter informing the judge about Stoffberg's October Surprise testimony. Because the letter had prompted the federal judge to free Stoffberg several months early, the Republicans claimed that Oliver had set loose a dangerous criminal. They sought to make Oliver an example by seeking his formal investigation and censure.

"This isn't an arms-for-hostages scandal," fumed McEwen. "It's an arms-dealers-for-hogwash scandal. And this action has put the House of Representatives right in the middle of the slop."

Though little known outside Congress, Oliver had long been the target of Republican hostility. Tall, dapper, and tough, Oliver had personal experience with the worst of Republican election-year tactics. In June 1972, it was Oliver's telephone—at the Democratic National Committee offices housed in the Watergate complex—which was bugged by burglars working for Richard Nixon's re-election campaign. One theory why Oliver's phone was chosen was that he was so well-connected that much of the political intelligence and gossip that the Watergate burglars wanted to know would likely be discussed over his telephone.

Oliver also had bedeviled the Republicans during the Iran-contra affair. He was one of the staff investigators who pushed hardest for a thorough investigation of CIA director William Casey's domestic political apparatus. Casey had promoted a special White House bureaucracy, under the direction of a top CIA propagandist, to intimidate journalists and politicians who got in Casey's way. The overriding goal, according to internal White House memos, was to shape American perceptions about key Casey causes, such as the contra war in Nicaragua.

The existence of the so-called "public diplomacy" apparatus—run under Casey's supervision—was soft-pedaled in the congressional Iran-contra report to gain a measure of Republican support. But Oliver continued pressing to expose what he considered Casey's extralegal operations to influence the American political debate. The CIA is, after all, forbidden to interfere with U.S. politics or policies.

Over the years, Oliver had come to suspect that the original sin for a decade-long degradation of U.S. democratic institutions was Casey's role in the hostage crisis during the 1980 campaign. So Oliver strongly urged a full-scale congressional investigation into the October Surprise mystery. On the other side, the Republicans thought that cooling down Oliver would take the steam out of the Democrats. But Oliver, an experienced political hand, had taken precautions. He had cleared his Stoffberg letter with both Rep. Dante Fascell, the Foreign Affairs Committee chairman, and Rep. Lee Hamilton, who had been tapped to oversee a preliminary review of the October Surprise evidence.

Reacting to the harsh GOP attack on Oliver, Fascell took to the floor and went jaw-to-jaw with the Republicans. "I authorized what was done," an angry Fascell shouted. "It was my staff member who did it under my direction." Fascell confronted one Republican, Rep. Henry Hyde of Illinois, and chastised him for going after a staff aide. "Why don't you pick on someone your own size," Fascell seethed.

The Democrats were energized by the fight and rallied emotionally to Oliver's personal defense. During the balloting, when one Democratic vote was recorded as siding with the Republicans, Democratic members raced to the computer readouts in the cloak room to see who had broken ranks and then rushed back to the floor to buttonhole their colleague into changing his vote. The Republican censure motion failed on a straight party-line vote, rare even for the nastily partisan House of Representatives.

The Democrats' anger lingered long enough to guarantee passage of the resolution authorizing a formal House investigation of the October Surprise issue. Always hovering over that debate was the ugly experiences of the 1980s when Democrats were deceived again and again by the Reagan administration on foreign policy issues. In one sense, the Iran-contra scandal had been a story of repeated government lies and coverups, a policy of stonewalling ordered by the highest levels of the executive branch. Congress, the press, and the American public had been systematically misled. But the withholding of information had not stopped with Iran-contra. More recently, Congress had been buffaloed by White House refusal to turn over documents about the administration's pre-Persian Gulf War policy of aiding Iraq's Saddam Hussein.

"What we had during this era in the 1980s was a policy of deceit and misrepresentation of the Congress of the United States and the American people," charged Rep. Bill Alexander, Democrat of Arkansas, who was an early inquirer into covert U.S. policy in Central America. "The Reagan administration formulated and carried out an official policy of deceit. The elected representatives of the people were denied the facts about the official policy and actions of our government. The constitutional process of government was compromised, subverted. The rule of law was replaced by the president's policy." Alexander argued that answers were needed to the many October Surprise questions.

Late in the evening of February 5, 1992, amid deep-seated partisan distrust and with every Republican voting in the negative, the House approved an official October Surprise inquiry. The vote was 217–192. But the personal attacks on anyone who dared investigate the October Surprise mystery were not over.

Throughout the difficult October Surprise investigation, one of the few bright spots had been the friendly presence of Martin Kilian, *Der Spiegel*'s Washington correspondent. But in late 1991 and early 1992, Kilian grew increasingly depressed. Kilian had been rudely interrogated several times by ex-CIA officer Frank Snepp, who was preparing a new story for the *Village Voice*. Snepp was the spy-turned-journalist who had been handed the documents proving Brenneke's lies about attending the Paris meetings.

But Snepp now wanted to go further. He was spinning his own counter-conspiracy theory. It held that the October Surprise allegations had been concocted entirely by Brenneke and a few of his arms-trafficking friends in 1988 as revenge for the 1986 "merchants of death" case. Snepp even postulated that Kilian had colluded with the fabricators to spread the story.

For weeks, Kilian's normally positive outlook was darkened by Snepp's nasty questions and offensive innuendos. Snepp accused Kilian of talking too much to Brenneke in 1990 about the various October Surprise allegations. Though Brenneke's controversial charges had been made two years earlier and his story of the alleged Paris meetings hadn't changed, Snepp followed in the footsteps of the *New Republic* and *Newsweek* with another debunking story. He unleashed his speculation in a rambling article in the February 25, 1992, edition of the *Village Voice*.

But pinning the origins of the October Surprise allegations on Brenneke made no sense. At *Frontline*, we had tracked the rumors about the October Surprise—on both the Republican and Iranian sides—back to 1980. *Chicago Tribune* reporter John Maclean told us that he had gotten a tip in mid-October 1980 that George Bush was going to Paris to meet with Iranians about the hostages. Maclean had passed on the rumor to State Department officer David Henderson, who recorded the date of the conversation as October 18, 1980. Though Maclean concluded that he had been given a bad tip, it was undeniable that the story was circulating that early.

On the Iran side, three individuals reported being told about Iranian-Republican contacts in 1980–81. They all said they had heard the story from Revolutionary Guard arms procurer Hamid Naqashan. And in September 1980, Iran's foreign minister Sadeq Ghotbzadeh was quoted by Agence France-Presse as claiming that Republicans were "trying to block a solution" to the hostage crisis. Other Iranians whom we interviewed also agreed that rumors about a Republican hostage deal were swirling around Tehran in 1980. Ex-Iranian president Abolhassan Bani-Sadr made his October Surprise allegations to Flora Lewis of the *New York Times* in 1987, a year before Brenneke entered the picture.

Though lacking evidence and logic, Snepp's article was lauded by Republicans as another reason to kill any investigation into the October Surprise. Snepp's assault also dampened Kilian's enthusiasm for getting to the bottom of a tough story. He discovered that in the new Washington it was dangerous for journalists even to examine controversial issues, especially when the stories might put the White House in a bad light. Kilian had risked his journalistic career and invested countless hours of his own time in an honest pursuit of the truth. His reward was to be ridiculed and insulted by an American press colleague.

At *Frontline*, our second hour-long documentary on the October Surprise controversy was set to air on April 7, 1992, nearly a year after the first program. But the growing clique of debunkers began denouncing the show even before it was broadcast. The update was attacked by the *New Republic*'s Steven Emerson before he had seen it. I was mocked this time as an "active proponent of the [October Surprise] theory." Emerson's pre-emptive strike suggested that PBS was wasting the public's money by looking at the issue after the *New Republic* already had declared the October Surprise unfit for respectable comment.

In the poisonous atmosphere of spring 1992—as President Bush cranked up his re-election campaign—the new show, entitled "Investigating the October Surprise," was like a breath of fresh air. It tried to restore some evenhandedness to the increasingly polarized debate. The documentary began by recounting the controversy that had followed the publication of Gary Sick's *New York Times* opinion article and the first *Frontline* broadcast a year earlier.

We then undertook an ambitious effort to block out as many days of Casey's known schedule as possible from the summer and fall of 1980. We established the campaign chairman's whereabouts for about two-thirds of the days between the Republican convention in July and the election in November. But we could not establish firm alibis for Casey for the time periods in question.

The program also pointed out the holes in the debunking articles by *Newsweek* and the *New Republic*. We showed that the records of the World War II historical conference in London were not conclusive. While not endorsing Jamshid Hashemi's Madrid claims, we concluded that Casey's whereabouts in late July remained "in question for a three-and-a-half day gap" prior to the first afternoon of the conference. We also divulged the cozy business relationship between Cyrus Hashemi and Casey chum John Shaheen.

Frontline landed hard on Brenneke for lying about his participation in October Surprise meetings. "Whether he lied for personal gain or for some other motive, it's a mystery why he presented his Paris story under oath before a federal judge in an unrelated case four years ago," we said. *Frontline* also recounted the peculiar case of Mr. Razine/Oswald LeWinter and his claim that he had been paid to spread disinformation about the controversy. The LeWinter segment, we noted, underscored how tough it was to solve the October Surprise mystery.

The program concluded on that down note: "Even with the power to compel testimony and to subpoena documents, [the congressional] investigation, born in bitter partisan debate, faces a daunting task. The overriding truth about 1980 may be that the American people may never know what happened."

24

"HONORABLE" MEN

By late spring 1992, the congressional investigators were collecting documents, interviewing witnesses, and listening to the hundreds of hours of FBI audiotape recorded in Cyrus Hashemi's office. But the Republicans continued to object furiously to the investigation.

Unprompted, President Bush raised the October Surprise issue at two news conferences. Although he was not the target of the investigation, he demanded that all allegations tying him to the mystery be repudiated. Speaking to the press on June 4, 1992, Bush snapped at a reporter who asked whether an independent counsel was needed to investigate the administration's pre-war courtship of Iraq's Saddam Hussein.

"I wonder whether they're going to use the same prosecutors that are trying out there to see whether I was in Paris in 1980," a peeved president responded. "I mean, where are we going with the taxpayers' money in this political year?" A surprised hush fell over the press corps. For Bush to connect the two sets of allegations was a stretch in logic.

"I was not in Paris, and we did nothing illegal or wrong here" on Iraq, the president added.

At another news conference at the world environmental summit in Brazil, Bush again brought up the October Surprise probe in reaction to an unrelated question. The president called the congressional investigation "a witchhunt" and demanded that Congress clear him of having traveled to Paris.

The House Republicans, taking their cue from Bush, threatened to obstruct continued funding for the October Surprise probe if the president's demand was not met. Since the investigation's money needed reauthorization on July 1, House task force chairman Lee Hamilton tried to be accommodating. In the hostile environment created by the *New Republic* and *Newsweek* debunking stories, the investigators saw the October Surprise issue as more mirage than oasis, anyway. So they didn't mind dismissing the most unlikely allegation, the Bush trip to Paris.

But still, the Secret Service was balking at releasing all the information about Bush's travels around Washington on October 19, 1980. The task force had not been told whom Bush supposedly visited that day on the morning and afternoon outings recorded by Secret Service supervisors on their daily reports. The afternoon trip to the home of a family friend remained completely secret. For the morning trip, the task force had the report showing that Bush's detail had gone to the Chevy Chase Country Club, but the investigators could not locate a reliable witness to corroborate Bush's presence at the club.

When congressional investigators questioned the Secret Service agents on the Bush detail, only one—supervisor Leonard Tanis—claimed a clear recollection of the trip to the Chevy Chase Country Club that Sunday. As he had in earlier statements, Tanis recalled Mr. and Mrs. Bush going to the Chevy Chase club for brunch with Justice and Mrs. Potter Stewart.

Then the congressional investigators got hold of Mrs. Bush's records, which *Frontline* had obtained earlier under the Freedom of Information Act. Those documents contradicted Tanis by showing Mrs. Bush going to the C&O Canal jogging path in Washington, not to the Chevy Chase club. Mrs. Stewart also told investigators what she had told me—that she had no recollection of the Chevy Chase brunch. So it appeared that Tanis was wrong about who attended the brunch. He possibly was remembering the two couples at a country club dinner on a totally different date.

The task force judged Tanis's error in placing Mrs. Bush and Mrs. Stewart at the brunch just an honest mistake, understandable given the passage of time. But House Foreign Affairs chief counsel Spencer Oliver was less generous. In a memo urging a closer look at the Bush question, Oliver noted that the Secret Service had doggedly withheld the uncensored Bush records from an inquiry by the congressional General Accounting Office that sought to clear up the Bush issue two years earlier.

Oliver asked: "Why did the Secret Service refuse to cooperate on a matter which could have conclusively cleared George Bush of these serious allegations [in 1990]? Was the White House involved in this refusal? Did they order it?"

Finally, on June 29, 1992, two days before the Republicans' deadline for clearing Bush, the House task force reached a compromise, of sorts, with the Bush administration. Task force chief counsel, E. Lawrence Barcella, Jr., was allowed to see the name of the person supposedly visited by the Bushes on the afternoon of October 19, 1980.

But in exchange for seeing the name, Barcella was barred from interviewing the witness or ever releasing the name. While one would think the White House should have welcomed the testimony of this witness to debunk the Paris suspicions once and for all, instead the Bush administration blocked access to the family friend. The friend could not even be questioned confidentially by congressional investigators.

Barcella was proud that he finally had extracted the name of the family friend but chagrined when I asked him about the value of knowing the identity of an alibi witness when the person is never questioned. "Well, we got the name," he stammered defensively. But Barcella would not reveal the name or provide other details about the person.

Because of this strange agreement to forego questioning the alibi witness, the House committee still had only one person who could recall George Bush's activities in Washington during the day—Secret Service supervisor Tanis. And Tanis had two women present at a brunch that they apparently did not attend.

Nevertheless, in a public statement on July 1, 1992, the task force's Democratic chairman, Lee Hamilton, declared that "all credible evidence leads to the conclusion that President Bush was in the United States continuously during the October 18–22 [1980] time period, and not attending secret meetings in Paris, France."[1]

* * *

---

[1] In the *New Republic* (December 23 and 30, 1991), Steven Emerson attacked me for reporting on *Frontline* that Bush's Secret Service records, released under the Freedom of Information Act contained deletions. "By describing the records as 'heavily censored,' Parry raised further suspicions about their authenticity," Emerson wrote. "Yet we obtained a perfectly clean set of records under FOIA. Nothing was hidden." However, Emerson's

The decision to absolve Bush, despite the nagging questions, fit Hamilton's career-long obsession with bipartisanship and compromise. Hamilton—known for his simple butch-style haircut, his Indiana twang, and his measured speech—impressed many in Washington as a man of substance and integrity. He won wide respect for his clear enunciation of constitutional principles. He could be a persuasive advocate for the democratic ideals of openness and honesty in government, as he was during the Iran-contra hearings in 1987.

But in reality, Hamilton had a sorry record for exposing the government lies and wrongdoing that were eating at the foundations of American representative democracy. Hamilton was chairman of the Middle East subcommittee in the mid-1980s when the secret policy of shipping arms to Iran was developed. He missed it completely. He was chairman of the House Intelligence Committee in 1986 when Oliver North's secret contra supply network was in full swing. He missed that, too.

I had been writing about North's activities for the Associated Press, and one of those stories, citing 24 sources, finally prompted the House Intelligence Committee to confront North. At the August 1986 meeting in the White House's Situation Room, North assured Hamilton and other members of the committee that the allegations about his contra work were false. North's superiors at the National Security Council also denied the charges. Without doing any independent investigation, Hamilton accepted the word of North and his superiors. I was informed that my stories hadn't checked out.

"Congressman Hamilton had the choice of accepting the word of

---

claim that he had "perfectly clean" copies was undercut by the Secret Service's adamant refusal to provide uncensored records even to Congress and federal prosecutors. When I called the Secret Service and asked how Emerson could have gotten the complete Bush file under FOIA, a public liaison official answered succinctly: "He's lying." The Secret Service checked and confirmed that Emerson's copies had deletions just like ours had. Despite my repeated written requests to his editors and lawyer, Emerson failed to produce copies of the "perfectly clean" copies he claimed to have. The only reasonable conclusion was that he never had them. Apparently, Emerson felt that even fabricating historical records was not too far to go in the noble cause of debunking the October Surprise and discrediting anyone who tried to keep an open mind.

honorable men or the word of your sources," one Democratic staff aide told me. "It wasn't a close call."

For me personally, Hamilton's decision to clear North was possibly the worst moment in the entire Iran-contra scandal. Then, it was not only the White House, State Department, and CIA denying my stories. The Democrats had joined the pack, too.

At that point, I decided that North's secret network might remain outside of Washington's official reality forever. Many of my journalistic colleagues had already dismissed the North stories as just one more crazy conspiracy theory. The few reporters who insisted on chasing this discredited tale were simply fools and dupes, unfit for mainstream Washington journalism.

Only a freak incident in Nicaragua on October 5, 1986, exposed the secrets. On that sleepy Sunday morning, a teen-age Sandinista draftee aimed a shoulder-fired SAM missile at a lumbering C-123 cargo plane, fired, and watched transfixed as the missile found its mark. One of North's contra supply planes crashed to earth, and one of the crew members, Eugene Hasenfus, parachuted into Sandinista custody. Suddenly, the pervasive deception at the White House—and the gullibility of Washington's insider community—was brought into clear focus.

But it was another sign of the times that no one in the press or Congress who missed the Iran-contra scandal suffered. Some even saw their standing rise because they had proven how "responsible" they could be by accepting the word of "honorable" men at the White House. Lee Hamilton was one such case. Despite his failure to catch on to either the Iran or the contra side of the scandal, he was rewarded with the plum assignment as chairman of the House Iran-contra investigation.

Hamilton again showed how responsible he could be. Hoping to avoid a Watergate-style impeachment crisis, his congressional probe quickly swallowed its skepticism and accepted the word of senior Reagan administration officials who blamed their subordinates. The new White House story was that North and a few accomplices had run wildly out of control. President Reagan, Vice President Bush, and other senior officials had been kept in the dark about most of the misdeeds, the story went. Bush claimed to be "out of the loop" on both the Iran arms-for-hostage scheme and the secret contra supply operation. When these top officials learned of the scandal, they sought out the facts and told the whole story. There had been no high-level cover-up.

This time, however, North blew the whistle. He testified that the new White House tale was a pre-arranged "fall guy" plan. His actions, he insisted, had been authorized by his superiors, including the president. The Oval Office was simply covering up the culpability of senior officials, North claimed. But Hamilton still couldn't believe that "honorable" men with high government titles might lie to him. So he and his committee accepted the new White House story. Hamilton's investigation blamed most of the trouble on North and a few other "men of zeal."

Years later, Iran-contra independent counsel Lawrence Walsh would establish that President Reagan and his top men had systematically lied about the scandal. After the Iran-contra scam was exposed in November 1986, those senior officials had continued to mislead Congress and the public. They gave perjurous testimony, falsified records, and concealed key documents that, when finally brought to light by Walsh's investigation, proved that Reagan had been aware of the illegality of his decision to ship arms to Iran through Israel in 1985. Other documents would show that then Vice President Bush helped secure third-country support for the Nicaraguan contras and also was in the loop on the Iranian arms-for-hostage deals, despite his adamant claims to the contrary.

Once more, Hamilton had taken the word of "honorable" men—and had been taken in. Though Hamilton's record as a congressional sleuth was unimpressive, it established him, ironically, as a responsible "wise man" who could be trusted with sensitive inquiries. Hamilton might not be a "profile in courage," but he could win bipartisan support for his investigative conclusions. Because of Hamilton's experience with the Iran-contra scandal, House Speaker Thomas Foley appointed the Indiana Democrat to run the October Surprise task force.

Larry Barcella was one of the first applicants in line for the job as chief counsel of the task force. Hamilton promptly hired him. Initially, Barcella did seem like a reasonable choice. An energetic and creative investigator, Barcella was the federal prosecutor who had won convictions against renegade CIA agent Edwin Wilson during the early years of the Reagan administration.

Balding and bearded, Barcella had the quick and cagey mannerisms of a hunter ready to pounce. As he had shown in the Wilson prosecution, Barcella could be imaginative in laying complex traps for his legal prey. He had tricked Wilson by luring him to a bogus meeting in the Dominican Republic where Wilson was apprehended and returned to the United States for trial on charges he illegally supplied Libya's Muammar Qaddafi with explosives.

Barcella had also been willing to listen to low-lifes, such as Wilson's former employee Kevin Mulcahy, a chronic alcoholic who supplied key evidence to break the case. A healthy tolerance for sleazy characters certainly would be a prerequisite for the October Surprise investigation.

But I was troubled by other parts of Barcella's background that suggested a tolerance for the back-scratching ways of Washington. According to *Manhunt*, Peter Maas's book on the Wilson case, Barcella entertained a nighttime visit in 1982 from Michael Ledeen, then a State Department consultant on terrorism and a personal friend of Barcella's. Ledeen had bought a house from Barcella, and the two aspiring Washington professionals shared a housekeeper. Ledeen was concerned that two of his associates had come under suspicion in the Wilson case. The associates, Theodore Shackley and Erich von Marbod, held high offices at the CIA and the Pentagon, respectively.[2]

Barcella saw nothing wrong with the out-of-channel approach. "He wasn't telling me to back off," Barcella told me about the Ledeen visit. "He just wanted to add his two-cents worth." Barcella felt the contact was appropriate because Ledeen "wasn't asking me to do something or not do something."

Ledeen agreed. "I told Larry that I can't imagine that Shackley [or von Marbod] would be involved in what you are investigating," Ledeen said in an interview. "I wasn't trying to influence what he [Barcella] was doing. This is a community in which people help friends understand things." Later, Shackley and von Marbod were dropped from the Wilson investigation.

But Barcella's friendship with Ledeen also raised questions about his objectivity on the October Surprise issue. As an expert on Iran and terrorism, Ledeen maintained close contact with European conservatives, especially French intelligence chief Alexandre deMarenches, who had met privately with Casey in July 1980. Several October Surprise

---

[2] Peter Maas, *Manhunt*, (New York: Random House, 1986), p. 247.

△ Friends don't let friends vote Republican.

"witnesses" alleged that deMarenches had provided security for the Paris meetings in fall 1980. Plus, in 1985, Ledeen helped initiate the Iran arms-for-hostage strategy which pulled in leading October Surprise figures—Cyrus Hashemi, Hassan Karrubi (Mehdi Karrubi's brother), John Shaheen, William Casey, and Robert McFarlane.

Barcella, too, had played his own bit role in the Iran-contra scandal. In 1985, as an assistant U.S. attorney in Washington, Barcella was contacted by a Pentagon official who wanted to get legal advice so retired Maj. Gen. John Singlaub could ship weapons to the Nicaraguan contra rebels. At the time, the Pentagon and the CIA were legally barred from "directly or indirectly" assisting the contras militarily. The call also should have raised serious questions about possible violation of the Neutrality Act, which prohibits the plotting of unauthorized acts of war against foreign nations.

The Pentagon official "asked me a hypothetical" about the potential illegality of an arms shipment to Central America, Barcella told me. "But it was clear to both of us that it was not a hypothetical."

Instead of objecting to the potential illegality of the Pentagon official's request, Barcella provided advice on how Singlaub could skirt the Arms Export Control Act by buying the weapons overseas. Following Barcella's advice, Singlaub obtained light assault weapons from Poland that were shipped to Honduras for the contras in July 1985.[3] Singlaub, however, was not acting on his own. He was part of the secret White House contra-support operation run by Oliver North and overseen by William Casey.

Again, Barcella had been approached by a federal official acting in a legally dubious way. But the Pentagon official's inquiry set off no moral alarm bells inside the prosecutor. Barcella even defended his arms shipment advice, arguing that it was the same sort of legal counsel he would give to Catholic charities like "the Little Sisters of the Poor" trying to raise money through "Monte Carlo nights" without breaking the gambling laws. Barcella's ethical antennae seemed to make no distinction between charity bingo games and international arms trafficking.

---

[3] Ironically, Israeli Ari Ben-Menashe has claimed that Singlaub's purchase tapped into a pipeline of Polish weapons that he had helped open for the Israelis in 1984.

Even more troubling, Barcella had entertained an approach by a Pentagon official seeking legal advice for what amounted to a private act of war. But the prosecutor raised no constitutional or legal objections to a military man circumventing a federal prohibition against the Defense Department aiding the contras. Barcella also had gotten a glimpse into the illegal White House arms network, which would later be exposed in the Iran-contra scandal, but took no follow-up action.

Though admitting the facts of the Pentagon approach (after they were disclosed in a news article in the *Hartford Courant* in Connecticut), Barcella refused to divulge the name of the Pentagon official who had contacted him. That was a piece of information that should have been shared with the Iran-contra special prosecutor and might have been relevant to the October Surprise probe. After all, some important Reagan campaign officials linked to the 1980 allegations had landed jobs at the Pentagon.

"The person who called me from the Pentagon had never come up on any paper, document or memo related to the October Surprise," Barcella insisted. But since he would not supply the name, there was no way to be sure.

After Barcella went into private practice, he represented the president of GMT, the Washington-based company that Singlaub had used to arrange the contra arms shipment. The shadowy firm, which employed a number of former intelligence officials, was closely linked to William Casey's rogue CIA operations and the clandestine activities of Oliver North. GMT prepared one of the three-way trade proposals that were designed to create a slush fund for unauthorized covert operations.

Barcella was no more finicky about his other private clients. He acted as an aggressive defense attorney for the scandal-plagued Bank of Credit and Commerce International as it sought to frustrate federal investigations into its worldwide fraudulent practices and drug-money laundering. Barcella's law firm, Laxalt, Washington, Perito & Dubuc, collected $2.159 million in legal fees from BCCI from October 1988 to August 1990, according to a Senate Foreign Relations Committee report on the BCCI scandal.

The lead partner in Barcella's law firm was former Senator Paul Laxalt, one of President Reagan's closest political allies. In 1980, Laxalt was chairman of the Reagan-Bush presidential campaign, which Barcella's House task force was assigned to investigate. The Senate BCCI report said Barcella worked directly with Laxalt on the lucrative BCCI account and had sought to enlist the politically well-connected Laxalt in pro-BCCI lobbying on Capitol Hill. Though this recent relationship with Laxalt raised other conflict-of-interest concerns about Barcella, it was a comment on the real-life ways of Washington that no one in Congress or the news media voiced any concern.

Beyond lawyering, Barcella served as a lobbyist and public relations man for BCCI and its high-powered Washington representatives, Clark Clifford and Robert Altman. Barcella buttonholed senators and congressional investigators. He tried to discourage journalists who were digging into the complex story. He warned one reporter, Larry Gurwin, that it would be improper to report that BCCI secretly owned First American bank in a ground-breaking article that Gurwin was writing for *Regardie*'s magazine. Barcella called the allegation "absurd," although it would later be established that BCCI had secretly gained control of the Washington-based First American.

"I suppose I was repeating the word used by Clifford, Altman, and the bank," Barcella said about his description of the early allegations as "absurd." But he told me that he had conducted his own investigation and found no credible evidence to support the allegations about BCCI and First American. Barcella's judgment looked gullible, at best, after the BCCI scandal broke wide open.

Still, Barcella argued that his work for BCCI created no conflict of interest on the October Surprise front even though FBI wiretaps had recorded major transactions between Cyrus Hashemi's First Gulf Trust and BCCI in 1980. Casey's friend, John Shaheen, also was tied to BCCI principals during this period. In January 1981, Shaheen opened his Hong Kong Deposit and Guaranty bank with $20 million secretly supplied by the shah's twin sister, Princess Ashraf, and with financial support from BCCI figures. One of the bank's directors was Abu Dhabi's investment director Ghanim Al-Mazrouie, who controlled 10 percent of BCCI's shares.

The Shaheen-Hashemi-BCCI connections were considered so suspicious that they were cited in the 1992 Senate report on the BCCI scandal.

But the BCCI tie-in would receive almost no attention in the House task force's October Surprise investigation.

At lower staff levels, the task force had almost no aggressive investigators inclined to prove the October Surprise allegations. In filling those jobs, Barcella and the Republicans repeatedly turned to veterans of the Reagan-Bush Justice Departments and other Executive Branch agencies. Barcella himself had worked for a Republican U.S. attorney, Joseph diGenova, and had become a trusted figure to the national security establishment. Barcella's chief aide, Michael Zeldin, held several posts in the Reagan-Bush Justice Departments.[4] So did two other task force lawyers on the Democratic side.

Less surprisingly, the Republicans pulled senior Reagan-Bush lawyers from main Justice and important U.S. attorney's offices to staff their side. Minority staff director John P. Mackey had been associate deputy attorney general before joining the task force. Deputy chief minority counsel Gregory W. Kehoe had handled the BCCI drug-money laundering case for the U.S. attorney's office in the middle district of Florida. That case ended in a controversial plea bargain that outraged some members of Congress as too lenient. Kehoe negotiated the plea bargain with BCCI attorney, Larry Barcella.

The Republicans' senior associate counsel, David H. Laufman, was recruited to the task force from the minority staff of the House Foreign Affairs Committee. But from 1980 to 1984 he had worked as an analyst at the CIA, a position that meant his bosses included William Casey and Robert Gates. The task force's chief minority counsel, Richard Leon, had represented Republican interests aggressively during the Iran-contra investigation and helped draft the minority report denying that any crimes had been committed. Throughout the October Surprise probe, Leon sought

---

[4] Zeldin was a longtime personal friend of reporter Steven Emerson, who had written the nasty October Surprise debunking article for the *New Republic*. House investigators told me that Emerson frequently visited the task force offices and advised Zeldin and others how to perceive the October Surprise evidence.

to discredit not only the shady witnesses, but the reporters and congressional staff who had dared examine the issue.

While ex-Reagan-Bush lawyers came to dominate both the majority and minority sides of the task force, fulltime Democratic congressional staff investigators were pushed to the sidelines or sent directly to the showers. Several Democratic aides complained about trouble getting access to the investigative evidence, which was kept highly classified by the task force staff. Even Democratic congressmen felt out of touch.

More than halfway through the investigation, one Democratic congressman on the task force, Rep. Sam Gejdenson of Connecticut, asked House Foreign Affairs chief counsel Spencer Oliver to act as his personal representative on the investigation. Oliver was possibly the most knowledgeable October Surprise investigator on Capitol Hill and was well-schooled in the ways of Washington. But Barcella and the Republican leadership objected to Oliver's appointment. Oliver was a *bête noire* to the Republicans because he had advocated the October Surprise inquiry in the first place and had questioned the premature clearing of President Bush.

In the spirit of bipartisanship, task force chairman Hamilton consulted with the ranking Republican, Rep. Henry Hyde of Illinois, about the Oliver appointment. Hamilton found the Republicans adamantly opposed. Oliver "raised a red flag with the minority," Hamilton told me in a telephone interview. "It was our judgment that it would not be a good idea to put him on as a task force staffer."

Hamilton then met with Gejdenson and Oliver's direct boss, Rep. Dante Fascell, and persuaded them that Oliver's appointment should be withdrawn. Otherwise, Hamilton argued, the Republicans would be "upset" and his hope for a bipartisan investigation disrupted.

When I asked Hamilton whether it wasn't unusual for the Republicans to be granted veto power over the choice of Democratic staff, he responded simply that "it was a decision that I take responsibility for. I don't think he [Oliver] was the right man for the job."

As the months wore on, the House task force and the Senate subcommittee kept asking questions, but the answers didn't push the story very far. The investigators did hear the Madrid allegation from Iranian/CIA man Jamshid Hashemi under oath. Though Jamshid shifted his story, claiming that

Casey was interested in negotiating freedom for the hostages, not in delaying it, Jamshid continued to insist that Casey had attended two rounds of meetings with Iranian cleric Mehdi Karrubi in the summer of 1980.

The investigators received some corroborative testimony from former Iranian defense minister Ahmad Madani, who recalled that Cyrus Hashemi told him about the Republican-Iranian contacts as they were happening in 1980. Madani said Cyrus had brought up Casey's name in connection with back-channel negotiations over the U.S. hostages. Cyrus had even urged Madani to meet Casey personally. But Madani said he declined on the grounds that Casey was not part of the existing American government. "We are not here to play politics," Madani remembered telling Cyrus.

Still, Cyrus defended his behind-the-back relations with the GOP campaign chief, Madani said. Cyrus argued that Casey was in line for a top job—either secretary of state or CIA director—if Reagan won. Based on Cyrus's apparent relationship with Casey over the hostages, Madani concluded that "Casey wanted to fish in troubled waters" and that Cyrus was "double-dealing" the Carter administration.

While Madani's testimony was second-hand, it came from a credible individual with no apparent reason to lie. That in 1980 Cyrus would have told a former Iranian government minister about his contacts with Casey also undermined the debunkers who had argued that the allegations were fabricated recently. Plus, Madani's testimony now meant that three senior Iranian officials from the 1979–80 period—President Bani-Sadr, Foreign Minister Ghotbzadeh, and Defense Minister Madani—had all claimed independent knowledge of Republican-Iranian contacts in 1980. The Senate investigators considered Madani's testimony important. The House task force did not.

The investigators also listened to former Israeli intelligence man Ari Ben-Menashe, but soundly rejected his October Surprise allegations. While acknowledging that some of Ben-Menashe's other information was on target and that he had worked for Israeli intelligence, the congressional probers discounted his value as a credible witness on the October Surprise. They had, after all, concluded that George Bush had remained in the United States during October 1980, though Ben-Menashe repeated under oath that he saw the vice presidential candidate shaking hands with Mehdi Karrubi in Paris.

The House task force tried to check out Ben-Menashe's other October Surprise allegations in Israel, including his claims that Prime Minister Begin collaborated with the Reagan-Bush campaign in arranging arms shipments to Iran. The Israeli government first stalled—citing scheduling conflicts over religious holidays—and then barred the U.S. investigators from making the trip altogether. Instead, the ever-accomodating Hamilton agreed to let Israeli authorities do the investigation themselves.

In a classified report to the task force, the Israelis denied that Begin's government had colluded with the Republicans and denounced Ben-Menashe as a liar. He had served only as a low-level translator with no access to sensitive secrets, the Israeli authorities insisted. He never traveled on official business and had no responsibility for Iran. The government also claimed that Ben-Menashe was in Israel throughout October 1980, contradicting his claims about the L'Enfant Plaza meeting and Paris.

Still, the report confirmed that Ben-Menashe had been assigned to a military signals intelligence unit in the mid-1970s, did work for the External Relations Department of Israeli Military Intelligence (ERD) from 1977 to 1987, and did spend three of those years as a "staff officer in the means of war [armaments] unit" of ERD.

The Israeli report cited senior military and intelligence officials to back up its attacks on Ben-Menashe. But Moshe Hebroni, former chief of staff to the military intelligence director, was not on the interview list. Hebroni was bypassed, although he had been quoted publicly by Israeli and American journalists as saying that Ben-Menashe *did* have access to highly sensitive Israeli intelligence secrets and *had* met with the military intelligence chief, Yehoshua Saguy.

"Ben-Menashe was directly under my authority," Hebroni told *Davar* foreign editor Pazit Ravina. "He was a desk man who worked in Foreign Flow. Within the framework of his role, I often called on him to take part in discussions with the head of the intelligence office," Saguy. Saguy told *Davar* that Ben-Menashe may have "sat in the second or third row" at meetings in the intelligence chief's office. But in the report, the Israeli government said that Saguy denied knowing Ben-Menashe.

The Israeli report also had no explanation for the effusive praise in Ben-Menashe's letters of reference. In those letters, dated September 1987, Ben-Menashe's ERD superiors commended him for handling "a task which demanded considerable analytical and executive skills" and holding "key positions." Those statements did not seem to mesh with the "low-level translator" story.

When I asked Barcella about Israel's earlier denials that Ben-Menashe had worked for military intelligence and the contradictory accounts in the letters, Barcella agreed that Israeli officials had not been fully forthcoming about their rogue operative. "They were low-balling it and Ben-Menashe was high-balling it," Barcella said about the competing claims over Ben-Menashe's importance. But brushing aside that history and Israel's obvious self-interest in discrediting Ben-Menashe, the House task force accepted the Israeli report as "credible."

The House team repudiated other October Surprise "witnesses" as well. None was telling the truth about Republican-Iranian contacts, the House investigators concluded. Yet, most of the so-called "allegators"—including pilot Heinrich Rupp, South African Dirk Stoffberg, intelligence freelancer Reiner Jacobi, American arms dealer William Herrmann, and Iranian intelligence operative Richard Babayan—stuck by their stories about Casey's supposed hostage initiatives. Several complained, however, that the House task force tried to bully them into retractions. A lawyer for one said his client was told that the task force had already concluded that the October Surprise claims were false and that repeating the accusations would lead to perjury charges.

While denying any rush to judgment, a senior House investigator told me that the witnesses, indeed, were viewed as two separate classes. The low-lifes associated with the allegations received harsher treatment than the higher-brow Republican figures who were denying any knowledge of Casey-Iranian contacts. This investigator added that throughout the process, the Republican lawyers acted openly as "defense attorneys" for the Reagan-Bush campaign officials. In this way, the GOP staff ensured that the Republican witnesses were never pressed too hard even when their stories were implausible. By contrast, both the majority and minority investigators hammered the "allegators," treating them as common criminals and battering them over any inconsistencies found in their testimony.

But Reagan campaign officials often seemed no more credible than the unsavory witnesses. In June 1991, while playing golf with George Bush in

Palm Springs, Reagan told reporters that he had "tried some things the other way" to free the hostages in 1980. But Reagan had declined to elaborate on grounds that "some of these things are still classified."

In an initial response to congressional inquiries about what his golf course remarks meant, Reagan said, through his lawyer, that "he has no recollection or other information relevant to the issues raised in any of your questions." In a later letter, however, Reagan claimed that his golf course comment referred only to his public support of President Carter's negotiating policy. As for his insistence that some of his efforts were "still classified," Reagan answered that "I cannot recall what I may have had in mind when I made that statement."

Max Hugel, a top Casey campaign aide and later Casey's choice to head the CIA clandestine services, startled the House task force when his lawyer demanded immunity from prosecution for Hugel in exchange for his October Surprise testimony. Normally, an immunity request is considered a breakthrough, suggesting that a witness is prepared to divulge incriminating information. The House investigators asked from what crimes Hugel needed immunity.

David Carmen, a spokesman for Hugel, told me that Hugel wanted immunity so he could not "be sent to jail for even an inadvertent perjurious statement."[5] An exchange of letters ensued between the House task force and Hugel's lawyer before alarmed Republicans intervened. They convinced Hugel to testify, without immunity, and simply say that he knew nothing about the October Surprise allegations. Hugel did exactly that, though repeating often that he had no recollection of events.

"I wanted to be sure that I would be protected from any kind of entrapment," Hugel told me. "I had nothing to hide or anything."

The pugnacious former national security adviser Richard Allen appeared defiantly before the Senate panel, still attacking the investigation. But Allen did come armed with a September 10, 1980 "confidential memorandum for the file" that he claimed described the curious L'Enfant Plaza meeting which had been the subject of much GOP forgetfulness.

Allen said the memo was the one that he had lost, but had hoped someday to recover. He found it while searching through some old files on

---

[5] Although this is what Carmen told me, perjury is the one offense to which such immunity does not generally apply.

the eve of his testimony. The only trouble with the memo was that it flatly contradicted the story that Allen and another Republican, Laurence Silberman, had given publicly about the meeting with an Iranian emissary who had proposed releasing the hostages to candidate Reagan. That proposal had brought an abrupt cutoff of the discussion, Allen and Silberman had claimed. But that was not the story the memo told:

"Today at 1142 Mike Butler, Senator Tower's office called me to ask me if I could meet with him to discuss a confidential matter. . . . Subsequently, at about 12 o'clock, he and Bud McFarlane came to the office and we drove back down to [Capitol] Hill. On the way, they told me about their meeting with a Mr. A.A. Mohammed, a Malaysian who operates from Singapore and who came to them via an old friend of Senator Tower's. . . . This afternoon, by mutual agreement, I met with Messrs. Mohammed, Butler and McFarlane. I also took Larry Silberman along to the meeting.

"As it turned out, Mr. Mohammed claims to have a scheme which has ostensibly received the approval of Ayatollah Khomeini to release the hostages once the son of the shah is returned to Iran and installed as a figurehead monarch. Larry and I indicated our scepticism [*sic*] about the possibility of such an exercise, especially since it also involves the release of the hostages. . . . Both Larry and I indicated that we would be pleased to hear whatever additional news Mr. Mohammed might be able to turn up, and I suggested that that information be communicated via a secure channel."

Nearly every important detail was different. Mike Butler—not McFarlane—initiated the contact. No pestering by McFarlane as Allen had claimed. Butler also took part in the meeting, a fourth Republican who had never been mentioned in any of the earlier accounts. The timing of the meeting also was off. Originally, Allen and Silberman had said the L'Enfant Plaza encounter followed a morning conference of foreign policy advisers which ended at noon. Silberman had said Allen told him about the planned hostage talk at the end of the morning meeting in Allen's office and the two men then drove together to the L'Enfant Plaza Hotel. Now, Allen didn't even hear about the proposed get-together until he was being driven to Capitol Hill by Butler and McFarlane. How could Allen have invited Silberman during a morning meeting when Allen didn't hear about it until after he left his office in the early afternoon?

The meeting's contents also didn't match. Gone was the proposal to release the hostages to candidate Reagan; gone was the abrupt cutoff of the meeting; gone was the Iranian or Egyptian—the man from the "Mediter-ranean littoral" in Allen's colorful phrase. Added was a Malaysian busi-nessman; added was a cockamamie scheme to restore the shah's son to the Peacock Throne; added was the possibility of future contacts "via a secure channel." The memo did not even say that the meeting was held at the L'Enfant Plaza Hotel.

A reasonable conclusion might be that Allen's memo was about a totally different meeting. But that would mean that Republican contacts with Iranian emissaries were more frequent than previously known and that Silberman was a more regular player than he had acknowledged. So the congressional investigators accepted the Allen memo as the final answer to the L'Enfant Plaza puzzle. The investigators felt that Houshang Lavi and Ari Ben-Menashe had such little credibility that pursuing the question further—and untangling the Republicans' twisted story—wasn't worth the trouble.[6] Silberman, McFarlane, and Butler, incidentally, disputed Allen's new version of the L'Enfant Plaza tale. They claimed no recollec-tion of the A.A. Mohammed discussion.

The task force also turned a blind eye to another tantalizing L'Enfant Plaza lead that emerged from contemporaneous notes supplied by Lavi's lawyer, Mitchell Rogovin. One page of Rogovin's notes cried out for expla-nation, but didn't get any. According to his calendar for September 29, 1980, Rogovin wrote down Lavi's latest proposal to trade war matériel for the U.S. hostages. Rogovin, a former CIA counsel and an adviser to John Anderson's independent presidential campaign, then recorded his telephone contact

---

[6] In dismissing Lavi and Ben-Menashe, the investigators cited their alleged claims that Cyrus Hashemi had been in Paris over the weekend of October 18–19, 1980. Based on the FBI wiretaps of Cyrus's home office, there was no question that Cyrus was in the New York area that weekend, so, the reasoning went, Lavi and Ben-Menashe were lying. But actually, neither Lavi nor Ben-Menashe had specifically put Cyrus in Paris that weekend. Ben-Menashe testified that he understood that Cyrus wanted to join those meetings but had been barred. The Israeli said he was told that Cyrus did travel to Paris several days after the main meetings, but Ben-Menashe claimed no first-hand information about Cyrus's whereabouts at all. Lavi had told me that he wasn't sure when Cyrus had traveled to Paris in October 1980, but that it might have been "around October 20." Lavi said he met Cyrus in London and they flew together to Paris. Lavi claimed Cyrus then talked with a variety of foreigners about Iranian arms deals, but Lavi did not say he saw any of the alleged American principals. FBI documents reported that Cyrus did travel to London and Paris on a trip beginning October 28.

North, McFarlane, Tower in April '86 Failed mission.

with senior CIA official John McMahon to discuss Lavi's plan and schedule a face-to-face meeting with a CIA representative on October 2.

The next entry, however, was stunning. It read: "Larry Silberman—still
very nervous/will recommend . . . against us this P.M. I said $250,000—he
said why even bother." When I called Rogovin about this notation, he said
it related to a loan that the Anderson campaign was seeking from Crocker
National Bank where Silberman served as legal counsel. The note meant
that Silberman was planning to advise the bank officers against the loan,
Rogovin said.

"This is a totally different issue," Rogovin explained. "We were trying
to borrow money from banks. Silberman was nervous about lending the
money."

But, I asked, could the Lavi hostage initiative have come up in the
conversation with Silberman? No, Rogovin was certain that he had not
mentioned Lavi's scheme to Silberman. "There was no discussion of the
Lavi proposal," Rogovin insisted. But Rogovin acknowledged that Silberman was a friend from the Ford administration. Both men had worked on
intelligence issues—Rogovin as CIA counsel and Silberman as deputy
attorney general. So there was at least the plausibility of two friends
interested in intelligence matters discussing Iran. Moreover, on September
29, 1980, Lavi's proposal to settle the crisis was fresh in Rogovin's mind,
and Rogovin knew that Silberman had an interest in the hostage issue as a
foreign policy adviser to Ronald Reagan.[7]

In a normal investigation, this set of coincidences would strain credu-
lity: Lavi's attorney, Rogovin, discusses his client's hostage plan with the
CIA and arranges a meeting; Rogovin next speaks with his friend, Silberman, a Reagan foreign policy adviser, and asks for campaign funds; Lavi
then claims that three days later, he meets with Silberman about the
hostage plan; and Silberman later admits to having discussed a nearly
identical hostage plan with a mysterious Iranian emissary whose name he

---

[7] Silberman was considered strongly pro-CIA while at the Justice Department and was
appointed to head Ronald Reagan's presidential transition team for the intelligence agencies. Rogovin told me that Silberman even had hoped to get the job as CIA director and was
disappointed when the post went to Bill Casey. After the election, Rogovin's friendship
with Silberman flourished. Silberman moved in next door to Rogovin, and the two men
bought a boat together.

can't recall. Logically, the chance that all these points would be sheer coincidence would be almost nil.

I also learned that after Rogovin's phone call to Silberman, Crocker National did establish a line of credit for the Anderson campaign. During the last half of October, the Anderson campaign drew advances almost daily, totaling in the tens of thousands of dollars, according to Federal Election Commission records. On October 6, Rogovin's law firm was paid $216,738 for arranging the bank advances and other legal services, the FEC records showed.

I remembered, too, that before his death in December 1991, Lavi claimed that Silberman had initiated the L'Enfant Plaza meeting and did most of the talking from the Republican side. Lavi's allegation now made more sense: Silberman had a plausible basis to know about Lavi's initiative, through Rogovin. But for that to be true, Silberman and Rogovin would have to be covering up their full knowledge about the L'Enfant Plaza meeting. That was a possibility the House task force emphatically rejected. After all, in 1992, Silberman was a judge on the U.S. Circuit Court of Appeals in Washington, D.C.,[8] and Rogovin was a respected Washington attorney in a major law firm.

Despite the House task force's shortcomings, the last best hope for solving the October Surprise mystery rested in the government files that had not been available to journalists and researchers. But even with subpoena power, the congressional investigators ran into trouble on that front, too.

Potentially, the most important documents were those belonging to William Casey. His calendars, passports, and other travel records should have shed light on where he was on key days in 1980 and when he left the country. Those records had not been found at the Reagan library because, as it turned out, Casey had taken them with him to the CIA in 1981. At CIA headquarters, they had been catalogued and indexed, the task force discovered. Then, after Casey's death in 1987, the records had been turned over to his family. The CIA's index showed that the files contained Casey's

---

[8] Silberman incidentally was the judge who wrote the opinion striking down the three Iran-contra felony convictions against Oliver North.

calendars, passports, and other personal records. Some files had gone to the family estate, Mayknoll, at Roslyn Harbor, New York. Others were sent to a family-owned house in McLean, Virginia.

With Sophia Casey's permission, congressional investigators searched the two homes, finding all the records except for Casey's passport, a "hostages" file, two personal calendars, and loose pages from a third calendar which covered the period of July 24, 1980, to December 18, 1980. When checked against the CIA's index, the only folders missing from Casey's files were the ones relevant to the October Surprise mystery.

After examining the file boxes, House investigator Richard Pedersen sat Sophia Casey and her daughter, Bernadette Smith, down at the kitchen table of the McLean house. Pedersen, a tall, trim, white-haired veteran from the Bureau of Alcohol, Tobacco and Firearms, was blunt. "We have a problem," he told the two women. But Casey's widow and daughter insisted that they had no idea where the missing documents might be.

Later, Pedersen urged Bernadette to search again for the missing records. His gentle pressure achieved some results. First, the "hostages" file was recovered, but the investigators found it stuffed with general campaign documents, not papers pertinent to the hostage crisis. Gradually, under Pedersen's continued prodding, the family turned over more likely papers from that file, but it was not clear if every document was delivered.

Then, on September 8, 1992, Bernadette Smith showed up at the House task force offices with some other missing material: the "Standard Diary-1980," the "Monthly Minder-1980," and most of the loose calendar pages. The family claimed that the missing documents were found under a box on a basement hearth in the McLean home. Pedersen called the Casey family explanation "incredible" in light of the earlier searches.

But there was even a bigger problem with the belated discovery. The loose calendar pages for about a dozen days were still missing, including those for the weekend of July 26–27, 1980, the days before the London historical conference—the weekend when some suspected that Casey snuck off to Madrid and others insisted he would not have had time. Other missing dates were October 21, October 29, November 3–11, and November 13.

Casey's 1980 passport, possibly the single most important document for the investigation, also had not reappeared. A CIA official told the task force that several cancelled passports had been handed to Bernadette Smith in 1987 after her father's death. From State Department records, the task force also knew that Casey had renewed his personal passport in 1979. But the Casey family delivered only two passports, one a diplomatic passport issued in 1981 and the other a personal passport from the 1950s. The passport that might have contained stamps from European capitals in 1980 never surfaced.

The task force had similar problems obtaining relevant business papers and a detailed calendar for Casey's pal, John Shaheen. Those were missing for the telltale year 1980, though found for years earlier and later. Shaheen's passport for 1980 also had disappeared. The Shaheen family could not explain what had happened to the missing documents.

The strange behavior of the Casey and Shaheen families would seem inexplicable if nothing had happened in 1980. Again, the investigators were encountering roadblocks to evidence that presumably could have cleared Casey and Shaheen of suspicion. Instead, key documents were disappearing. Though convinced the families were withholding documents, the House task force saw little reason to be suspicious since it was already inclined to reject the allegations of the witnesses who were considered disreputable.

By mid-1992, whatever momentum the investigation ever had was gone. After the nasty debunking articles and the ugly debates in Congress, everyone seemed more interested in finding cover than the truth. The October Surprise mystery had become a dangerous political quagmire. The Republicans and their allies in the press had made clear that they would exact a high price from anyone who pressed too deeply toward finding evidence to prove the allegations. No one was likely to achieve any career advancement by charging forward. Instead, the congressional investigators were struggling toward the most graceful route to extract themselves from the morass called the October Surprise.

25

THE MAN WHO WASN'T THERE

On a late summer evening in 1992, I convinced Spencer Oliver to meet me for drinks at Bullfeathers, a popular dark-wood-and-brass watering hole on Capitol Hill. Three blocks to the north was the U.S. Capitol and its lighted white dome. We sat at one of the outdoor tables and ordered a bottle of wine and sandwiches.

In shirtsleeves, Oliver was winding down from a tough day battling with the administration over congressional subpoenas in the so-called Iraqgate investigation into U.S. assistance to Iraqi dictator Saddam Hussein in the years before the Persian Gulf war. As usual, Oliver felt the Democrats needed to be firmer in their demand that an unwilling White House surrender documents on the failed policy.

In his 50s, Oliver was part of a political generation that still remembered how the institutions of Washington once worked constructively toward solving the nation's problems. The son of a labor union official, Oliver had responded to the calls to national service from John and Robert Kennedy. He had joined the civil rights movement in his youth. During one voter registration drive in the Deep South, he was injured in a car crash, the effects of the accident still visible in a slight scar on his forehead.

But in recent years, Oliver's idealism had been sapped. He had become disillusioned by the lies and distortions that were now the acceptable currency of political discourse in Washington. As he sipped a Chardonnay wine and chomped into a thick hamburger at Bullfeathers, Oliver called the October Surprise investigation the latest example of the government's failure to confront wrongdoing and discover the truth. He felt the inquiry was going nowhere because of unrelenting political pressure from the White House.

Oliver's rich experience with political misdeeds dated back to Watergate, when his phone at the Democratic National Committee was the one chosen by Republican burglars for tapping. But in his view, the great Republican lesson from Watergate was not the imperative to obey the law. It was an appreciation for more effective coverups. During the Reagan and Bush administrations, that skill was well-honed, Oliver believed. The Republicans who had held the White House for nearly 12 years—from 1981 to 1992—knew how to punish those who got too close to the secrets. The GOP defense was most aggressive when the Republican power base at the White House was at risk, as it was in the 1992 presidential contest.

"When corruption reaches the highest precincts of government, the protection mechanisms for the people who inhabit those precincts are so powerful that they are almost impenetrable," the seasoned veteran of Washington political wars commented. "What we saw in Watergate and what we saw in Iran-contra and what we saw in October Surprise—we saw these defense mechanisms used to discredit honest politicians and honest journalists.

"The result is that the word has been conveyed that if you take on people with positions of power, you have to be prepared to pay the highest price in terms of your job, your career, and even your friends. You find that there are fewer and fewer people willing to pay that price, and for democracy that is a very dangerous development. The tools that are available to people of great power in the U.S. government are so frightening in their impact on an individual that it has the effect of making most people conclude that it is just not worth the candle to fight the battle.

"It is like the old saying about striking the king, that when you strike at the king, you better not miss, because if you miss, the king will destroy you. When you seek to expose duplicity and corruption of the highest levels of American power, you invite the kind of retaliation that will almost certainly destroy you and, if not destroy you, cause you serious damage from which you will surely never recover."

As Oliver philosophized about the retaliatory powers of Washington's great and powerful, he seemed neither angry nor depressed, but almost matter-of-fact, like an entomologist reciting the disturbing mating habits of the black widow spider.

"Watergate was the most devastating blow that any political party has suffered in modern history," Oliver continued. "The president was driven out of office. The Republicans were repudiated at the polls. They took enormous losses in Congress.

"What they learned from Watergate was not 'don't do it,' but 'cover it up more effectively.' They have learned that they have to frustrate congressional oversight and press scrutiny in a way that will avoid another major scandal. They have learned how to withhold documents, create cover stories, throw scapegoats over the side, and prevent the truth from ever coming out. They've become experts in convincing officials to perjure themselves to protect their dirty little secrets and attacking the investigators either in Congress or the press.

"It's all politics to them—the pursuit and maintenance of power. It is the ultimate example of the ends justify the means and the means are so abhorrent to democracy that they cannot let the people know."

As for the October Surprise mystery, Oliver had grown convinced that the only logical explanation for the ferocious Republican counterattacks was that the allegations were essentially true.

"If the October Surprise did happen, whoever did it committed treason and then everyone who was implicated is bound together in a conspiracy forever. Whatever corrupt act they engage in, they have to go along. They can never leave. It is like joining the Mafia in a novelistic sense. Once you've taken the pledge, you're inextricably bound.

"None of the people who would have known about October Surprise has been thrown over the side. They've all been kept in the bosom of this power structure. They have all been well cared for in the government or outside with consultancies. You have to ask this question: Why? The conclusion you have to reach is that they have to be taken care of. The attacks on those who have sought the truth have been so extreme that the conclusion must be that the allegations are true. While we pursue nothing more than the truth, to them it is a death sentence."

We paid the check. The night was warm, but not as muggy as Washington often gets in summer. I walked Oliver a block back to his Capitol Hill townhouse. I suspected that he was right at least in part. There was something about the October Surprise mystery that demanded a relentless cover-up. The attacks against the press and government investigators who had dug into the story were excessive even by modern Washington standards.

I also agreed with him about the imbalance of power between those who wanted to get to the bottom of the mystery and those who wanted the investigation contained. For a powerful politician, like the president or his top men, the best defense often is simply to deny an allegation no matter how truthful and then punish those who try to prove it. As Saudi financier M.K. Moss once told me, "It's not true if it can't be proven."

But I still didn't feel confident that I knew what had happened a decade ago. I still didn't trust the sources who were alleging the wrongdoing. As a journalist, I wanted the hard facts that could clear away the torturous ambiguity. Perhaps, though, in an age when deception has evolved into a high art form, endless uncertainty will be the fate of all our political controversies. Climbing back into my car for the drive back to Arlington, I still wasn't satisfied that I knew the answer to the mystery.

As the summer faded into fall, Washington's attention turned to politics. President Bush, saddled by an economic recession and a growing distrust of him by the American people, struggled toward the November election far behind Democratic challenger, Bill Clinton. Independent candidate Ross Perot was nipping, rhetorically, at Bush's heels. Members of Congress faced their own troubles. Public disgust with Washington gamesmanship was running high, and the House was looking at a possible 25 percent turnover in members. Even congressmen assigned to the October Surprise task force were paying the issue little heed.

While Congress tended to its political needs, Barcella's investigators continued to interview witnesses and review documents. Possibly, the task force's most daunting job was to listen to 1,800 hours of the FBI electronic surveillance of Cyrus Hashemi's home and office from September 1980 through February 1981. Those tapes offered the possibility of an unguarded comment that might prove or disprove the allegations.

The House investigators who listened to the Cyrus Hashemi wiretaps found that most conversations dealt with routine business and personal matters; there were no references to meetings between Casey and Iranians. Though Cyrus frequently warned his callers that he suspected his phones were wiretapped, the task force counted the absence of an offhand incriminating comment important evidence against Jamshid Hashemi's claims about Madrid meetings.

But several tape-recorded conversations corroborated the close relationship between Cyrus and Casey's friend, John Shaheen. On October 23, 1980, for instance, Shaheen placed a call from Cyrus's New York office to a Swiss business associate, Dick Gaedecke. Shaheen was overheard saying that Cyrus had been working on the hostage issue that day since 5:00 a.m. and that the hostages could be released at "any hour." A woman's voice, presumably belonging to a Shaheen assistant, interrupted with the comment, "Frankly, I wish they'd wait two weeks."

Other tapes suggested—but didn't prove—that Cyrus and Casey knew each other personally. On November 8, 1980, four days after Reagan's electoral victory, Shaheen offered Cyrus a helping hand from Casey, who had just been named director of Reagan's transition team. On the phone to Cyrus, the street-smart Shaheen said he had already told Cyrus's lawyer, Stanley Pottinger, that "if Cyrus wants anything in his stuff, let me know because, you know, we're one team that works together."

Then in an apparent reference to Casey, Shaheen told Cyrus, "I want you to lunch with the guy." Shaheen added that he had told Casey that "I was getting into a banking venture with you, and you know, what the hell, you might as well have a direct one-to-one relationship."

The remark about a "direct one-to-one relationship" puzzled the congressional investigators. Did it mean that Casey and Cyrus had met previously through Shaheen or did Casey and Cyrus get acquainted only after the election? The first interpretation would bolster Jamshid's story of prior Casey-Cyrus contacts; the second would undercut it.

On another FBI tape, Cyrus Hashemi bragged about a long-standing association with Casey. On November 20, 1980, in a conversation in Persian, Cyrus told Iranian associate Mahmood Moini that: "I have been close friends . . . with Casey for several years . . . and I am now a very good friend of his . . . I have spoken so far to them several times." But was that to be believed?

Other evidence of a Casey-Cyrus connection was equally hazy. In the early 1980s, Shaheen told FBI investigators who were examining Cyrus's arms dealing, that he, Shaheen, had introduced Casey and Cyrus before Casey became CIA director in 1981. But Shaheen didn't say exactly when or where the two men met.

A CIA memo dated February 4, 1984, was another piece of the puzzle, suggesting that Casey may have dealt with Cyrus Hashemi as far back as mid-1979. The CIA memo recounted a conversation with Hashemi attorney Elliot Richardson when the former U.S. attorney general was urging the CIA to block Cyrus's arms-trafficking indictment because of the Iranian's past help to the spy agency. Richardson told CIA lawyers that in mid-1979, Shaheen had shown Cyrus a letter in which Casey designated Cyrus as the middleman for the purchase of a New York City building belonging to the Pahlavi Foundation, a wealthy private organization controlled by Iran's deposed royal family.

In 1979, Iran's new Islamic government was trying to seize the Pahlavi Foundation's assets, and the royal family was seeking to liquidate property into cash. At the time, Casey was a lawyer with the powerful New York-Washington firm of Rogers and Wells, which did represent the Pahlavi Foundation. Cyrus Hashemi also would have been a clever choice for the assignment, since he was associated more with the new government than the old. I recalled that Shaheen's former bookkeeper, Roy Furmark, had acknowledged working on a New York real estate deal with Cyrus around 1980. Shaheen and Cyrus had also tapped into Pahlavi money for their business schemes in fall 1980. Princess Ashraf had financed Shaheen's Hong Kong bank with a $20 million investment in January 1981. So Richardson's account made some sense, but was still not conclusive proof of a direct Casey-Cyrus relationship.[1]

The FBI wiretaps also had gaps in coverage. One tape jumped eight days without explanation of why no phone calls had been recorded. The FBI men who had handled the bugging recalled no period that long when

---

[1] In May 1993 I tracked down an American businessman who had served with Casey and Shaheen in the OSS. He said Casey introduced Shaheen to Princess Ashraf when Casey represented the Pahlavi Foundation. He added that Casey did help the Foundation sell off or conceal its assets. He said Casey brought in Saudi financier Adnan Khashoggi as well as Cyrus Hashemi and Shaheen for this operation.

the tape recorders were shut down. But the congressional investigation saw no reason to be suspicious. For the tapes to have been doctored, either the FBI or the Justice Department would have had to do the tampering, and there was no evidence that had happened.

Still, in one dispatch after the Hashemi tapes had been recovered from a warehouse in Newburgh, New York, Reuters, the British news agency, quoted New York-based FBI sources who claimed to have heard Ronald Reagan on one tape talking to an Iranian, presumably Cyrus Hashemi. But Reagan's voice was not found on any of the tapes that arrived at the congressional offices. In a formal statement, the FBI insisted that the tapes had not been played in New York, thus refuting the Reuters story. But the FBI refused to let Congress interview the individual FBI agents in New York.

Since the bugs were installed in September 1980, the tapes did not cover the July and August time period of the alleged Madrid meetings. But the investigators obtained phone company records of these months for Cyrus Hashemi's New York office and Connecticut home and for his lawyer/ adviser, Stanley Pottinger, a former Nixon administration official. Pottinger worked with Cyrus on the hostage project and was in frequent contact with the Iranian wheeler-and-dealer.

The records showed regular phone communications between Cyrus and Pottinger. But for the likely Madrid meeting dates of July 27–28, 1980, there was no evidence of significant phone traffic. The only relevant calls from Saturday night, July 26, through Monday evening, July 28, the "window" that would give adequate time for the two-day meeting described by Cyrus Hashemi's brother, Jamshid, were a one-minute phone call from Pottinger's house to Cyrus's home at 8:05 p.m., Sunday, and a one-minute call back at 8:54 p.m. While the House task force considered those calls important evidence placing Cyrus in the United States and not in Madrid, the timing and length of the calls could equally, if not more strongly, suggest a call from Pottinger to Cyrus's family about when Cyrus was expected back and then a return call to give Pottinger the answer.

The House investigators also dismissed the possibility that CIA officer Donald Gregg could have gone to Madrid as Jamshid Hashemi had alleged. But again, the evidence on Gregg's whereabouts for July 27–28 was thin. Gregg's wife had a diary entry showing a brunch with her sister and brother-in-law on Sunday, July 27, but she had no recollection of her husband being home that day. Gregg testified that he went to the CIA's training center at Camp Perry, near Williamsburg, Virginia, on Monday, July 28. But Camp Perry was a highly secure facility, and its directors declined *Frontline*'s request for clear evidence that Gregg had attended a scheduled conference that day.

But the big question remained the old one: "Where was Bill?" What was Casey doing in the days before the London historical conference where he arrived at 4:00 p.m., Monday, July 28? Could he have traveled to Madrid for a two-day meeting on July 27–28 before jetting to London?

On this crucial timing question, *Newsweek* and the *New Republic* had concluded that Casey was in London by Sunday night, July 27, and attended the historical conference Monday morning, July 28. That meant, the magazines agreed, that the Madrid allegations were bogus and the October Surprise story was a myth. But at *Frontline*, we had concluded that Casey's presence in London could not be established before late afternoon on Monday, when the conference secretary jotted down the notation "came at 4 p.m." That would have left enough time for the Madrid meetings.

After reviewing the evidence, the House and Senate investigations reached the same conclusion we did. The British general in charge of the Royal Army Medical College—where the two magazines were certain Casey had stayed for two nights at the start of the conference—told investigators that the two-day charges for a bed and breakfast did not mean that Casey had slept in the bed or eaten the breakfasts. The charges just meant, the general informed the investigators, that the college was instructed to provide Casey with a room and a morning meal for the two days. Casey would have been charged whether he was there or not. And the two-day charge totaled only £6, roughly $10, a pittance for a millionaire who might need a cover story.

The congressional investigators also interpreted the conference records as we had—to say that Casey arrived at London's Imperial War Museum for the first time at 4:00 p.m. on Monday, July 28. The collapse of the London alibi put the congressional investigation in line with *Frontline*'s conclusion: the London evidence did not preclude the possibility of the

Madrid meetings. The *Newsweek* and *New Republic* "myth" stories had themselves been debunked. But the stories had left behind a toxic residue that continued to contaminate any openminded assessment of the October Surprise allegations.

The investigators did locate one document that shed some new light on Casey's presence in London by mid-afternoon on Monday, a receipt from a London bookstore. Apparently, before going to the Imperial War Museum at 4:00 p.m., Casey stopped at a Piccadilly bookstore called Hatchard's and bought four books about World War II and intelligence operations. One was entitled, *Who Dares Wins*, another was called *Master of Deception*.

On November 3, 1992, the American voters soundly repudiated George Bush. Giving the sitting president only 38 percent of the popular vote, the voters elected Bill Clinton and ended a dozen years of Republican rule. The weekend before the election, Bush's furious comeback drive had stalled when Iran-contra independent counsel Lawrence Walsh disclosed notes by former Defense Secretary Caspar Weinberger showing that Bush had lied when he claimed to be "out of the loop" on the scandal. Bush, it turned out, had been an advocate of the arms-for-hostage swaps that had so enraged the American people in 1986. The Weinberger case established that the White House had engaged in a cover-up of the scandal and that Congress and the Washington press corps had missed the story again.

But the revelation of new Iran-contra deceptions and official Washington's gullibility had little impact on the October Surprise investigators. Two weeks after Bush's defeat, Senate counsel Reid Weingarten issued his report, largely accepting the word of government officials and dismissing the allegations of a 1980 hostage deal as not credible.

In his report, Weingarten lamented the disappearance of key pieces of evidence—Casey's passport, the dozen calendar pages, John Shaheen's 1980 records—and stressed the difficulty of judging complex events from a decade's distance. His work had also been hampered by Republican pressure. Sen. Jesse Helms, a conservative from North Carolina, had exercised his power on the Senate Foreign Relations Committee to block any travel by Weingarten or his investigators. The total cost of his inquiry was only $75,429.

While acknowledging the frustrating limits of his investigation, Weingarten still concluded that "the great weight of the evidence is that there was no . . . deal" to delay the release of the 52 American hostages. But Weingarten felt the assertions about Casey's extraordinary activity on the hostage issue weren't entirely fictitious. He cited credible testimony from former Iranian defense minister Ahmad Madani and the FBI wiretaps to suggest that Casey had conducted secret initiatives on the hostages.

"The evidence supports the conclusion," Weingarten wrote, "that William Casey, while director of the Reagan campaign, was intensely involved in the hostage crisis and likely was dealing with Cyrus Hashemi either directly or indirectly through John Shaheen. . . . The totality of the evidence does suggest that Casey was 'fishing in troubled waters' and that he conducted informal, clandestine, and potentially dangerous efforts on behalf of the Reagan campaign to gather intelligence on the volatile and unpredictable course of the hostage negotiations between the Carter administration and Iran."

Weingarten had charted a middle course between the believers and the debunkers, doubting the likelihood of a deal to delay release of the hostages, but suspecting that Casey had made clandestine contacts with Iranian emissaries. That was a possibility even voiced by Casey's widow, Sophia, who told me once: "Oh, he would talk to Iranians, sure. He had no reason not to. . . . He would do it for information. How would he get it? He'd want to know what the other fellows knew about the Iranians or the situation there or what was gonna happen."

But the House report was still to come, and with the Republicans working congenially with Barcella's investigators, the outcome was clear. The investigators had decided months earlier that barring the discovery of an incontrovertible piece of evidence, they would conclude that nothing had happened in 1980—no deal, not even Weingarten's "fishing in troubled waters" formulation.

Although the missing Casey documents were troubling, the witnesses— no matter how numerous—were dismissed as liars or frauds or knownothings. Even though the *New Republic* and *Newsweek* had gotten the London alibi wrong, the two magazines had established a powerful conventional wisdom against anyone who claimed that the October Surprise had happened.

Certainly, some of the "witnesses" had been their own worst enemies, giving contradictory or implausible accounts. But neither had the investigators found reliable alibis for Casey on the handful of dates named by the "witnesses." There was no solid evidence about where Casey was on July 27–28; there was an opening on August 9, too, so the possible second Casey-Madrid meeting could not be ruled out. August 17, the alleged date of the Stoffberg-Jacobi-Casey get-together in London, could not be shut down, either. And October 19, the supposed date of the Paris rendezvous, was open as well.

Yet, without clear-cut alibis, the October Surprise allegations were likely to linger in some limbo between unlikely and impossible. So to put the story to rest with finality, the task force still wanted firm conclusions about Casey's whereabouts. The Republicans lobbied energetically for two alibis—one that would cover the July 27–28 opening and another that would fill in Casey's whereabouts for October 19.

As the House investigation neared its end in December 1992, the task force agreed to the two alibis. The case, the investigators said, was now closed. The alibis were the commitment papers that would wrap the October Surprise story in a straightjacket and lock it up in an asylum for crazed conspiracy theories forever. But before the iron gate to the asylum slammed shut, there were still some questions about the task force's own grasp on reality. How good were the new alibis?

The first alibi went as follows, the House task force said: on Friday, July 25, Casey flew from Washington to Los Angeles, where he met Republican activist Darrell Trent at the Reagan-Bush campaign offices. Later in the day, Casey and Trent flew to San Francisco, got a car, and drove the 90-minute trip to the exclusive Bohemian Grove encampment on northern California's Russian River. (They arrived, the investigators believed, sometime after dark.) Casey stayed at the men-only club as Trent's guest on Saturday, July 26. Then, on Sunday, July 27, Casey left with Trent and drove back to San Francisco. Trent dropped Casey off at the airport for an overnight flight to London, where the Republican campaign chief arrived at midday, Monday, July 28, for the historical conference.

That itinerary, the relieved House investigators decided, made a sidetrip to Madrid an impossibility and proved, once and for all, that Jamshid

Hashemi was a liar. The "Bohemian Grove alibi" was a neat package that satisfied the investigators' desire for a final answer.

The "Bohemian Grove alibi" rested on the testimony of two Grove members: Darrell Trent, who was Casey's host, and Bernard Smith, a Casey associate from New York who also belonged to the Bohemian Club. Trent told the task force that he traveled with Casey from Los Angeles to the Grove either the last weekend of July or the first weekend of August. Trent attended only those two weekends in 1980, and Casey was his guest for one of them. But Smith testified that he attended the Grove in 1980 only on the last weekend of July and remembered seeing Casey with Trent at the Grove's Parsonage camp. That meant, the House task force decided, that Casey was at the Grove on the last weekend of July. Case closed.

But under close inspection the "Bohemian Grove alibi" collapsed. It was not only a selective reading of the evidence. It was flatly contradicted by a solid record of documentary proof.

First, it was Trent's recollection that he left for the Grove around noon on Thursday, July 24, and, indeed, three dated-and-signed bar receipts established that Trent was at the Grove that Thursday. However, Casey was filmed collecting a matching-fund check at the Federal Election Commission in Washington on July 24th. On the same day, according to his financial records, Casey was charged for using the telephone at the Metropolitan Club, also in Washington. Even the House task force agreed that Casey could not have flown to Los Angeles until Friday. So Casey could not have left Los Angeles with Trent on Thursday. By themselves, Trent's bar receipts and the evidence putting Casey in Washington made the "Bohemian Grove alibi" an impossibility. But there was much more.

On Friday, July 25, Trent stayed at the Grove, according to the club's financial records. He signed two more Grove bar tabs and was charged for skeet shooting, a daytime activity. Trent never claimed that he made another round-trip to Los Angeles to pick up Casey, and the record supports Trent's presence during the day at the Bohemian Grove.

But a theoretical return trip to Los Angeles was irrelevant because the documentary record shows that Casey never went to the West Coast that Friday. Casey's personal calendars list two meetings in the GOP campaign headquarters in Arlington, Virginia, on Friday morning. And while the task force found no documentary evidence that Casey flew to Los Angeles (no tickets, no receipts, no notations, no calendar entries), the investigators discovered a ticket that Casey bought for the Eastern Airlines' Washington-to-New York shuttle on Friday, July 25. It was the type of shuttle ticket that is purchased and signed at the airport before a passenger gets on the plane. So instead of flying to Los Angeles and then San Francisco, the documentary record shows Casey going to New York City.

Two days into Casey's supposed Bohemian Grove visit, his calendar for Saturday, July 26, cites a meeting with a "Mrs. Tobin." The investigators identified the woman as Mary Jane Tobin, a New York-based right-to-life advocate. She confirmed meeting with Casey at his estate on Roslyn Harbor, Long Island, but could not remember the precise date. When I called her, Mrs. Tobin did say that the weather was very hot. The temperature on July 26 in New York was in the 90s. So her memory matched the documentary record of Casey going to New York for this meeting.

But nothing, not even solid documentary evidence, would stand in the way of the House insistence on the "Bohemian Grove alibi." The House task force was not even deterred when it obtained a group photograph of the men staying with Trent at the Parsonage camp on Sunday, July 27. Casey was not in the photo. The imaginary San Francisco-to-London flight also was supported by no documentary evidence—no ticket, no boarding pass, no receipt. That was just more speculation.

But as consistent as all the documentary evidence was that Casey remained on the East Coast from July 24–26 and was not at the Bohemian Grove, the evidence was even stronger that Casey traveled to Los Angeles and to the Grove the *following* weekend.

For starters, Casey's calendar showed that he was in Los Angeles on Friday, August 1. Meeting notes taken by Reagan foreign policy adviser Richard Allen put Casey at a campaign strategy session in Los Angeles on that date. Allen's diagram of where the meeting's participants sat showed Darrell Trent across the table from Casey. So while Trent could not have left with Casey for the Grove on July 24 because Casey was in Washington, Trent and Casey were together on August 1 in Los Angeles before Trent went to the Grove that weekend.

Trent's Bohemian Grove bill showed him with three more bar tabs at the resort on August 1. Also, on that date, both Trent and Casey were charged $9 apiece for the Grove "play book" which commemorates the annual play put on by Bohemian Club members that last weekend of the encampment.

At *Frontline*, we already knew a great deal about the "Bohemian Grove alibi" because producer Jim Gilmore had examined the possibility in preparing the second October Surprise documentary. As diligent as ever, Gilmore called many of the members who stayed at the Parsonage camp in 1980. Gilmore located two members who had attended the Grove only on the last weekend of July 1980, and they had no memory of Casey being there. Their recollection matched the group photograph which also showed Casey not present.

But Gilmore also found a Bohemian Club member, San Francisco businessman Matthew McGowan, who had been at the Grove each weekend that summer and kept a diary on each day. For August 3, the last Sunday of the Grove encampment, McGowan wrote: "1980 Bohemian Grove encampment closed this date. A very good encampment for me. We had Bill Casey, Gov. Reagan's campaign mgr., as our guest this last weekend." So besides the Bohemian Club financial records, there was even a contemporaneous written record of Casey attending the Grove the first weekend of August, not the last weekend of July.

McGowan's diary entry, buttressed by the large body of documentary evidence and testimony, should have settled the issue once and for all. Casey was on the East Coast for July 25–26, not at the Bohemian Grove. He was in Los Angeles on August 1 and went to the Grove later that day for the weekend. The documentary record could not account for Casey's whereabouts from Saturday evening, July 26, until Monday afternoon, July 28, when he appeared in London. That still left two mornings open for the alleged Madrid meetings.

Even the House investigators admitted that "on its face" McGowan's notation placed Casey at the Grove on the first weekend of August, not the last weekend in July. Astonishingly, however, the House task force concluded that "the great weight of evidence" put Casey at the Grove from July 25–27. To reach this judgment, the investigators decided that: McGowan must have made a mistake in his diary; Trent's signed-and-dated Grove bar tabs for July 24 must be in error; Casey must not have taken the Eastern shuttle to New York on July 25; the three meetings listed on his calendar for July 25–26 must have been cancelled; Casey must have been out for a walk when the group photo was snapped on the last weekend in July.

The House task force would not be dissuaded from the "Bohemian Grove alibi." To counter the documentary evidence, Barcella's team made much out of Darrell Trent's statement that after leaving the Grove, he understood that Casey was planning to fly from San Francisco to London. Relying on this recollection, the investigators rejected contrary testimony from Casey's chauffeur, who remembered picking Casey up at Washington's Dulles airport on the Sunday that Casey returned from the Bohemian Grove. The chauffeur's testimony would have debunked the theory of a San Francisco-to-London flight because Casey would not have had enough time to stop first in Washington.

But Trent's memory that Casey had mentioned London should not have been taken seriously at all. When Jim Gilmore interviewed Trent nearly a year before his congressional testimony, Trent had no memory of Casey going to London. The London memory was added to Trent's recollection only after Gilmore told Trent the significance of the question about the Bohemian Grove dates. Indeed, in his testimony, Trent freely admitted that he might have inserted London into his story after he heard about the controversy over Casey's whereabouts.

"I don't know whether [that recollection of London] was triggered by some of the information that I have heard since on the reason for the investigation, or whether in fact he did say that he was going to London," Trent acknowledged. So Trent conceded that his memory might well have been tainted and that Casey might never have mentioned London.

But this important admission was buried in the House final report as a footnote, as was the chauffeur's conflicting testimony. So unless a reader pored over the fine print of the footnote section, he would not know how flimsy the speculation about a San Francisco-to-London flight was.

The task force's other key argument for the "Bohemian Grove alibi" was Bernard Smith's recollection of seeing Casey and Trent together at the Parsonage camp. That sighting must have been on the last weekend of July, the House investigators argued, because Smith only attended the 1980 Grove that weekend. But Smith's memory was not for 1980, but rather for 1981 when Smith, Trent, and Casey were all at the Bohemian Grove encampment again. That year, Casey stayed at the Mandalay, a neighboring camp to the Parsonage, so Casey could easily have visited Trent several times in the Parsonage as Smith recalled.

While the plausibility of Smith recalling Casey and Trent in 1981 was high, the chance that Smith saw Casey in 1980 was nil. Not only did two other Grove members tell Gilmore that Casey was not there the last weekend in July, and not only did the group photo back that up, but the documentary record—most notably Trent's signed-and-dated bar tabs for July 24—made Casey's arrival on July 25 with Trent impossible.

Still, the House task force's fact-defying commitment to the "Bohemian Grove alibi" was not over. Barcella's team found their own piece of paper which they claimed overcame the overwhelming documentary evidence to the contrary. That proof was a handwritten sheet of phone calls made by Richard Allen on August 2, 1980. At the bottom of the page was scribbled a Long Island phone number for Casey. That meant, the investigators concluded, that Casey must have been on Long Island for the first weekend in August, thus nixing it as the Bohemian Grove weekend. That would mean that Casey must have been at the Grove on the last weekend of July and, thus, not in Madrid.

But the Allen phone-call sheet did not support that conclusion at all. Other phone calls recorded on the page show times for the various conversations and include notations about what was said. The Casey number is accompanied by neither a time for the presumed call nor any notation of a conversation.

Indeed, Allen had no recollection of talking with Casey on that date. "I can't tell you whether or not I got through," Allen testified. The Reagan foreign policy adviser said only that he believed he asked his secretary for Casey's home number and wrote it down. He presumed he called it, but Allen had no memory of the call being answered. Allen also had no telephone bill showing a completed call and no notes.

Normally, this "evidence" would be dismissed as proving nothing. Just because someone writes down a person's phone number does not mean the person is at the phone's location. But in the anything-goes world of October Surprise debunking, Richard Allen suddenly had been granted magical powers to transport Bill Casey to Long Island simply by scribbling down Casey's home number. Any child could have spotted the flaw in this "logic," but not the House task force.

So the new question was, how could a staff of experienced lawyers and investigators accept this paper as proof of Casey's location on Long Island in defiance of solid documentary evidence—Bohemian Club records and McGowan's diary—putting Casey in California? There seemed to be only two plausible answers: either the House investigators were very stupid or they were very biased. But nobody could be that dumb. So the only possible conclusion was that the House task force was willing to twist any evidence to disprove the October Surprise allegations. Evidence that fit that bias, no matter how flimsy or contradicted, was accepted; any that went the other way, no matter how strong, was thrown out.

The "Bohemian Grove alibi" and the theory of Dick Allen's magical transporting powers were so ludicrous that they put into doubt the handling of the entire investigation. If the investigators were so determined to debunk the October Surprise story that they would embrace these arguments, how fairly did Barcella's team question witnesses or evaluate the FBI wiretaps of Cyrus Hashemi's office? What other evidence had been read through the same distortive prism of investigative bias? Why should anyone give credence to a task force that believed that writing down a person's phone number automatically proved that the person was sitting next to the phone?

Still, the phoniness of the "Bohemian Grove alibi" did not mean that Jamshid Hashemi was telling the truth about the alleged Madrid meetings. To me, that allegation remained very much in doubt. The collapse of the Bohemian Grove alibi only destroyed the task force's certainty that Casey could not have been in Madrid.

The same debunking bias was on display when the task force tried to plug the hole for October 19, the date for the supposed Paris meeting. Again, at Republican urging, the investigators seized on more dubious testimony about Casey's activities. This time, the alibi came from Casey's nephew, Larry, who claimed that he remembered his father calling Uncle Bill on Sunday, October 19. Bill Casey was hard at work at the campaign office in Arlington, Larry Casey said, and thus could not have gone to Paris.

Larry Casey insisted that his recollection of the phone call was clear, but he had no phone records because it had been a local call. Larry's father had since died, so he could not corroborate the conversation. Still, the House investigators were now satisfied that they had driven a stake through the heart of the original October Surprise allegation of a Casey trip to Paris in mid-October.

But there was one problem with Larry Casey's testimony, besides the implausibility of remembering the precise date of a telephone call made a dozen years ago. Larry Casey had given Robert Ross and me a videotaped interview in fall 1991—and the nephew had told a completely different story. Then, Bill Casey's alibi was that he was at dinner with Larry Casey's father and mother in the dark-woody Jockey Club in Washington on the evening of October 19. "It was very clear in mind even though it was 11 years ago, my uncle actually taking them to dinner at the Jockey Club," Larry Casey said in the videotaped interview.

With the camera rolling, I then handed Larry Casey the visitor logs for the GOP headquarters, which showed that his mother and father had actually picked up Bill Casey at his office on the night of October 15, not 19. Later, Casey's American Express receipts would also establish the date of the Jockey Club dinner as October 15. Larry Casey's recollection of the dinner at the Jockey Club was four days off.

A year later, Larry Casey had dropped his Jockey Club story and was now offering a new alibi—the phone call—to congressional investigators. He had made no mention of the telephone call when he talked to Ross and me a year earlier. Although I informed both Republican and Democratic investigators about the contradiction, they still accepted Larry Casey's account as credible and relied on it as proof that William Casey had spent the day in the Washington area.

Focused on re-election and then the inauguration of a new president, the congressmen assigned to the task force paid little attention to the details of the investigation. Few Democrats on the task force—or their staffs—had any idea what was going into the report or how strong the evidence was or wasn't. In effect, they had put their faith in Barcella, who was vowing by late December to bury the October Surprise allegations under the new alibis.

One task force member, however, was uneasy. Rep. Mervyn Dymally, a California Democrat who was retiring from Congress, was annoyed by how hard the task force staff had made reviewing the evidence even for congressmen. Though the October Surprise story was presumably a myth, the report was kept highly classified and could be read by congressmen only under guard or if they went to the task force offices in a remote Capitol Hill building.

After finally seeing a censored version of the report, Dymally had a staff aide prepare a dissent. Submitted on January 3, 1993, the dissent complained about selective handling of evidence to clear the Reagan campaign. Dymally cited the investigation's reliance on shaky circumstantial data and its uncritical acceptance of accounts from Casey's associates.

Dymally told me that the day his dissent was submitted, he received a call from Lee Hamilton warning him that if the dissent was not withdrawn, "I will have to come down hard on you." The next day, Hamilton, the new chairman of the House Foreign Affairs Committee, dismissed the staff of the Africa subcommittee that Dymally had headed. The firings were billed as routine, and Hamilton told me that "the two things came along at the same time, but they were not connected in my mind." Hamilton said his warning related only to a toughly worded written response that he would have made to Dymally's dissent. That response would have criticized Dymally for missing task force meetings and assigning a staff aide who lacked security clearances.

But out of office and hoping to help some of his old staff win back their jobs, Dymally decided that discretion was the better part of valor. He dropped his dissent, though he refused to sign the final report.

The bipartisan task force report was released on January 13, 1993. It concluded that there was "no credible evidence" to support allegations that the Reagan-Bush campaign had struck a deal to delay the release of the hostages or that Casey had even contacted Iranian emissaries.

In a *New York Times* opinion article defending the findings, Lee Hamilton said one of the keys to debunking the October Surprise suspicions was proving where Casey was on days when the meetings in Madrid and Paris were alleged to have happened. Having established solid Casey alibis for the last weekend of July (the Bohemian Grove) and on October 19 (the phone call), Hamilton wrote, the task force's findings "should put the controversy to rest once and for all."[2]

---

[2] Lee H. Hamilton, "Case Closed," *New York Times*, January 24, 1993, p. 17.

26

TRICK OR TREASON?

So what really did happen? Did William Casey strike a deal with the radical Iranian mullahs to keep the 52 Americans hostage in Tehran until Ronald Reagan was safely ensconced in the White House? Or did a loose-knit band of arms dealers and low-lifes invent the whole scenario and play out the charade for some convoluted motive? Was the October Surprise, on one side, a trick played by some master deceivers or, on the other side, treason committed by some Republicans whose electoral blind ambition had run wild?

Throughout the two-year October Surprise investigation, I had remained agnostic about the conspiracy allegations, or perhaps ambivalent might be a better word. Sometimes I thought Casey probably had contacted the Iranians; other times I didn't. One of my problems was that I couldn't picture these meetings actually happening. From my middle-American background, the scenarios seemed too fantastic, too melodramatic: night flights to foreign capitals for secret meetings in luxury hotels. One of the strongest arguments against the October Surprise story was simply its implausibility.

On the other hand, the Republicans linked to the allegations were not exactly run-of-the-mill characters. William Casey and John Shaheen had been World War II spies. George Bush had been Director of Central Intelligence. Others, too, had spent years in the CIA or had lived in the world of high-finance where private jets and international travel were the norm. These men were not strangers to the idea of secret diplomacy. They also saw the stakes as monumental, the chance to wrest the power of the U.S. government away from a naive ex-governor who, they felt, had failed to protect America's national security and the broader interests of the Western alliance.

I also could not forget former Secretary of State Alexander Haig's lecture when I had questioned why government officials might lie about a national security issue. "Jesus! God!" he had exclaimed. "You'd better get out and read Machiavelli or somebody else because I think you're living in a dream world! People do what their national interest tells them to do and if it means lying to a friendly nation, they're going to lie through their teeth." The Iran-contra scandal had proven that these same Republicans were not above lying to Congress and to the American people as well.

Nevertheless, the even worse credibility of the "witnesses" remained a fundamental flaw of the October Surprise story. There was no one who inspired unrestrained confidence, no one who erased the nagging doubts, no one who could be trusted to tell the inside story under the Klieg lights of a congressional hearing. In many ways, our investigation had been a long and frustrating search for a source who would be widely accepted as reliable. But finally—strangely enough from the House task force report—such a credible individual emerged from the fog. He told a story which just might be true.

The House investigators had heard from reporters at ABC News that there might be a former journalist who had important information about Casey meeting Iranians in Paris in October 1980. The ex-journalist was David Andelman, a former correspondent for the *New York Times* and CBS News. Recently, he had been the biographer of Count Alexandre deMarenches, Casey's old friend who was the head of the *Service de Documentation Exterieure et de Contre-Espionage* (SDECE), French intelligence, in 1980. Andelman had written deMarenches's English-language autobiography, *The Fourth World War*.

DeMarenches had always been a mysterious figure lurking on the fringes of the October Surprise story. Robert Ross and I had discovered early in our work that Casey had met privately with deMarenches during a brief trip to Paris on July 4, 1980. We also knew that deMarenches was one of the first foreign officials to sit down with Ronald Reagan after the 1980 election. The two had a private discussion at Reagan's home in California just weeks after the election. The meeting was revealed only years later in Bob Woodward's *Veil*, a book about Casey's swashbuckling adventures at the CIA.

In his sworn testimony to the House task force, Andelman said the October Surprise issue had come up in his discussion with deMarenches about the book they were writing together. Andelman wanted to know the background for the curious meeting with Reagan in December 1980 in California. Why, Andelman wondered, did the president-elect meet so early with a foreign intelligence chief?

DeMarenches told Andelman that the honor of the early get-together with the newly elected president resulted from assistance that he, de-Marenches, had given to the Reagan-Bush campaign. That help had been meetings which deMarenches claimed he arranged between Casey and Iranians in the summer and fall of 1980 to discuss the hostage issue. One of those meetings had been held in Paris in October, Andelman recalled. But the biographer added that deMarenches provided no other details and ordered that the story be kept out of the book because it could damage William Casey and George Bush.

Prior to interviewing Andelman, the task force had received a dismissive response from deMarenches about the October Surprise allegations. DeMarenches denied knowing anything when he spoke with House investigator Michael Zeldin over the phone. DeMarenches said he had not even seen Casey in the summer or fall of 1980—though two Casey associates, Albert Jolis and Richard Allen, had confirmed that Casey and deMarenches did talk in early July. DeMarenches grudgingly agreed to a face-to-face meeting with Zeldin in Paris. But the ex-spy chief barely gave Zeldin time to take off his coat before again denying any knowledge about the October Surprise and sending Zeldin packing.

Despite deMarenches's early denial, the task force had reasons to believe Andelman. A well-connected French investigative reporter, Claude Angeli, testified that his sources inside the French secret service confirmed that deMarenches had provided "cover" for a meeting between American Republicans and Iranians in France on the weekend of October 18–19, 1980. Martin Kilian had received a similar account from one of deMarenches's top aides. So Andelman's testimony did not stand alone.

The allegation of a Paris meeting was, of course, not new. Ross and I had interviewed French arms dealer Nicholas Ignatiew, who worked closely with deMarenches's intelligence service on Middle East hostage negotiations. Ignatiew stated that he checked with his government contacts in 1988 and was told that Republican-Iranian meetings had occurred in mid-October 1980 in Paris.

As early as 1987, Iranian ex-president Bani-Sadr had made similar claims. So had American arms dealer William Herrmann and Israeli Ari Ben-Menashe. *Chicago Tribune* reporter John Maclean was told by a well-placed Republican source in mid-October 1980 that then vice presidential candidate George Bush was on his way to Paris for hostage talks with Iranians. Pilot Heinrich Rupp even claimed he flew Casey from Washington to Paris in October 1980. The House task force, of course, judged these accounts untrue. But why would credible individuals around French intelligence be making matching claims?

The task force also received testimony from Iranian arms merchant Ahmed Heidari linking deMarenches to a secret French-Israeli arms shipment to Iran in fall 1980. Heidari said he approached de-Marenches in September 1980 to seek help obtaining weapons for the Iranian military, which then was confronting the Iraqi army in oil-rich Khuzistan province. Though deMarenches refused to provide the arms directly, he did put Heidari in touch with a French middleman named Yves deLoreilhe, Heidari testified. The connection led to an Iranian arms shipment that left France by plane on October 23. During a stop in Tel Aviv, 250 tires for U.S.-built F-4 fighters were loaded on the plane by Israeli government agents. Back in France, spare parts for M-60 tanks and other military equipment were added to the load before the shipment was flown on to Tehran on October 24. President Carter protested the violation of the arms embargo to Israel's prime minister Menachem Begin, but Begin allowed the flight to go ahead.

In his early interview with the House task force, deMarenches denied ever meeting Heidari. But Heidari's account of French intelligence collaboration was corroborated, in part, by a memo written in 1981 by a

French participant in the shipment, Jacques Montanes, president of a Paris-based air cargo firm. In the memo, Montanes claimed that one of deMarenches's top assistants, Alain deMarolles, SDECE's director of operations, had given "the tacit agreement" for the deliveries. Montanes wrote that the shipments then were coordinated with an Israeli diplomat in Paris. Montanes also claimed that the British gave the operation the code name "Pharoah" because some Scorpio tank engines were diverted to Iran from a contract with the Egyptian defense ministry. From reading Montanes's memo, it seemed as if Heidari's arms flight was on the radar scopes of many key governments even before it left the ground.

Most important to the October Surprise story, Heidari's testimony put French intelligence operatives in league with the Israeli and Iranian governments on an arms shipment at the same time October Surprise "witnesses" were alleging the French and Israelis were cooperating with Republican hostage initiatives. Based on Heidari's testimony, it appeared that deMarenches may have been the linchpin that held the four-sided operation together, connecting the Republicans with the Israelis, Iranians, and French.

The House task force, however, dismissed the French-Israel-Iran shipment as simply a scheme "to make money" and "serve the strategic needs of Israel." The cocky investigators declared that "no linkage between this deal and the release of the American hostages could be found because none exists." Though noting the alleged overtures to French intelligence, the task force concluded that "it would be disingenuous to use this attempt to reach representatives of French intelligence, particularly Count deMarenches, as a basis for concluding that Bill Casey was the hand behind this operation." One might have thought Andelman's testimony would have raised fresh doubts among the House investigators, but it didn't.

In January 1993, I reached Andelman by phone at Burson-Marsteller, a Washington-based public relations firm where he worked as an executive. Andelman was cooperative in responding to my questions, but he was not eager to be dragged into the spotlight about the October Surprise story. He said he had simply answered the questions put to him by the task force investigators and freely acknowledged that his information was second-hand.

"I'm quite confident that the count [deMarenches] will deny it because that is what he does," Andelman told me. "He thought the world of Casey and Bush, and never wanted anything to come out that would hurt Bush's chances for re-election or Casey's legacy."

As for Bush possibly joining the Paris meetings, Andelman said de-Marenches made no mention of that, causing Andelman to assume that the vice presidential candidate had not gone. But Andelman added that when he raised the Paris issue with deMarenches during a 1992 book promotion tour, the French spymaster refused to discuss the October Surprise publicly because "I don't want to hurt my friend, George Bush," who was then campaigning for re-election.

To the House task force, the Andelman testimony was just an annoying last-minute diversion. Having already rejected the possibility of a Paris meeting, the House task force did not even bother to re-interview de-Marenches about the startling new allegation. Zeldin placed a few phone calls to deMarenches's office to ask for comment on Andelman's disclosures. But deMarenches did not call back, and the follow-up stopped there. The new account about deMarenches arranging Paris meetings between Casey and Iranians was not "outcome-affecting," Zeldin told me.[1] Andelman's account was dismissed, although the task force conceded that the ex-journalist was a credible witness.

In one of its more imaginative explanations, the task force reasoned that the story lacked "probative value" because Andelman could not rule out the possibility that deMarenches had lied about the Casey meeting in Paris so that, in case the October Surprise allegations turned out some

---

[1] While working on the October Surprise investigation, Zeldin was also scouting for future work. Zeldin landed that job with former Republican U.S. Attorney Joseph diGenova, Larry Barcella's old boss, who had been named as independent counsel to examine the so-called Passport-gate case. That scandal erupted in the closing days of the 1992 campaign when officials for President Bush's State Department searched Bill Clinton's passport file apparently digging for dirt that could be used to challenge the Democratic nominee's patriotism. Zeldin was hired by diGenova for the Passport-gate probe along with David Laufman, a Republican veteran of the October Surprise investigation and ex-CIA official. DiGenova told the *Washington Post* (January 27, 1993) that Zeldin recommended Laufman for the job.

day to be true, the old French spy chief would not lose face with his biographer.

That sort of fear did not seem to fit the personality of the imperious deMarenches who had directed the powerful French intelligence services for more than a decade. DeMarenches was anything but loose-lipped. In his book, *The Fourth World War*, deMarenches cited the "code of silence" that a senior intelligence official accepts. "It is as profound as any blood fealty sworn by a tribal chieftain," he said. "The knowledge and power wielded by those in my chosen profession are accompanied by a need to guard our crown jewels in the most profound secrecy."[2]

In the book, deMarenches gave the reader a glimpse of a few jewels but always in settings favorable to conservative causes. He described his post-election meeting with Reagan in California when the spy chief lectured the president-elect about the coming Apocalypse. DeMarenches said he warned Reagan, an interested student, about the growing dangers of international communism and Third World terrorism. At another session after Reagan entered the White House, deMarenches stressed the need for bold and imaginative action to protect Western interests. He then outlined a plan dubbed "Operation Mosquito," which involved a joint U.S.-French covert action to smuggle drugs into Afghanistan to addict the Soviet soldiers.

"If this works, you will upset the Russians," deMarenches said he told the president. "There will be considerable pressure on them to pack up and go home to avoid moral and physical disintegration."[3] The French spy-master said an enthusiastic Reagan quickly reached for the secure phone to call Casey. DeMarenches wrote that Casey then asked the French spy chief to undertake the drug operation. With discreet White House backing, Operation Mosquito was put in place but ultimately was dropped for fear of public disclosure, deMarenches said. Still, in their commitment to aggressive covert operations against the Soviets, Casey, Reagan, and deMarenches appeared to have been of like minds.

In his book, deMarenches also praised President Bush for his work at the CIA in 1976–77 and for his understanding that intelligence operations

---

[2] DeMarenches and Andelman, *op cit.*, p. 16.

[3] *Ibid.*, p. 16.

must be performed with utmost secrecy. In an early meeting with Bush in 1976, deMarenches proposed "some joint system of cooperation with the Americans, similar to the loose working arrangements we had with our European allies."[4] Bush was sympathetic but cautious, deMarenches noted.

The French spymaster, however, felt nothing but contempt for Bush's successor, Stansfield Turner. "It was not surprising that the Carter administration all but succeeded in destroying America's human intelligence capability," deMarenches said of Turner's four years at the CIA's helm.

DeMarenches, the hardline conservative ideologue, was forced into retirement in May 1981 with the election of Socialist president François Mitterrand. But deMarenches remained close to Reagan and Casey. When Oliver North needed to raise money for the Nicaraguan contras in 1985, deMarenches volunteered his services soliciting money at pro-contra fundraisers in Texas. In deMarenches, there was a man with the motive, means, and temperament to make October Surprise meetings happen. Andelman's testimony should not have been cavalierly dismissed as it was by the House task force.

My personal evaluation of the October Surprise story changed with the testimony of David Andelman. Finally we had encountered an undeniably credible witness with a modest story that possessed the ring of truth. Further, the story was supported by other witnesses' testimony and a large body of circumstantial evidence, including deMarenches's relationship with Casey and his alleged hand in the Israeli-French military shipment to Iran in October 1980.

Andelman's testimony left me little choice but finally to come down on the side of believing that Casey had met with Iranian representatives in Paris during the election campaign. And once I had reached that opinion, I came to suspect that other accounts of Casey's travels—his reputed trips to Madrid and his Stoffberg-Jacobi meeting in London—might well be true, too. Buttressing those accounts from the more suspect sources was the inability of the House task force to construct credible alibis for Casey's whereabouts on those dates.

Concluding that Casey met with Iranians, however, did not mean that I

---

[4] *Ibid.*, p. 248.

believed the Reagan-Bush campaign chief necessarily had struck a deal to *delay* the hostages' freedom. Casey could have been seeking intelligence about the Carter-Iranian hostage negotiations, as the Senate report suggested, or he might have been trying to engineer an early hostage release. If accomplished early enough, freeing the hostages would have eliminated the possibility that President Carter could time a welcome-the-hostages-home extravaganza as an October Surprise to boost his re-election hopes.

A Republican bid to guarantee a hostage release after the elections but before the inauguration would also have made sense. After all the tough talk about Tehran being three feet deep and glowing in the dark, Ronald Reagan might have had no choice but to take precipitous action if the crisis had not been resolved. But in a violent clash, the hostages might have died, oil supplies might have been disrupted, and the thirst for revenge might have spread throughout the Middle East.

So there were logical alternative explanations for Casey meeting with Iranians other than thwarting Carter's hostage negotiations. Still, intended or not, Casey's actions could have disrupted efforts by legitimate authorities to win the hostages' freedom.

Then there was the other big October Surprise question: Did George Bush join Casey in Paris to prove to the Iranians the seriousness of the Republican overture? This was the allegation that I had long considered the most implausible of all. The idea that the Republican vice-presidential candidate snuck out of the United States for a trip to Paris just three weeks before the election sounded outlandish. Not only would Bush have needed to slip away from his campaign aides, but he would have required collaboration from the Secret Service. That was hard to accept even as a remote possibility.

Plus, Israeli intelligence man Ari Ben-Menashe and pilot Heinrich Rupp were the primary sources claiming to have seen Bush in Paris. Neither was considered credible. Even when many of Ben-Menashe's other unlikely allegations—from the cozy U.S.-Iraqi ties to his Iran-contra secrets—were checking out, it was his Bush story that devastated Ben-Menashe's believability. In both *Frontline* programs we had cited Secret Service records placing Bush in Washington on October 19, 1980, to challenge Ben-Menashe's claim.

But still, there were troubling anomalies about Bush's alibi. First, we had located *Chicago Tribune* reporter John Maclean, who had been told by a Republican source in mid-October 1980 that Bush was on his way to Paris to talk to Iranians about the hostages. It was a remarkable coincidence that intelligence operatives would allege exactly that same set of events years later, yet have had no contact with Maclean.

Second, President Bush never fully explained what he was doing on that Sunday in October, despite his repeated public declarations that he was not in Paris. His Secret Service records reflected two seemingly innocuous trips—one to the Chevy Chase Country Club in late morning and the other to the home of a family friend in the afternoon. The only Secret Service agent who claimed to remember the first trip put Mrs. Bush and Mrs. Potter Stewart at the brunch, but the two women were apparently not there.

Then, the congressional investigation was given the name of the family friend for the afternoon trip only after agreeing not to divulge the name or interview the witness. At that point in mid-1992, President Bush was publicly demanding that he be cleared of any suspicion that he had flown to Paris. Logically, Bush should have wanted this family friend to eliminate any remaining doubts about the October Surprise story. Instead, the Bush administration kept investigators away from the alibi witness.

Despite these gaps in the investigation, Hamilton's task force rushed to endorse Bush's Paris denial under duress, a Republican threat to block continued funding if that judgment was not reached in the interim report on July 1, 1992. But ironically, because of Bush's success in frustrating a thorough examination of his whereabouts, the "Where was George?" question might never be answered with finality.

The same might be true of the whole October Surprise mystery. The congressional failure to consider the possibility that "respectable" figures in Washington might be lying prevented the kind of aggressive investigation that could have laid the allegations to rest for good. In addition, a credible inquiry required some politically experienced investigators who believed that the accusations were true. If these proponents could be convinced that the story was bogus, then the findings would have carried much more legitimacy. Instead, pro-October Surprise figures, such as

Spencer Oliver, were barred from the investigation, while committed debunkers and investigators with pro-Reagan-Bush conflicts of interest were not.

From Watergate to Iran-contra, White House stonewalls crumbled only because of tenacious digging by open-minded investigators in the government and the press. These investigators were willing to get their hands dirty and risk soiling their reputations to get at the truth. There was no comparable determination among the congressional investigators on October Surprise, and there were only a few reporters who dared put their mainstream careers in jeopardy.

The House task force conclusion, dismissing the October Surprise allegations as impossible and denouncing the "witnesses" as liars, might be reassuring to many. It might make Reagan-Bush partisans happy. It might justify a new round of Washington snickering about "conspiracy theories." But for me, it will always carry with it the question: Is this official reality or real reality? As French spymaster deMarenches wrote, "there are two sorts of history. There is the history we see and hear, the official history; and there is the secret history—the things that happen behind the scenes, in the dark, that go bump in the night."

In my personal search through the dark that had enveloped the October Surprise story, I discovered how painful—how bumpy—the quest for historical truth could be. Many times, I had regretted accepting *Frontline*'s assignment in 1990. I faulted myself for risking my future in mainstream journalism. After all, that is where the decent-paying jobs are. I had jeopardized my ability to support my four children out of an old-fashioned sense of duty, a regard for an unwritten code that expects reporters to take almost any assignment.

The damage to my reputation from the two-year investigation had been substantial. Even friends told me that because of my work on the October Surprise story, I had gotten a reputation around Washington as a "conspiracy theorist." Doors for possible jobs slammed in my face.

My mood would darken when the personal attacks accelerated, as they did with the nasty debunking stories in fall 1991 and the House report in early 1993. My minority dissents against the many errors and the staggering illogic contained in those findings opened me to vilification, most notably from Steven Emerson and Lawrence Barcella, who chose to defend themselves by smearing me, my motives, and my credibility.

Emerson, who refused to acknowledge his own journalistic errors such as putting Casey in London at the wrong times in July 1980, continued to invent opinions for me to hold. He insisted that I was an October Surprise "adherent," thus disparaging my professional objectivity. Barcella claimed I had slipped into a "conspiratorial miasma" because I would not accept his October Surprise judgments, including the Bohemian Grove and phone call alibis.

In this poisonous environment, I often found myself depressed for no other reason than that my faith in the profession of journalism had been shaken. Nearly all my Washington colleagues stayed away from the October Surprise story as if it were a new strain of the plague. I found that by the early 1990s, there was more careerism among journalists than honest commitment to get the facts to the American people.

In the 1980s and 1990s, the Washington press corps had failed, again and again, to confront government deceit and get to the truth. Part of the reason was fear; another part was laziness; a third was coziness with government officials. Too many historical questions—many of which swirled around Casey's controversial actions at the CIA—were left unanswered or ignored outright.

I could not forget that the Iran-contra scandal had broken open in Washington in 1986 not because of the investigative reporting that a few of us were doing into Oliver North's secret network. The story finally cracked through the government denials because a teenaged army draftee in Nicaragua shot down a supply plane in October 1986. A month later, again no thanks to American reporters, a newspaper in Lebanon disclosed President Reagan's arms-for-hostage deals in Iran.

Given those embarrassments, one might have expected that the Iran-contra scandal would have sparked a renaissance in investigative reporting. Instead, as the White House deliberately delayed the official investigations and covered up the roles of senior officials, the Washington press corps quickly grew bored with Iran-contra. Over time, reporters and columnists began grumbling over independent counsel Lawrence Walsh's dogged attempts to dig out the facts and to expose the long-running obstruction of justice that had been organized inside the White House.

Like those of us who examined the October Surprise mystery, Walsh often found himself the target of journalists who adopted the troubling position of opposing the honest pursuit of truth. A number of columnists even praised President Bush's pardoning of six Iran-contra figures on Christmas Eve 1992, a move that effectively ended the Iran-contra probe and protected the White House cover-up. By the end of the Reagan-Bush era, it seemed, journalists were not only acquiescing in the theft of Ameridan history, they sometimes were advocating it.

My wife Diane once likened my state of mind at the end of the investigation to that of a person disillusioned by a religion. In a sense, she was right. Journalism—the daily chaotic pursuit of the facts and the news—had been a central part of my adult life and a profession that I considered more a public trust than a job. I believed that honest reporting was vital to a democratic system. It was the means of conveying information to the public so the voters could hold elected officials accountable. Too often in this era, my profession had fallen woefully short.

At noon, on January 20, 1993, the 12-year Reagan-Bush era formally came to an end. George Bush, a man who relished the intrigue of foreign policy but had neglected the nation's declining economy, watched as 46-year-old Bill Clinton was sworn in as the 42nd president of the United States. Clinton, whose only government service had been as governor of the provincial state of Arkansas, assumed the nation's chief executive office. He carried with him an ambitious domestic agenda but possessed little experience on the international gameboard.

Two days before Clinton's inauguration, my father passed away. He had been in poor health for several years, so his death was not entirely unexpected. He also had been a staunch Republican and had dreaded the prospect of another Democrat in the White House. Losing him brought my spirits to a very low point. I was packing my suitcase and preparing to drive my family to Massachusetts for my father's funeral as I watched Clinton's inaugural address on television.

The day was sunny and unseasonably warm, matching the nation's hopefulness at the start of a new presidential era. But the traditional pomp and circumstance, the comforting continuity that custom brings, took my mind back to that hectic day a dozen years earlier when Ronald Reagan heralded another new era by taking the oath of office. At that moment, 52 American diplomats and servicemen waited at Mahrabad Airport as their plane prepared to fly out of Iran to freedom. They were ending an agonizing 444 days in captivity.

On that cold day in 1981, Ronald Reagan addressed a nation seeking quick answers to America's decline in world respect. Twelve years later, Bill Clinton spoke to a people tired of the excesses and deceits that had accompanied those solutions. Emphasizing his break with the recent past, Clinton celebrated "the mystery of American renewal." The young president noted that the inaugural "ceremony is held in the depth of winter, but by the words we speak and the faces we show the world, we force the spring—a spring reborn in the world's oldest democracy, that brings forth the vision and courage to reinvent America."

But Clinton's promise to renew American democracy did not include a commitment to get to the truth about the national security scandals and mysteries that had spanned the Reagan-Bush era. Already, Clinton had decided to look forward, not backward. He saw his political future resting on his ability to revitalize the American economy and reduce the federal budget deficits, not to answer the controversial historical questions of the Republican era.

In that approach, Clinton was following the majority opinion of his inner circle, which urged him to let bygones be bygones; "don't stop thinking about tomorrow," in the words of his campaign theme song. Pursuing the truth about the Iraqgate courtship of Saddam Hussein or the Iran-contra coverups or even the Bush administration's clumsy attempt to unearth damaging evidence from Clinton's passport file would be a distraction, these advisers thought. Those investigations might sow the seeds of partisanship and dissension. The new administration might reap a bitter harvest of Republican obstructionism against Clinton's economic programs. As for October Surprise, Lee Hamilton assured the incoming administration that his investigation had laid those troubling allegations to rest.

Having won the presidency, and controlling both houses of Congress, the Democrats chose to be magnanimous. The plugs were pulled on the congressional spotlighting of Iraqgate. Not a peep of protest was heard when ex-President Bush refused to submit to a free-ranging interview by Iran-contra prosecutor Lawrence Walsh. The Clinton Justice Department even supported Bush's last-minute arrangements to keep control of his White House's computerized messages, a blow to historians seeking a truthful record of decision-making for the entire 12-year period.

But Clinton got no thanks for turning his back on investigations into GOP misdeeds. Instead of bipartisan peace, he faced unrelenting Republican opposition to his economic program. During his first six months in office, House and Senate Republicans cast party-line votes against Clinton's budget proposals, his job-creation bill, and his tax plans. Clinton was left scrambling to scrape together barely enough Democratic votes to keep his administration from suffering crippling defeats. His approval ratings and popularity plummeted to historic lows for a new president. As it had so often during the Reagan-Bush era, Democratic bipartisanship had backfired.

With official Washington preoccupied with the present, piecing together an honest history of the Reagan-Bush era again was left to the occasional private researcher or out-of-the-mainstream journalists. In spring 1993, for instance, I was asked by a small independent filmmaking firm, K-Video Productions of New York City, to conduct some interviews in Israel for a documentary the company was making on the secret history of the Reagan-Bush era. Planning a 90-minute film, the firm was concentrating on the period's three major mysteries—Iran-contra, Iraqgate, and October Surprise—and was following the trail of Ari Ben-Menashe to show how treacherous the path toward the truth could be. The project's goals were ambitious, probably beyond the company's limited resources, but I agreed to go once more to Israel.

Assisted by Israeli journalist Pazit Ravina, the K-Video team landed its first interview with Yitzhak Shamir, who recently had been forced into retirement as prime minister when his Likud Party lost national elections. On May 13, in a rented van, the documentary crew drove from the American Colony hotel in East Jerusalem to Shamir's office in a modern building in downtown Tel Aviv, near Israel's military headquarters. After a brief wait and a security check of the video gear, we were ushered in to talk with Shamir, a short man in his late 70s whose public image in the United States was that of a dour conservative.

In person, however, Shamir struck me as casual and witty, even charming. In reaction to some questions, the deep lines of his face would turn up in silent amusement. Other times, he would smile or laugh in finessing a question. He was not at all the rigid character who appeared on U.S. television screens throughout the 1980s, arguing for a hardline reaction to Palestinian protests. His conservatism also was not the anti-communist or free-market variety of the West; it was a heartfelt commitment to retain the West Bank and the Golan Heights for Israel.

As for our questions about the Iranian revolution in 1979, Shamir agreed that the upheaval "constituted a danger for us until this day. . . . We are worried all the time about what is going on there." Shamir added that Israel had sought "to be of help to the United States" in its dealings with Iran after the Islamic revolution.

"We did what we could," explained Shamir, a Zionist independence fighter and longtime Mossad official before his political career. "This was the principle. I don't know many details about it. I was not involved in the details, and you know, I am used to forgetting details I don't need."

But Shamir, who had risen to be Israel's foreign minister in 1980, had a startling assessment of the larger October Surprise issue. "I know about all the efforts of the Carter administration," the ex-prime minister said in response to a question about the 1980 hostage impasse. "And well, I read this interesting book of Gary Sick's," a reference to Sick's account of his investigation, published in fall 1991 and entitled *October Surprise*.

"What do you think?" Pazit Ravina asked, picking up on Shamir's opening. "Was there an October Surprise?"

"Of course, it was," Shamir responded without hesitation. "It was," he repeated. My eyebrows rose in amazement. Here was a senior Israeli official, who had been in a clear position to know the truth, first praising Sick's account of the 1980 intrigue and then asserting that he believed the October Surprise events had happened.

But also immediately, Shamir thought better of his answer and moved to add some gray to the coloring of his declaration. "I think it was," he continued, after a brief pause. He also moved quickly to dispel any suspicion that the Israeli government had collaborated in a scheme to influence the outcome of an American presidential election. "I don't think there was any special Israel activity in this framework," the former prime minister said. As Shamir backpedaled, he also insisted that he did not know anything specific and suggested that perhaps the coincidence of the hostage release with Ronald Reagan's inauguration was merely "an accident."

But were his hasty equivocation and sudden assertion of ignorance to be believed, considering his long experience with Israel's covert foreign policy both as a senior Mossad official stationed in Paris and as foreign minister? It had crossed my mind that the joint French-Israeli military shipment to Iran in October 1980 had started with intelligence contacts in Paris and almost certainly would have interested Shamir as the Israeli foreign minister. In 1983, Shamir succeeded fellow Likud Party member, Menachem Begin, as prime minister, so Shamir also would have had access to historical records explaining what the Israelis did about Iran in 1980. Known for his conspiratorial outlook forged during decades of clandestine operations, Shamir loved reading raw intelligence reports on important events.

"You did say at one point, that you thought there probably was an October Surprise," I cut in. "What makes you think there was?"

"Well, I think that this revolution, the Iranian revolution, was a very influential event in the life of our area, and it was a very, very dangerous event for Israel," Shamir responded, trying to turn the question in another direction.

"But the allegation, sir, is that the Republicans interjected themselves into the negotiations in some way—either to help resolve the crisis or prolong it," I reminded him.

"Well, I know in America, they know it," Shamir answered cryptically. "I have not been interested in it, and I don't remember anything that could help."

"Did the Israelis send any kind of delegation to meet with Iranians in Europe during this period, during the fall of 1980?"

"I don't think so," Shamir answered. "Anyhow, I don't know about it, I didn't know about it. Maybe, you know, people tried to get information.

There are all kinds of contacts, but it depends if these contacts are important or not important, you know. You can see that in Europe there are many Iranians who try to sell some secrets to interested factors [*sic*]. But it is not always serious and important."

"Do you have any knowledge of any specific event like that, where Israeli officials or Israeli contacts played such a role?" I asked.

"No, I don't remember," he said, unflustered by my pressing.

"If you did know about it, would you tell us?" I inquired.

"No, no, I don't remember such matters, you know," he answered, amused with the give-and-take.

Whatever his real knowledge, Shamir had opened the window slightly and then closed it. As often had been the case in the long investigation, an interview had provoked new questions: was Shamir speaking knowledgeably when he praised Sick's book and asserted that "of course, it was" true about the October Surprise? Or had he voiced an off-the-cuff opinion that he quickly corrected? He certainly had been in a position to know a great deal about the U.S.-Iranian back-and-forth on the hostages. But I had come never to expect any easy answers.

As for Ari Ben-Menashe, Shamir's response was sharp and unequivocal. "I don't want to hear his name," he said, without a smile on his face this time. But Shamir added, with the twinkle returning to his eyes, "Does this man even exist?"

Three days after the Shamir interview, we drove to the home of retired General Yehoshua Saguy, who had been chief of the Aman, Israeli military intelligence, in 1980. Saguy lived north of Tel Aviv, in a modern apartment overlooking the Mediterranean Sea. Saguy was a burly man with white hair, a white mustache, and teeth slightly discolored from a fondness for pipe-smoking.

Saguy shared Shamir's strong disdain for Ben-Menashe's talking out of school, and belittled his allegations. But, as with Shamir, and perhaps equally inadvertently, he offered some information that bolstered Ben-Menashe's broad description of events in 1980. When I asked the general about the Israeli hand in the October 1980 France-to-Israel-to-Iran weapons shipment, Saguy claimed no knowledge of that flight. But he recalled that Israel made two other military shipments to Iran during 1980, sending mortar shells, ammunition, Uzis, and light weaponry by sea. Ben-Menashe had long claimed that the Israelis sent Iran one batch of military supplies in spring 1980 and another in the fall.

What was even more intriguing about Saguy's account was his understanding that Prime Minister Begin had obtained approval from the United States for the shipments. Ben-Menashe had claimed that the American clearance came from the professionals within the CIA and the Republicans, after President Carter had demanded Begin's compliance with a Western arms embargo. Saguy told us that he wasn't sure exactly whom Begin approached.

"At that time, he was at the same time prime minister and defense minister," Saguy recalled. "He had weekly meetings of the highest level of intelligence and the defense ministry and so on every Friday morning dealing with such things at Tel Aviv, at the defense minister's office. . . . The [military shipment] was raised by the defense ministry . . . a man there raised the subject: 'There is a demand for a shipment of so and so—' Begin's answer was, 'Hold it, not until next week.' "

The following week, on Friday, Saguy said, Begin returned, claiming to have secured approval from the Americans. Begin limited the value of the shipment to $20 million and restricted it to light Israeli-manufactured armaments.

"Prime Minister Begin did not tell you at that time exactly who gave him the permission?" I asked.

"No," answered Saguy.

"So it could have been someone other than President Carter?"

"Could be."

But while unclear precisely which Americans were contacted by Begin, Saguy was certain "that such a shipment had been made. I know we did it twice, at least, in 1980." For the second shipment, the same pattern was followed, with a $20 million arms proposal arising from the Defense Ministry and Begin again returning the following week with the supposed U.S. sanctioning.

"And what was the policy rationale for the decisions?" I inquired.

"Look," the blunt-speaking Saguy continued, "Israel had strategic interests that the Iraqis would be busy in this war that they started. That is for sure. Israel had a commitment also to the previous Iranian regime when she sold the shah such equipment before. So when the successors came, we also had in mind that maybe one day we can renew our good relations that we had for so many years with Iran after the war would be over. . . .

"We were aware very much that we were touching a very touchy subject by doing it, so we went to the Americans. As a matter of fact, I think we informed the Americans that such a deal is going to be concluded and asked their opinion about it."

But President Carter had denied approving any weapons shipment to Iran during the hostage crisis, as had other senior officials of the Carter administration. Carter had imposed a strict arms embargo and had scolded Begin twice when U.S. intelligence learned of planned Israeli arms shipments to Iran. So how did Saguy's recollection make sense? Was Saguy simply mistaken? Or did Begin consciously mislead his senior intelligence and military officials by falsely claiming that the Americans had approved the shipments? Or did Begin have informal U.S. support from career levels of the American foreign policy establishment—and possibly from the Republicans?

Israel refused to let the October Surprise investigators question Israeli officials about the 1980 issue. Instead, the Jerusalem government submitted its own report to the House October Surprise task force. The Israeli account acknowledged only the late October 1980 arms flight to Iran through France which sent 250 F-4 tires from Israel. That deal, however, had been previously documented, and Saguy insisted that it was not one of the two he knew about. The Israeli report made no mention of those two seaborne shipments described by Saguy.

The Israeli report noted that the Iranian arms requests began flooding into the offices of Israeli arms salesmen in Europe and elsewhere after the Iran-Iraq war erupted in September 1980. Begin, who had approached President Carter about this issue in the spring, again urged Carter to permit the sales. They were needed, Begin argued, partly to thwart the Iraqis and partly to increase U.S. diplomatic leverage on the hostage crisis.

U.S. Ambassador Samuel Lewis testified before the House October Surprise task force that one "high-level Israeli official" told him that if Israel were allowed to strike several arms deals with Iran "under strict cover," Israel could use that goodwill to ensure that Iran addressed the hostage issue. Carter, however, insisted that the American hostages must be freed first and that premature arms shipments would lessen allied pressure on the Khomeini regime.

Despite Carter's clearly stated position, a frustrated Begin continued to press for permission to sell weapons to Iran before the hostages' release. Already annoyed by Carter's perceived pro-Arab tilt in negotiations with Egypt and the Palestinians, Begin had a clear motive to go behind the president's back and collaborate with Carter's opponents inside and outside the administration. But the Israeli report insisted that except for the one French-Israeli flight, Carter's embargo was respected. According to Saguy, however, Begin told his top military and intelligence advisers that he had found someone in the United States who gave him a green light for "at least" two seaborne military shipments.

Though barred from going to Israel, the House task force accepted the Israeli government's self-investigation as credible. The task force already had dismissed Ben-Menashe as a liar and gave no credence to his wild stories about secret Israeli weapons shipments that supposedly had clandestine American backing.

But even the Israeli report contradicted the House investigators who had concluded, without doubt, that the French-Israeli-Iranian arms shipment had "no linkage" to the hostage crisis. The Israeli account described Begin arguing with Carter that the deal would generate goodwill and help bring the hostages home. Begin specifically had linked the arms sales to the hostages.

Saguy's claim of seaborne shipments in 1980 rang another faint bell in my mind. I remembered that Jamshid Hashemi had told ABC's *Nightline* that the arms shipments resulting from the Madrid meetings had gone from Israel by ship to Iran. There were differences in the stories, however. Hashemi had mentioned four boatloads of equipment—compared to Saguy's two—and cited a value several times higher than Saguy's total of $40 million. Still, Saguy's comments were the first confirmation from a senior Israeli official that Jamshid's assertion was not completely preposterous.

In summer 1993, after returning from Israel, I completed the final pages of this manuscript. Though the trip had added some new clues and chipped away at the official story, I felt frustrated that the history of 1980 might never be written clearly. Certainly, in the near future, the purveyors of Washington's "conventional wisdom" would not allow the issue to be taken seriously. It had been ridiculed for too long. Each new clue would be rejected as "lacking probative value." Each new witness would fail to measure up to the yardstick of perfection demanded of anyone suggesting that something might have happened in 1980. Almost by definition in the official inquiries, witnesses only could be "credible" if they insisted that there was nothing to any of this.

But I, too, was frustrated by the fuzziness of much of the evidence and the weirdness of many of the witnesses. I was tired of fitting together the pieces of a complex puzzle that never looked more than half done. But I had come to recognize that my desire for a precise story was naïve. In an era so pervaded by duplicity, truth had become more a distant goal than an immediate ending.

Still, as I had learned from my experience with the early stories about Oliver North's secret network, sometimes when the lies look most certain to prevail, a plane falls out of the sky. There remains a chance that some impeccable witness or clear-cut document might still come crashing into public view. I'm not betting on that possibility, but I still harbor a hope that historians someday will find a crucial missing clue and solve the October Surprise mystery, finally.

INDEX